DEBARATI GUHA-SAPIR is [...] demiology of Disasters at the Univ[...] de Louvain, Institute of Health an[...] in Brussels. She trained at Calcutta University and Johns Hopkins School of Public Health and holds a PhD in Epidemiology from the University of Louvain. Dr. Sapir currently heads the internationally renowned World Health Organization Collaborating Centre for Research on the Epidemiology of Disasters (CRED), where she and her team conduct field and policy research on disasters and their impacts.

INDHIRA SANTOS is an Economist at the World Bank, where she has worked on labor markets and social protection and has continued her research on how households respond to shocks, including natural disasters. She was a Research Fellow at Bruegel, a European policy think tank in Brussels, between 2007 and 2009. Previously, she was a Researcher for the Economic Research Center of PUCMM University (Dominican Republic) and worked for the National Ministry of Finance. She holds a PhD in Public Policy from the Kennedy School of Government at Harvard University.

ALEXANDRE BORDE is the founder and CEO of Carbonium, a leading climate change and renewable energy consulting company. He holds a PhD in Economics from the University of Versailles. He started his career as an environmental economist at the World Bank before joining the FAO in 1997. From 2000 to 2003, he was a Senior Research Fellow within the French Ministry of Environment. He regularly advises corporations, governments, and international organizations such as the UNDP and the European Commission about climate change mitigation and adaptation. Dr. Borde has lectured at the Institut d'Edudes Politiques de Paris and the University of Versailles.

The Economic Impacts of Natural Disasters

The Economic Impacts of Natural Disasters

Edited by
Debarati Guha-Sapir
and Indhira Santos

Managing Editor
Alexandre Borde

OXFORD
UNIVERSITY PRESS

Oxford University Press is a department of the University of Oxford.
It furthers the University's objective of excellence in research, scholarship,
and education by publishing worldwide.

Oxford   New York
Auckland   Cape Town   Dar es Salaam   Hong Kong   Karachi
Kuala Lumpur   Madrid   Melbourne   Mexico City   Nairobi
New Delhi   Shanghai   Taipei

With offices in
Argentina   Austria   Brazil   Chile   Czech Republic   France   Greece
Guatemala   Hungary   Italy   Japan   Poland   Portugal   Singapore
South Korea   Switzerland   Thailand   Turkey   Ukraine   Vietnam

Oxford is a registered trade mark of Oxford University Press
in the UK and certain other countries.

Published in the United States of America by
Oxford University Press
198 Madison Avenue, New York, NY 10016

Library of Congress Cataloging-in-Publication Data
The economic impacts of natural disasters / edited by Debarati Guha-Sapir, Indhira Santos,
Alexandre Borde.
    p. cm.
    Includes bibliographical references and index.
    ISBN 978-0-19-984193-6 (cloth : alk. paper)   1. Natural disasters—Economic aspects.
I. Guha-Sapir, Debarati. II. Santos, Indhira. III. Borde, Alexandre.
    HC79.D45E23 2013
    363.34—dc23
                    2011044533

CONTENTS

FOREWORD

The number of disasters and the scale of their impact continue to grow, driven largely by the increasing vulnerability to natural hazards, but also by the effects of climate change, threatening the lives and livelihoods of ever more millions of people and the achievement of the Millennium Development Goals. There is growing urgency to increase efforts to implement the Hyogo Framework for Action 2005-2015: Building the Resilience of Nations and Communities to Disasters. Without the joint efforts of the academics, practitioners, and policy makers, it will be difficult to achieve substantive reduction in disaster losses by 2015.

Catastrophic disasters in areas where people and economic activities are intensely concentrated and exposed to large-scale geological and climatic hazard events, such as earthquakes and tropical cyclones, can set the development process back for decades. In addition to the immediate effects, low-intensity asset loss and livelihood disruption over extensive areas where people and economic activities are exposed to localized hazard events, steadily erode the coping capacity of families and communities, pushing them into increasing marginalization.

Poor communities living in high-risk areas typically do not have the economic or institutional support to face unexpected shocks caused by a hurricane or an earthquake (e.g., loss of livelihood assets such as homes, livestock, and crops), resulting in a permanent or temporary loss of the communities' productive base, aggravating their level of poverty, and, in some cases, triggering migration. To cope with poverty aggravated by disasters, communities repeatedly need to accept external aid and to call upon interfamily solidarity and networks.

While death is often the immediate and tragic consequence of a disaster, economic losses and the inability of the underprivileged to recuperate over the medium and long term add additional burdens. The interplay of economic systems, both informal and formal, and—equally important—the appropriate tools to measure the economic impact of natural hazards are poorly understood. The dependence on family aid transfers and the "crowding out" effect or the robustness of classical cost-benefit techniques in these very specific situations, as well as the evidence required for long-term, sustainable preparedness policy, situations in developed countries where natural disasters are also on the increase and where preparedness is still inadequate—are all issues that need debate, both on theory and practice.

This book is a major step in bringing together both theory and practice, particularly in terms of measuring economic losses caused by disasters. This is a subject that must draw on sound theory that will root it in graduate and postgraduate education for future generations of environmental and development economists. But it also requires evidence from the field from different settings around the world to ground theory in reality.

This collection is an important contribution to the research literature on economics of disasters, not only for students and researchers but also for global, national, and local policy makers and practitioners of disaster risk reduction.

Margareta Wahlstrom
Assistant Secretary-General
International Strategy for Disaster Reduction

ABBREVIATIONS

AC	averting cost
ADB	Asian Development Bank
CARICOM	Caribbean Community and Common Market
CBA	cost-benefit analysis
CCFSC	Central Committee for Flood and Storm Control
CCRIF	Caribbean Catastrophe Risk Insurance Facility
CE	choice experiment
CFSC	Committees for Flood and Storm Control
CLP	Chars Livelihoods Programme
CPB	Centraal Planbureau
CRED	Centre for Research on the Epidemiology of Disasters
CV	contingent value
DALY	disability adjusted life year
DC	discrete choice
DEFRA	Department for Environment, Food and Rural Affairs
DFID	Department for International Development
DRM	disaster risk management
EAR	Economic Amplification Ratio
ECLAC	Economic Commission for Latin America and the Caribbean
EGS	Employment Guarantee Scheme
EM-DAT	Emergency Disasters Database
ERL	Emergency Recovery Loan
FEMA	US Federal Emergency Management Agency
GCMs	General Circulation Models
GDP	Gross Domestic Product
GFDRR	Global Facility for Disaster Reconstruction and Response
GHG	greenhouse gas
HDFC	Housing Development and Finance Corporation
HP	hedonic price
HPF	household production function
IADB	Inter-American Development Bank
IPCC	Intergovernmental Panel on Climate Change
IRR	internal rate of return
ISDR	International Strategy for Disaster Reduction
LSMS	Living Standards Measurement Studies
MCII	Munich Climate Insurance Initiative
MDGs	Millennium Development Goals

NAIS	national agricultural insurance program
NNI	net national income
NOAA	US National Oceanic and Atmospheric Administration
NPV	net present value
NRDA	Natural Resource Damage Assessment
OFDA-USAID	Office of United States Foreign Disaster Assistance from the United States Agency for International Development
OMB	Office of Management and Budget
PRSP	Poverty Reduction Strategy Paper
RP	revealed preferences
SOP	standard operating procedure
SRES	Special Report on Emission Scenarios
SP	stated preferences
TC	travel cost
TCIP	Turkish Catastrophe Insurance Pool
TE	transfer error
TEV	total economic value
UNDP	United Nations Development Programme
UNDRO	United Nations Disaster Relief Organization
UNFCCC	United Nations Framework Convention on Climate Change
VSL	value of a statistical life
WHO	World Health Organization
WINCROP	Windward Islands Crop Insurance
WTP	willingness to pay
WTAC	willingness to accept compensation

CONTRIBUTORS

Sabari Bandyopadhyay is District Coordinator at the District Programme Management Unit for Strengthening Rural Decentralisation (SRD) Cell, West Bengal State Rural Development Agency (WBSRDA), Government of West Bengal, India.

Alexandre Borde is the Managing Director of Carbonium, a climate change and carbon finance consulting company based in Paris, France.

Roy Brouwer is Professor in the Department of Environmental Economics at the Institute for Environmental Studies, VU University Amsterdam, The Netherlands.

Debesh Chakraborty is a retired Professor in the Department of Economics, at Jadavpur University, Calcutta, India.

Ajay Chhibber is Assistant Secretary-General and Assistant Administrator of the United Nations Development Programme and Director of UNDP's Regional Bureau for Asia and the Pacific.

Olivia D'Aoust is a Ph.D. candidate in Economics at the Catholic University of Louvain.

Debarati Guha-Sapir is Director of the WHO Collaborating Centre for Research on the Epidemiology of Disasters (CRED) and Professor at the Institute of Health and Society (IRSS) at Université Catholique de Louvain.

Ivy Das Gupta is a Lecturer of Economics at Bhawanipur Education Society College, Calcutta, India.

Stéphane Hallegatte is an economist with Météo-France and the Centre International de Recherche sur l'Environnement et le Développement (CIRED). He is currently on special assignment with the World Bank as a Lead Climate Change Specialist.

Philippe Hoyois has worked as Senior Research Fellow at the Centre for Research on Epidemiology of Disasters (CRED) and for the Mental Health Service of the Free University of Brussels.

K. M. Nabiul Islam, Ph.D., is a Senior Research Fellow at the Bangladesh Institute of Development Studies (BIDS), Dhaka.

Rachid Laajaj is a Ph.D. candidate in Agricultural and Applied Economics at University of Wisconsin–Madison, USA.

Kristin Magnussen holds a Ph.D. in Environmental and Resource Economics and works for Sweco Norway.

Reinhard Mechler is leader of the research group on "Disasters and Development" in the "Risk and Vulnerability programme" (RAV) at the International Institute for Applied Systems Analysis (IIASA), Laxenburg, Austria. He is a lead author on IPCC's upcoming special report on adaptation to extreme events and the fifth assessment report.

Debabrata Mitra is an Officer in Secretarial and Corporate Legal at Family Credit Limited, Calcutta, India.

Ståle Navrud is a Professor of Environmental and Resource Economics in the Department of Economics and Resource Management, at the Norwegian University of Life Sciences.

Indhira Santos was a Research Fellow at Bruegel, a Brussels-based think tank, at the time of writing. She has now joined the Human Development division at the World Bank, working on matters related to the Eastern European and Central Asian regions.

Yasuyuki Sawada is a Professor at the Faculty of Economics, University of Tokyo.

Marije Schaafsma is a Senior Research Associate at the Centre for Social and Economic Research on the Global Environment (CSERGE), University of East Anglia, UK.

Sayanti Sen is a teacher in the Department of Geography at Bangabasi College, Calcutta University, India.

Bui Dung The, Ph.D., is the chair of the Department of Environmental and Agricultural Economics and the director of the Office of Science-Technology, International Cooperation and Postgraduate Education, College of Economics, Hue University, Vietnam.

Tran Huu Tuan is Vice Dean of the Faculty of Economics and Development Studies, College of Economics, Hue University, Vietnam.

Femke Vos is a data analyst and researcher at CRED specializing in natural disasters and their impacts.

Angelika Wirtz is head of NatCatSERVICE at Munich RE.

Ricardo Zapata-Marti is an Economist at the United Nations Economic Commission for Latin America and the Caribbean (ECLAC).

The Economic Impacts of Natural Disasters

INTRODUCTION

Since the turn of the millennium, more than 2.3 billion people have been directly affected by natural disasters—several of these have killed nearly 100,000 people within a matter of 24 hours. Moreover, the global alarm generated during the last decade by events such as the 2004 tsunami in Asia, Hurricane Katrina in the United States in 2005, the Sichuan earthquake in China in 2008, and more recently the 2011 tsunami in Japan—together with a rising concern worldwide over climate change—has renewed the policy and academic interest on understanding the economic causes and consequences of natural disasters.

While recognizing that improved rescue, evacuation, and disease control are key to reducing the effects of natural disasters, in the final analysis, poverty remains the main risk factor determining the long-term impact of natural hazards. Furthermore, natural disasters have themselves a tremendous impact on the poorest of the poor, who are often ill-prepared to deal with natural hazards and for whom a hurricane, an earthquake, or a drought can mean a permanent submersion in poverty. It is with these concerns for poverty and vulnerability that we present this volume.

This book has two parts. Part I begins with an overview of the general trends in natural disasters and their effects, before going on to critically analyze different methodologies to assess the economic impact of natural disasters, as well as on the *ex-ante* and *ex-post* mechanisms to deal with the effects of disasters and the relationship between extreme natural events and climate change. Part II presents six case studies, covering three different continents and both the developed and the developing world: Bangladesh, Vietnam, India, Nicaragua, Japan, and the Netherlands. Using both country-level data and household surveys, these case studies analyze and quantify the impact of natural hazards—hurricanes, floods, earthquakes, among other types of disasters—on household welfare and macroeconomic performance.

Part I starts with a discussion of the recent trends in natural disasters. During the last fifty years, better reporting of disasters, population growth, growing population density in risky areas, and changes in land use have led to an increasing number of natural disasters being reported worldwide. Hoyois and Guha-Sapir highlight as well the probable role of climate change in these trends.

The increasing frequency of natural disasters and the rising reported economic losses associated with them present policy makers with important challenges. In chapter 2, Ajay Chhibber and Rachid Laajaj provide an overall view of the long-term economic impact of natural disasters and their interaction with economic development, especially in the case of Africa. It outlines desirable policy actions both for preventing and coping with disasters.

However, one of the main difficulties in assessing the economic impact of natural disasters relates to the valuation of the losses. How is one supposed to measure the impact on nonmarketed goods like the environment? How can one balance the risks, costs, and benefits in disaster management? Chapters 3 and 4 complement each other very well in exploring these questions. Ståle Navrud and Kristin Magnussen in chapter 3 do so by analyzing the different loss valuation methods and their applicability to developing countries. While they find that there is no single valuation method that is valid for assessing all types of damages, they recommend specific methods that are relevant for the existing constraints in a developing country context. In chapter 4, on the other hand, Reinhard Mechler and Nabiul Islam apply a cost-benefit analysis of disaster management and adaptation in Bangladesh, drawing some general insights for the modeling of risks of extreme events that should contribute to better planning and climate adaptation policies in disaster-prone regions.

Natural hazards, however, do not need to become disasters. Various challenges, nevertheless, present themselves in disaster management, preparedness, and adaptation, as discussed in chapters 5 and 6.

Stéphane Hallegatte in chapter 5 focuses on the increasing risk and uncertainty arising from climate change and is concerned not only with the intrinsic difficulties in estimating future climate and the related risks but also with the financial and institutional limitations for adaptation. These obstacles are not exclusive of developing countries, however, as the case of Hurricane Katrina in the United States illustrates.

These institutional, financial, and information obstacles in disaster management are further exacerbated by the lack of appropriate formal mechanisms to share the risks arising from natural hazards. Angelika Wirtz in chapter 6 argues that, while the insurance industry plays an important role in compensating for losses due to natural disasters in developed economies, its role is still extremely limited in less developed countries—where the majority of natural hazards take place. This poses important challenges for both domestic and international policy makers in terms of designing effective insurance schemes that are adequate for settings where credit and ability to pay are limited. Regional insurance schemes—like the Caribbean Catastrophe Risk Insurance Facility (CCRIF)—and microinsurance represent two different (micro and macro) innovative approaches to these issues.

The final chapter in Part I, chapter 7, has Ricardo Zapata-Marti taking a comprehensive view of the different public policy options available to mitigate the impact of natural disasters. Hazard reduction rules and norms, information systems, insurance, and calamity funds, are all put in perspective.

In the second part of the book, we examine specific cases in developing and industrialized countries worldwide in light of the theory presented in the previous part.

The first two chapters explore Vietnam and India. Vietnam, a country at very high risk of natural disasters especially floods, has recently established a flood preparedness plan for mitigation and response. Direct disaster-related deaths, injuries, or disease outbreaks are also registered by the provincial system and with the exception of major catastrophes; these are handled at community levels. The indirect effects of these disasters, especially recurring floods on the economy at household and district levels are less well known. Tran Huu Tuan and Bui Dung The discuss the economic effects of floods in Vietnam, critically analyzing the existing studies and identifying the priority gaps in the literature on the economic costs of floods in Vietnam.

The next case study focuses on Orissa, an Indian state that is also exposed to frequent disasters. The authors first present the history of disasters in India and propose an index to classify states according to their vulnerability. In their view, vulnerability is not only determined by the frequency of occurrence of catastrophic events but also by the economic or social fragility of households or communities that render them more likely to suffer from disasters. Based on their definition of vulnerability, Debesh Chakraborty, Sabari Bandyopadhyay, Ivy Das Gupta, Sayanti Sen, and Debabrata Mitra provide new empirical evidence on the economic impact of floods at the household level and attempt to value and measure the losses experienced by families based on an original survey conducted by the authors.

Both of the above chapters propose policies to governments for mitigating the economic impact of disasters in these circumstances. Both also reveal that not only the scope of economic impacts of natural disasters in developing countries is wide and potentially long-lasting but also that our current capacity to satisfactorily measure them is fairly limited.

Chapters 10 and 11 provide further microeconomic evidence of the impact of natural hazards on household consumption and the instruments used to deal with their effects. The analysis of changes in consumption patterns and coping capacities is carried out for both developing and industrial country contexts. Poor communities, in general, tend to help each other more in the absence of institutionalized mechanisms for relief and recovery present in wealthier countries. Indhira Santos examines the case of Nicaragua after Hurricane Mitch, looking at informal mechanisms of interhousehold transfers and their capacity to cover some of the losses after the disaster. She further explores the interrelations between these transfers and public aid schemes, suggesting that more of the latter leads to reductions in interfamilial solidarity. In Japan, Yasuyuki Sawada also uses a micro-level approach, but analyzes consumption and insurance patterns captured through formal mechanisms for household recovery. The author compares the contrasting experiences in the aftermath of two earthquakes in two different Japanese regions in terms of formal insurance penetration and coverage, illustrating some of the advantages of the availability of insurance, as discussed in Part I. Although the impacts of the 2011 tsunami are not directly discussed, his analysis can be used to further improve our understanding and ability to identify and target future channels of vulnerability. Both case studies provide valuable insights for public policy on relief and recovery, in both poor and wealthy settings, and point to a research agenda for the future on the welfare impacts of natural disasters.

Finally, this section ends with case studies of floods in the Netherlands and Bangladesh, also contrasting the management and impact of natural disasters in developed and developing economies. Nabiul Islam, and Roy Brouwer and Marije Schaafsma in chapters 12 and 13, respectively, look at the case of floods in two countries that are at high risk of this particular type of hazard. In the Netherlands, major engineering projects on flood management have been successfully implemented over decades, making the country a leader on hydrological engineering techniques. Bangladesh, with much fewer resources and at equal risk of floods, has made significant progress in the last decade on designing and implementing low-cost community-based flood mitigation programs. Here, Nabiul Islam explores the urban impact of floods, an area relatively neglected in the literature. The patterns of impact in urban settings can be fundamentally different. High poor and ultra-poor concentrations, political limelight, and different profiles of economic activity question the accepted views on disaster impact. Islam further explores the implications of flood loss management for adaptation options in the country. Roy Brouwer and Marije Schaafsma, on the other hand, apply cost-benefit analysis to flood disaster management in the Netherlands and highlight the main challenges for policy makers in developed economies that worry about spatial differentiation of flood calamity risks.

There is still much more work to do to strengthen the existing evidence and policy base for the economic and social impact of disasters. Although path-breaking work has been undertaken by several researchers in the past decades, the uncovered ground still remains vast. This has made our task of selecting topics and maintaining a publication at book length extremely challenging. The subjects addressed here do not, by any means, cover all areas that require attention in the study of the economics of disasters.

We would like to emphasize that the ideas put forward in this book are not set in stone. We hope, however, that this work opens new avenues for thinking and debate, pushing forward the frontiers of knowledge in this area.

An Overview of Natural Disaster Trends, Risk Management Analysis, and Mitigation Policies in a Changing Climate

1 }

The Frequency and Impact of Natural Disasters

Debarati Guha-Sapir, Olivia D'Aoust, Femke Vos, and Philippe Hoyois

Introduction

The world is facing the impact of natural disasters on human lives and economies on a colossal scale. In 2011, 302 disasters killed 29,782 people, affected 206 million others, and cost a total of US$366 billion. The Millennium Declaration recognizes the risk to development arising from disasters and calls on the global community to "intensify our collective efforts to reduce the number and effects of natural hazards and man-made disasters" (United Nations 2000). One of the key activities of the Hyogo Framework for Action (UN ISDR 2005) is defined as the development of systems of indicators of disaster risk and vulnerability at national and subnational scales, which will enable decision makers to assess the impact of disasters on social, economic, and environmental conditions and disseminate the results to other decision makers, the public, and populations at risk. Systematic disaster data are necessary for evidence-based risk assessment and for measuring progress in the reduction of disaster losses. The Centre for Research on the Epidemiology of Disasters (CRED) provides standardized disaster occurrence and loss data. This is embedded in the overall goal of information dissemination for disaster management in order to enhance regional, national, and local capacity to prepare for, respond to, and mitigate disaster events.

The Emergency Events Database (EM-DAT) (CRED 2012), held by CRED since 1988, was created with the initial support of the World Health Organization (WHO), United Nations Disaster Relief Organization (UNDRO), and the Belgian Government. It has been sponsored by the Office of US Foreign Disaster Assistance from the US Agency for International Development (OFDA-USAID) since 1999 (Guha-Sapir and Vos 2009). CRED defines a disaster as "a situation or event which overwhelms local capacity, necessitating a request to a national or international level for external assistance; an unforeseen and often sudden event that causes great damage, destruction and human suffering."

This chapter has been partially funded by the European Commission FP6 Contract No. 036877 (MICRODIS project).

TABLE 1.1 } Definition of EM-DAT Disaster Types

EM-DAT disaster type	Disaster subgroup[a]	Definition
Earthquakes Volcanoes Mass movements (dry)	Geophysical	Events originating from solid earth
Storms	Meteorological	Events caused by short-lived/small to meso scale atmospheric processes (in the spectrum from minutes to days)
Floods Mass movements (wet)	Hydrological	Events caused by deviations in the normal water cycle and/or overflow of bodies of water caused by wind setup
Droughts Extreme temperatures Wildfires	Climatological	Events caused by long-lived/meso to macro scale processes (in the spectrum from intraseasonal to multidecadal climate variability)
Epidemics Insect infestations	Biological	Disaster caused by the exposure of living organisms to germs and toxic substances

Source: EM-DAT: The OFDA/CRED International Disaster Database, Université Catholique de Louvain, Brussels, Belgium. http://www.emdat.be.

[a] Climatological, hydrological, and meteorological disaster subgroups together are hydrometeorological disasters.

CRED and Munich Re have recently led a collaborative initiative on a disaster category classification for operational databases (CRED and Munich Re 2009) in order to create standardized terminology for global and regional databases on natural disasters, for the use of comparing and exchanging disaster data. Table 1.1 presents clarifications of the terms used by EM-DAT and their definitions.

Media often refer to disaster data for purposes of informing the public or dispersing messages on climate and disasters. The correct interpretation of information on disasters is one of the major pitfalls of these kinds of data, as was recently shown when Al Gore tried to underpin the possible effects of climate change on disasters using CRED EM-DAT statistics (Revkin 2009). Although global warming is partly responsible for the global increase in disasters, much of these are due to environmental and other factors such as zoning laws and urban migration.

The purpose of this chapter is to review and analyze the occurrence and consequences of natural disasters with an emphasis on global economic damage data. It focuses on the occurrence of natural disasters during the period of 1950 to 2011, studies the human impact of natural disasters (in terms of the number of people killed and affected), emphasizes economic loss from hazards (globally and in terms of Gross Domestic Product (GDP)), and summarizes the main conclusions that can be drawn from these numbers.

The Occurrence of Natural Disasters

Statistics on disaster data can provide insight in the evolution of disaster occurrence in time. Natural disaster data from EM-DAT are compiled from a variety of public sources, which include governments, insurance companies, press agencies, and humanitarian aid agencies. Although methodology within EM-DAT has been standardized to make data consistent over its time span, the disaster data compiled remain strongly dependent on the information provided by the sources. Information provision has vastly improved in the last decennia. However, when interpreting disaster data, one has to take into account the inherent complexity of disaster occurrence, human vulnerabilities, and statistical reporting and registering.

Since 1950, more than 11,800 natural disasters have been reported worldwide. Figure 1.1 might lead us to believe that disasters occur more frequently today than in the 1950s. One of the main contributors to this apparent increase of natural disasters is the launch of active disaster data collection by OFDA in 1960 and CRED in 1973. Furthermore, the development of telecommunications and media, increased humanitarian funds, and reinforced international cooperation have all contributed to a better reporting of disasters.

Historically, Asia is the continent that is most hit by natural disasters. Since 1950, Asia has counted over 4,600 disasters, which represents 39 percent of the global disaster occurrence in this period. These disasters killed over 5,721,000 (78 percent) people and affected over 5,989,771,000 (89 percent) others. Globally, floods (33 percent), storms (28 percent), and earthquakes (9 percent) are the most frequent disaster types that occurred during the period of 1950 to 2011.

The increase in occurrence of disasters is not equally distributed among continents (figure 1.2). Asia and Africa show the greatest growth. The Americas and Europe show a similar evolution, whereas disaster occurrence in Oceania remains rather stable over time.

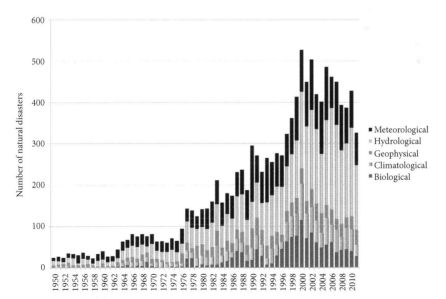

FIGURE 1.1 Natural disaster occurrence, 1950–2011

Source: Data from EM-DAT: The OFDA/CRED International Disaster Database. Université Catholique de Louvain, Brussels, Belgium. http://www.emdat.be.

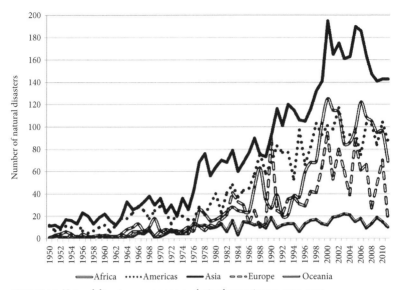

FIGURE 1.2 Natural disaster occurrence, evolution by continents, 1950–2011

Source: Data from EM-DAT: The OFDA/CRED International Disaster Database. Université Catholique de Louvain, Brussels, Belgium. http://www.emdat.be.

Figure 1.3 shows the occurrence of natural disasters, as aggregated into two main categories, which make a clear difference in the hazards at the origin of the disasters. Climatological, hydrological, and meteorological disasters, as defined in table 1.1, are usually linked to significant variations of ordinary rainfall, wind, or temperature conditions, whereas geophysical disasters are linked to important soil movements that are in numerous cases of seismic origin.

Data from 1950 onward show a significant increase in the number of reported weather-related events, compared to geophysical disasters. The increase can mainly be attributed to the increase in floods and storms in recent years.

As mentioned earlier, increased reporting of disasters partly explain this rise in disasters. Disasters are the convergence of hazards with vulnerabilities. As such, an increase of physical, social, economic, or environmental vulnerabilities (i.e., population growth, change in land uses, climate change) can contribute to an increase in the occurrence of disasters (Guha-Sapir, Hargitt, and Hoyois 2004).

The growth in geophysical disaster occurrence appears slow but regular. The impact of climate change can be excluded here and, unless tectonic activity patterns change, human factors (demographic pressure, land use changes, spread of information) mostly explain the progressive evolution in the number of such disasters.

When considering the overall distribution of natural disasters according to their types (vertical analysis), the continents show different profiles (figure 1.4). The greatest differentiation appears among droughts (Africa), extreme temperatures (Europe), and wildfires (the Americas). All other disasters (i.e., earthquakes, floods, storms) are most frequent in Asia.

When looking at disaster occurrence in each continent (horizontal analysis), floods are most frequent in Asia, Europe, and Africa, whereas storms occur most in Oceania and the Americas.

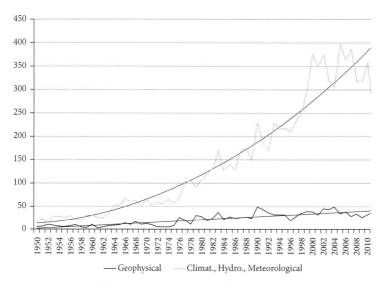

FIGURE 1.3 Natural disaster occurrence, evolution by main groups, 1950–2011

Source: Data from EM-DAT: The OFDA/CRED International Disaster Database. Université Catholique de Louvain, Brussels, Belgium. http://www.emdat.be.

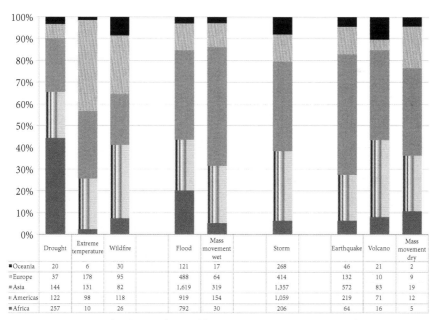

	Drought	Extreme temperature	Wildfire	Flood	Mass movement wet	Storm	Earthquake	Volcano	Mass movement dry
■Oceania	20	6	30	121	17	268	46	21	2
▨Europe	37	178	95	488	64	414	132	10	9
▩Asia	144	131	82	1,619	319	1,357	572	83	19
▨Americas	122	98	118	919	154	1,059	219	71	12
■Africa	257	10	26	792	30	206	64	16	5

FIGURE 1.4 Percentage distribution of natural disasters occurrence, by subtypes and continents, 1950–2011

Source: Data from EM-DAT: The OFDA/CRED International Disaster Database. Université Catholique de Louvain, Brussels, Belgium. http://www.emdat.be.

The Human Impact of Natural Disasters

In EM-DAT, the human impact of natural disasters is essentially measured by two parameters: the number of people killed, missing, or presumed dead and the number of people affected by the events, which means people requiring immediate assistance to provide basic survival needs (food, water, shelter, sanitation, medical assistance) during a period of emergency and includes people injured, homeless, displaced, or evacuated.

Figure 1.5 presents the evolution in the number of casualties and people affected by natural disasters worldwide between 1990 and 2011. Over time, the patterns of these two parameters show great variability. The mortality peak of 1991 is explained by a storm in Bangladesh that left a death toll of almost 140,000 people; the one of 1999, by a flood in Venezuela that caused 30,000 deaths, as well as the Izmit earthquake in Turkey that killed over 17,000 people; the peak of 2004 relates to the Indian Ocean tsunami with more than 225,000 deaths; the peak of 2008 relates to cyclone Nargis in Myanmar and the earthquake that hit China; finally, the mortality peak of 2010 is explained by the earthquake in Haiti, which killed over 222,000 people.

The total number of deaths for the period was 1.5 million. More than 68 percent of them occurred in Asia, with earthquakes, tsunamis, storms, and floods accounting for 97 percent of the fatalities.

Nevertheless, raw numbers are not a very good indicator of the reality and make comparisons difficult. Therefore, we examine these data by standardizing per 100,000 inhabitants.

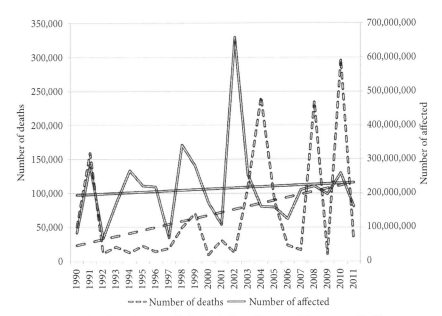

FIGURE 1.5 Number of people reported killed and affected by natural disasters worldwide, 1990–2011

Source: Data from EM-DAT: The OFDA/CRED International Disaster Database. Université Catholique de Louvain, Brussels, Belgium. http://www.emdat.be.

In 2008, the death toll in Asia was particularly high: considered as a proportion of total population, six deaths per 100,000 inhabitants were reported in this continent, compared to less than one person killed per 100,000 inhabitants in the Americas, Africa, Europe, and Oceania. This high figure is to a great extent due to the cyclone in Myanmar and the earthquake in China. In 2010, 24 deaths per 100,000 inhabitants were reported in the Americas, an extremely high figure, due to the devastating earthquake in Haiti. These are good examples of the influence of single catastrophic events on disaster statistics. Often, these events completely change a disaster profile, as was also seen in the case of the Kobe earthquake in 1995 and the 2004 Indian Ocean tsunami.

In terms of people affected, the high numbers for 1991 are attributable to a flood in China, as well as a storm in Bangladesh, affecting respectively 210 and 15 million people. In 1994, two floods, a drought, and a storm in China affected a total of 122 million; a flood in India affected 12 million. In 1998, three floods in China, India, and Bangladesh affected 240, 30, and 15 million people respectively, a storm in China affected 11 million, and a drought in Brazil 10 million people. The extremely high number of people affected in 2002 is explained by several events: a drought in India (300 million people affected); a storm (100 million), drought (60 million), and two floods in China (80 and 20 million, respectively); a flood in India (42 million); and a drought in Ethiopia (14 million). Finally, in 2010, China was hit by a flood affecting 134 million people.

The cumulated number of people affected by natural disasters (some people may have been affected several times during the period) reaches over 4.7 billion. Again, most of them (90 percent) lived in Asia, of whom 61 percent were affected by floods.

Asia remains the most affected continent when the number of victims is related to the total population of the continent. In 2011, 4,200 people per 100,000 inhabitants were affected by disasters in Asia, which was 2 to 880 times higher than in the other continents.

For both indicators, the time trends show a small increase, associated with the peaks of 2002, 2004, 2008 and 2010. With the floods that affected more than 188 million people in 2010 and 106 million in 2011, mainly in China, Pakistan, Thailand, and India, and the estimated high numbers of people killed or reported missing after the 2010 earthquake (222,000) in Haiti and the 2011 earthquake and tsunami (19,800) in Japan, it is to be feared that the number of people killed and affected by natural disasters will continue their slow progression.

When considering the number of people killed and affected by natural disasters in light of the growing world population, both figures appear relatively stable over time (figure 1.6). For the period of 1990 to 2011, the annual average death toll per 100,000 inhabitants was 1.1 while the annual average number of people reported affected per 100,000 inhabitants is around 3,500.

Economic Losses Due to Natural Disasters

Information on the direct economic damages caused by natural disasters is far from being readily available for all disasters.

In EM-DAT, for the period of 1990 to 2011, damage data are present for 37 percent of disasters. However, using the EM-DAT classification for disaster impact, it appears

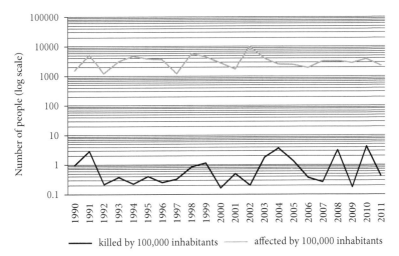

FIGURE 1.6 Numbers of people killed and affected by natural disasters, per 100,000 inhabitants, worldwide, 1990–2011

Source: Data from EM-DAT: The OFDA/CRED International Disaster Database. Université Catholique de Louvain, Brussels, Belgium. http://www.emdat.be.

that the proportion of reported damage data increases with the severity of disasters, going from around 18 percent in small-scale disasters to 88 percent in catastrophes.

Such figures highlight the fact that the cumulated economic impact of natural disasters for the years 1990 to 2011, amounting to 2011 US$2,521 billion, is probably underestimated. Despite the low proportion of available damage data for small- and medium-scale disasters, the major part of the underestimation can be attributed to more severe disasters, ranking from upper medium scale disasters to catastrophes.

The increase in the proportion of damage data availability linked with disaster severity appears in all continents. However, in Africa damage reporting is low compared to other continents.

With a more detailed figure, it appears that the propensity to report damage data is not only linked with disaster severity but also varies greatly between regions (UNSD 2008) (figure 1.7). In EM-DAT, countries are automatically linked to one of the following regions: Eastern Africa, Middle Africa, Northern Africa, Southern Africa, Western Africa, Caribbean, Central America, Northern America, South America, Central Asia, Eastern Asia, South-Eastern Asia, Southern Asia, Western Asia, Eastern Europe, Northern Europe, Russian Federation, Southern Europe, Western Europe, Australia and New Zealand, Melanesia, Micronesia, or Polynesia (see table 1.2 for a list of countries in each region). In Middle and Western Africa, economic damages are reported for less than one in 10 disasters. In only five regions, Northern America, Eastern Asia, Northern and Western Europe, and Australia and New Zealand, the proportion of disasters with economic data reported is over 50 percent. Four of these regions belong to the developed world. In Eastern Asia, which combines developed and developing countries, the proportion of disasters with reported damage varies between 38 percent (Democratic People's Republic of Korea) and 78 percent (Taiwan).

TABLE 1.2 } List of Continents, Regions (UNSD definition), and Countries as Used in EM-DAT

Continent	Region	Country
Africa	Eastern Africa	Uganda
		Tanzania Uni Rep
		Comoros
		Ethiopia
		Reunion
		Mozambique
		Mauritius
		Somalia
		Kenya
		Madagascar
		Malawi
		Zambia
		Rwanda
		Zimbabwe
		Djibouti
		Burundi
		Eritrea
		Seychelles
		Mayotte
	Middle Africa	Chad
		Zaire/Congo Dem Rep
		Congo
		Cameroon
		Central African Rep
		Angola
		Sao Tome et Principe
		Equatorial Guinea
		Gabon
	Northern Africa	Morocco
		Algeria
		Egypt
		Sudan
		Libyan Arab Jamah
		Tunisia
	Southern Africa	South Africa
		Botswana
		Lesotho
		Namibia
		Swaziland

(Continued)

TABLE 1.2 } (*Continued*)

Continent	Region	Country
	Western Africa	Cape Verde Is
		Niger
		Burkina Faso
		Gambia The
		Guinea Bissau
		Mali
		Mauritania
		Senegal
		Ghana
		Togo
		Nigeria
		Benin
		Cote d'Ivoire
		Sierra Leone
		Liberia
		Guinea
		St Helena
Americas	Caribbean	Jamaica
		Martinique
		St Vincent and The Grenadines
		Haiti
		Puerto Rico
		Anguilla
		Bahamas
		Cuba
		Guadeloupe
		Montserrat
		St Kitts and Nevis
		Dominican Rep
		Dominica
		Trinidad and Tobago
		Antigua and Barbuda
		Netherlands Antilles
		Barbados
		St Lucia
		Grenada
		Turks and Caicos Is
		Virgin Is (US)
		Virgin Is (UK)
		Cayman Islands

TABLE 1.2 } (*Continued*)

Continent	Region	Country
	Central America	El Salvador
		Guatemala
		Nicaragua
		Mexico
		Costa Rica
		Honduras
		Belize
		Panama
	Northern America	United States
		Canada
		Bermuda
		Northern Mariana Is
	South America	Ecuador
		Colombia
		Chile
		Peru
		Brazil
		Bolivia
		Venezuela
		Argentina
		Paraguay
		Uruguay
		Suriname
		Guyana
		French Guiana
Asia	Central Asia	Tajikistan
		Kyrgyzstan
		Uzbekistan
		Kazakhstan
		Turkmenistan
	Eastern Asia	Japan
		Taiwan (China)
		China P Rep
		Hong Kong (China)
		Korea Rep
		Mongolia
		Macau
		Korea Dem P Rep

(*Continued*)

TABLE 1.2 } (*Continued*)

Continent	Region	Country
	South-Eastern Asia	Myanmar
		Philippines
		Indonesia
		Viet Nam
		Thailand
		Malaysia
		Lao P Dem Rep
		Cambodia
		Singapore
		Brunei Darussalam
		Timor-Leste
	Southern Asia	India
		Bangladesh
		Iran Islam Rep
		Pakistan
		Nepal
		Afghanistan
		Sri Lanka
		Maldives
		Bhutan
	Western Asia	Turkey
		Jordan
		Cyprus
		Iraq
		Lebanon
		Saudi Arabia
		Syrian Arab Rep
		Israel
		United Arab Emirates
		Oman
		Bahrain
		Palestine (West Bank)
		Georgia
		Yemen
		Azerbaijan
		Armenia
		Kuwait
		Qatar
Europe	Eastern Europe	Romania
		Belarus
		Bulgaria
		Russia
		Poland

TABLE 1.2 } (*Continued*)

Continent	Region	Country
		Czechoslovakia
		Hungary
		Ukraine
		Moldova Rep
		Czech Rep
		Slovakia
	Northern Europe	United Kingdom
		Denmark
		Norway
		Ireland
		Sweden
		Finland
		Iceland
		Lithuania
		Estonia
		Latvia
	Russian Federation	Soviet Union
	Southern Europe	Italy
		Spain
		Greece
		Portugal
		Azores
		Canary Is
		Yugoslavia
		Albania
		Malta
		Croatia
		Serbia Montenegro
		Macedonia FRY
		Slovenia
		Bosnia-Hercegovenia
		Serbia
		Montenegro
	Western Europe	Belgium
		France
		Germany

(*Continued*)

TABLE 1.2 } (*Continued*)

Continent	Region	Country
		Netherlands
		Switzerland
		Austria
		Luxembourg
Oceania	Australia and New Zealand	New Zealand
		Australia
	Melanesia	Papua New Guinea
		Fiji
		Solomon Is
		New Caledonia
		Vanuatu
	Micronesia	Guam
		Kiribati
		Micronesia Fed States
		Marshall Is
		Palau
	Polynesia	Tokelau
		Cook Is
		Tonga
		French Polynesia
		Niue
		Samoa
		Wallis and Futuna Is
		American Samoa
		Tuvalu
		Wallis

When considering natural disaster types, the proportion of disasters with reported amounts of damage is only above average for storms, with data available for more than 50 percent of them, and around average for earthquakes (figure 1.8). In floods, droughts, and wildfires, proportions of disasters with reported damage data are 3 to 6 percent below the average. In all other disaster types, economic damages are reported in less than 20 percent of the cases. Many of the storms occur in industrialized regions such as Europe and the southwestern and southeastern United States. Both property values as well as insurance penetration are high in these regions, along with institutional frameworks to capture these losses. Most events occur in places where systematic attribution of monetary value to assets is deficient.

When geographic areas of occurrence and disaster type are considered together, the proportion of disasters with amounts of damage reported show high variations between both regions and disaster types. For example, economic damages from droughts are reported for at least 50 percent of disasters in Central and Northern America; Central and South-Eastern Asia; Eastern, Northern, Western, and Southern

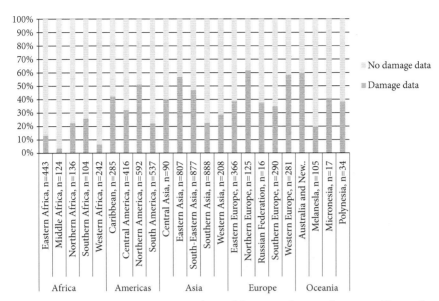

FIGURE 1.7 Damage reporting: proportions of natural disasters with reported amounts of damage, by region, 1990–2011

Source: Data from EM-DAT: The OFDA/CRED International Disaster Database. Université Catholique de Louvain, Brussels, Belgium. http://www.emdat.be.

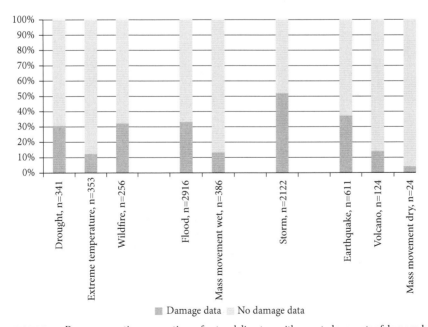

FIGURE 1.8 Damage reporting: proportions of natural disasters with reported amounts of damage, by natural disaster types, 1990–2011

Source: Data from EM-DAT: The OFDA/CRED International Disaster Database. Université Catholique de Louvain, Brussels, Belgium. http://www.emdat.be.

Europe, and Australia and New Zealand. For floods, it is only in Central and Eastern Asia; Eastern and Northern Europe, and the Russian Federation, and Australia and New Zealand and Polynesia, that damage data are reported for more than one out of two cases. Damage data from earthquakes and tsunamis are reported at similar rates only in Northern America, Western and Northern Europe, and Australia and New Zealand, Polynesia, and Micronesia.

The unequal distribution of available damage data across regions and disaster types makes it difficult to obtain an accurate global estimation of total amount of damage for the period under consideration.

By disaster type, the largest cumulative losses during the period of 1990 to 2011 correspond to storms (2011 US$927 billion). An amount of US$752 billion has been reported for earthquakes and of US$619 billion for floods. It has to be noted that these are also three frequently occurring types of events, where damages are most often reported.

In total, storms have cost US$606 billion in the Americas, which represents 24 percent of worldwide losses due to all natural disasters and about three quarters of the losses reported for the continent. In Asia, earthquakes have cost $598 billion (24 percent of worldwide losses), floods $385 billion (15 percent of all losses), and storms $196 billion (8 percent of all losses), 93 percent of all Asian costs. In Europe, floods cost $114 billion and storms $108 billion, totaling about three quarters of losses reported for this continent. In Oceania, earthquakes and storms generated losses of $27 and $15 billion, respectively, or 65 percent of the total damages documented for this continent. In Africa, where economic damages are poorly reported, the largest losses registered in the period were related to earthquakes ($8.9 billion), followed by floods ($5.8 billion), and droughts ($3.3 billion); all three representing 87 percent of all losses in the continent (figure 1.9).

The lack of damage data for many disasters, as well as the variations in their availability across regions and disaster types, make analysis complex and may result in more pronounced underestimations of damage for some regions of the world. When implementing risk reduction efforts, stakeholders should be aware of cases where bias is likely to occur.

To relate the amounts of damage caused by a disaster to the annual GDP of the country where it occurs is a classical way of accounting for the extent of a disaster. The International Monetary Fund (IMF 2003) defines large disasters as "causing economic damages corresponding to, at least, 0.5 percent of annual GDP."

The Economic Commission for Latin America and the Caribbean (ECLAC) proposes a more refined definition of damage assessment. Their methodology, recently modified by the World Bank, allows estimation of damage to capital stocks, losses in the production of goods and services, as well as the disaster impacts on living conditions, economic performance, and environment. It also allows assessment of changes in the main macroeconomic indicator such as GDP (ECLAC and World Bank 2003).

We can notice that the value of life is systematically excluded when calculating damage costs. Indeed, quantifying the economic costs of human loss would require specific assumptions and thereby give rise to uncertainties in the calculations. An approach derived from a human capital perspective is known as the Disability Adjusted Life Year (DALY) calculation, where one DALY represents the equivalent

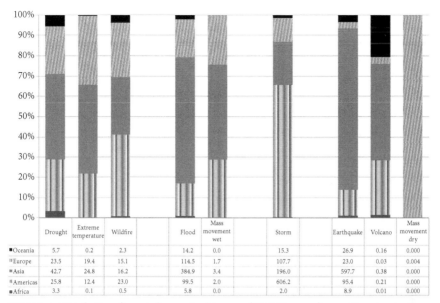

	Drought	Extreme temperature	Wildfire	Flood	Mass movement wet	Storm	Earthquake	Volcano	Mass movement dry
■Oceania	5.7	0.2	2.3	14.2	0.0	15.3	26.9	0.16	0.000
░Europe	23.5	19.4	15.1	114.5	1.7	107.7	23.0	0.03	0.004
▨Asia	42.7	24.8	16.2	384.9	3.4	196.0	597.7	0.38	0.000
▨Americas	25.8	12.4	23.0	99.5	2.0	606.2	95.4	0.21	0.000
■Africa	3.3	0.1	0.5	5.8	0.0	2.0	8.9	0.01	0.000

FIGURE 1.9 Distribution of reported amounts of damages (US$ billion, 2011) caused by natural disasters, by disaster types and continents, 1990–2011

Source: Disaster data: from EM-DAT: The OFDA/CRED International Disaster Database. Université Catholique de Louvain, Brussels, Belgium. http://www.emdat.be. World population data: from The World Bank: Open Data Catalogue. http://data.worldbank.org/indicator.

of the loss of one year of full health. From an economic point of view, the value of one DALY is set to the annual average productivity of a worker and can then be extended to calculate the economic cost involved in the reduction of DALYs (Brandon 1997).

For those reasons, more than other impact measurements, economic damage data remain weak indicators in EM-DAT, as there is no universal and sound methodology to calculate the exact overall impact of a natural hazard.

In figure 1.10, the reported annual amounts of damage and their proportion of the world GDP (World Bank Group 2012) are presented. In six years—1995, 1999, 2004, 2005, 2008, and 2011—natural disasters caused damages of more than 2011 US$150 billion. The Kobe earthquake in 1995 and Hurricane Katrina in 2005 account for 64 percent and 57 percent of damages reported for those two years, respectively. The 18 catastrophes, making US$1 billion damages or more, in 1999 and the 22 catastrophes in 2004 explain the high level of losses reported for these years. In 2005, besides Katrina, the 23 other catastrophes pushed the amount of losses to tremendous levels. The total damage costs of US$196 billion in 2008 can be mainly attributed to the Sichuan earthquake and extreme winter conditions in China, as well as Hurricane Ike in the United States. In 2011, damages from natural disasters reached unprecedented levels, when the earthquake and tsunami in Japan cost US$210 billion, contributing to a total of US$366 billion for this year.

At the world GDP level, the amount of damage exceeds or is close to the IMF threshold for large disasters in 1995, 2005, and 2011, when the Kobe earthquake, Hurricane Katrina and the Tohoku earthquake and tsunami in Japan caused each country more than US$100 billion damages.

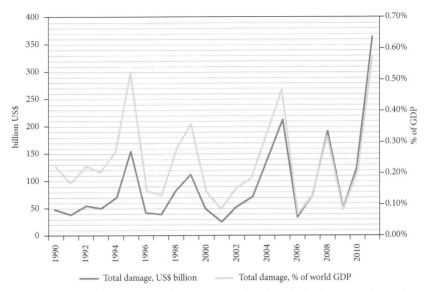

FIGURE 1.10 Natural disasters reported damages: annual total (US$ billion) and annual percentage of world GDP, 1990–2011

Source: Disaster data from EM-DAT: The OFDA/CRED Emergency Disaster Database. Université Catholique de Louvain, Brussels, Belgium. http://www.emdat.be. World GDP data: from The World Bank: Open Data Catalogue. http://data.worldbank.org/indicator.

Using the IMF threshold and considering only disasters with damage data and countries with GDP available (World Bank Group 2012), we computed the proportion of disasters that should have been defined as large by the IMF for each region of the world. Data for Middle Africa and Micronesia were inconsistent.

Of the 2,481 disasters, 336 (14 percent) caused damages equal to or greater than 0.5 percent of the annual GDP of the country of occurrence. Again, as figure 1.11 shows, the variations between regions appear to be high. In Northern America, large disasters appear very infrequently, but the large geographic area and economic wealth of the United States and Canada has to be considered. In such a context, the consequences of some disasters recede, which otherwise would make a large economic impact. Similar explanations can be given for Eastern Asia. According to the number of natural disasters occurring in this region, it seems also to have been spared by large disasters. Here, the superficies of China and the wealth of Japan and South Korea have to be taken into account. This pleads in favor of the use of regional GDP, at least for the largest or wealthiest countries. The complete lack of natural disasters causing damages equal or greater than 0.5 percent of the annual GDP in Middle Africa is merely a result of the very poor monitoring of disaster impact in this region. Of the 124 natural disasters reported in this region during the period of 1990 to 2011, only five events included information on damage costs.

Inversely some regions appear to be economically more sensitive to natural disasters. In Eastern Africa, the Caribbean, Central Asia, Melanesia, and Polynesia, at least one disaster of three makes damages equal or greater than 0.5 percent of GDP.

		0%	10%	20%	30%	40%	50%	60%	70%	80%	90%	100%
Oceania	Polynesia											
	Micronesia											
	Melanesia											
	Australia and New Zealand											
Europe	Western Europe											
	Southern Europe											
	Northern Europe											
	Eastern Europe											
Asia	Western Asia											
	Southern Asia											
	South-Eastern Asia											
	Eastern Asia											
	Central Asia											
Americas	South America											
	Northern America											
	Central America											
	Caribbean											
Africa	Western Africa											
	Southern Africa											
	Northern Africa											
	Middle Africa											
	Eastern Africa											

▦ Percentage

FIGURE 1.11 Proportions of natural disasters with reported amount of damage equal to or greater than 0.5 percent of GDP, by region, 1990–2011

Source: Disaster data from EM-DAT: The OFDA/CRED International Disaster Database. Université Catholique de Louvain, Brussels, Belgium. http://www.emdat.be. Regional GDP data: calculated from The World Bank: Open Data Catalogue. http://data.worldbank.org/indicator.

The small superficies of the involved countries may explain some of these results. However, it may be that in many countries of these regions poverty is the best explanation for such worrying results.

When considering the economic impact of disasters according to their types and only those with information on damage and GDP available (total n = 2,481), droughts appear to have impacts on economies generally greater than other types of disasters. Almost 40 percent of droughts provoke damages equal to or greater than 0.5 percent of the GDP of the country of occurrence. Droughts are typically slow-onset events with a long duration and high spatial coverage, which have a high impact on welfare and food security of countries depending on agriculture as their main resource. Earthquakes also appear to be more economically destructive than other disaster types. Their impact is most heavily felt in densely populated urban areas where preventive measures such as earthquake-resistant buildings have not been implemented.

These results should be examined in light of their geographic distribution. But they also show that the economic impact of a disaster should not only be considered in absolute terms but also within the context of the economy of the country where it occurs.

Conclusions

Natural disaster statistics are essential for policy makers. Effectiveness of resource allocation, especially in poor countries, is fully dependent on understanding of risk profiles and severity of impact. Enhanced collection of disaster data, improved tele-communication and media flow, and reinforced international collaboration have all contributed to better disaster reporting, hereby partly explaining the global upward trend in reported disasters. Compared to geophysical disasters, which have remained stable in the last couple of decades, reported weather-related disasters show a rela-tively strong increase. Trends in the number of people that are killed or affected by natural disasters are highly influenced by single extreme disaster events. Different regions present different disaster profiles and regional policies should reflect these.

There are limitations on disaster data that have to be taken into account. Information on disaster occurrence and impact is often collected for relief fundrais-ing rather than statistical purposes. The lack of standardized methods and defini-tions diminishes the quality of analysis and findings.

The lack of damage reporting leads to underestimation of the true economic costs arising from disasters, especially for poorer regions. Finally, a lack of standard methods to measure impact on economy or humankind seriously compromises comparison across time and space. Progress in disaster risk reduction becomes dif-ficult to measure in the absence of benchmarks.

References

Brandon, C. (1997). *Economic Valuation of Air and Water Pollution in Bangladesh*. Washing-ton, D.C.: The World Bank.

CRED (2012). EM-DAT: The OFDA/CRED International Disaster Database. Université Catholique de Louvain, Brussels, Belgium. Accessed January 1, 2012. http://www.emdat.be.

CRED and Munich Re (2009). *Disaster Category Classification and Peril Terminology for Oper-ational Purposes*. CRED Working Paper No. 264. Brussels and Munich: Centre for R.

Economic Commission for Latin America and the Caribbean (ECLAC) and International Bank for Reconstruction and Development (The World Bank) (2003). *Handbook for Esti-mating the Socio-economic and Environmental Effects of Disasters*. Santiago, Chile.

Guha-Sapir, D., and Vos, F. (2009). "Quantifying Global Environmental Change Impacts: Methods, Criteria and Definitions for Compiling Data on Hydro-Meteorological Haz-ards." In *Coping with Global Environmental Change, Disasters and Security—Threats, Challenges, Vulnerabilities and Risks*, Hexagon Series on Human and Environmental Security and Peace, Vol. 5, edited by H. Brauch et al. Berlin, Heidelberg: Springer-Verlag.

Guha-Sapir, D., Hargitt, D., and Hoyois, P. (2004). *Thirty Years of Natural Disasters 1974–2003: The Numbers*. Brussels: UCL Presses Universitaires de Louvain.

International Monetary Fund (IMF) (2003). *Fund Assistance for Countries Facing Exogenous Shocks*. Washington, D.C.: US International Monetary Fund.

Revkin, A. (2009). "Gore Pulls Slide of Disaster Trends." *New York Times*, February 23. Accessed on March 1, 2009. http://dotearth.blogs.nytimes.com/2009/02/23/gore-pulls-slide-of-disaster-trends/?ref=science.

UN ISDR (2005). *Hyogo Framework for Action 2005–2015: Building the Resilience of Nations and Communities to Disasters*. Paper for the World Conference on Disaster Reduction, Kobe, Hyogo, Japan, January 18–22.

United Nations (2000). *United Nations Millennium Declaration*, General Assembly Resolution 55/2, New York.

UNSD (2008). Composition of Macro Geographical (Continental) Regions, Geographical Sub-regions, and Selected Economic and Other Groupings, United Nations Statistics Division. Accessed January 22, 2008. http://unstats.un.org/unsd/methods/m49/m49regin. htm.

World Bank Group (2012). World Development Indicators Database. Washington, D.C. Accessed January 1, 2012. http://www.worldbank.org/data/onlinedatabases/ onlinedatabases.html.

2 }

The Interlinkages between Natural Disasters and Economic Development
Ajay Chhibber and Rachid Laajaj

Introduction: The Increasing Costs and Frequency of Natural Disasters

Worldwide, the risks linked to natural hazards have increased sharply in recent years. The number of recorded natural disasters has increased exponentially from around 50 per year in the early 1970s, to almost 400 in 2005 (figure 2.1). In constant dollars, natural disasters between 1996 and 2005 resulted in more than $650 billion in material losses, more than 15 times higher than the cost over the period 1950 to 1959.[1] Between 1996 and 2005, natural disasters affected some two billion people. Natural hazards increasingly hinder the development of poor countries. The degree to which human activity contributes to the growing vulnerability to disasters has been the subject of some debate. This chapter argues that nature creates hazards, but disasters are largely man-made, and development and disasters are closely interlinked. Moreover, while there is a natural tendency to focus on very visible cataclysmic events such as earthquakes, floods, and tsunamis, we must become more aware that disasters also result from the slow buildup of human pressure on resources. This leads to natural resource degradation and increased frequency of disasters such as floods or famines. And while many disasters are considered a product of underdevelopment, many are also the result of strategic development choices.

As chapter 1 of this book discusses in detail, the increase in the frequency of disasters has not been uniform. In particular, there have been huge increases in hydrometeorological disasters such as floods and windstorms, while the frequency of other categories of natural disaster has not changed markedly, though there is a small but perceptible increase in droughts (see figure 2.1).

There is also growing evidence of links between conflict, security, and disasters, with pressure on resources often leading to increased likelihood of conflict. Disasters can be part of a vicious spiral: recurring floods, for example, can add to the pressure on resources and create greater vulnerability to future disasters. This is evident in some of the conflicts in Central Africa and more recently in the Darfur region of the Sudan, where the rebellion began in the 1970s, right after Africa's greatest famine.

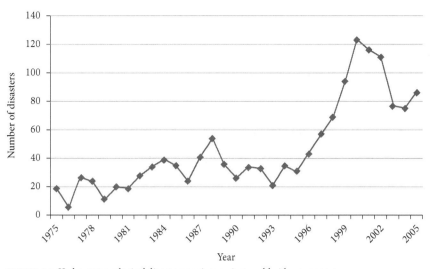

FIGURE 2.1 Hydrometeorological disasters are increasing worldwide, 1975-2005

Source: R. Parker (2007). "Development Actions and the Rising Incidence of Disasters." Washington, D.C.: The World Bank Independent Evaluation Group.

This chapter argues that a much more comprehensive link should be made between disasters, security, and economic development.

This will help policy makers to better prepare countries to deal with natural disasters and to understand how development policy choices affect vulnerability to disasters. The second section shows that while it is easier to understand the short-term impact of natural disasters, their long-term economic impact remains uncertain. This chapter presents a framework for looking at the long-term impact of disasters and summarizes available theoretical and empirical literature. The third section stresses the reciprocal influence of development and vulnerability, highlighting the possibility of a vicious circle: a highly vulnerable and poor country may suffer frequent disasters that prevent it from development and thus from improving its resilience. The fourth section provides case studies of both poorly and well-managed disasters. These cases, combined with theory and other evidence, provide the basis for discussion about better mechanisms for coping with natural disasters. The focus here is on better financial mechanisms and on better measures for preparedness that are currently overlooked. Finally, we end with some suggestions on how disaster response can be factored into long-term development strategies.

The Short- and Long-Term Economic Impact of Natural Disasters

Several studies have evaluated the short-term cost of natural disasters. An exhaustive assessment of the short-term costs must include both direct costs (damage to buildings, crops, social infrastructure) and indirect costs (lost output and investment, macroeconomic imbalances, increased indebtedness). The World Bank estimated that from 1990 to 2000, natural disasters caused damage representing between 2 and 15 percent of an exposed country's annual GDP (World Bank 2004).

Natural disasters thus have severe short-term consequences on economies and cause tremendous human suffering. The costs of human life, capital, and economic losses from large and small disasters are huge and, if avoidable, could lead to large welfare gains. For this reason alone, it would be important to study ways in which the short-term impact of natural disasters could be reduced. But it seems even more important if we can demonstrate that natural disasters have long-term impact. Decisions on how to cope with natural disasters can have consequences for future generations. But very few studies assess these long-term consequences. This chapter outlines the findings of past studies, developing theoretical, as well as empirical, analysis of the long-term economic impact of natural disasters.

THEORY AND ALTERNATE SCENARIOS: THE POSSIBILITY OF A POSITIVE IMPACT ON THE GROWTH PATH

Because natural disasters frequently usher in periods of higher growth, which seem to compensate for the economic impact of the disaster, one might expect that disasters temporarily disrupt development processes but have no impact on long-term development. Aghion and Howitt (1998) provide a theoretical explanation of this observation with a Schumpeterian model of endogenous growth. In the model, technological change that is embedded in new capital replacement needed after the disaster generates growth. As a result, a natural disaster can even lead to a positive overall impact on the economy.

Some authors have tried to model the long-term effects of disasters. Using arguments on economic linkage and substitution effects, Albala-Bertrand (1993a) constructed the first macroeconomic model of the economic impact of a natural disaster. In this model, the first step was to set an upper limit for the impact of a one-off disaster on output, assuming that all losses are to capital stocks, which are homogeneous and irreplaceable in the short term. The result was that the reduction in output was proportional to the reduction in capital stock. The author then modified some assumptions, considering, for example, that loss is split between capital and output, that capital loss is estimated at replacement cost, and that capital is heterogeneous. As a result, the author found a much smaller impact on output, considering this to be much more realistic than the first result. The implication is that a natural disaster is unlikely to have a long-term impact on growth. The model explained why macroeconomic indicators improved during the years following the disaster, quickly returning to their normal level.

Benson and Clay (2004) came to the opposite conclusion by arguing that resources used following a disaster are not necessarily additional and can have a high opportunity cost. The authors identified a number of ways in which natural hazards can influence growth and development paths:

- The capital and human resources stock can be damaged (through migration and death), or their productivity reduced by disruption of infrastructure and markets.

- Spending increases can lead to higher fiscal deficits and cause inflation.
- Reallocation of expenditures draws funds from planned investments.
- Even when funded by aid, this aid may not be entirely additional: donors tend to advance commitments within existing multiyear country programs and budget envelopes. As a result, the amount of aid provided following a natural disaster is diverted from development aid flows.
- Consecutive natural disasters create an atmosphere of uncertainty that discourages potential investors.

Different Possible Scenarios

A common problem in preparing an economic assessment following a disaster is the confusion caused by mixing stock losses with changes in flows. It is necessary to distinguish between the impact of the disaster on stocks and flows. Physical and human capital, and public debt are examples of such stocks; they can be affected directly (destruction of infrastructure, livestock) or indirectly, in which case the variation of a flow causes the variation of the corresponding stock. An increase in the public deficit (a flow) would help add to the public debt; or a diversion of investments (a flow) to fund the relief costs would reduce the stock of physical capital. In return, annual flows are dependent on stocks: physical and human capital stocks are determinants of GDP (a flow). These multiple and complex interactions need to be considered when evaluating the economic impact of a disaster.

Because of contradictory effects, theory does not provide clear-cut conclusions about the impact of natural disasters on the long-term growth rate. It may be useful to outline different scenarios that would then need to be tested.

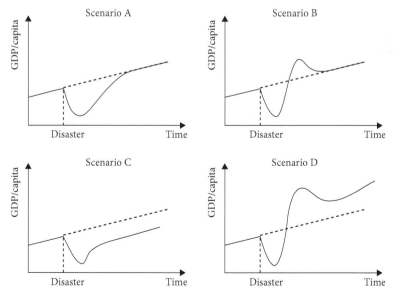

FIGURE 2.2 Possible long-run impact of a disaster on GDP per capita
Source: Authors.

Disasters reduce the stock of human and physical capital, leading to immediate losses in annual production. This short-term reduction of GDP can also be direct, for example, when a drought reduces agricultural production. While a negative impact is commonly observed in the short term, the impact of disasters over the medium and long term is still subject to debate. Scenarios A, B, C, and D of figure 2.2 are graphic representations of the possible impacts of a disaster on the long-term growth rate. In scenarios A and B, the disaster does not influence the long-run income growth path: the shock has a negative impact on GDP, eventually followed by an expansion during the reconstruction (in order to match the initial stock of capital), and the production level returns to its long-run state of equilibrium. In scenario C, because the disaster has permanently reduced the capital stock, the new long-run equilibrium is established at a lower level of GDP. Finally, in scenario D, the recovery of human capital and physical capital brings with it technological change that enhances the long-run economic growth rate.[2] It should be noted that different types of disasters could be associated with different scenarios. For example, an earthquake is more likely to be associated with scenario B or D because it is generally followed by considerable reconstruction that may trigger an expansion, and eventually technological change. But an earthquake might also lead to large loss of human capital, which will reduce the long-run economic growth rate. Conversely, Scenario A or C could correspond to a drought, because when the loss is restricted to the annual production and the household's livelihood, it is unlikely to lead to greater production potential unless it leads to major investments in irrigation or other drought-reducing technologies. Empirical testing of these assertions would be useful.

EMPIRICAL EVIDENCE

One of the first empirical evaluations of the long-term economic impact of disasters was provided by Albala-Bertrand (1993b). In a statistical analysis of 28 disasters in 26 countries from 1960 to 1976, he found that the long-run growth rate and some other key variables were not affected by disasters (similar to Illustrative Scenarios A and B). Benson and Clay (1998) noted the lack of assessment of the nonagricultural or economy-wide macroeconomic impacts of droughts in sub-Saharan Africa. Even if the direct impacts of droughts are easily observable, indirect and secondary impacts on the nonagricultural and macro-economy should not be neglected. They are often not examined as recurrent issues that could potentially affect the rate and pattern of development. Benson and Clay found that drought shocks have large economy-wide impact but that the extent of the impact varies tremendously according to a number of factors, the main ones being the level of complexity of the economy and increased intersectoral linkages.

Benson (2003), in a cross-sectional study covering 115 countries, found that the average growth rate from 1960 to 1993 was lower in countries that experienced more natural disasters (as in Illustrative Scenario C). A main criticism of this study was that the more developed countries have experienced less disaster and therefore the results might reflect Quah's (1993) finding of a polarization toward a bimodal distribution. Indeed Quah observed a long-term divergence of income between developed and developing countries, hence the lower long-term growth rate in countries with frequent disasters (mostly developing countries) is not sufficient to draw conclusions regarding the direction of causality. It is generally difficult to isolate the impact of natural hazards from other factors influencing the growth and development path, because countries with stronger institutions exhibit higher growth and also are better able to handle natural hazards, and therefore are better able to reduce the probability of huge disasters.

Another main channel deserves investigation but seems absent from most of the studies: natural disasters increase the risk of civil war through their economic and social impacts. Using a panel of 41 African countries from 1981 to 1999, Miguel, Satyanath, and Sergenti (2004) found that a negative growth shock of 5 percentage points (instrumented by extreme rainfall variations) increases the likelihood of conflict by 50 percent the following year.

Some models focus specifically on one of these transmission channels. For example, the International Institute for Applied System Analysis modeled the potential impact of disaster on capital accumulation, while Cochrane (1994) explored the impact of disasters on a country's indebtedness. Using a recursive Keynesian growth model, the author assumes that the recovery costs are entirely funded by external borrowing and hence generate an increase in interest rates. The consequence is an increase in debt stock, as well as a reduction of long-term investment and growth.

Nonetheless, all the studies mentioned have been subject to some criticism. Lavell (1999) points out that models such as those presented here should be submitted to an *a posteriori* analysis and evaluation in order to compare real with projected performance. Insufficient empirical work has been done on these issues.

Another problem that has received insufficient attention is that different types of natural disaster have different consequences: for example, Benson and Clay (2004) note the need for a distinction between geological and hydrometeorological disasters. While geological events, being less frequent but often more cataclysmic are more likely to generate Schumpeterian innovation and stimulate postdisaster growth, hydrometeorological disasters are generally more frequent, creating an atmosphere of uncertainty that hurts the investment climate and requires adaptation costs. Indeed in the Albala-Bertrand study mentioned earlier, most of the countries that achieved higher growth rates in the two years following a disaster compared with the two preceding years, had experienced earthquakes. Most other disasters were followed by a lower postdisaster growth rate.

Empirical studies have shown that natural disasters can have a positive long-run impact on economic growth. Skidmore and Toya (2002) showed that a higher frequency of climatic disasters (as opposed to geologic disasters) was associated with higher rates of human capital accumulation, increases in total factor productivity, and economic growth (as in Illustrative Scenario D). Because disaster reduces the expected return to physical capital, and thereby increases the relative return to human capital it can lead to faster growth. Moreover, as capital is replaced, it comes embedded with new technology and thereby helps increase the rate of economic growth. They also argue that natural disasters increase adaptability and readiness to adopt new technology. But the opposite could also be true: people subject to repeated disasters could adopt more risk-averse behavior regarding new ideas and new technology. In the case of geologic disasters, the same study found a negative impact on long-run growth but the coefficients are not statistically significant. Okuyama (2003) and Okuyama, Hewings, and Sonis (2004) even suggest that older capital is more likely to be exposed when a disaster hits the capital stock, and therefore the replacement of this capital stock would create a positive productivity shock and might affect positively the permanent growth rate of the economy.

The argument that natural disasters act as a tool for Schumpeterian creative destruction has been criticized by, for example, Cuaresma, Hlouskova, and Obersteiner (2007) who used gravity models to study the technology spillovers in imports. They found that countries with higher exposure to natural disasters (especially climatic disasters over the medium term and geologic disasters over the short run) get fewer technology spillovers. They also show that the relatively more developed developing countries benefit more from technology spillovers following a disaster. Therefore, catastrophe risk tends to affect technology absorption negatively and the effect is stronger the less developed a country is. Furthermore, catastrophe risk variables tend to be significant determinants of cross-country differences in the long-run patterns of knowledge spillovers to developing countries.

This raises the issues of how analysis of the effect of disasters on growth fits in with analysis of the policies and institutions that determine long-run growth. Popp (2006) argues that a country's ability to cope with disasters also depend on the strength of its institutions, especially those charged with disaster response. The author emphasizes the distinction between risk and uncertainty, and the importance of systematic information on types of disasters, their frequency, and impact. Risk arises from being highly disaster-prone, but uncertainty arises from not knowing about the risks with sufficient precision, and therefore adds a premium to the likelihood of a disaster. Insurance companies factor risk premiums into disaster insurance policies; however, where adequate information is lacking, uncertainty premiums are also added, often making insurance costs prohibitively high. The uncertainty premium affects all investment decisions and may in the long run be a bigger hindrance to development than the cost of the disaster itself.

Given the difficulties faced by macroeconomic studies in isolating the impact of natural disasters, microeconomic results can provide valuable insights into the long-term consequences of disasters. Using a panel dataset from Zimbabwe, Alderman, Hoddinott, and Kinsey (2004) found that children aged between 12 and 24 months during the 1982/84 drought had a higher probability of their growth being stunted[3] during preschool years—a manifestation of malnutrition. The cohort affected by the drought was found to be 2.3 centimeters shorter and to have attained 0.4 fewer grades of schooling when measured 13 to 16 years later. This study highlights the long-term irreversible consequences of natural disasters on human capital in poor countries. Carter et al. (2006) use longitudinal panel data from Ethiopia (for the 1998/2000 drought) and Honduras (following Hurricane Mitch in 1998) to study how different household categories cope with the disasters. Their study shows the existence of "poverty traps"—threshold levels below which households were unable to cope and recover to their original level of well-being. Richer households in Honduras were able to re-establish their assets some three years after the hurricane, but those with annual incomes below $250 were not and fell into a low level of equilibrium. In Ethiopia, poorer households recovered faster than richer households, but to a lower level of equilibrium, suggesting the existence of poverty traps. Dercon (2007) explains that this suggests the existence of poverty traps linked to human capital, resulting in a permanent state of low human capital and earnings.

Using simulation-based econometric methods, in a growth model applied to panel data from rural Zimbabwe, Elbers and Gunning (2003) found that risks associated with disasters reduced the mean capital stock in the observed region by 46 percent. The most innovative part of their work comes from the distinction between *ex-post* (observed directly after the shock) and *ex-ante* effects of risk (the costly behavioral response to risk, such as discouragement of investment). They show that the *ex-ante* effect represents two thirds of the negative effects of risk, stressing the inadequacy of most existing studies, which focus on the *ex-post* effect of risk. This also explains how frequent disasters can generate significantly different effects to a one-time huge disaster (which would have no *ex-ante* effect). Moreover, these studies also show the intergenerational effects of a one-time disaster, if it leads to irreversible decisions such as increased dropout rates from schools or inadequate attention to health care leading to disease. Disaster response mechanisms must be designed with such shocks in mind.

When estimating the overall cost of natural hazards, too much attention has been paid to the major events. Lavell (1999) stresses the importance of smaller scale, more frequent disasters. These may not be registered in the statistical databases because they are small enough not to involve central government authorities. According to Lavell, "the cumulative losses associated with the 'smaller disasters' may be as significant as that attributed to large-scale disasters."

Moreover, in many cases, little action is taken to address smaller but recurring disasters. Land degradation and soil erosion, for example, are also accentuated by climate change and human behavior, and have ever-greater consequences for the poor, such as reduced crop yields. In the Ugandan districts of Kabal, Kisoro, and Mbale, which are densely populated with more than 250 inhabitants per square kilometer, 80 to 90 percent of the area is estimated to be affected by soil erosion (Uganda National Environment Management National Authority 2008). Land degradation is a worldwide issue. A World Bank report (1997) estimated that 80 percent of the poor in Latin America, 60 percent of the poor in Asia, and 50 percent of the poor in Africa lived on marginal lands characterized by poor productivity and high vulnerability to degradation and natural disaster.

Given the methodological difficulties linked to empirical analysis, let us see what is offered by studies that focus on qualitative evidence. Benson and Clay (2004) provide a number of case studies, highlighting the long-term negative effects of disasters. For example, Khan and Hossain (2009: 144) found that in Bangladesh, the "inadequate infrastructure to deal with floods have been a constraint on investment in productive activities as well as on utilization of installed capacity." Similarly, the Philippines has had tremendous difficulty improving its transport system and meeting its social infrastructure needs because of extremely high exposure to natural hazards, mainly floods and windstorms. Dominica in 1979 and Montserrat from 1995 to 1998 are examples of considerable loss of human capital through emigration linked to natural disasters. Clearly more work, both qualitative and quantitative, is needed to explore these issues.

The Interaction between Development and Vulnerability

Before going forward with the analysis, the concept of vulnerability needs to be clarified. Vulnerability to natural hazards can be broken down into two main components: the exposure to shocks and resilience. The degree of exposure to shocks is a function of the frequency and magnitude of natural hazards affecting the population, and the proportion of the population affected by the hazard, in part determined by choices made by people in where they live. In some cases, these choices are voluntary, for example, people prefer to live by the coast or beside rivers. In other cases, the choices are involuntary, as when population pressure drives people into marginal areas. Resilience is the capacity to cope with natural disasters, including both preparedness (land and building codes, better forecasting) and response to disasters (such as financing mechanisms, postdisaster relief). Therefore,

$$V = f(NH, P, R)$$

where V is vulnerability, NH is the number and intensity of natural hazards, P is the population exposed to disaster, and R is the level of resilience. It is expected that NH and P increase vulnerability, while R reduces it. Note that in this framework climate change can affect V by increasing the intensity and frequency of NH and by increasing the proportion of population that disasters affect.

DEVELOPMENT STRATEGIES AND THEIR IMPACT ON VULNERABILITY TO DISASTERS

Hewitt (1983) and Blaikie et al. (1994) have made major contributions to the recent study of natural disasters and development. They stress the role of social structures in shaping vulnerability. Sen (1981) and Drèze and Sen (1989), meanwhile, were pioneers in considering famine not just a natural disaster but also an avoidable economic and political catastrophe. They show that famines were caused not so much by lack of food but by lack of entitlement to resources based on access to economic, social, and political power. This work has strongly influenced thinking about prevention and management of famines in the developing world, and the idea that disasters are man-made or policy-induced.

To pursue the analysis, it is crucial to understand that a natural disaster is not a completely exogenous event. A natural disaster is used as shorthand for humanitarian disaster with a natural trigger. Or, as stated by Wisner in a more provocative way, a natural disaster is a failure of human development (Pelling 2003). Natural disasters make populations more vulnerable because of lack of preparedness. Therefore, the risks of natural disasters must no longer be considered as exogenous factors but as central to development planning.

Determinants of Vulnerability to Natural Hazards

Well-managed and sustainable economic development typically reduces exposure to natural hazards. A reduction of the proportion of the population working in the agricultural sector increases a country's resilience, since the overall level of production becomes less sensitive to hydrometeorological conditions. The inter-sectoral linkages are another determining factor of resilience: countries with a high degree of dualism, with a large capital-intensive extractive sector are less sensitive to natural hazards. For example, droughts had limited effects on the macro-economies of Botswana, Namibia, or Zambia, all of which draw most of their resources from mining. But some types of development can increase expo-sure. For example, there has been a huge migration of people and assets to coastal areas all over the world and this has led to greater exposure to hurricanes, torna-does, and tsunamis. Parker, Little and Hueser (2007) show that about one quarter of the world's population now lives within 100 km of the coast. Of the 25 mega cit-ies around the world, 14 are on the coast and seven are within a few hours' drive of the coast. Unplanned urban development and lack of effective building codes have made many urban areas in the world highly vulnerable to disasters. Migration is also a coping strategy whereby people are forced to move out of harm's way, as in Montserrat due to the volcano or in the Darfur region due to dwindling resources.

THE FINANCIAL SYSTEM

Development is generally linked to a better financial system, which allows a wider diffusion of the impact of a disaster, especially when it facilitates small-scale sav-ings and transfers. In Zimbabwe, for example, after the 1991/92 drought, a well-developed financial system facilitated transfers from urban to rural regions. Later we will discuss the role and importance of micro-credit.

TRADE OPENNESS

Economies that are more open have fewer exchange constraints. Consequently, any increase in imports for relief and reconstruction will not displace normal imports. Moreover, local inflation can be contained more easily in a more open economy following a disaster. But again, more research is needed on how openness to trade helps or hinders recovery from natural disasters.

INSTITUTIONS

One of the most important factors determining a country's resilience is the willing-ness of the government to prioritize preparedness for natural hazards. This includes making a long-term commitment to mitigation and preparedness, even when no disaster has occurred during the preceding years. Such a commitment should also include transparency, better reporting of relevant expenditures, postdisaster real-locations, and the enforcement of appropriate land-use and building codes.

However, the coincidence of a natural disaster and political instability can have dramatic consequences. A recent example is the case of Zimbabwe in 2002. Angola, Lesotho, Malawi, Mozambique, Swaziland, Zambia, and Zimbabwe have all suffered from food shortages because of drought combined with flooding in some areas. Zimbabwe, however, which was considered to be the "breadbasket" of southern Africa a few years ago, became the most vulnerable country in the region. Political violence, fueled by inflation, unemployment, racial tensions, land reform issues, and soaring HIV/AIDS rates have greatly weakened the country's capacity to provide effective relief. The government took control of the distribution of mealie meal (basic food), with the objective of ensuring that mealie meal was supplied only to the supporters of the ZANU-PF ruling party (Osborne 2002). Sen observed that famines result from human behavior, stressing that they do not happen in democracies, where a free press and free speech create excellent early warning systems. While Sen gave Zimbabwe as an example of a democracy that had successfully prevented famines despite sharp declines in food output, he recognized himself that by 2002, Zimbabwe could no longer be labeled as such. Sen also compared the response to droughts in India and China, arguing that India avoided famines because of its free press, whereas China suffered a major famine in 1984 because information on the drought was withheld, problems were not admitted, and assistance was not sought.

PUBLIC AWARENESS AND INSTITUTIONAL RESPONSES

Only an informed population concerned by risks related to natural hazards can create the appropriate incentives for governments to invest sufficiently in preparedness and mitigation. In Turkey, public awareness was very low despite frequent events. The Marmara earthquake (1999) created a new level of public awareness not only because of the unprecedented scale of the disaster but also because it was mainly urban, making it difficult for the politicians, local municipalities, building contractors, and civil engineers to ignore their responsibility (Özyaprak 1999). Turkey has seen a series of earthquakes with each one followed by some improvements in disaster response. But by the time the Marmara earthquake struck, Turkey's disaster response systems had fallen into disrepair and its main agency for disaster response had become a small department under the Ministry of Reconstruction.[4] Since Marmara, Turkey has taken a more active approach to disaster preparedness, in particular planning for the city of Istanbul to be able to handle a large earthquake.

Toya and Skidmore (2007) using cross-country econometric analysis have shown that countries with higher income, higher educational achievement, greater openness, more complete financial systems, and smaller government expenditures experience fewer losses from natural disasters.

An Example of Vulnerability Due to Human Factors

In 1972/73, the Sahel experienced a catastrophic drought during which thousands of people and millions of animals died (de Waal 1997; Mortimore 1998). This catastrophe was the result of both natural and human factors. The preceding droughts in the late 1960s and early 1970s increased people's vulnerability, especially in the rural areas, by depleting their stock of physical capital (savings, grains, animals), as well as human capital, through health deterioration or rural-to-urban migration. Rural communities were the most vulnerable because of:

- isolation due to poor communication and transport links;
- an urban bias in policy making resulting from poor rural representation;
- a focus on short-term stabilization rather than long-term economic development; and
- an emphasis on industrial investment and the conversion of agriculture to cash crops at the expense of the production of food for local consumption (Baker 1987; Shaw 1987; Rau 1991).

The relevance of those human factors is highlighted by the fact that subsequently, the Sahel endured many droughts comparable to those of the early 1970s, but none led to such a massive regional-scale famine (Mortimore 2000). Natural hazards increased vulnerability in the short term, but in the long run the population developed many strategies to cope with drought, such as agricultural diversification and migration.

In this case, the emphasis on industrialization, cash crops, and export earnings in countries that were primarily rural, where most of the population could not afford or lacked access to imported foodstuffs, increased vulnerability. This example illustrates the existence of a local-level adaptive capacity and the danger inherent in a "top-down" approach to development, especially when it is based on global economic paradigms disconnected from the reality of rural communities (Pelling 2003).

THE COMPLEX RELATIONSHIP BETWEEN VULNERABILITY AND DEVELOPMENT

Considerable development effort can be wasted when vulnerability is not taken into consideration. In Honduras, after Hurricane Mitch (1998), President Carlos Flores stated that his country's development was set back 30 to 50 years. Indeed 70 to 80 percent of the transport infrastructure was destroyed, including almost all bridges and secondary roads. One fifth of the population was left homeless, crops and animal losses led to food shortages, and there were outbreaks of malaria, dengue fever, and cholera (National Climatic Center 2004).

Mohamed H. I. Dore and David Etkin (Pelling 2003) point out the importance of having an adaptive capacity at an institutional level. They define the necessary conditions for adaptation by observing the ways in which developed countries are responding to current climate conditions. The authors observed six conditions:

- Developed countries have the technical know-how to understand climate.
- They have resources to devote to research on climate and the related risks.
- They develop the necessary technology to cope with climate change.

- They share risks through government disaster-assistance programs and through the insurance market.
- The insurance market mediates moral hazard problems through mechanisms such as deductible minimums, rebates for minimizing damages, or premium reductions for making no claims.
- They invest resources in emergency response at all government levels.

Fulfilling the six conditions is generally costly and requires high-quality institutions and human capital. A country must therefore be relatively developed to meet the necessary conditions for a high resilience to natural hazards. At the same time, a vulnerable country is highly exposed to disasters that would be harmful to its development process. Consequently, there is a risk that poor countries will be locked into a vicious circle, in which they are vulnerable because of their low level of development, and this vulnerability regularly brings them back to their initial level of development through natural disasters. We earlier summarized the literature on "poverty traps" for individual households, but one can imagine an entire country falling into a low-level equilibrium trap because of repeated disasters, making it unable to lift its per capita growth rate. As represented in figure 2.3a, high vulnerability would result in frequent large-scale natural disasters. Even if one disaster would generally not have long-term effects (as represented in Scenario A of figure 2.2, for example), the

a. Possible Long-Run Impact of Successive Disasters on Income

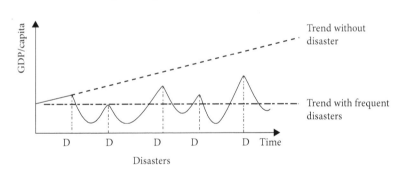

b. Possible Long-Run Impact of Climate Change on Income

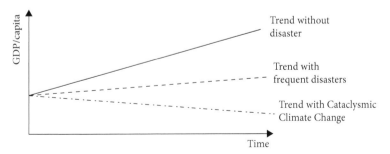

FIGURE 2.3 Possible long-run impacts on income

Source: Authors.

succession of disasters does not allow the country to reconstitute its capital and other productive capacities. The result is high instability but also inability to get onto the growth path that would have been expected in the absence of disasters. This could, for example, be the case for Ethiopia, which is particularly vulnerable, since agriculture accounts for 41 percent of its GDP, 80 percent of its workforce, and 80 percent of exports. Repeated droughts in Ethiopia lead to a lower level growth equilibrium than would be the case without droughts. Undoubtedly, vulnerability is only one of the numerous factors that can explain the stagnation of a least-developed country, but its role should not be neglected, including its role through indirect channels, such as discouraging private investments or increasing the risk of political instability. Further work on the link between vulnerability and development would be valuable, although the establishment of a counterfactual would be difficult.

In order to emerge from this situation progressively, a highly exposed country needs to very consciously build resilience and reduced vulnerability into its development policy. Some authors, such as Katrina Allen (Pelling 2003), go even further and argue that the distinction between resilience to natural hazards and development is mainly theoretical and has more meaning for government bodies than for local communities. At a local level, both are strongly related to the lack of livelihood. Similarly, humanitarian crises cannot be separated from the sociopolitical context. According to Allen, isolating vulnerability from the wider social background risks treating symptoms rather than the cause. The final case study under the heading of case studies illustrates how vulnerability and poverty can be tackled jointly.

If Lord Nicholas Stern (2007) is correct in his forecasts, which incorporate the impact of more severe climate change, then we must also allow for the possibility of a sharp drop in income and consumption. Figure 2.3b illustrates such a scenario without any prevention or coping action. This grim scenario would lead to a huge increase in poverty, malnutrition, and even famine, as well as serious disruption to development. Climate change would be the ultimate natural disaster, with such large negative impacts that countries would face sharp GDP per capita drops.

Case Studies

THE LA JOSEFINA LANDSLIDE IN ECUADOR

In 1993 there was a huge landslide in La Josefina, located in the mountainous southern region of Ecuador near the city of Cuenca. The landslide covered the entire valley, blocking the river for 33 days, during which 1,000 hectares were flooded. In all, about 200 persons were killed by the flood and 14,000 persons displaced, with damage to land and buildings. The damage to agricultural lands, factories, and residential infrastructure amounted to several million dollars.

This case is a good example of a natural disaster caused by a combination of human and natural factors. The area was constantly vulnerable to landslides; below the landslide site, there are about 35 scars from past slides. But this should not obscure the human responsibility. The area has a dense rural population and, following land reforms, land was divided into excessively small plots, worked by farmers with little experience of intensive agriculture. Mono cultivation of maize in rows following the slope was a frequent practice, though this leads to heavy erosion.

After the disaster, during the 33 days of flood, NGOs and the provincial government were criticized for their ineffectiveness and passivity. Codevilla (1993) argued that there was an excess of aid-dependence on the part of the locals, who simply waited to be helped. No structure was in place capable of handling the disaster.

A solution recommended by Morris (Pelling 2003) was to promote a soft engineering (making low-energy adaptations) rather than a hard engineering approach (trying to match the power of nature). These suggestions spring from Abramovitz's recommendations (2001), advocating greater control over land use, the limitation of intensive farming, and the development of forestry in critical zones. This implies recognition of the significant risks presented by natural hazards, which cannot be totally controlled, and the acceptance of a trade-off between higher short-term productivity brought about by intensive farming, and the long-term benefits resulting from the maintenance of a more resilient ecosystem.

SUCCESSFUL DISASTER RECOVERY IN MOZAMBIQUE

In a vulnerable country, one disaster can set back hard-won development efforts. Mozambique is one of the poorest countries in the world, with 69 percent of the population below the poverty line. A 17-year-long civil war ended in 1992, after which GDP per capita growth averaged 6 percent until the flood of 2000. The flood killed 700 people, 650,000 were displaced, and 4.5 million (a quarter of the population) were affected. It devastated 140,000 hectares of crops and their irrigation systems, 350,000 head of livestock were lost or seriously injured, 6,000 fishermen lost at least 50 percent of their boats and equipment, and about 500 primary schools and seven secondary schools were destroyed.

However, Mozambique seems to have recovered successfully from the disaster. Recovery programs have provided an opportunity for improving services and infrastructure (Cosgrave et al. 2001), many affected people have been assisted, and the rehabilitation and the rebuilding of schools and health facilities has encouraged the development of new social structures, such as associations and community committees.

This success can be explained by different factors (see World Bank 2005 for more details), among them the creation of the National Disaster Management Institute in 1999, and the development of a culture of prevention. There were also immediate and massive flows of aid and, above all, determination on the part of the government to establish a recovery program to strengthen national reconstruction and development policies. The objective was not simply to restore the previous level of development, but to generate social and economic improvements to increase resilience against future disasters. A clear sign of progress is that UNICEF (2002) noted significant improvements in responses to the 2001 flood. Preparedness measures had been taken, including the pre-placement of food, boats, and other relief facilities. Neighboring countries were contacted to coordinate the displacement of affected populations.

One of the key elements in the success of the reconstruction was the extraordinarily high level of donor commitment, representing around $450 million in May 2000, combined with the commitment of the government to maintain macroeconomic stability. These aid flows dampened the negative impacts of the disasters, allowing a rapid return to high levels of growth. Therefore, the 2000 and 2001 floods are not considered to have had a lasting negative economic impact.

REDUCING VULNERABILITY AND POVERTY IN COMBINATION

Instead of thinking of disaster response and development as two separate activities, can programs and projects inherently combine these aims? An example of such an approach comes from Niger, one of the poorest countries in the world, where the project was implemented by the Small Rural Operation. It took 11 years (from 1988 to 1998) and targeted an area with a chronic food deficit. The aim was to reduce vulnerability to drought by intensifying off-season crop production through widespread use of existing, simple, low-cost technologies. Around 35,000 farmers benefited from the significant increase in production resulting from higher cropping intensities, cultivation of higher value crops, and diversification toward noncrop activities. In this case, the two objectives of poverty reduction and food security could not have been achieved separately because they were strongly connected to the livelihood of the rural population. More such combined approaches are needed if the vicious cycle of disasters and low-level development is to be broken. Much of the microeconomic evidence that we presented under the heading of the short- and long-term economic impact of natural disasters earlier in this chapter showed the existence of poverty traps, whereby households fall into poverty due to a disaster. If these households fall temporarily into poverty because of a natural disaster, they become chronically poor. Therefore, antipoverty schemes must help households avoid the poverty trap, through special safety-net mechanisms that are triggered by a natural disaster.

Coping with and Preparing for Natural Disasters

FINANCIAL MECHANISMS

When governments do not resort to higher fiscal deficits to fund disaster relief and reconstruction, they generally turn to international aid or reallocation of expenditure. However, other solutions are available for spreading risks. This section discusses the strengths and weaknesses of each solution.

Current Approach

FISCAL DEFICITS

When a government has to meet emergency needs, higher expenditure leading to a bigger fiscal deficit is an easy answer. Nonetheless, the long-term costs of indebtedness are well known, making this choice the last resort. Benson and Clay (1998,

2004) found no impact of natural disasters on the overall budget deficit except in drought-affected sub-Saharan economies, where five of the six case studies showed a noticeable increase in government borrowing after a drought.

REALLOCATION OF EXPENDITURE

One of the most common ways to cope with urgent postdisaster needs is reallocation of budgetary resources. This solution rapidly provides funding while keeping domestic credit and money supply under control. Still, it diverts funds from planned investments and thus hampers development. A main concern is that reallocation of funds after a disaster should follow a formal process rather than emergency decisions, so that funds are not diverted from projects essential to the country's long-term development. But often this is not the case, and vital long-term development is affected.

INTERNATIONAL AID

International agencies play a major role in helping countries with limited resources cope with disasters. However, Benson and Clay (2004) suggest that postdisaster aid flows are not additional. In their three case studies (Dominica, Bangladesh, and Malawi), they observed that disasters had little impact on the overall level of aid. Donors bring forward commitments and thus reduce aid for the subsequent years. The World Bank (2006) IEG report confirms that, despite the existence of an Emergency Recovery Loan (ERL), loan reallocations are the most frequent response to disasters in highly vulnerable countries, with such reallocations rarely leading to good outcomes.

Considerable flows of aid from different donors also cause management difficulties in the receiving country. Recipients must observe different donor-stipulated conditions, which take time and limit the recipient's freedom of action by diminishing its ability to determine the allocation of reconstruction funds or set its own priorities.

Increasingly, countries are taking greater ownership over donor coordination during the relief and recovery period. But where institutional capacities are limited, coordination can also be provided by a donor. After the 1989 Sudan drought, the World Bank worked with other donors to organize the relief and avoid unnecessary overlaps. The international community must pay special attention when a natural disaster occurs in a politically unstable country, or in a country with weak institutions.

Benson and Clay (2004) denounce excessive reliance on international aid when disasters happen. Natural disasters often substantially increase the gap between commitments and actual aid disbursements. In an emergency, small delays may result in severe social and economic consequences. Moreover, more generally, aid flows might not be able to cope with the rapid increase in the annual cost of disasters. There is a need to look at alternatives. And if natural disaster management must be seen as part and parcel of economic development, then special funding mechanisms for disasters may actually lead countries to avoid the fundamental choices they must make about building disaster management into their development strategies.

Financial Risk Mechanisms

INSURANCE

As noted by Freeman et al. (2002), currently less than 1 percent of the losses from natural disasters are formally insured in the world's poorest countries. Financial risk mitigation mechanisms could certainly be developed to reduce aid dependency for managing disasters. The expansion of insurance, however, has been limited by its high cost: catastrophe insurance premiums can be several times higher than the actuarially determined expected losses (Froot 1999). Furthermore, to manage insurance schemes, strong institutions are required. Regulations must ensure that insurance companies are sufficiently cautious and are large enough to diversify the risk or to obtain reinsurance. Moreover, clear and agreed triggers are needed for payment of claims, which are often difficult to finalize.

A closer look at developed countries shows that, in most cases, the market for insurance for natural hazards is not fully private. Governments play a major role, generally by providing catastrophe reinsurance to the companies. As a consequence, the agents are encouraged to adopt risky behavior, knowing that they would not bear the full costs in case of a disaster. To limit the moral hazard, insurance can be provided on condition of implementation of loss-reduction measures and respect for building and land-use zoning codes. In that way, insurance companies can contribute to national efforts for preparedness and mitigation by creating appropriate incentives.

A second problem with the government providing a backstop facility is that this does not eliminate the risk, but transfers it from local to national level. While a rich country's government may have the ability to absorb the costs, a poor country might not have the same capacity. In order to cope with the additional pressure on its budget, the government itself would need to resort to other sources of funding, such as international aid.

DETERMINING CLAIMS TRIGGERS

A possible solution would be to establish a so-called "index" insurance system in which payouts would be triggered by parametric observations such as extreme rainfall. Settling claims without damage assessment procedures can accelerate transfers and reduce transaction costs, but it is currently difficult to find simple instruments strongly related to economic costs. Further agro-meteorological research, as well as good historical data, is necessary for insurance companies to be able to calculate accurate premiums. Good institutions are also required; for example, many difficulties relating to land titles might arise without a strong institutional context.

Because of the difficulties of implementation, few examples of index insurance currently exist. The Windward Islands Crop Insurance (WINCROP), which covers the export of bananas from Dominica, Grenada, St Lucia, and St Vincent and the Grenadines, has a verification system close to the parametric trigger (Benson and Clay 2004). Evaluation of losses is easy because the insurance covers one crop against one hazard. When a disaster occurs, a 5 percent physical survey of affected growers gives the proportion of damaged plants, avoiding lengthy damage assessment procedures. The claim amount is calculated on the basis of the average exports during the preceding three years. Payment of premiums is guaranteed, since payments are directly deducted from export revenues. However, the scheme faces some difficulties, such as the high covariance risk, the fact that premiums are too low but cannot be raised for political reasons, and the long-term decline in banana prices. So far, WINCROP has been unable to extend the insurance scheme to other crops because of legislative restrictions and extremely high reinsurance rates.

In January 2006, the World Bank initiated preparatory studies for the establishment of the Caribbean Catastrophe Risk Insurance Facility (CCRIF). It aims to allow governments of the Caribbean Community and Common Market (CARICOM) to have access to insurance coverage at lower rates than each state could have obtained on its own for three main reasons:

(1) participating governments will pool, and thus diversify, their risk;
(2) donor partners will contribute to a reserve fund in order to reduce the need for international reinsurance; and
(3) the use of a predetermined parametric trigger will reduce transaction costs and moral hazard.

Parametric triggers will allow immediate cash payments after the occurrence of a major earthquake or hurricane, helping governments fund immediate postdisaster recovery, while mobilizing additional resources (World Bank 2007). High exposure to natural hazards has encouraged Caribbean governments to look for creative solutions.

INSTRUMENTS FOR SPREADING RISKS DIRECTLY
TO THE CAPITAL MARKET

Instruments such as "catastrophe bonds" could reduce postdisaster pressure on fiscal and external balances. The principle is very simple, in that the owner of the bond would receive regular payments. However, if the catastrophe occurs, an amount is taken from the principal or interest of the bond. Bonds can provide funds quickly, but because of high transaction costs this solution is twice as expensive as insurance (Swiss Reinsurance Company 1999). When compared to postdisaster assistance, which is generally highly concessional, it is not surprising that the demand for risk transfer mechanisms in the private market is very low in developing countries. But in countries with repeated disasters, one could consider using part of the aid flows to invest in market-based risk spreading options like insurance, with part of the aid being used as a backstop facility. The Turkish earthquake insurance scheme (box 2.1) is an example of this, together with other mechanisms that allow risk to be spread more efficiently.

MICRO-CREDIT INSTITUTIONS

Micro-credit institutions can help cushion the impact of disasters for the part of the population that is highly vulnerable and not reached by other institutions. Natural disasters have a profound impact on households including human losses but also loss of housing, livestock, food stores, and productive assets such as agricultural implements. These assets have to be replaced and households must meet

BOX 2.1 } Giving Countries Access to Catastrophe Risk Financing, Some Successes

Earthquake insurance for homeowners in Turkey. The Turkish Catastrophe Insurance Pool (TCIP) was established in the aftermath of the 1999 Marmara earthquake. It offers efficiently priced earthquake insurance to homeowners. The World Bank provided the initial capitalization of the TCIP through a committed contingent loan facility of $100 million, enlarged to $180 million in 2004. The full risk capital requirements of TCIP are funded through commercial reinsurance (currently in excess of $1 billion) and the build-up of surplus. The TCIP sold more than 2.5 million policies (i.e., 20 percent penetration) in 2006, compared to 600,000 households that were covered when the pool was set up.

Sovereign budget insurance for Caribbean governments. At the request of CARICOM, the World Bank assisted in developing the Caribbean Catastrophe Risk Insurance Facility (CCRIF). The CCRIF allows Caribbean governments to purchase insurance, based on parametric triggers, to provide immediate liquidity and budget support after the occurrence of a major earthquake or the nearby passage of a hurricane. This Caribbean-owned, regional institution is the first regional disaster insurance facility in the world. It currently has 16 participating governments, with policies effective as of June 1, 2007, and is managed by the private sector. The CCRIF was able to secure $110 million of reinsurance capacity on attractive terms prior to the hurricane season.

Index-based livestock insurance for herders in Mongolia. A livestock insurance program was designed and implemented by the government of Mongolia to protect herders against excessive livestock mortality caused by harsh winters and summer drought. A Livestock Insurance Indemnity Pool was established, whereby insurance companies build collective reserves and the government offers public reinsurance, backed by a $5 million World Bank contingent credit facility. The viability of index-based livestock insurance was piloted in 2005-2008 in selected areas to test the preparedness of private insurance companies to offer this product and the herders' willingness to purchase. In the second sales season (April–July 2007), about 600,000 animals were insured (a 10 percent insurance penetration).

Weather index-based insurance for farmers in India. The government of India requested World Bank technical assistance to further improve its national agricultural insurance program (NAIS) and help the state-owned agriculture insurance company to develop innovative products such as weather-based parametric insurance. New weather-based index insurance products were piloted in the State of Karnataka during spring 2007 and more than 40,000 policies were sold. The state agriculture insurance company expanded weather-based insurance to other states in the autumn 2007, largely to provide an early claim payment mechanism under the NAIS.

Catastrophe bond in Mexico. Following the successful example of Taiwan in 2003, an arm of the government of Mexico, with technical assistance from the World Bank, issued a $160 million three-year catastrophe bond with a historically low interest spread. Its purpose is to cover against the risk of earthquakes

(Continued)

BOX 2.1 } Continued

affecting Mexico City, as part of an overall strategy to secure $450 million in the aftermath of a major disaster. If an earthquake above defined intensities hits in designated areas of the country within a certain time period, the government will be able to draw from these funds. If no disaster occurs during the life of the fund, the money will be returned to investors. This is the first time a sovereign entity has issued a catastrophe bond.

Contingent credit facility against natural disasters in Colombia. The Colombian government arranged in 2005 a $150 million contingent credit line with the World Bank. This will provide the government with immediate liquidity in the event of a major disaster.

Source: Lester and Mahul (2007).

basic needs until they are able to earn income again. In the absence of micro-credit institutions, poor households might be forced to rely on money lenders who charge considerably higher rates of interest.

However, micro-credit institutions are highly exposed. In Bangladesh, after the 1998 floods, considerable refinancing from the Bangladesh Bank prevented many micro-credit institutions from falling into bankruptcy. The government guarantee is essential because the high covariance risk would result in micro-credit agencies facing problems during a disaster. In order to avoid repercussions for the users of micro-credit, a contingent liability from the governments or donors will constantly be required. A risk-pooling arrangement with micro-credit institutions from different parts of the world could be another way of diversifying the risk.

INCREASING THE FLEXIBILITY OF AID DISBURSEMENTS

The term "moral hazard" has often been used when accusing poor country governments of not doing enough for disaster mitigation as part of their development strategy because of the expectation of postdisaster external assistance. The cost of insurance can be so high, however, that it could have long-run economic effects through diversion of capital from investment or other spending with a high opportunity cost. In this case, it is not only rational to rely on international aid at a national level, but it is also rational at a collective level because international assistance is the solution that minimizes the long-run negative economic impact of natural disasters. It is likely that the capacity of a country to handle the risks linked to natural hazards without international assistance will depend heavily on its stage of development. For this reason, insurance and instruments for spreading risk linked directly to the capital market—such as catastrophe bonds—might be accessible mainly to middle-income countries. In the least developed countries, however, where the insurance industry is reticent because of risk aversion, the only solution might be an appropriate intervention: aid flows must be adapted to meeting the urgent needs following a disaster.

The limits of aid mentioned previously (such as delays or the lack of coordination) are essentially due to the donor community tending to be reactive rather than anticipating disasters. Guillaumont (2006) suggests that aid could provide a guarantee to countries that accept some predefined rules of shock management. This shift from *ex-post* conditionality to *ex-ante* conditionality could considerably reduce both delays and moral hazard. We know disasters will occur, but we do not know when and where. In this case, one option would be a regional or a global disaster facility. Following a recent evaluation, the World Bank has established a Global Facility for Disaster Reconstruction and Response (GFDRR), which assists several countries, regional and international organizations in identifying disaster risks, developing risk-mitigation and risk-financing strategies, establishing institutional and legal systems for risk reduction and strengthening regional cooperation in early warning, knowledge-sharing, and emergency preparedness. If procedures for accessing the facility are agreed up front, then such a facility (once scaled up) would also reduce problems of donor coordination often seen in postdisaster reconstruction programs.

Even when disaster relief is reactive, it can be made more effective if it is provided more flexibly. Until recently, much postdisaster aid was given in the forms of goods and services, such as food, clothing, and material donations. This can cause logistical nightmares and is in any case not the most effective way to help disaster-stricken families. Cash assistance is often much better because it allows families to make better choices about what they need, keeps families and communities intact, as people do not need to move to search for income, helps families who have fallen into a temporary poverty trap to keep their assets, and ensures much faster recovery and reconstruction. Cash injections into a devastated local economy also help revive business activity, thereby creating opportunities for work—a process of recovery that would normally take much longer. But cash assistance is not the preferred choice of most donor organizations, though this is changing.

Another solution deserving more attention, although it has already been implemented, is the use of debt relief as a way to rapidly reduce financial pressure on the country where the disaster takes place. This can circumvent regular delays related to funds being released by donors. This solution is particularly useful for Heavily Indebted Poor Countries, where debt servicing can crowd out other important uses of scarce resources.

DISASTER PREPAREDNESS MUST BE IMPROVED

The Predictability of Natural Hazards

Most natural hazard risks are foreseeable in the sense that it is possible to predict where events are more likely to occur in the near future; and yet this forecasting is very infrequently included in country development strategies, even in highly vulnerable countries. Even some of the most advanced countries in Africa, such as South Africa, spend only about $5 million per year on forecasting research as against estimated economic costs of natural hazards of $1 billion per year. If forecasting research can make even a small contribution to better public decisions on mitigation, preparedness, and crisis management, it would justify sustaining the climatic forecasting research effort. Investments in early warning systems for flooding, tsunamis, and hurricanes can also help save thousands of lives and even

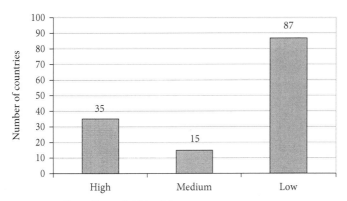

FIGURE 2.4 Natural hazard risk levels by country

Note: high = over 50 percent of GDP at risk; medium = 30–50 percent; low = < 30 percent.

Source: Based on data from M. Dilley (2005). "Natural Disaster Hotspots: A Global Risk Analysis." Washington, D.C.: World Bank Publications.

reduce the financial cost of disasters. There is much room for improvement in climate forecasting: the density of weather watch stations is eight times lower than the minimum level recommended by the World Meteorological Organization, and reporting rates in Africa are the lowest in the world (Washington, Harrison, and Conway 2004). But even without waiting for better forecasting, we can already classify countries into categories of vulnerability on the basis of existing *ex-post* disaster data (figure 2.4).

Planning the Relief and Reconstruction Efforts

As mentioned in the previous section, it is possible to identify a number of countries that are highly exposed to natural hazards. For example, in figure 2.4, we can classify countries as high risk where over 50 percent of GDP is at risk, and as medium risk where between 30 and 50 percent of GDP is at risk. Out of 137 countries, 50 countries fall into the medium- to high-risk category. Figure 2.5 shows the most exposed African countries, where at least 10 disasters occurred between 1996 and 2005. In countries in which disasters are known to occur with repeated periodicity, disaster preparedness must be a central part of the development strategy and not an afterthought. The infrastructure in these countries should be disaster resistant. Yet we find repeatedly that in most of these high-risk countries, infrastructure built after one disaster must then be rebuilt after the next one. We also find very poor enforcement of existing building codes. For example, in the 1999 Marmara earthquake in Turkey, which killed more than 15,000 people, lack of housing code enforcement by local authorities was a major cause of death and destruction.

In afflicted countries, the probability that another disaster will occur during the next decade is very high. However, table 2.1 shows that even among the countries with a high frequency of disasters, only two have incorporated aspects of hazard risk management into their Poverty Reduction Strategy Papers (PRSPs).

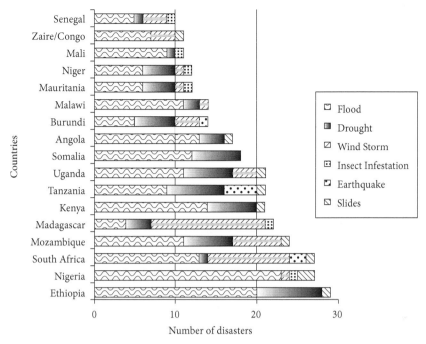

FIGURE 2.5 Natural hazard risk levels by country in Africa

Source: Authors.

TABLE 2.1 } Neglecting Natural Disasters in Development Strategies in Africa

Number of disasters (1966–2005)[a]	Number of countries	Number of countries including a discussion of disasters in the PRSP
21 to 29 disasters	7	1 (Mozambique)
11 to 19 disasters	6	1 (Malawi)
1 to 9 disasters	18	1 (Ghana)
TOTAL	31	3 (10%)

Source: Authors.

[a] This table only includes those sub-Saharan countries that have a PRSP.

A more ambitious agenda would involve preventing or reducing the frequency of natural disasters by designing development approaches and strategies that reduce vulnerability. Of course, development itself, by reducing the exposure of the population to agro-climatic conditions, reduces vulnerability; but more specific actions can be taken, such as better water and land management, better infrastructure and housing, and more careful attention to actions that increase vulnerability to natural hazards.

Disasters must be anticipated in order to make rational choices, even in emergency situations. In highly exposed countries, governments should prepare a clearly defined policy framework for meeting urgent needs, as well as for minimizing the long-term negative consequences of disasters. Such a framework should include a system of prioritization of individual development projects and programs to ensure that any budget reallocation does not harm the projects with the highest development impact.

Stern (2007) also recognizes development as a key to long-term adaptation to climate change; moreover, he points out some particular areas of development that are essential to foster climate-change adaptation capability:

- income and food security;
- education and health systems;
- urban planning and provision of public services and infrastructure; and
- gender equality.

The cost of climate change adaptation in the developing world is hard to estimate, but it will be up to tens of billions of dollars. However, this is far less costly than the consequences of inaction. Firm measures to strengthen adaptation include the integration of climate change impacts in all national, subnational, and sectoral planning processes and macroeconomic projections. The involvement of a core ministry, such as finance, economics, or planning, which would be accountable for mainstreaming adaptation, would be a sign of government commitment (Sperling 2003).

Conclusions

The objective of this chapter is to draw attention to the growing impact of natural hazards on long-term development, as well as the reciprocal effect of development on vulnerability. After a review of the existing literature, many areas for further research have emerged.

First, there is no consensus about the long-term economic impact of natural disasters. Some authors argue that while a consequent negative impact is observed during the year of the shock, it is generally followed by economic expansion, allowing a rapid return to the long-term equilibrium. Others say that the reduction of human and physical capital can hinder the long-term development of a country, especially when disasters are frequent. Because of technical difficulties, few previous studies have provided compelling empirical evidence to confirm either perspective. Both theoretical and better empirical work is needed.

Second, further theoretical, as well as empirical, studies of the long-term impact of natural disasters will have analysis of disasters in more detail. It is very likely that impacts will differ according to the type and frequency of disaster, and the contribution of international aid and the socioeconomic conditions of the affected country. Less detailed approaches could be misleading.

Third, the link between conflict, natural disasters, and vulnerability needs more attention, especially in parts of sub-Saharan Africa where population pressure, land degradation, and desertification are increasing rapidly.

Fourth, the role of alternative funding mechanisms needs more research, including research on how they could be expanded and how inherent moral hazards and covariance could be reduced. Funding mechanisms include market-based facilities like insurance and bonds, local funding such as micro-credit schemes to reduce vulnerability, and prearranged global or regional funding mechanisms.

Fifth, current development plans appear largely to ignore disaster risks. Is this caused by a lack of incentives due to limited public awareness? Much more attention must be paid to how economic development plans and strategies can incorporate disaster risk mitigation more visibly and centrally through national plans.

Notes

1. Based on a report on natural disasters prepared by the World Bank's Independent Evaluation Group.

2. Postwar reconstruction has also seen this type of feature with the rapid recovery of countries devastated by World War II attributed to, among other factors, new capital stock embedded with better technology.

3. A child is considered as stunted if his height given his age is two standard deviations below international norms (ACC/SCN (2000). *Fourth Report on the World Nutrition Situation* Geneva: ACC/SCN in collaboration with IFPRI).

4. The Turkish agency's role in coordination had fallen into disrepair similar to the problems encountered by the US Federal Emergency Management Agency (FEMA) once it came under the overall US security apparatus after 9/11. As a result, FEMA, which was once held up as a model for disaster response, became ineffective and was unable to respond effectively during the Hurricane Katrina disaster in Louisiana.

References

Abramovitz, J. (2001). "Averting Unnatural Disasters." In *State of the World 2001*, edited by L. R. Brown. London: Earthscan.

Aghion, P., and Howitt, P. (1998). *Endogenous Growth Theory*. Cambridge, Mass.: MIT Press.

Albala-Bertrand, J. M. (1993a). "Natural Disaster Situations and Growth: A Macroeconomic Model for Sudden Disaster Impacts." *World Development* 71(9): 1417–1434.

———. (1993b). *The Political Economy of Large Natural Disasters with Special Reference to Developing Countries*. Oxford: Clarendon Press.

Alderman, H., Hoddinott, J., and Kinsey, B. (2004). "Long-Term Consequences of Early Childhood Malnutrition." Department of Economics, Dalhousie University at Halifax, Canada. Mimeographed.

Baker, R. (1987). "Linking and Sinking: Economic Externalities and the Persistence of Destitution in Africa." In *Drought and Hunger in Africa: Denying Famine a Future*, edited by M. H. Glantz. Cambridge: Cambridge University Press.

Bangladesh, Economic Relations Division, Ministry of Finance and Panning Commission (2000). "Memorandum for Bangladesh Development Forum 2000–2001." Dhaka.

Benson, C. (2003). "The Economy-wide Impact of Natural Disasters in Developing Countries." Draft Ph.D. diss., University of London.

Benson, C., and Clay, E. (1998). "The Impact of Drought on Sub-Saharan African Economies: A Preliminary Examination." *World Bank Technical Paper*, No. 401.

———. (2004). "Understanding the Economic and Financial Impacts of Natural Disasters." *World Bank Disaster Risk Management Series*, No. 4.

Blaikie, P., Cannon, T., Davis, I., and Wisner, B. (1994). *At Risk: Natural Hazards, People's Vulnerability, and Disasters*. London: Routledge.

Carter, M., Little, P., Mogues, T., and Negatu, W. (2006). "Poverty Traps and Natural Disasters in Ethiopia and Honduras." *World Development* 35(5): 835–856.

Cochrane, H. C. (1994). "Disasters, Indebtedness and Faltering Economic Growth." Prepared for the 9th International Seminar on Earthquake Prognostics, September 9–23, San José, Costa Rica.

Codevilla, U. (1993). *Antes que las Aguas nos Alcancen*. Cuenca: Rumbos.

Cosgrave, J., Fidalgo, L., Hallam, A., and Selvester, K. (2001). *Independent Evaluation of Expenditure of DEC Mozambique Floods Appeal Funds March 2000–December 2000*. London: Valid International and ANSA.

Cuaresma, J., Hlouskova, J., and Obersteiner, M. (2007). "Natural Disasters as Creative Destruction? Evidence from Developing Countries." *Economic Enquiry* 46(2): 1–13.

Dercon, S. (2007). "Fate and Fear: Risk and Its Consequences in Africa." Paper prepared for the African Economic Research Consortium, Oxford University, Oxford.

De Waal, A. (1997). *Famine Crimes: Politics and the Disaster Relief Industry in Africa*. Oxford: James Currey.

Drèze, J., and Sen, A. (1989). *Hunger and Public Action*. Oxford: Clarendon Press.

Elbers, C., and Gunning, J. (2003). "Growth and Risk: Methodology and Microevidence." *Tinbergen Institute Discussion Papers*, 03–068/2.

Freeman, P., Martin, L., Mechler, R., and Warner, K., with Peter Hausman (2002). "Catastrophes and Development: Integrating Natural Catastrophes into Development Planning." *World Bank Disaster Risk Management Working Paper Series*, No. 4.

Froot, K. (1999). *The Financing of Catastrophe Risk*. Chicago: University of Chicago Press.

Guillaumont, P. (2006). "Macroeconomic Vulnerability in Low-Income Countries and Aid Responses." In *Securing Development in an Unstable World*, edited by F. Bourguignon, B. Pleskovic, and J. Van der Gaag. Annual World Bank Conference on Development Economics—Europe, 2005. Washington, D.C.: World Bank.

Hewitt, K. (1983). *Interpretations of Calamity*. London: Allen and Unwin.

Khan, A. R., and Hossain, Mahabub (1989). *The Strategy of Development in Bangladesh*. Basingstoke and London: Macmillan.

Lavell, A. (1999). "The Impact of Disasters on Development Gains: Clarity or Controversy." Latin American Social Science Faculty (FLACSO) and The Network for the Social Study of Disaster Prevention in Latin America-LA RED. Paper presented at the IDNDR Programme Forum, Geneva, July 5–9, 1999.

Lester, R., and Mahul, O. (2007). "Facilitating Countries' Access to Catastrophic Risk Financing Some Recent Successes." Mimeo. World Bank.

Miguel, E., Satyanath, S., and Sergenti, E. (2004). "Economic Shocks and Civil Conflict: An Instrumental Variables Approach." *Journal of Political Economy* 112(4): 725–753.

Mortimore, M. (1998). *Rots in the African Dust*. Cambridge: Cambridge University Press.

———. (2000). "Profile of Rainfall Change and Variability in the Kano-Maradi Region 1960–2000." Working Paper, No. 40, Drylands Research, Crewkerne, Somerset, UK.

National Climatic Center (2004). "Mitch: The Deadliest Atlantic Hurricane since 1780." Accessed December 28, 2008. http://lwf.ncdc.noaa.gov/oa/reports/mitch/mitch.html.

Okuyama, Y. (2003). "Economics of Natural Disasters: A Critical Review." Research Paper 2003-12, Regional Research Institute, West Virginia University.

Okuyama, Y., Hewings, G., and Sonis, M. (2004). "Measuring Economic Impacts of Disasters: Interregional Input-Output Analysis Using Sequential Inter-Industry Model." In *Modeling the Spatial and Economic Effects of Disasters*, edited by Y. Okuyama and S. Chang. New York: Springer.

Osborne, P. (2002). *Is Zimbabwe on the Brink of Genocide?* London: Chameleon Press.

Özyaprak, S. (1999). "Yapisal Degisim Zamani mi?" (Is It Time for Structural Changes?) *Financial Forum* 11: 9.

Parker, R., Little, K., and Hueser, S. (2007). "Human Actions and the Rising Incidence of Disasters." Independent Evaluation Group Evaluation Brief, No. 4. Washington, D.C.: World Bank.

Pelling, M. (2003). *Natural Disasters and Development in a Globalizing World.* London: Routledge.

Popp, A. (2006). "The Effects of Natural Disasters on Long Run Growth." *Major Themes in Economics* 8: 61–81.

Quah, D. (1993). "Empirical Cross Section Dynamics in Economic Growth." *European Economic Review* 37: 426–434.

Rau, B. (1991). *From Feast to Famine.* London: Zed Books.

Sen, A. (1981). *Poverty and Famines: An Essay on Entitlements and Deprivation.* Oxford: Clarendon Press.

Shaw, T. (1987). "Towards a Political Economy of the African Crisis." In *Drought and Hunger in Africa: Denying Famine a Future*, edited by M. Glantz. Cambridge: Cambridge University Press.

Skidmore, M., and Toya, H. (2002). "Do Natural Disasters Promote Long-Run Growth?" *Economic Enquiry* 40: 664–688.

Sperling, F. (ed.) (2003). *Poverty & Climate Change: Reducing the Vulnerability of the Poor Through Adaptation.* African Development Bank, Asian Development Bank, UK Department for International Development, European Commission, German Federal Ministry for Economic Cooperation and Development, Netherlands Ministry of Foreign Affairs, Organization for Economic Cooperation and Development, United Nations Development Programme, United Nations Environment Programme. Washington, D.C.: World Bank.

Stern, N. (2007). "The Economics of Climate Change." *The Stern Review.* Cambridge: Cambridge University Press.

Swiss Reinsurance Company (1999). "Alternative Risk Transfer (ART) for Corporations: A Passing Function of Risk Management for the 21st Century?" Swiss Re sigma No. 2.

Toya, H., and Skidmore, M. (2007). "Economic Development and the Impact of Natural Disasters." *Economics Letters* 94-1: 20–25.

Uganda National Environment Management National Authority (2008). *State of the Environment Report for Uganda.* Kampala: Republic of Uganda. http://www.nemaug.org/national_s_o_reports.php.

UNICEF (2002). *Mozambique: Energy Preparedness and Response Plan 2002.* New York: UNICEF.

Washington, R., Harrison, M., and Conway, D. (2004). *African Climate Report: A Report Commissioned by the UK Government to Review African Climate Science, Policy and*

Options for Action. London: UK Department for Environment, Food and Rural Affairs, and the Department for International Development.

World Bank (1997). *World Disaster Report*. Oxford: Oxford University Press.

———. (2004) "Natural Disasters: Counting the Cost." March 2, 2004. Accessed December 28, 2011. http://go.worldbank.org/BD449R1HY0.

———. (2005). "Learning Lessons from Disasters Recovery: The Case of Mozambique." *Disaster Risk Management Working Paper Series*, No. 12.

———. (2006). "Hazards of Nature, Risks to Development, An IEG Evaluation of World Bank Assistance for Natural Disasters." Independent Evaluation Group, Washington, D.C.: World Bank Publications.

———. (2007). "Results of Preparation Work: Caribbean Catastrophe Risk Insurance Facility." Washington, D.C.: World Bank. http://siteresources.worldbank.org/OECSEXTN/Resources/ResultsofPreparationWorkontheDesignofaCaribbeanCatastropheRiskInsuranceFacility.pdf.

3 }

Valuing the Impacts of Natural Disasters and the Economic Benefits of Preventing Them
METHODS AND APPLICATIONS

Ståle Navrud and Kristin Magnussen

Introduction

Natural disasters such as flooding, wind storms, volcanic eruptions, and earthquakes cause economic welfare losses to households through impacts on private, market goods and public, nonmarket goods. These impacts include:

- damage to public health in terms of loss of lives (mortality) and reduced health status due to injuries and illnesses (morbidity);
- damage to private manufactured goods such as houses and household items, agricultural production, small businesses;
- damage to the environment such as like water quality, soil, biodiversity, and ecosystems; and
- damage to other public goods such as the electricity supply, drinking water supply, schools, hospitals and other public buildings, built cultural heritage, roads, bridges, and other infrastructure.

Economic assessments of damage caused by extreme events are conducted both *ex-post* in order to assess the need for compensatory and alleviating measures, and *ex-ante* in cost-benefit analyses of preventive/mitigating measures that will prevent natural hazards or reduce their impact.

While damage to public goods could make up a large part of the overall economic damage caused by natural disasters, few studies of their economic value exist. This is due to their nonmarket nature and lack of market prices, which make assessments of their economic values difficult. Therefore, this chapter aims at describing both market and nonmarket valuation methods that can be used to value the impacts

Department of Economics and Resource Management at the Norwegian University of Life Sciences and SWECO Norway are the affiliations for Ståle Navrud and Kristin Magnussen, respectively. This chapter is written as part of the project *Microdis* (Integrated Health Social and Economic Impacts of Extreme Events: Evidence, Methods and Tools), which is financed by the European Commission, 6th Framework Programme on Research, Technological Development and Demonstration.

of natural disasters; and especially how they can be adapted in order to estimate the social benefits arising from the prevention of damage from natural disasters in developing countries.

Whereas private goods can be valued using market prices, nonmarket valuation methods are used for the economic assessment of impacts on public goods like public health (mortality and morbidity), environmental quality (air, soil, and water quality), ecosystem services, and built cultural heritage. These methods try to elicit individuals' (or households') preferences for public goods through their behavior in markets for private goods that are related to the public goods (i.e., revealed preferences), or their behavior in constructed, hypothetical markets (stated preferences) for the public goods.

Since the majority of empirical nonmarket valuation studies have been conducted in developed countries and in contexts not related to natural disasters, there is a great need for new primary nonmarket valuation studies in developing countries in the context of natural disasters. An alternative to these new studies would be to transfer values from previous valuation studies in developed countries (and the few studies found in developing countries). This practice is most often referred to as "benefit transfer," but since damage costs can also be transferred, a more general term is "value transfer" (Navrud and Ready 2007). While benefit transfer is less costly and faster than conducting an original study, the resulting values, which have been transferred across time and space, and across social, cultural, and environmental contexts, are less certain. Thus, we will also review benefit transfer techniques, the evidence on how well economic values of public goods transfer both within and across countries, and the potential for benefit transfer when assessing damage costs arising from extreme events, or the benefits of preventing these damages.

Nonmarket Valuation Methods

The welfare loss to households due to, for example, damage to ecosystem goods and services from natural disasters can be estimated on the basis of how much individuals are willing to pay (willingness-to-pay, WTP) to avoid incurring this damage, which is defined as the total economic value (TEV). TEV can be divided into:

- use value, motivated by individuals' actual use of the public good; and
- nonuse values motivated by the wish to preserve the option for future use (i.e., option value), the wish to preserve the existence of the good (i.e., existence value), and the desire to pass on the good to future generations (i.e., bequest value) (figure 3.1).

The different nonmarket valuation methods can be used to estimate some, or all, parts of the TEV. Thus, the economic valuation of environmental quality, cultural heritage, and health impacts would typically be based on individual preferences, either observed behavior (revealed preferences, RP) toward some marketed good with a connection to the nonmarket good of interest; or stated preferences (SP) expressed in surveys about the change in nonmarketed goods. Table 3.1 provides an overview of the different types of RP and SP valuation techniques.

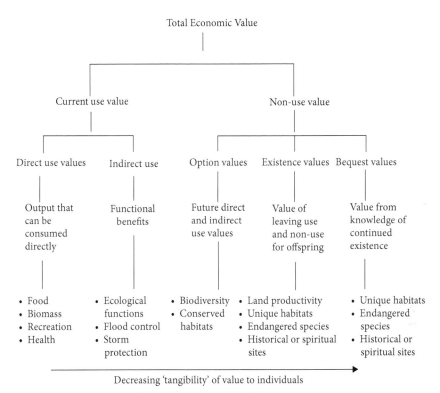

Total Economic Value

Current use value

Non-use value

Direct use values   Indirect use   Option values   Existence values   Bequest values

| Output that can be consumed directly | Functional benefits | Future direct and indirect use values | Value of leaving use and non-use for offspring | Value from knowledge of continued existence |

- Food
- Biomass
- Recreation
- Health

- Ecological functions
- Flood control
- Storm protection

- Biodiversity
- Conserved habitats

- Land productivity
- Unique habitats
- Endangered species
- Historical or spiritual sites

- Unique habitats
- Endangered species
- Historical or spiritual sites

→ Decreasing 'tangibility' of value to individuals

FIGURE 3.1 Decomposition of total economic value (TEV) of ecosystem goods and services

Source: Based on M. Munasinghe and E. Lutz (1993). "Environment Economics and Valuation in Development Decision-Making." Washington, D.C: World Bank, Environment Working Paper No. 51.

RP techniques can be divided into direct and indirect methods. *Direct methods* include the use of market prices to value productivity losses in, for example, crops due to inundation and soil erosion. In its simplest form this approach would collect data on the physical consequences of a disaster based on reported damages from farmers (e.g., crop losses); or would predict this based on a generalizable and transferable dose-response function (which describes the functional relationship, e.g., between the "dose" in terms of how severe the flooding is, when it occurs, and how

TABLE 3.1 } Classification of Nonmarket Valuation Methods

	Direct	Indirect
Revealed Preferences (RP)	Market prices/Productivity Loss Approach Replacement Costs (RC)/Restoration Costs	Household Production Function (HPF) Approach – Travel Cost (TC) method – Averting Costs (AC) Hedonic Price (HP) analysis
Stated Preferences (SP)	Contingent Valuation (CV)	Choice Experiments (CE)/Choice Modelling

Source: Authors.

long it lasts; and the "response" in terms of annual loss of different crops due to this flooding). A monetary measure of damage is obtained by multiplying the observed market prices of the affected crops by the magnitude of the physical or biological response. Thus, neither behavioral adaptations nor price responses are taken into account. Simple multiplication provides an accurate estimate of economic behavior and value—in this case changes in gross revenue—only if economic agents are limited in the ways in which they can adapt to the environmental effect, and if the effect is small enough to have little or no impact on relative prices. These assumptions might be fulfilled in cases where the shock is very localized and where the crop is widely traded in competitive markets, so that the price is exogenous to the region or farmers affected. However, if crop damages from flooding affect a larger area and increase prices, changes in consumer and producer surpluses have to be calculated. If farmers undertake preventive measures, such as switching to crops that are less sensitive to extreme events (e.g., switching from growing rice to shrimps in mangrove forest areas with salt water intrusion due to storms and flooding); then the simple multiplicative approach will overestimate damage costs. Thus, this approach should be used with great care and clearly stated assumptions.

Another direct RP method is the *replacement cost method*, which is also termed the *restoration cost method*. This method is frequently used to estimate economic damage caused by soil erosion, by using market prices for soil and fertilizers to calculate what it would cost to replace the lost soils and its nutrients. This approach has also been used to calculate value of lost ecosystem functions, such as flood protection provided naturally by mangrove forests. It has also been used to estimate the economic value of the flood prevention and waste water treatment functions of wetlands by calculating the costs of building embankments and water treatments plants, respectively (see, e.g., Byström 2000). This procedure assumes that the replacement projects are perfect substitutes for the lost ecosystem services and do not cause their own negative impacts. This is not always the case. Embankments, for example, might not fully protect the threatened areas, and if they are flooded the embankments might increase the time an area is inundated and thus increase damages. Also, one should bear in mind that these replacement or restoration costs might bear little relationship to the welfare loss suffered by the affected households.

The greatest advantage of these direct RP methods is that they are relatively simple to use. But as noted earlier, the methods ignore the behavioral responses of individuals to changes in environmental amenities. They also obscure the distinction between benefits and costs—there is no guarantee that people are actually willing to pay the estimated cost of the replacement project as their welfare loss might be much smaller than the replacement costs. Their welfare loss could in some cases also be larger than the replacement costs.

There are two main groups of *indirect RP methods*: the household production function approach (including the travel cost and averting cost methods) and the hedonic price analysis.

The *household production function* (HPF) approaches involve investigating changes in consumption of commodities that are substitutes or complements for the public good in question. HPF approaches include the travel cost (TC) and the averting cost (AC) methods, and use actual behavior as the basis for valuation. However, they are limited to use value. Nonuse values, that do not entail direct consumption, cannot be estimated by looking at marketed complements or substitutes.

The *travel cost* (TC) method has been widely used to measure the economic value of recreational activities (Bockstael and McConnell 2007). The costs of travelling to a recreational site (e.g., beach, river, national park, or cultural heritage site), together with participation rates, visitor attributes, and information about substitute sites, are used to derive a measure for the use value of the recreational activity at the site. Travel can be used to infer the demand for recreation, only if it is a necessary part of the visit, or in economic terms is a *weak complement*. TC models build on a set of strict assumptions, which are seldom fulfilled, and the results are sensitive to the specification of the TC model, the choice of functional forms, treatment of travel time and substitute sites, and so on. However, the TC method can be relatively cheap to use (compared to SP methods) and can give reasonably reliable estimates for use values of natural resources (e.g., recreational use values of beaches, rivers, national parks, etc.) for the *current* quality of a site. Thus, they could be used to assess lost recreational value from the flooding of rivers used for recreational activities, or loss of beach recreation due to cyclones, by assessing the number of visitor days lost due to the extreme event multiplied by the estimated recreational value per visitor day (assuming this value to be the same before and after the event). In the same way the TC method could be used to assess the loss in beach recreation value at popular tourist destinations in Thailand due to the Asian tsunami.

Another HPF approach is the *averting cost* (AC) method; also known as *defensive or preventive expenditures*. Averting inputs includes, for example, buying bottled water and water purification systems, and other means of mitigating personal impacts from flooding. Such inputs substitute for changes in environmental attributes; in effect the quality of a consumer's personal environment is a function of the quality of the collective environment and the use of averting inputs. We measure the value of changes in the collective environment by examining costs incurred in using averting inputs to make the personal environment different from the collective environment. A rational consumer will buy averting inputs to the point where the marginal rate of substitution between purchased inputs and the collective environment equals the price ratio. By characterizing the rate of substitution and knowing the price paid for the substitute, we can infer the price that consumers would be willing to pay for a change in the environment. The common element in household production methods is the use of changes in the *quantities* of complements to estimate the value of a change in environmental quality.

Hedonic price (HP) analysis refers to the estimation of implicit prices for individual attributes of a market commodity. Some environmental goods and services can be viewed as attributes of a market commodity, such as residential property (Bockstael and McConnell 2007, chapter 7). For example, when a residential property is bought, the purchase may be said to include attributes such as proximity to noisy streets, noisy airports, and polluted waterways; the smell from pig farms, factories, sewage treatment plants, and waste disposal sites; exposure to polluted air; and access to parks or scenic vistas. Part of the variation in property prices is due to differences in these amenities. Another application (termed *hedonic wage model*) analyses wages for different jobs that entail different levels of mortality risks to reveal how much people must be compensated with higher wages for them to do a job with a higher occupational mortality risk. These wage and risk differentials can be combined to estimate the value of a statistical life (VSL), which can be viewed as the economic value of preventing a fatality.

One obvious way in which natural disasters affect welfare is related to loss of life, injuries, and reduced health status. These costs include loss of production, medical expenditures, hospital costs, and welfare loss to the households that are directly and indirectly affected. The economic VSL can depend on whether the exposure to the fatality risk is voluntary (whether you have decided to live on a floodplain, despite warnings; or have decided to stay behind during a flood when others have been evacuated), whether you have some control of the risk (e.g., driving a car versus flying in an airplane), the degree of pain and suffering prior to death, the age at which you die (and thus the lost number of life years), and the ability to pay (which depend on both the income (net after taxes) and the cost of living). Hedonic wage models can be used to estimate VSL, but these analyses often rely on industry-specific data on salaries and fatal risks, which hides the fact that within the same industry there are many types of jobs with different job risks. Shanmugan (2006) used a hedonic wage model in the Chennai (Madras) district of southern India to estimate VSL at US$1.34–1.47 million (this study will be discussed in more detail later in this chapter). However, this might not be representative of VSL of the general population affected by natural disasters in the same area.

HP data can be quite costly to collect, as there is often no database of residential properties that includes detailed data on the attributes of the property and its environment, including public goods, which determine the property price. The HP function is very sensitive to the specification and functional form, and it is often difficult, where data exist, to find a measure for the environmental amenity of a property, in which the bidders for residential properties can recognize marginal changes and have complete information about them at the time they bid for the property. Two examples:

1. There are often no data on traffic noise levels, and using the annual average number of vehicles on the nearest road or distance to this road as a proxy variable for noise levels could easily value all road traffic related externalities (including accident risks, health impacts from air pollution, barrier effects, and soiling).

2. Properties are typically shown to potential buyers on Sundays when there is little traffic on the nearby road, and thus they place their bid on the property with incomplete information about the road traffic noise level. In developing countries there are usually even more imperfect markets for property than in developed countries, with less data available on property prices and characteristics of the house and its environment. As an approximation, however, one could use the assessed value (or market prices where they exist, corrected for market imperfections), conduct field surveys to register characteristics that could have a potential effect on property prices, and, for example, use distance to the river as a proxy for flood risk.

While (indirect) RP methods are based on actual behavior in a market for goods related to the nonmarket good in question (and thus the value of the nonmarket good is drawn out based on sets of strict assumptions about this relationship), SP methods measure the value of the environmental good in question by constructing a hypothetical market for the good. The hypothetical nature is the main argument against SP methods. However, no strict assumptions have to be made about their market behavior, the relationship between marketed complements or substitutes, or attributes of a marketed good and a nonmarket good. This is an advantage compared to the RP methods. SP methods also have the advantage of being able to measure the TEV including both use and nonuse value, of deriving the "correct" welfare measure, and of being able to measure future changes in the quality or quantity of the public good.

The Stated Preference methods can be divided into direct and indirect approaches. The direct contingent valuation (CV) method is by far the most used, but in recent years the indirect approaches of choice experiments (CE)/choice modeling have gained popularity. The main difference between these two approaches is that while the CV method typically is a two-alternative (referendum) approach, CE employs a series of questions/choices between two alternatives (and often a status quo alternative) described by different characteristics/attributes including the cost of providing the alternative. CE is designed to identify preferences and values for different attributes of the public good, while CV values the good as a whole.

A *contingent valuation* (CV) survey constructs scenarios that offer different possible future government actions (Mitchell and Carson 1989; Bateman and Willis 1999). Under the simplest and most commonly used CV question format, the respondent is offered a binary choice between two alternatives, one being the status quo policy, the other an alternative policy (e.g., a flood protection scheme) with a cost greater than the status quo. The respondent is told that the government will impose the stated cost (e.g., increased taxes, higher prices associated with regulation, or user fees) if the non status quo alternative is provided. The respondent is then asked whether he would vote for or against implementing the alternative government policy at the stated cost. What the alternative policy will provide, how it will be provided, and how much it will cost, and how it will be paid for (i.e., payment vehicle) have to be clearly specified. This way of measuring willingness-to-pay is termed binary *discrete choice* (DC). In such a closed-ended version of CV, respondents can also be asked to value multiple discrete choices in double- and multiple-DC WTP questions. Open-ended questions can also be used. Respondents are asked directly about the most they would be willing to pay for the alternative policy. A payment card with amounts ranging from zero to some expected upper amount is often used as a visual aid. Then the data could be treated statistically as interval data, for example, if you say "yes" to paying $50 as the highest amount, but say "no" to $100, we know that the respondent has a willingness-to-pay within this range.

One of the main challenges in a CV study is to describe the change in the nonmarket good brought about by the new policy/program in a way that is understandable to the respondent and at the same time scientifically correct. Another challenge is to find a realistic and fair payment vehicle, which does not create protest behavior, in terms of people stating zero WTP even if they have a positive WTP for the change in the nonmarket good. People might object to paying for the new policy in terms of increased income taxes because they think these taxes are too high already or they might find a proposed new environmental tax unrealistic (and thus their answers do not express their correct welfare gain from this new policy). However, an increase in existing charges that are linked to environmental improvement, such as an increase in sewage treatment charges in exchange for improved water quality, is likely to be considered realistic and fair, and respondents' stated WTP then better reflects their "true" WTP.

Concerns raised by CV critics over the reliability of the CV approach (especially over if people would actually pay their stated "true" WTP) led the US National Oceanic and Atmospheric Administration (NOAA) to convene a panel of eminent experts cochaired by Nobel Prize winners Kenneth Arrow and Robert Solow to examine the issue. In January 1993 the panel issued a report that concluded that "CV studies can produce estimates reliable enough to be the starting point for a judicial or administrative determination of natural resources damages—including lost passive use value" (Arrow et al. 1993). The panel suggested guidelines for use in Natural Resource Damage Assessment legal cases (NRDA are assessments of the economic value of damage done to natural resources from, e.g., accidental marine oil spills, to be paid by the polluter to compensate users and nonusers affected by the event) to help ensure the reliability of CV surveys on nonuse values (which they term passive use values) including the use of in-person interviews, a binary discrete choice question, a careful description of the good and its substitutes, and several different tests.

Since the panel's report, several key theoretical and methodological issues have been tested and clarified. The simplest test corresponds to a well-known economic maxim, that is, the higher the cost, the lower the demand. This price sensitivity test can easily be tested in the binary DC format, by observing whether the percentage favoring the project falls as the randomly assigned cost of the project increases, which rarely fails in empirical applications. The scope test is the one that has attracted the most attention in recent years. It involves testing whether people are willing to pay more for a larger quantity or quality improvement of the good being valued rather than a small one. CV critics often argue that insensitivity to scope results from what they term "warm glow," by which they mean getting moral satisfaction from the act of paying for the good, independent of the characteristics of the actual environmental good. There have now been a considerable number of tests of the scope insensitivity hypothesis (also termed "embedding"), and a review of the empirical evidence suggests that the majority of CV studies testing for scope find that WTP is sensitive to scope; that is, people pay more for a larger amount of the public good, although at a marginally decreasing rate (Carson 1997).

Producing a good CV survey instrument requires substantial development work, typically including focus groups, in-depth one-to-one interviews, pre-tests, and pilot studies. These help determine if people find the good and scenario presented plausible and understandable. The task of translating technical material into a form understood by the general public is often a difficult one. The recommended mode of one-to-one interviews for surveys adds to the high costs of CV surveys (Arrow et al. 1993). Mail, internet, and telephone surveys are dramatically cheaper, but mail and internet surveys suffer more from sample selection bias (i.e., those returning the survey are typically more interested in the issue than those who do not) and phone surveys have severe drawbacks if the good is complicated or visual aids are needed. In many developing countries, one-to-one interviews are the only viable option. When illiteracy rates are high, visual aids should be carefully designed with this in mind. When questionnaires have to be translated into the local language, they should afterwards be translated back to the original language (often English) and checked to see if the questions had the same meaning as originally intended. In developing countries where income levels are low, WTP could also be framed in terms of willingness to contribute in kind instead of money, for example, contributing labor (person-days) to a program that will provide the public good in question (see, e.g., Hung, Loomis, and Thinh 2006 for a successful application of this technique to a forest fire prevention program in Vietnam).

CV results can be quite sensitive to the treatment of potential outliers. Open-ended survey questions typically elicit a large number of so-called protest zeros and a small number of extremely high responses. In discrete choice CV questions, econometric modeling assumptions can often have a substantial influence on the estimated mean and median WTP. Any careful analysis will involve a series of judgmental decisions about how to handle specific issues involving the data, and these decisions should be clearly noted.

Carefully designed and administered CV surveys can provide useful estimates. The reliability of estimates and validity of results depend on the survey design and implementation. Much experience has now been gained in the design of cost-effective and robust CV surveys, also in developing countries (see, e.g., Whittington 1998 for a review of issues and lessons learned in administering CV surveys in developing countries). Although the approach has been widely applied for cost-benefit analysis of projects with environmental impacts, examples of use in assessing damage caused by extreme events are few (see chapter 14 for an application).

Choice experiments (CEs) have been employed in marketing, transportation, and psychology literature for some time and arose from conjoint analysis, which is commonly used in marketing and transportation research. CEs differ from typical conjoint methods in that individuals are asked to choose from alternative bundles of attributes instead of ranking or rating them. Under the CE approach respondents are asked to pick their most favored out of a set of three or more alternatives and are typically given multiple sets of choice questions, for example, they are asked to choose between the current situation with no Flood Prevention Plan and no additional costs to households, and two flood prevention plans, one costing €50/household/year that leads to the avoidance of all future flooding of Rivers X and Y, while the other plan costs €20 and avoids half of the current floods in River X only. Because CEs are based on attributes (i.e., in the previous example these attributes are monetary costs, number of rivers, and percentage reduction in number of floods in each of the two rivers), they allow the researcher to value attributes, as well as situational changes. Furthermore, in the case of damage to a particular attribute, compensating amounts of other goods that are attributes (as well as compensation based on money as in CV surveys since money is one of the attributes) can be calculated. This is also one of the approaches that can be used in NRDAs. An attribute-based approach is necessary to measure the type or amount of other "goods" that are required for compensation (Bennett and Blamey 2001). This approach can provide substantially more information about a range of possible alternative policies, as well as reduce the sample size needed compared to CVs. However, survey design issues with the CE approach are often much more complex due to the number of goods that must be described and the statistical methods that must be employed.

SP approaches can also be used to value morbidity and mortality. For morbidity the health episodes/symptoms must be described in detail and in a manner understandable to the respondents (see, e.g., Ready et al. 2004). SP methods can also be used to estimate VSL. For a developing country application, see Bhattacharya et al. (2007), which we will discuss later in this chapter.

To conclude, both RP and SP methods can be used to value damage arising from natural disasters in both developed and developing countries, but in developing countries certain adaptations of the methods are needed, for example, measuring WTP in terms of contributing labor instead of money (and we do both in the flood damage assessment surveys conducted in selected Asian countries as part of the EU project "Microdis").

Value Transfer Methods

Since there are very few RP and SP studies valuing damages from natural disasters in developing countries, we often rely on transfer of values from similar type studies in developed countries. Often there is not enough time or money to conduct primary valuation studies, and we opt for value transfer. There are two main approaches to value transfer:

1. Unit Value Transfer
   a. Simple unit value transfer
   b. Unit value transfer with adjustment for income differences
2. Function Transfer
   a. Value function transfer
   b. Meta-analysis.

In approach (1) the unit value at the site of the primary study (often termed the study site), is assumed to be representative for the policy site (being the site we want to transfer to); either without (a) or with (b) adjustment for differences in income levels between the two sites using equation (3.1).

$$\text{WTP}_p' = \text{WTP}_s \ (Y_p/Y_s)^\beta \tag{3.1}$$

where WTP_s is the mean WTP estimate from the primary study (often termed the study site), Y_s and Y_p are the income levels at the study and policy site, respectively, and β is the income elasticity of WTP for the public good in question (e.g., if this elasticity is 0.8, then WTP increases by 0.8 percent when income increases by 1 percent).

In approach (2) a WTP function is estimated at the early study site and transferred to the policy site (a), or a benefit function is estimated from several study sites using meta-analysis (b) then values for the independent variables at the policy site are used in the function to calculate WTP at the policy site. A benefit function from a CV survey would be WTP as a function of site and good characteristics and characteristics of the respondent. Meta-analysis would also include characteristics of the different studies as a variable, since estimated values could be affected by even small methodological differences.

There are few detailed guidelines on value transfer. In the United States, there exist guides that cover the key aspects of conducting a value transfer; notably, Desvouges et al. (1998) aimed at creating a transfer guideline for valuing environmental and health impacts of air pollution from electricity production. We would propose the following eight-step guideline adapted to the economic valuation of environmental and other public goods affected by natural disasters (according to Navrud 2007):

1. Identify the change in the environmental good to be valued at the policy site.
2. Identify the affected population at the policy site.
3. Conduct a literature review to identify relevant primary studies (based on a database).
4. Assess the relevance and quality of study site values for transfer.
5. Select and summarize the data available from the study site(s).
6. Transfer value estimate from study site(s) to policy site.
7. Calculate total benefits or costs.
8. Assess uncertainty and acceptable transfer errors.

Validity of Value Transfer and Acceptable Transfer Errors

Transfer errors arise when estimates from study sites are adapted to policy sites. These errors are inversely related to the degree of correspondence between the study site and the policy site. Assume there is an underlying meta-valuation function that links the values of a resource (such as a lake) or an activity (such as swimming or recreational fishing) with characteristics of the markets and sites, across space and over time. Further, hypothesize that a primary research project samples from this meta-function. The meta-valuation function is based on estimates from existing studies (where each estimate or each study is an observation) and relates site values to characteristics or attributes associated with each site, including market characteristics, physical site characteristics, spatial characteristics, and time. The degree to which any of these sets of factors affects value transfer accuracy is an empirical question. The greater the correspondence (or similarity) of the policy site with the study site, however, the smaller is the expected error.

In the value transfer validity tests, two or more parallel valuation studies are conducted at different sites. Then an imaginary transfer is made from a study site (or a pooled data set from several study sites) to a policy site, where we have also per-formed an original/primary study. The transferred value, WTP_T, is then compared to the value estimated in the original valuation study at the policy site, WTP_P. The *transfer error* (TE) is calculated as the percentage difference between the transferred estimate and the policy site estimate

$$\mathrm{TE} = \frac{\left|\mathrm{WTP}_T - \mathrm{WTP}_P\right|}{\mathrm{WTP}_P} \tag{3.2}$$

Ready et al. (2004) show in their transfer tests of CV estimates of respiratory illnesses in five European countries that even if the distribution of WTP had been the same in all countries, they would have measured an average transfer error of 16 percent. Thus, they point out the average transfer error of 38 percent they did find should be assessed relative to this background level of random sampling error.

Much academic work has been done in the past 10 years to test the validity of alternative value transfer methods for different environmental goods. However, even fairly small transfer errors can be rejected using the classical statistical tests; usually t-tests where we hypothesize that the transferred policy site values are equal to the "true" values found in a new primary study at the policy site. Bergland, Magnussen, and Navrud (1995) rejected value transfers statistically in cases of average transfer errors of less than 20 percent in two simultaneously performed CV studies that looked at similar water quality improvements in two closely located and similar lakes. The standards of accuracy required in academic work, however, may exceed those viewed as tolerable by policy makers, especially in cost-benefit analysis. Kristofersson and Navrud (2005) suggest the use of equivalence testing as being more appropriate and offering a clear complement to the shortcomings of the classical tests. Equivalence tests examine the null hypothesis of *difference* between the original and transferred value estimates (which is in most cases what we would expect rather than similar values). Equivalence tests also combine the concepts of statistical significance and policy significance into one test, by defining an acceptable transfer error prior to the validity test. Applications of these tests are found in Kristofersson and Navrud (2007) and Muthke and Holm-Mueller (2004).

Several studies have tested the validity and reliability of cross-country benefit transfer in the context of developing countries. Alberini et al. (1997) and Alberini and Krupnick (1997) transferred to Taiwan US WTP estimates to avoid an episode of ill health and found an average transfer error across four different possible transfers of 34 percent (calculated by Ready and Navrud 2006). Chestnut et al. transferred the US estimates of median WTP to Bangkok, Thailand, and found transfer errors ranging from 18 percent to 35 percent, depending on the ill-health episode valued (cited in Ready and Navrud 2006). Barton and Mourato (2002) found transfer errors of 87 to 130 percent when transferring WTP values to avoid ill-health episodes from Portugal to Costa Rica. About-Ali and Belhaj (2006) transferred WTP for air quality improvements between Morocco and Egypt and found transfer errors of 60 to 220 percent.

Ready and Navrud (2006) reviewed cross-country benefit transfer studies conducted to date and found that the average transfer error for cross-country benefit transfers was in the range of 20 to 40 percent, but individual transfer error was as high as 100 to 200 percent. Function transfer does not seem to perform better than unit value transfer. Meta-analyses of international studies could be useful when we lack similar domestic valuation studies but could also produce high transfer errors. The validity tests also support the hypothesis that it is preferable to find a study site located close to the policy site of interest. The closer the study site is to the policy site, the more likely that both the good being valued and the user population affected will be similar, and therefore the transfer errors would be lower. Transfer validity tests also suggest that transfer errors are smaller if people have had experience with the environmental good in question, but the transfer errors do not seem to be lower for use than for nonuse values. Lindhjem and Navrud (2008) review this recent literature on benefit transfer validity tests and perform an empirical comparison of meta-analysis and unit value transfer for use and nonuse values of forests, showing that the simple technique of unit value transfer (especially from domestic studies) performs just as well as the more complex meta-analyses.

Even if we cannot determine general levels of acceptable transfer errors for different policy use, some general decision rules for how to determine the acceptable transfer errors in cost-benefit analyses (CBA) (e.g., of flood prevention measures) can be outlined.

There are two main sources of error in estimated values from value transfer:

- errors associated with estimation of the unit value/value function at the study site;
- errors from transferring the study site value(s) to the policy site.

By using "best practice" guidelines for original valuation studies, we can minimize the first type of error. The second type of error arises because we usually would need to transfer estimates both in space and time. Results from validity tests of different value transfer procedures for different type environmental goods have shown that individual transfer errors in spatial value transfer vary from a few percent to several hundred percent. Average transfer errors, however, both for national and international value transfer, seem to be about ± 20 to 40 percent (Ready and Navrud 2006). In many cases this would be an acceptable transfer error in CBA. Sensitivity analysis should be performed to see if this interval for the estimated values would influence the outcome of the CBA. The size of the critical transfer error (i.e., the magnitude of the transfer error to make the net present value (NPV) of the project zero) should also be calculated, especially in cases where we suspect the transfer errors could be large. These cases include international value transfers of complex environmental goods from study sites that are quite different from the policy site, in terms of magnitude and direction of change, initial level of environmental quality, availability of substitutes (scarcity), different size of affected areas, different type of population (locally most affected population versus the national population), etc.

Examples of Applications of Valuation Methods to the Impacts of Natural Disasters

In this section we will review selected empirical studies that have used methods most applicable to valuing the effects of natural disasters. We will focus on developing countries as they are most prone to disasters.

VALUING MORTALITY USING THE HEDONIC WAGE AND THE CONTINGENT VALUATION METHODS

One of the most severe effects of natural disasters is loss of life. The value of a statistical life (VSL), or rather the economic value of a prevented fatality, is derived from how much people are willing to pay to obtain a small reduction in mortality risks. The VSL can be obtained either from surveys (contingent valuation and choice experiments) or by analyzing labor market data to determine how much less workers will accept in wages for a job with a lower mortality risk (hedonic wage). For example, if respondents in an SP survey on average are willing to pay $500 as a one-time amount to get a risk reduction of five in 10,000 we must multiply $500 by 2,000 (to get a 10,000 in 10,000 chance of dying, which is equivalent to a statistical life). This means a VSL of $1 million. We will use two studies from India to illustrate these SP and RP approaches to estimate VSL, respectively.

Shanmugam (2006) derives the VSL in India from workers' revealed willingness to incur mortality risks at work in exchange for higher wages, using an original data set from the Indian labor market. The main objective of the study was to discuss the appropriate discount rate for comparing the long-term health benefits of policies from a developing country's perspective. Shanmugam estimates the implicit discount rate that the Indian workers use in making their life-cycle job decisions, estimates VSL, the implicit value per additional expected life year, and the value of marginal life years.

Shanmugan (2006) uses the discounted expected life-years approach developed by Moore and Viscusi (1988, as reported in Shanmugan 2006) which is an extension of the Hedonic wage approach, "resting on Adam Smith's proposition that risky jobs command risk compensating differentials" (Shanmugan 2006).

Data for the study were collected in a 1990 survey of 522 blue-collar male workers in manufacturing industries in the Madras district of southern India.

The study found an implicit discount rate that the workers place on inter-temporal health risk and the quantity-adjusted value of life. The estimated implicit value per year of life ranges from 0.97 million to 1.06 million rupees ($54,000 to $59,000) (1990 prices). From this estimate Shanmugam calculates an implicit value of one's future life of about 24.3 million to 26.5 million rupees ($1.34 million to $1.47 million). This estimate greatly exceeds the workers' annual earnings. The author argues that this is not necessarily inconsistent, since it represents the rate of risk-money trade-off for very small risks, not the amount the workers would pay for a certain life extension.

Shanmugan compares his VSL estimate with studies listed in Viscusi (1993, as reported in Shanmugan 2006) and concludes that his estimates are lower than reported values from developed countries, but closer to estimates for Taiwan calculated by Liu et al. (1997, as reported in Shanmugan 2006), who estimated the Taiwanese value at $135,000 to $589,000 (1990 dollars).

Shanmugan further found that the implicit discount rate that the workers use in discounting their future life years, ranges between 7.6 and 9.7 percent. This range was close to the market interest rate on debt to private creditors of 8 percent, but lower than the bank interest rate of 12 percent and consistent with earlier field studies from developed nations, supporting the use of the market interest rate in evaluating health benefits. The author concludes that these estimates hopefully can aid policy makers and others in evaluating health projects in India and other developing countries, and carrying out comparisons with values obtained for developed nations.

Bhattacharya et al. (2007) value mortality risk reductions in Delhi, India. They interviewed commuters and estimated their WTP to reduce their risk of dying in road traffic accidents. The authors note that in Delhi, as in cities in most developing countries, half of all traffic fatalities are pedestrians. Bicyclists and the drivers and passengers of two-wheelers make up 30 percent of fatalities, while car drivers/passengers account for only 5 percent of fatalities. This is a very different distribution compared to developed countries, and suggests that methods used for valuing traffic accidents in developed, high-income countries may not be applicable. They suggest that a more reasonable approach is to present scenarios including the types of choices respondents actually face in daily life—for example, whether to buy a safer motorcycle helmet—and estimate VSL from such choices.

The study includes 1,200 commuters who were asked what they would pay to reduce their own risk of dying

(1) as a pedestrian;
(2) as a driver of a two-wheeler; and
(3) as a commuter, regardless of travel mode.

Their preferred VSL estimate is about 1.3 million rupees, which is based on the mean WTP of a commuter with a high school degree who drives a two-wheeler and travels while on the job. This estimate is preferred by the authors because it represents the benefits to a person with high exposure to traffic risks from a reduction in risk of death. This number exceeds the VSL currently used in evaluating the benefits of road safety projects by the World Bank (generally based on foregone earnings) or other Indian studies (Mohan 2001 uses 535,000 rupees according to Bhattacharya, Alberini, and Cropper 2007). On the other hand, Bhattacharya, Alberini, and Cropper find that their estimated value is smaller than the VSL that would be used if VSL values used in public project appraisals in high-income developed countries were transferred to India using unit value transfer with income adjustment and assuming an income elasticity of one; see equation (3.1).

VALUATION OF FLOOD RISK EXPOSURE AND FLOOD RISK REDUCTION USING THE CONTINGENT VALUATION METHOD

Brouwer et al. (2009) applied a contingent valuation (CV) study in order to value flood risk reductions in Bangladesh. Individual households were asked to state their WTP to reduce the risk of flooding and the corresponding impacts on life and livelihood. The sensitivity of stated WTP to varying risk exposure levels was tested by targeting flood plain residents who face regular annual floods and a disaster flood once every five to ten years. The authors suggest that the fact that the respondents "know" the risks they face helps to avoid many of the difficulties one might otherwise face in communicating risk exposure and risk reduction. They note that risk communication is of particular concern when a substantial share of the target population (and hence sample) is illiterate. In their case study, Brouwer et al. find that there are some problems related to the use of CV, particularly concerning the lack of financial resources among respondents. They find that half the respondents who are unable to pay money to reduce their risk are willing to contribute in kind. This suggests that these respondents actually have a positive WTP, which could be taken into account if they were allowed to contribute in other ways (such as working hours/days, etc.).

In another paper based on data from Bangladesh, Brouwer et al. (2007) investigate the relationship between environmental risk, poverty and vulnerability. They asked 700 flood plain residents, who lived without any flood protection along the river Meghna, about their flood risk exposure, flood problems, flood damage, and coping mechanisms. They found that the people who face the highest risk of flooding are the least well prepared, both in terms of household-level *ex-ante* preparedness for flood events and community-level *ex-post* flood relief. Households with lower income and less access to productive natural assets face higher exposure to risks of flooding. The study results further imply that individually vulnerable households also are collectively more vulnerable because disparities in income and asset distribution at community level tend to be greater in areas with higher risk exposure.

VALUATION OF ECOSYSTEM FUNCTIONS USING THE REPLACEMENT/RESTORATION COST APPROACH

Badola and Hussain (2005) valued the storm protection function of the Bhitarkanika mangrove ecosystem in India. Their point of departure for the study was that ecosystem services provided by mangroves are often ignored in the process of mangrove ecosystem conversion in the case of development projects. They assessed the avoided damage costs using a replacement costs approach to value the storm protection function of the Bhitarkanika mangrove ecosystem. The actual damages avoided due to mangrove forests were estimated after a cyclone hit the area in October 1999. Socioeconomic data pertaining to local demography and economic conditions were collected from 35 villages in the area. Data on demography, land use and occupational patterns, resource use, and perceptions and attitudes were gathered through a questionnaire survey from 10 percent of the households in three of the villages. These villages were selected as follows: one was protected by mangrove, one was unprotected by mangroves, and the third had an embankment on its seaward side. Data were collected to compare damages in the different villages with different protection. In door-to-door surveys, the authors collected data to assess the socioeconomic status of the villages, the actual damage to houses, livestock, fisheries, trees, and other assets owned by people, and the rate, level, and duration of flooding.

The authors estimated losses for each household in terms of damage to houses (0–19 scale), tree damage (percent), damage to other personal property (money), damage to livestock in monetary terms, flooding in premises and fields, water logging in fields (days), cost of repair and reconstruction, yield for the year of the storm, and loss of young fish (fingerlings) released prior to the cyclone (in monetary terms). The total loss in monetary terms was calculated for each of the households in the three villages by combining the value of the cost of repair and reconstruction, damage to other personal property such as boats, fishing nets, and household goods, damage to livestock, and loss of agricultural products.

The authors found that in the mangrove-protected village, variables had either the lowest values for adverse factors (such as damage to houses), or the highest values for positive factors (such as crop yield). The loss incurred per household was greatest in the village that was not sheltered by mangroves but had an embankment ($153.74), followed by the village without mangroves and embankment ($44.02) and the village that was protected by mangrove forests ($33.31). This clearly shows that embankments are not a perfect substitute for the mangrove forest, which the replacement methods assumes, but rather create more damage than having neither embankments nor mangroves (as it takes longer for the water behind the embankment to subside). Thus, the negative effects of the measure aimed at replacing this lost ecosystem service, makes the replacement cost method less suitable for estimating the welfare loss in this case.

The study also found that the local people were aware of and appreciated the functions performed by the mangrove forests in protecting their lives and property from cyclones, and were willing to cooperate with the forest department in restoring the mangroves.

VALUATION OF ECONOMIC BENEFITS AND COSTS OF HAZARD MITIGATION PROJECTS

Rose et al. (2007) summarize the economic analysis of benefits and costs of the US Federal Emergency Management Agency (FEMA) Hazard Mitigation Projects. In this study, future savings, in terms of losses avoided, were estimated for hazard mitigation activities related to earthquakes, wind, and floods, funded through three major natural hazard mitigation programmes in the US, as well as various supplemental programmes. Two types of mitigation activities were addressed: "project" and "process" mitigation. Project activities include physical measures to avoid or reduce damage from disasters. Typically they involve acquiring, elevating, or relocating buildings, lifelines or other structures threatened by floods; strengthening buildings and lifelines to resist earthquake or wind forces, and improving drainage and land conditions. Process mitigation, on the other hand, includes activities resulting in policies, practices, and projects that reduce risk and loss. These efforts typically focus on assessing hazards, vulnerability

and risks: conducting planning to identify mitigation efforts, policies, and practices and set priorities; performing research to develop new technology-based
mitigation strategies; educating decision-makers and building constituencies;
and facilitating the selection, design, funding and construction of projects (Rose
et al. 2007).

The authors note that, while the cost side is rather straightforward to estimate,
the benefit, or avoided losses from hazards, are more difficult to assess "because
they are not limited to a single structure or moment in time and are highly uncertain over the short term." They note two complications in particular. The first is
discounting future values to present and the second is the need to express avoided
losses in probability terms to capture their uncertain frequency and severity of
occurrence. The study aims at expanding the range of losses considered, including the business interruption loss from utility outage, environmental and historic
benefits and benefits from grants for process mitigation activities. They use different methods in order to arrive at the estimated benefits, including market prices,
direct property damage losses, and benefit transfer for environmental and historical losses avoided.

MARKET PRICE BASED METHODS

Chapter 9 examines the nature and extent of flooding disasters, magnitude, and
extent of damages in West Bengal, India. The chapter gives an example of how
market prices can be used to value damages from natural disasters.

VALUATION OF FLOOD RISK USING
THE HEDONIC PRICE METHOD

Daniel, Florax, and Rietveld (2007) discuss hedonic price methods to assess the
benefits of reducing flood risk. According to the authors, it is well documented that
housing prices are reactive to flood risk, and that devaluation of housing prices
due to flood risk is greater in the wake of a recent flood. As an example of this
divergence between *ex-ante* and *ex-post* valuations, they show that *ex-post* evaluations of flood risk were twice as high as before the Meuse River flooded in 1993 in
the Netherlands. In addition, they refer to earlier work that has shown that prices
for houses located in an area that was flooded in 1993 were *ex-ante* 7 percent lower
than a similar house located in a safe zone and were about 14 percent lower after
the 1993 flood.

The authors use a hedonic price model for several cities along the Meuse River,
including house sales in the period 1990 to 2004. They find that the total impact of
flooding on house values in the areas affected by the recent flooding event is substantial, with a price reduction of 7 to 13 percent. They find that this reduction does
not disappear after some years, as some had suggested it would. The authors suggest
that this may be due to the increasing focus on climate change, and hence increased
attention given to flood (and other extreme climate events) risks.

ECONOMIC VALUATION OF EVACUATION USING
THE CONTINGENT VALUATION METHOD

Zhai and Ikeda (2006) study the economic value of evacuation and its relationship
with flood risk acceptability in Japan using the contingent valuation (CV) method.
The term "flood risk acceptability" is used to indicate to what extent people accept
the occurrence of floods, in terms of scale and frequency. The study collects people's
WTP for avoiding the inconvenience of evacuation, and the potential for certain
losses as a result of evacuation. More than half of the people who were evacuated in
a real flood situation reported inconvenience. The greatest inconveniences reported
were shortage of information and shortage of food. The estimated WTP for avoiding current inconvenience was approximately half of the calculated economic value
of evacuation. The authors find that "flood risk acceptability" and "home ownership" are important determinants of people's WTP. They find that those who accept
flood risk have a lower WTP for flood risk control (*ex-ante*) measures than those
who do not, who are more willing to pay for *ex-ante* than *ex-post* measures.

Concluding Remarks

This chapter has reviewed and briefly described several valuation methods that can
be used to value the impacts of natural disasters. We have described how values can
be transferred if we lack time and resources to conduct new original valuation studies and have provided a few examples of original studies valuing impacts of natural
disasters, mainly from developing countries as natural disasters are most frequent
there, and there is a great need for more original studies in these countries.

   Although we have provided only a few examples of applications of valuation
methods to natural disasters, some conclusions can be drawn.

   First, we need more original valuation studies in order to fully comprehend and value
all impacts of different types of natural disasters. This is particularly true for developing countries, where such primary studies are scarce. Because there are few nonmarket
valuation studies of damage caused by natural disasters, and the corresponding social
benefits of preventive measures, there are also few valuation studies to transfer from,
and the possibility for benefit transfer is limited. Hence, new, primary valuation studies
constructed, conducted, and reported with benefit transfer in mind are needed.

   Different valuation methods must be used in order to value different effects of
natural disasters. There is no single method capable of capturing damages to both
marketed goods (e.g., houses, livestock, or crops) and nonmarketed goods (ecosystems, environmental quality, and social and health impacts) from all effects from
all natural disasters. Using several independent methods to value the same impacts
would also be good in order to test the validity and reliability of the valuation methods, and thus reduce the uncertainty of the estimate.

   For valuation of damage to public goods (such as health, environment, or cultural
heritage), the impacts must be specified in physical units (e.g., lives lost), which can
be valued. New primary valuation studies (using the stated and revealed preference

methods discussed earlier in this chapter) are needed both for impacts identified in impact assessments (IAs) and for preventive (and adaptive) programs to avoid impacts identified in IAs.

Since valuation studies have been done mainly in developed countries and adapted to the conditions there, one should carefully consider if and how the methods can be adapted to the institutional, cultural, religious, and social contexts of developing countries. For example, SP methods asking for WTP may be adapted, but allowing for in-kind payment in addition to or as an alternative to monetary payments, in order to also allow households with the most severe financial restraints to express their preferences. These households are also often those which may benefit the most from risk reductions. It is also important that the payment mechanism chosen (whether monetary or in kind) is credible and not voluntary.

Likewise, developing relevant scenarios is important for obtaining valid results, as shown by Bhattacharya et al. (2007). Scenarios of traffic-related deaths in developing countries should take into account that fatalities are much more related to pedestrians and cyclists in these countries than in developed countries (where most fatal accidents affect car drivers and passengers). If there is distrust of the government and governmental agencies, scenarios should avoid using governmental programs as the supplier of the good/preventive program and should instead use, for example, NGOs or other organizations or scenarios that people trust. The program chosen as the provider of the good in question should have high probability of provision. Fairness is important in all SP scenarios and surveys. However, this may be of particular importance for disaster prone populations in developing countries.

The studies reviewed above show that it is possible to carry out valuation studies of prevented fatalities also in developing countries, but there are currently few empirical studies. These studies suggest that just counting foregone earnings of persons that die does not account for the total economic value of a statistical life lost. The Bhattacharya study further suggests that one should be careful in transferring VSL estimates from developed countries (where there are many empirical studies), because the numbers differ even when corrections are made for income differences. Thus, the VSL does not depend only on income but probably also on other socioeconomic, cultural, religious, and institutional factors. Furthermore, the studies suggest that people actually do discount future benefits related to risk reduction. Neither of these studies was carried out for scenarios particularly relevant for natural disasters. Bhattacharya et al. (2007) suggest that the scenarios and context for valuation may be of importance. Still, these numbers, and numbers from similar studies, could be used as a first approximation to value lives lost due to disasters in order to avoid using "foregone earnings," which could greatly underestimate damage and lead to underinvestment in measures to mitigate impacts from natural disasters. Studies valuing prevented fatalities from disaster prevention measures are, however, much needed.

The case studies cited above further show that it is possible to carry out valuation studies and even present difficult scenarios involving risk reductions in disaster-prone areas where the majority of the population has a low income and/or is illiterate. However, they also show that one should use local knowledge when constructing and conducting surveys and interpreting the results. We saw that there was a large proportion of people who stated zero WTP for flood protection, but many of these zero-respondents were willing to pay if they had the opportunity to pay in kind. This is due to the fact that people with the lowest income live in the most flood exposed areas and are most vulnerable due to both lack of preparedness to floods and lack of disaster relief *ex-post*. This should have implications for how such valuation studies are carried out and used. Misconduct and/or misinterpreted valuation studies may be more misleading than enlightening. Well-conducted studies, such as the ones cited above, however, may help us to better understand the mechanisms and values related to disaster mitigation and prevention.

Due to a lack of primary studies in developing countries, benefit transfer techniques should be considered. However, transfers from developed to developing countries show potentially large transfer errors. Thus, transfer from developed to developing countries must be made with much care. For example, Daniel, Florax, and Rietveld (2007) showed that transferring VSL values from developed countries to India would greatly overestimate VSL. On the other hand, using different VSL values in different parts of the world raises some important ethical questions that cannot be answered by the choice of the correct valuation method.

There is a need to generalize from the few existing primary valuation studies in developing countries to other areas in the same country or also to other countries. Before we can do this and be reasonably content that the results are plausible, we need to carefully test the transferability within and across countries in the context of an extreme event, and establish more context-specific transfer errors and transfer guidelines. In addition, care should be taken in order to cover as many as possible of the effects, in an attempt to estimate the total economic value (TEV) *ex-ante* of preventing disasters, or *ex-post* of the effects of the disaster. At the same time one should be aware of the risk of double counting when pieces of TEV using different methods and estimates are put together.

Finally, in addition to the spatial dimension of transfer discussed above, there is also a time dimension. The studies presented mainly give us a snapshot of the values at one particular point in time. However, if we want to find (*ex-ante* or *ex-post*) "the total economic picture" of a natural disaster, the time variable will be of great importance. Some effects may be valued differently before and after the event, and "just after" or "some time after" an event. Daniel, Florax, and Rietveld (2007) showed that *ex-post* valuations of floods in the Netherlands were twice as high as before the actual flood, and that this effect did not disappear even years after. It is hard to make general recommendations as to *ex-ante* and *ex-post*, and short- and long-term *ex-post* effects based on the existing studies, but this is clearly something to carefully consider if the purpose is to give the full picture.

This also tells us that, although it is of interest to get the full picture of extreme events, it is not easy to get it correct. In particular, for disasters in developing countries where data and valuation studies are still scarce, we believe one should primarily identify the major impacts and the value of them. Then, gradually, one can strive to complete the picture by including more impacts and more complex short- and long-term effects, and so on. This is exactly what we try to do in the multicountry damage assessment studies within the Microdis project.

References

About-Ali, H., and Belhaj, M. (2006). "A Multi-Country Analysis of the Consistency of Benefit Transfer." Paper presented at the Third World Congress of Environmental and Natural Recourse Economics, July, Kyoto, Japan.

Alberini, A., and Krupnick, A. (1997). "Air Pollution and Acute Respiratory Illness: Evidence from Taiwan and Los Angeles." *American Journal of Agricultural Economics* 79: 1620–1624.

Alberini, A., Cropper, M., Fu, T., Krupnick, A., Liu, J., Shaw, D., and Harrington, W. (1997). "Valuing Health Effects of Air Pollution in Developing Countries: The Case of Taiwan." *Journal Environmental Economics and Management* 34: 107–126.

Arrow, K. J., Solow, R., Leamer, E., Portney, P., Radner, R., and Schuman, H. (1993). "Report of the NOAA Panel on Contingent Valuation." 58 Fed. Reg. 58,4601–4614 (January 15, 1993).

Badola, R., and Hussain, S. A. (2005). "Valuing Ecosystem Functions: An Empirical Study on the Storm Protection Function of Bhitarkanika Mangrove Ecosystem." *India, Environmental Conservation* 32(1): 85–92.

Barton, D. N., and Mourato, S. (2002). "Transferring the Benefits of Avoided Health Effects from Water Pollution between Portugal and Costa Rica." *Environment and Development Economics* 8: 351–371.

Bateman, I. J., and Willis, K. G. (1999). *Valuing Environmental Preferences: Theory and Practice of the Contingent Valuation Method in the US, EU, and Developing Countries.* Oxford: Oxford University Press.

Bennett, J., and Blamey, R. (eds.) (2001). *The Choice Modelling Approach to Environmental Valuation.* Northampton, Mass.: Edward Elgar.

Bergland, O., Magnussen, K., and Navrud, S. (1995). "Benefit Transfer: Testing for Accuracy and Reliability." Discussion Paper D-03/95, Department of Economics, Agricultural University of Norway. Revised version in Florax, R. J. G. M., Nijkamp, P., and Willis, K. (eds.) (2000). *Comparative Environmental Economic Assessment: Meta Analysis and Benefit Transfer.* London: Kluwer Academic Publishers.

Bhattacharya, S., Alberini, A., and Cropper, M. L. (2007). "The Value of Mortality Risk Reductions in Delhi, India." *Journal of Risk and Uncertainty* 34: 21–47.

Bockstael, N. E., and McConnell, K. E. (2007). *Environmental and Resource Valuation with Revealed Preferences: A Theoretical Guide to Empirical Models.* Dordrecht, The Netherlands: Springer.

Brouwer, R., Akter, S., Brander, L., and Haque, E. (2007). "Socio-economic Vulnerability and Adaptation to Environmental Risk: A Case Study of Climate Change and Flooding in Bangladesh." *Risk Analysis* 27(2): 313–326.

Brouwer, R., Akter, S., Brander, L., and Haque, E. (2009). "Economic Valuation of Flood Risk Exposure and Flood Risk Reduction in a Severely Flood Prone Developing Country." *Environment and Development Economics* 14(3): 397–417.

Byström, O. (2000). "The Replacement Value of Wetlands in Sweden." *Environmental and Resource Economics* 16(4): 347–362.

Carson, R. C. (1997). "Contingent Valuation Surveys and Tests of Insensitivity to Scope." In *Determining the Value of Non-Marketed Goods: Economic, Psychological, and Policy Relevant Aspects of Contingent Valuation Methods*, edited by R. J. Kopp, W. Pommerhene, and N. Schwartz. Boston: Kluwer.

Daniel, V. E., Florax, R. J. G. M., and Rietveld, P. (2007). "Long Term Divergence between Ex-Ante and Ex-Post Hedonic Prices of the Meuse River Flooding in The Netherlands."

Paper presented at the meeting of the European Regional Science Association, August 29–September 2, 2007, Paris.

Desvousges, W. H., Johnson, F. R., and Banzhaf, H. S. (1998). *Environmental Policy Analysis with Limited Information: Principles and Applications to the Transfer Method*. Cheltenham, UK: Edward Elgar.

Hung, L. T., Loomis, J. B., and Thinh, V. T. (2006). "Comparing Money and Labour Payment in Contingent Valuation: The Case of Forest Fire Prevention in Vietnamese Context." *Journal of International Development* 19(2): 173–185.

Kristofersson, D., and Navrud, S. (2005). "Validity Tests of Benefit Transfer—Are We Performing the Wrong Test?" *Environmental and Resource Economics* 30(3): 279–286.

———. (2007). "Can Use and Non-Use Values be Transferred across Countries?" In *Environmental Value Transfer: Issues and Methods*, edited by S. Navrud and R. Ready. Dordrecht, The Netherlands: Springer.

Lindhjem, H., and Navrud, S. (2008). "How Reliable Are Meta-Analyses for International Benefit Transfer?" *Ecological Economics* 66: 425–435.

Liu, J.-T., Hammitt, J. K., and Liu, J.-L. (1997). "Estimated Hedonic Wage Function and Value of Life in a Developing Country." *Economic Letters* 57: 353–358.

Mohan, Dinesh (2001). "Social Cost of Road Traffic Crashes in India." *Proceedings 1st Safe Community Conference on Cost of Injuries*. Viborg, Denmark.

Mitchell, R. C., and Carson, R. T. (1989). *Using Surveys to Value Public Goods. The Contingent Valuation Method*. Washington, D.C.: Resources for the Future.

Muthke, T., and Holm-Mueller, K. (2004). "National and International Benefit Transfer Testing with a Rigorous Test Procedure." *Environmental and Resource Economics* 29(3): 323–336.

Navrud, S. (2007). "Practical Tools for Benefit Transfer in Denmark—Guidelines and Examples." Report to the Danish Environmental Protection Agency, Copenhagen.

Navrud, S., and Ready, R. (eds.) (2007). *Environmental Value Transfer: Issues and Methods*. Dordrecht, The Netherlands: Springer.

Ready, R., and Navrud, S. (2006). "International Benefits Transfer: Methods and Validity Tests." *Ecological Economics* 60(2): 429–434.

Ready, R. C., Navrud, S., Day, B., Dubourg, R., Machado, F., Mourato, S., Spanninks, F., and Rodriquez, M. X. V. (2004). "Benefit Transfer in Europe. How Reliable Are Transfers between Countries?" *Environmental and Resource Economics* 29 (August): 67–82.

Rose, A., Porter, K., Dash, N., Bouabid, J., Huyck, C., Whitehead, J., Shaw, D., Eguchi, R., Taylor, C., McLane, T., Tobin, L., Ganderton, P., Godschalk, D., Kiremidjian, A., Tierney, K., and Taylor, C. (2007). "Summary of Economic Analysis of Benefits and Costs of FEMA Hazard Mitigation Projects." Accessed February 20, 2009. http://bechtel.colorado.edu/~porterka/Rose-et-al-2007-NHR-BCA.pdf.

Shanmugan, K. R. (2006). "Rate of Time Preference and the Quantity Adjusted Value of Life in India." *Environment and Development Economics* 11: 569–583.

Viscusi, W. K. (1993). "The Value of Risks to Life and Health." *Journal of Economic Literature* 31(4): 1912-1946.

Whittington, D. (1998). "Administering Contingent Valuation Surveys in Developing Countries." *World Development* 26(1): 21–30.

Zhai, G., and Ikeda, S. (2006). "Flood Risk Acceptability and Economic Value of Evacuation." *Journal of Risk Analysis* 26(3): 683–694.

4 }

Cost-Benefit Analysis of Disaster Risk Management and Climate Adaptation

THE CASE OF BANGLADESH

Reinhard Mechler and K. M. Nabiul Islam

Introduction

A major decision-supporting tool commonly used for estimating the efficiency of development projects is cost-benefit analysis (CBA). CBA is used to organize, appraise, and present the costs and benefits, and inherent trade-offs of projects to increase public welfare undertaken by public sector authorities such as local, regional, and central governments, and international donor institutions (Kopp et al. 1997). There is specific literature, including manuals, on using CBA and other appraisal methods in the context of natural disaster risk (see Benson and Twigg 2004). In the United States, CBA of flood control projects was mandated by Congress under the 1936 Flood Control Act and has been used for evaluation of risk reduction projects since the 1950s. It has, in effect, been standard practice for more than half a century for organizations such as the US Federal Emergency Management Agency (FEMA) and the US Army Corps of Engineers. The UK government's Department for Environment, Food and Rural Affairs (DEFRA) and the World Bank also generally advocate the use of CBA for projects and policies including those related to disaster risk management (see, e.g., Ministry of Agriculture 2001; Penning-Rowsell et al. 1992).

Preventive disaster risk management measures have been found to generate considerable returns. In a retrospective analysis, investments in 4,000 disaster risk reduction programs in the United States, including the retrofit of buildings against seismic risk and physical flood defense options, on average exhibited a benefit-cost ratio of four (MMC 2005). A review of 21 studies on disaster risk management projects undertaken in different developing countries, such as planting mangrove forests to protect against tsunamis and relocating schools out of high-hazard areas, reported, with few exceptions, similarly high benefit-cost ratios (Mechler 2005). A prospective study examining the cost and benefits of improving or retrofitting residential structures in highly exposed developing countries—St. Lucia, Indonesia, Turkey, and India—against hurricane, flood, and earthquake hazards as well indicated high returns to those investments. This study also showed the manifold challenges involved in quantifying the key costs and benefits, as well as using probabilistic analysis, a key requirement in order to properly account for the *fat-tailed* disaster risks (see World Bank and United Nations 2010; Hochrainer-Stigler et al. 2010).

Partially explained by these technical challenges, overall there is still surprisingly little evidence regarding the efficiency and benefits of preventive measures; as a consequence, this leads to a serious bias toward relying on *ex-post* response rather than *ex-ante* risk management. "In the absence of concrete information on net economic and social benefits, and faced with limited budgetary resources, many policy makers have been reluctant to commit significant funds to risk reduction, though they have continued pumping considerable funds into high-profile, postdisaster response" (Benson and Twigg 2004).

This chapter is meant to add to this literature and evaluates the potential, as well as challenges, for applying CBA to natural disaster risk management and climate adaptation in a development assistance context. This is done through an assessment of the risks and benefits of reducing risk in Bangladesh, probably the world's most flood-prone country, and also one with huge development challenges, with about a third of its population living on less than $1 per day. The UK government's Department for International Development (DFID) piloted in Bangladesh a project (the ORCHID project[1]) to assess vulnerability to natural hazards and climate change in connection with development and donor assistance. This chapter is based on the experience of ORCHID in Bangladesh.

People and societies continuously brace themselves for natural hazards and aim to the greatest extent possible to reduce their vulnerability to natural hazards and other exogenous shocks. For Bangladesh, for which good information and data are available, these vulnerability-reducing efforts can readily be discerned in the statistics. Table 4.1 presents information on the impact of selected flood disasters in Bangladesh between 1974 and 2004 in terms of event.[2]

While the 1998 flood was larger, more violent, and more extensive than the 1974 flood, it caused fewer fatalities (around 900 compared to 29,000 in 1974), and less damage to assets relative to GDP (asset losses of 4.8 percent of GDP compared to

TABLE 4.1} Selected Impacts for Worst Riverine Floods in Bangladesh over the Last Four Decades

Year	Fatalities	Affected (million)	Flooded country area (1,000 sq km)	Asset losses (million current US$)	Asset losses as % GDP	Estimated recurrence (years)
1998	918	31	100	2,128	4.8%	90
1988	2,379	47	90	1,424	5.5%	55
1987	1,657	30	57	1,167	4.9%	13
2004	285	33	56	1,860	3.3%	12
1974	28,700	30	53	936	7.5%	9
1984	1,200	30	Na	378	2.0%	2

Source: Islam 1997, 2000, 2005, 2006; CRED 2007; World Bank 2006.

7.5 percent in 1974). A major reason for this significant decrease in vulnerability was heavy investment into physical disaster risk management between the two events. Yet the benefits of specific interventions, compared to their costs, have not been assessed.

Cost-benefit analysis is one tool that can provide such quantitative information about the prioritization of risk management and climate adaptation options. This chapter takes a probabilistic approach in order to inform the prioritization and implementation of cost-effective disaster risk management and climate adaptation ("no-regret") options that could help Bangladesh cope with current and future extreme events.

A key finding of this chapter is that in order to meaningfully discuss current and future disaster risks, and the potential for risk management and adaptation, analysis has to be based on an estimate of risk as a function of climatic drivers (hazard, climate change) and socioeconomic drivers (exposure, vulnerability). Sufficient information is not always available on all components of risk and, consequently, the results will be sensitive to key assumptions. Yet, substantial progress has been made over the last few years in modeling extremes in a risk-based, more geographically explicit manner, harnessing recent innovations and improvements in modeling techniques and data. Regional climate modeling and statistical downscaling methods, as well as climate and socioeconomic downscaling techniques, which are more appropriate for analyzing localized extreme event patterns, can increasingly be used (Goodess et al. 2003). We argue that it is important to apply these methods within a risk-analytic approach for assessing natural disaster risk as a combination of geophysical signals, socioeconomic drivers, and vulnerability that generates natural hazards via loss-frequency functions. Such a probablistic representation (with a discussion of parameter uncertainties) of extreme event risks more appropriately reflects the low-probability, high consequence nature of such events and their associated potential socioeconomic impacts.

This chapter is organized as follows. We first discuss the essentials of CBA and its advantages and limitations for assessing disaster risk management. Then, we provide more detail on the application of CBA to disaster risk management and systematic steps to be taken. This is followed by a presentation of two frameworks for estimating risks and costs and benefits. The forward-looking framework is then applied in an example of an analysis of a risk management option in Bangladesh. Finally, we conclude with insights gained from the study process.

Advantages and Limitations of CBA for Assessing Disaster Risk Management

CBA is the main technique used by governments and public authorities for appraising the societal benefits of public investment projects and policies. Generally, it is used to organize and present the costs and benefits, and inherent trade-offs, and to ultimately estimate the economic efficiency of projects. CBA has been widely used for this purpose (see, e.g., Dasgupta and Pearce 1978). Although there are different levels of detail and complexity, the general features and principles of CBA are described in box 4.1.

BOX 4.1 } The Main Principles and Features of CBA

- **With and without approach.** CBA compares the situation with and without the project/investment, not the situation before and after.
- **Focus on selection of the "best option."** CBA is used to single out the best option rather than calculating the desirability of undertaking a project per se.
- **Societal point of view.** CBA takes a societal welfare approach. The benefits to society have to outweigh the costs in order to make a project desirable. The question addressed is whether a specific project or policy adds value to all of society, with the balance between winners and losers usually unaccounted for.
- **Revealed versus expressed preferences**. In the revealed preference approach, market prices for the goods under scrutiny (such as the value of material used for reconstructing a building after a disaster) can be observed and used. Those values often cannot directly be observed, however (e.g., a general value for "protection" against natural disasters), and the expressed preference approach is used, where preferences are gathered through surveys.
- **Clear definition of the boundaries for the analysis**. Count only losses within the geographical boundaries in the specified community/area/region/ country defined. Impacts or offsets outside these geographical boundaries should not be considered.

Several limitations of CBA must be taken into account. One important issue is the lack of accounting for the distribution of benefits and costs in CBA.[3] CBA takes a utilitarian approach, holding that social welfare is derived by aggregating individual welfare and changes therein due to projects and policies.[4] If preferences are measured through market prices or "willingness to pay,"[5] it should be kept in mind that more weight is given to those with a higher ability to pay. Moreover, CBA cannot resolve strong differences in value judgments that are often present in controversial projects (e.g., nuclear power, biotechnology, river management; see also Wenz 1988; Gowdy 2007). Another difficulty is the assessment of nonmarket values such as those related to health, the environment, or public goods in general. Although valuation methods exist in those cases, this often involves making contentious assumptions, particularly regarding the value of human life. Another important issue is the question of discounting, which by applying high discount rates for future benefits and costs expresses a strong preference for the present while potentially shifting large burdens to future generations. While CBA's main function is to inform the actual project appraisal stage and select the most suitable options among alternatives, it is of importance for the other phases of the project cycle, specifically for identifying projects and preselecting potential projects and rejecting others (Brent 1998). Also, in the evaluation phase, CBA is regularly used for assessing *ex-post* if a project really has added value to society.

Overall, keeping these limitations related to the valuation of intangibles and the distribution within society in mind, CBA can be a useful tool. Its main strength can be seen in that it is an explicit and rigorous accounting tool for measuring those costs and benefits, gains and losses, that can be effectively monetized, and in so doing, for making decisions more transparent. In this fashion, CBA is a framework supporting coherent and systematic decision making and providing a common yardstick with a money metric against which to measure projects (Kopp et al. 1997). To many (government) decision makers economic efficiency is a very important aspect, also for disaster-related policies. In the United States, for example, cost-benefit considerations have "at times dominated the policy debate on natural hazards" (Burby 1991). CBA, however, has to be seen as a guide to decision making and leading to an approximation of the preferences of society rather than an expression of the exact economic benefit of a given investment. Consequently, CBA and economic efficiency considerations should not be used in isolation, but form part of a larger decision-making framework incorporating social, economic, and cultural considerations.

Application of CBA to Disaster Risk Management

The main application of CBA in the context of disaster risk is for evaluating disaster risk management (DRM) options. This application is extended in this analysis to climate change adaptation, which shares many of the characteristics of DRM (Sperling and Szekely 2005). Key elements of the process are broken down into four steps as shown in figure 4.1.

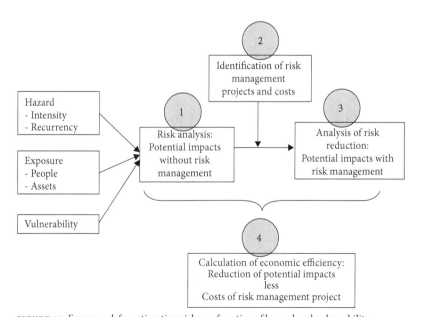

FIGURE 4.1 Framework for estimating risk as a function of hazard and vulnerability

Source: R. Mechler (2005). "Cost-Benefit Analysis of Natural Disaster Risk Management in Developing Countries." Disaster Risk Management in Development Cooperation, Working Paper, GTZ, Eschborn, Germany.

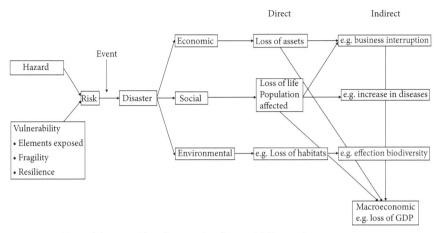

FIGURE 4.2 Natural disaster risk and categories of potential disaster impacts

STEP 1: RISK ANALYSIS

Risk, in terms of potential impacts without risk management, has to be estimated in order to set the stage for identifying and defining the problem. This entails estimating and combining hazard(s), exposure, and vulnerability. Also, the potentially changing hazard burden due to the impact of global climate change is estimated using best available science, noting the high degree of uncertainty. Disaster risk is commonly defined as the probability of potential impacts affecting people, assets, or the environment. Natural disasters may cause a variety of impacts, which are commonly classified into social, economic, and environmental categories, as well as according to whether they are triggered directly by the event or occur over time as indirect or macroeconomic effects (figure 4.2).

The standard approach for estimating natural disaster risk and potential disaster impacts is to understand natural disaster risk as a function of hazard, vulnerability, and exposure. *Hazard* analysis involves determining the type of hazards affecting a certain area with a specific intensity and return period, in order to derive a probabilistic representation of the hazard. In order to represent weather systematically, a weather generator is a useful tool generating future weather based on observed weather. As climate change is occurring and already significantly affecting extreme weather-related events in terms of frequency and/or severity in many places (IPCC, 2011), its effect on hazard needs to be factored into the analysis. In order to derive a representation of regional or local future weather, information of global climate models has to be downscaled to local conditions, a task involving considerable expertise, resources, and data.

Next, the *exposure* of people, assets, and the environment to a certain hazard needs to be identified. This involves assessing current and future socioeconomic trends. Accounting for changes in exposure is important, as reductions in future damages and losses[6] often may be compensated for by the sheer increase in the number of people and value of assets in harm's way.

Furthermore, the *vulnerability* of exposed people to hazard, and elements associated with a certain hazard intensity and return period has to be assessed. Different definitions exist for vulnerability, which is a multidimensional concept encompassing a large number of factors that can be grouped into physical, economic, social, and environmental factors. In order to operationalize and estimate vulnerability for CBA purposes, it can be defined more narrowly as the degree of impact observed on people and exposed elements as a function of the intensity of a hazard (see GTZ 2004).

A standard statistical concept for the probabilistic representation of disaster risk is the *loss-frequency function*, which indicates the probability of an event exceeding (*exceedance probability*) a certain level of losses. The inverse of the exceedance probability is the *return period*, that is, an event with a return period of 100 years on average will occur only every 100 years. It has to be kept in mind, that this is a standard statistical concept allowing the calculation of the occurrence events and their consequences in a probabilistic manner. A 100-year event could also occur two or three times in a century, but the probability of this would be low. In order to avoid misinterpretation, the exceedance probability is often a better concept than the return period.

Another important property of loss-frequency curves is the area under the curve. This area (the sum of all losses weighted by its probabilities) represents the expected annual losses, that is, the annual amount of losses that can be expected to occur over a longer time horizon. This concept helps when translating infrequent events and loss values into an annual number that can be used for planning purposes.

Potentially, there are a large number of impacts. In practice, however, only a limited amount of these can be and is usually assessed. The focus of this chapter, and this book, is those impacts that are quantified in monetary terms. These are usually grouped into three categories: direct, indirect, and macroeconomic effects (ECLAC 2003). *Direct* economic losses are mostly due to the immediate damage to, or destruction of, assets (or "stocks") in the event. Direct stock losses have *indirect* impacts on the "flow" of goods and services affecting households and firms. Finally, assessing the *macroeconomic* impacts involves estimating the aggregate impacts on economic variables like GDP, consumption, inflation, and government expenditures related to relief and reconstruction efforts. As the macroeconomic effects reflect indirect effects, as well as the relief and restoration effort, these effects cannot simply be added to the direct and indirect effects without causing duplication, as they are partially accounted for already (ECLAC 2003). Care also needs to be taken not to double count when including direct and indirect impacts.

STEP 2: IDENTIFICATION OF RISK MANAGEMENT MEASURES AND ASSOCIATED COSTS

Based on the assessment of risk, potential risk management projects and alternatives can be identified.

The costs in a CBA are the specific costs of conducting a project—investment and maintenance costs. There are the financial costs, the monetary amount that has to be spent on the project. Of more interest, however, are the so-called opportunity costs, which are the benefits foregone from not being able to use these funds for other

BOX 4.2 } Disaster Risk as Represented by the Loss Frequency Function

As an example, table 4.2 and figure 4.3 list values calculated for the case of flood risk in Piura, Peru as calculated in Mechler (2005).

In this case, losses due to 10, 50, 100, and 200 year events were estimated. For example, the 100 year event, an event with an annual probability of 1 percent, was estimated to lead to losses of around 1.7 billion Peruvian Soles. The last column shows the product of probability times the losses; the sum of all these products is the expected annual loss.

TABLE 4.2 } Risk as Represented by the Loss-Frequency Function for the Case of Peru

Return period (years)	Annual probability	Losses (million 2005 Peruvian soles)	Risk: Probability losses (million 2005 Peruvian soles)
10	10.0%	0	0.0
50	2.0%	675	13.5
100	1.0%	1,672	16.7
200	0.5%	3,344	16.7
Annual expected losses			46.9

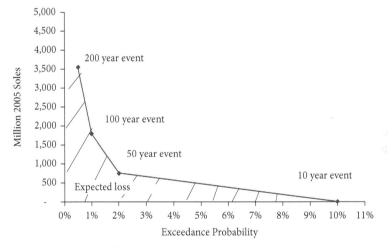

FIGURE 4.3 Example of loss-frequency distribution

important objectives. There is a wide spectrum of potential prevention prepared-ness, and risk financing measures that can be taken in order to reduce or finance risk. Table 4.3 lists a selection of these measures.

These measures reduce risk (prevention and preparedness) or transfer and spread it (risk

financing). While prevention and preparedness *reduce* the losses, insurance and other risk financing instruments lessen the *variability* of losses, but do not directly reduce them. Rather they spread and pool risks.[7]

TABLE 4.3 } Overview of Risk Management Measures

Type	Prevention	Preparedness	Risk financing
Effect	Reduces risk	Reduces risk	Transfers risk (reduces variability)
Key options	Physical and structural mitigation works (e.g., irrigation, embankments)	Early warning systems, communication systems	Risk transfer (by means of (re-) insurance) for public infrastructure and private assets, microinsurance
	Land-use planning and building codes	Contingency planning, networks for emergency response	Alternative risk transfer
	Economic incentives for pro-active risk management	Shelter facilities, evacuation plans	National and local reserve funds

Source: Modified based on IDB 2000.

STEP 3: ANALYSIS OF BENEFITS RISK REDUCTION

Whereas in a conventional CBA of investment projects, the benefits are the additional outcomes generated by the project compared to the situation without the project, in the case of disaster risk management, benefits arise due to the savings in terms of avoided direct, indirect, and macroeconomic costs, as well as due to the reduction in variability of project outcomes. Often, an attempt is made to monetize costs or benefits that are not given in such a metric, such as loss of life, environmental services, or the impacts of extreme events. However, some effects and benefits will be left out of the analysis due to estimation problems. Generally, *revealed vs. expressed preference* approaches can be distinguished (Parker, Green, and Thompson 1987). In the revealed-preference approach, available market prices for goods, such as the material cost of reconstructing a damaged building are used; in practice, this involves adding up potential avoided impacts in terms of reconstruction costs. Alternatively, in the expressed-preference approach, the value of a nonmarketed good, such as the value of flood safety, is directly elicited by asking those at risk. The revealed-preference approach is more common and followed for disaster risk management due to the general availability of data, while for the expressed-preference method, specific surveys would be required.

STEP 4: CALCULATION OF ECONOMIC EFFICIENCY

Finally, economic efficiency is assessed by comparing costs and benefits over the lifetime of the considered project. Costs and benefits arising over time need to be discounted to render current and future effects comparable. From an economic point of view, one dollar today has more value than one dollar in 10 years' time, thus future values need to be discounted. Last, costs and benefits are compared under a common economic efficiency decision criterion to assess if the benefits exceed the costs. Basically, three decision criteria are of major importance in CBA (see Dasgupta and Pearce 1978; Dinwiddy and Teal 1996):

- Net present value (NPV): costs and benefits arising over time are discounted and the difference is taken between benefits and costs, which leads to the net discounted benefit in a given year. The sum of the net benefits over the lifetime is the NPV. A fixed discount rate is used to represent the opportunity costs of using public funds for the given project. If the NPV is positive (benefits exceed costs), then a project is considered desirable.

- The benefit cost (B–C) ratio is a variant of the NPV: total discounted benefits over the lifetime of the project are divided by its discounted costs. If the ratio is larger than one, that is, benefits exceed costs, a project is considered to add value to society.
- Internal rate of return (IRR): whereas the former two criteria use a fixed discount rate, this criterion calculates a discount rate (or internal rate of return) discounting net benefits to zero. A project is rated desirable if the IRR surpasses the average return of public capital determined beforehand (e.g., the Asian Development Bank (ADB) uses a rate of 12 percent (Hecker 1995)).

In most circumstances, the three methods are equivalent.[8] In this assessment, due to its intuitive appeal, the B–C ratio will be used.

Frameworks for Estimating Risks: Cost and Benefits Associated with Natural Disaster Management

In order to estimate disaster risk, the potential and the costs and benefits of DRM, and climate adaptation, two assessment frameworks can be distinguished. The appropriate approach to be used depends on the objectives of the specific CBA conducted, the data situation, and available resources and expertise (table 4.4 and figure 4.4).

TABLE 4.4 } Types of Assessments in Context of CBA under Risk and Related Case Studies

Type of assessment	Methodology	Data requirements	Costs and applicability
Forward-looking assessment— risk-based	Estimate risk as a function of hazard, exposure, and vulnerability	Locale and asset-specific data on hazard, exposure, and vulnerability	More *accurate*, but *time and data-intensive* (up to several person years). More applicable for small-scale risk management measures, e.g., retrofitting a school/building against seismic shocks *Input to:* Pre-project appraisal or full project appraisal
Backward-looking assessment— impact-based	Use past losses as manifestations of past risk, then update to current risk	Data on past events, information on changes in hazard exposure and vulnerability	Leads to rougher estimates, but *more realistic and typical* for developing country context. More applicable for large-scale risk management measures like flood protection for river basin with various and different exposed elements. Need experience with losses in the past *Input to:* Evaluation (*ex-post*) or informational study

Source: Mechler 2005.

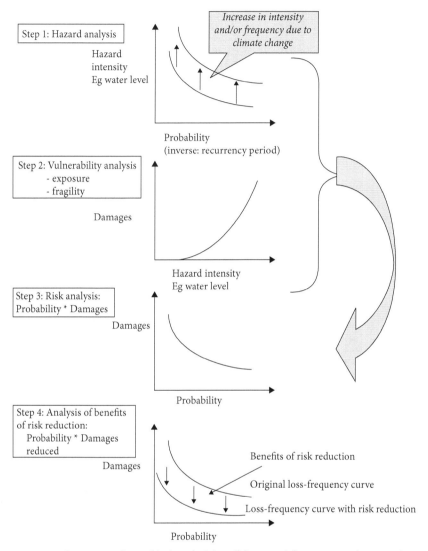

FIGURE 4.4 Quantitative forward-looking (risk-based) framework for estimating disaster risk

Source: R. Mechler (2005). "Cost-Benefit Analysis of Natural Disaster Risk Management in Developing Countries." Disaster Risk Management in Development Cooperation, Working Paper, GTZ, Eschborn, Germany.

In a more resource-intensive, *forward-looking* and *risk-based* framework, data on hazard and vulnerability are combined and can be used to produce estimates of risk and risk reductions. Ideally in a forward-looking risk assessment, risk can be estimated by combining information on hazard, exposure, and vulnerability as discussed above. Often such full-blown risk assessments are not feasible due to data, time, and money constraints, particularly when the area at risk is large, is exposed to more than one hazard, or there are a large number of exposed assets with different vulnerabilities. In the case of limited data availability, in a *backward-looking* and *impacts-based* framework, past losses are often used as the basis for coming to an understanding of current vulnerability, hazard, and risk. Such assessments are more applicable when loss functions are not developed or the scale under investigation is too broad to use loss functions.

Estimating extreme event risk and the benefits of risk reduction is fraught with a substantial amount of uncertainty, particularly so in this case, as disasters by definition are low-frequency, high-consequence events. A key limitation is data. Table 4.5 provides an overview of key data sources for estimating risk. Often, finding data on the elements of risk can be time-intensive and difficult. In particular, information on the degree of damage due to a certain hazard (vulnerability) is usually not readily available. As a consequence, in many instances, estimates need to be simply based on past impacts.

While we suggest that disaster impacts should be assessed in terms of risk as the probability of impacts occurring, it is important also to think about uncertainties involved in these risk estimates.[9] Uncertainties are inherent in:

- The recurrence of hazards: estimates are often based on a limited number of data points only.
- Incomplete loss assessments: data will not be available for all relevant direct and indirect and secondary effects, particularly so for the non-monetizable effects.
- Vulnerability: vulnerability curves often do not exist.
- Exposure: the dynamics of population increase and urban expansion, as well as welfare improvements need to be accounted for.
- Benefits of risk management options are often difficult to accurately measure.
- Discounting: the higher the discount rate used, the lower the benefits over the lifetime of a project; discounting thus has a very important impact on the result.

TABLE 4.5 } Data Sources for Hazard, Exposure, Vulnerability, and Impacts Information

Component	Data source	Comment on data availability
Hazard	Scientific publications and official statistics, postdisaster publications, geological meteorological and water authorities, local governments. Disaster management authorities. For climate change: global circulation models, regional downscaling	Often data available, for weather related events, may need to create a weather generator, climate change adds considerable complexity
Exposure	Statistical agencies, private firms. Disaster management authorities	Often some data available
Vulnerability	Specialized engineering reports. Disaster management authorities	Usually not available, often approximated by using information from other sources or from past events. Need to do survey or use expert assessment

- Valuation issues: exchange rates, deflators, and different cost concepts (replacement, market values) used.
- Additionally, for climate change, uncertainties are due to estimated changes in the frequency and intensity of natural hazards, which are considered likely by the latest report of the IPCC, yet today are still difficult to quantify (see IPCC 2011).

The specific sources of uncertainty are discussed in more detail in the assessment of the adaptation option in the next section. For Bangladesh and the ORCHID assessment of selected DRM options under dynamic conditions including climate change, both frameworks were used. While the backward-looking analysis focused on the broad-brush assessment of current and future countrywide risk in Bangladesh under climate change (see box 4.3), forward-looking risk-based CBAs were conducted for specific ongoing and planned DRM options. We will present the latter in the next section.

Forward-looking Framework for Assessing the Costs and Benefits of Specific Adaptation Options

The estimates presented in box 4.3 from the backward-looking analysis indicate the importance of adaptation (and assumptions about it for thinking about climate change and climate change policy). The representation of adaptation in this top-down assessment of adaptation is broad-based, locale-unspecific, and based on adaptation that occurred in the recent past. Furthermore, adaptation is not cost-

BOX 4.3 } Using a Backward-Looking Approach for Assessing Countrywide Risk Management and Adaptation Measures

The ORCHID project used a backward-looking approach toward disaster risk and potential changes due to climate change with a countrywide resolution, in order to set the stage for the later detailed CBA and specific adaptation options, and to study the importance of adaptation and associated modeling assumptions.[18] The project studied aggregate asset risk for all of Bangladesh for the present day, in 2020 and 2050 under possible climate change scenarios for

(1) a no-adaptation case with no additional adaptation taking place; and
(2) the adaptation case, where significant adaptation is occurring extrapolated from past adaptation.

The analysis indicates that without adaptation, a worsening climate will lead to increases in (direct) risk to assets. Meanwhile, with significant adaptation, despite a changing frequency of hazards, asset (direct) losses as a share of GDP could be reduced. The results in terms of asset risk for Bangladesh for the respective scenarios are shown in figures 4.5 a and b.

Note: The return period (in years) is the reciprocal of the exceedance probability, e.g. a 10 percent exceedance probability denotes a 10-year return period.

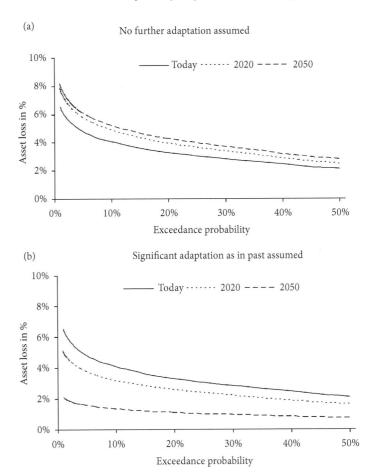

FIGURE 4.5 Asset risk measured in terms of GDP for baseline, 2020 and 2050 without and with significant adaptation assumed

Note: The return period (in years) is the reciprocal of the exceedance probability, e.g., a 10 percent exceedance probability denotes a 10-year return period.

Source: Authors' calculations.

free and may come at a significant price in terms of opportunity costs, which are not captured in the analysis. A key question for this assessment and the adaptation discussion in general (Stern 2007) is the scope for such adaptation and the extent to which it will occur autonomously or require specific planning and intervention.

In order to shed more light on these crucial issues, in what follows, a more forward-looking (risk-based) and bottom-up approach is applied using CBAs to analyze ongoing and planned adaptation options in Bangladesh. For measuring risk and the benefits arising due to selected adaptation or risk reduction options in a risk-based framework, the four steps discussed above are followed. The option under consideration involved the raising of homesteads on riverine islands (*Chars*)[10] in Northern Bangladesh by means of constructing raised earth platforms.[11]

RIVERINE FLOOD RISK IN THE CHARS

The riverine areas of Bangladesh are home to the poorest and most vulnerable communities in the country, with over 80 percent living in extreme poverty. Inhabitants of these areas live with a serious flood risk. The lives of the Char people are closely related to the dynamics of the river flows and the resulting formation and erosion of Chars. Thus, Char communities are extremely vulnerable to erosion and flooding. Against this background, DFID supported the Chars Livelihoods Programme (CLP), which aims to improve the livelihood of the poor in the Char areas by reducing their vulnerability. However, these people have the least resources to pay for the necessary infrastructure. The Bangladesh National Water Management Plan emphasizes coping with inland floods rather than managing them. In the past, greater reliance has been placed on embankments and drainage schemes, which are primarily designed for protection of agriculture. But beyond agriculture, in areas such as housing and other infrastructure, *ex-ante* preparation has received far less attention despite significant flood loss potential. In the 1998 and 2004 floods, for example, the direct losses to residential sectors accounted for 20 to 33 percent of the total loss, and 40 to 44 percent of the total nonagricultural loss (Islam 2006).

Quantifying the risks Char dwellers are exposed to is difficult given the high degree of uncertainty in terms of depths, duration, and frequency of flooding, as well as land levels and floor heights of individual houses. Direct (structural, inventory, and other) losses in terms of reconstruction costs and indirect (income) losses are included in the analysis based on Islam (2005, 2006).[12] Baseline probabilities are also based on Islam (2005, 2006).

The shaded area (losses up to the 20-year event, or with an annual probability of 5 percent) indicates the risks up to a 20-year event, which the option discussed in the following pages is supposed to manage and for which we calculate benefits. The forecasting of risks into the future, in order to account for changes in hazard frequency and/or intensity, draws on the results of the natural science components of the ORCHID study, which builds on the IPCC SRES B1 future climate scenarios for 2020 and 2050 for Bangladesh (see Nakicenovic et al. 2000). Based on the climate scenarios, in the ORCHID project the following changes in flooded area and associated probabilities were calculated (see figure 4.6), which then lead to the following risk curves in 2020 and 2050 compared to today's risks.

Changed flood recurrence intervals were used to modify the recurrence of flood losses (see figure 4.6). For example, according to this analysis a total loss of $80.8 associated with an annual probability of 20 percent or a return period of five years, would in 2020 occur more frequently and become a three-year event (33 percent probability).

IDENTIFYING THE OPTION AND ITS COSTS: RAISING OF HOMESTEADS ABOVE CRITICAL FLOOD LEVELS

The *Homestead Raising* option (in the following called HS) supported by the CLP in the Char areas is concerned with providing proven technologies in the form of raised homesteads (up to the maximum flood depth on record in the respective

TABLE 4.6 } Flood Risk and Benefits of Avoiding/Reducing Risk Now and in 2020 and 2050 as Projected

Flood return period (years)	Structural damage (main house) (US$)	Inventory damage (US$)	Other damages (US$)	Income loss (US$)	Total (US$)	Probability baseline	Prob. 2020	Prob. 2050
2	8.4	0.0	0.0	5.1	13.5	50.0%	67.0%	67.0%
5	33.8	30.0	6.8	10.1	80.8	20.0%	33.0%	43.0%
10	73.7	79.9	27.3	20.3	201.2	10.0%	20.0%	25.0%
20	106.7	129.3	54.6	25.3	315.9	5.0%	11.0%	13.0%
50	160.0	194.0	81.9	38.0	473.9	2.0%	3.0%	4.0%
100	320.1	387.9	163.8	76.0	947.8	1.0%	1.5%	2.0%
Expected loss (US$)	30.1	28.2	10.1	9.4	77.8		139.1	173.1
Expected loss avoided—up to 20-year event (US$) = benefits in the CBA	19.5	20.5	6.8	2.7	52.1		101.7	126.1

Note: For (indirect) income losses, we assumed that the physical homestead option reduces losses by half, as work conducted at home will be made feasible irrespective of flooding, yet there will be some disruptions in economic activity due to affected infrastructure, such as roads.

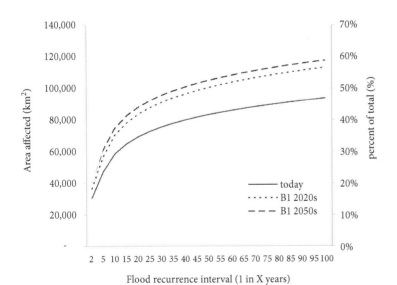

Flood recurrence interval (1 in X years)

FIGURE 4.6 Increase in area affected by flood from today to the 2020s and 2050s

Source: T. M. Tanner et al. (2007). "ORCHID: Piloting Climate Risk Screening in DFID Bangladesh." Summary Research Report, Institute of Development Studies, University of Sussex, UK.

location). The basic idea for this option is to construct earthen platforms on beneficiaries' land to protect against the height of a flood with a recurrence interval of 20
years by establishing a unit for a "bari" (homestead)—comprising four houses with
a total of 20 people on an area of 600 square meters.

The adaptation option presented here considers that the flood proofing of an area
will cover four dwellings, a hand tube well, and a toilet. It is assumed that the inhabitants will dismantle their individual houses and reconstruct them on a common platform. As erodible soils can be washed away by wave action during floods, protection
and/or regular maintenance may be required.

The Char areas in this adaptation option refer to one of the main Char areas
comprising five districts along the Brahmaputra River.[13] About 1,000 villages in 20
Upazilas (an administrative unit equivalent to a subdistrict) in the Brahmaputra
Char lands are expected to be covered under the option, totaling some 2.5 million people. As regards working life, the Government of the People's Republic of
Bangladesh (2001) generally suggests a 25-year life for such options. Flood proofing
by raising houses, roads, water supply/sanitation facilities, and other infrastructure
above flood level reflects traditional practice in Bangladesh.[14] Not all households
have the resources to do this, particularly in the unprotected Char areas near the
major river channels. We assume that support could be extended within the DFID-
supported CLP to generally focus on improved livelihoods for Char dwellers.

This adaptation option would provide an earth platform to protect against a minimum flood level, so that flooding does not affect households' day-to-day functioning. The level to which the land is raised takes into account not only the maximum
observed flood level, but the effects of sea level rise due to climate change. Knowledge
of the maximum flood level in Char areas is critical for the planned height of the
homesteads to be raised. It is difficult to assess exactly to what extent individual
homesteads have to be raised as land levels vary considerably from house to house,
and location to location. Furthermore, due to spatial variability, the precise return
period (flood frequency) associated with a flood level is difficult to determine. As a
consequence, there is no satisfactory scientific basis for any assessment unless there
is a detailed land use, land level, and hydrological survey for the area. In the absence
of this, the maximum flood level has been based upon the living memory of the local
population.

Following a field survey done with local people, all the Char inhabitants are found
to be vulnerable even to a two-year flood event. Moreover, 33 percent of inhabitants
reported vulnerability to higher flooding levels. Houses should on average be raised
by 0.9 meters in order to be protected from a flood, such as the 2004 flood, for which
a return period of about 15 years was established. An additional 0.6 meters has to
be added to this level to allow for even greater safety. Therefore a level of 1.5 meters
above ground level is expected to provide sufficient protection for dwellings against
a flood having a return period of 20 years (assessed by CLP).

The HS option can be divided into two suboptions depending on whether the
community will bear any associated costs. Under the HS Option (A), the project will
raise one common platform for four dwellings, with each dwelling having an area
of 150 square meters, and will reconstruct individual houses. Other infrastructure

provision such as tube wells and sanitation will also be constructed by the project. Under the HS Option (B), the project will only raise the common platform while the beneficiaries will reconstruct their individual houses, including making other infrastructure provision such as tube wells and sanitation. The analysis is carried out for both the cases. Cost estimates for these two suboptions are provided in table 4.7.

According to the estimates, the capital investment extended by the donor-supported project per household benefited amounts to about $233 for the first suboption and to $143 for the second one. Raising land for buildings above flood levels is assumed to eliminate the loss caused by flooding up to that respective flood level, but raising other facilities can also reduce or eliminate the disruption caused by the floods. Finally, 2 percent of the total cost will be required for operation and maintenance costs, which is to be borne by the project.

ASSESSING THE BENEFITS OF DISASTER RISK MANAGEMENT IN THE CHARS

The benefits in terms of avoided or reduced losses are assessed to be equal for both the two suboptions, HS (A) and HS (B). As is generally the case when implementing local adaptation measures in the face of uncertainty, any broad assumptions made should ideally be based on dialogue with vulnerable Char dwellers and Char managers. We used the triangulation method for cross-checking information from various sources.[15] Perceptions of local Char people were useful in collecting information on floods, their frequency, depth, and duration.

The following factors are of specific importance and have implications for the engineering design of flood protection structures and flood response strategies:

- frequency of flooding;
- depth of flooding;
- duration of flooding;
- land levels and height of platform;
- the susceptibility of building materials to water.

Two types of houses in Char areas are considered: (1) earthen floor and corrugated iron sheet wall (EC); and (2) earthen floor and thatched wall (ET). These two low-cost types of houses are currently occupied by 33 and 67 percent of the Char dwellers, respectively.

The benefits associated with avoiding losses up to the 20-year flood (5 percent chance of recurrence) are shown in the shaded area of table 4.6 for the individual loss categories, alongside total losses for the baseline (today), 2020, and 2050.[16] For the total losses these amounted to about $52, $102, and $126 per household potentially affected for today, 2020, and 2050, respectively. In order to calculate annual benefits, and the option's lifetime of 25 years, a climate-change induced annual increase of 2.6 percent in avoided losses as benefits based on these figures was used up to the year 2032 (2008–2032) (figure 4.7).

There are some additional potential benefits not included in the calculations. In particular, adverse impacts of floods on health are considerable because, for

TABLE 4.7 } Information and Costs for Homestead Raising Option

Item	Estimates (cost estimates in current US$ if not indicated otherwise)	Major assumptions
Population in Char areas under CLP	2,500,000	
Average household size	5	
No. of "bari" platforms (consisting of 4 dwellings) to be raised	125,000	
Average size of each platform (4 dwellings @ 150 m²)	600	
No. of dwellings served	500,000	
No. of people served	2,500,000	
Working life	25 years	
Average quantity of earthwork (for each "bari" platform consisting of 4 dwellers) (600 m² × 1.22 m)	732 m³	Construction on beneficiaries' land
Cost of earthwork per m³	0.8	
OPTION A		Cost of water supply, toilets and reconstruction of buildings will be borne by the Project
Cost for each bari platform		
Cost of earthwork	564.7	
Cost of compaction, turfing, & plantation [1]	9.2	
Cost of dismantling/reconstruction	61.4	
Cost of CLP-type (raised) tube well (1 for 4 dwellers) [2]	69.1	
Cost of CLP-type tube-well platform (1 for 4 dwellers)	26.1	
Cost of CLP-type latrine (4 for 4 dwellers @ TK3,300) [3]	202.7	
Total cost for each bari (4 dwellers)	933.3	
Total cost for each household	**233.3**	
OPTION B		Cost of water supply, toilets and reconstruction will be borne by the beneficiaries.
Cost for each bari platform (2007 price)	564.7	
Cost of compaction, turfing, & plantation	9.2	
Total cost for each bari (4 dwellers)	573.9	
Total cost for each household	**143.5**	
Total cost of the option in Char areas		
OPTION A	116,657,143	
OPTION B	71,742,857	
Operation and maintenance cost	2 percent of project	To be borne by the Project

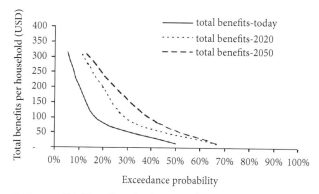

FIGURE 4.7 Total benefits today, in 2020 and 2050

example, there is a close correlation between flooding and the incidence of water-borne diseases such as diarrhea and dysentery[17] (Islam 2006; Islam 1998). The proposed option has introduced some low-cost and improved water supply and sanitary measures, which help to provide protection against water-borne diseases.

CALCULATING ECONOMIC EFFICIENCY

Tables 4.7 and 4.8 present estimated B–C ratios, for the two options, HS (A) and HS (B), respectively. The estimates are carried out for a range of discount rates from 0 to 20 percent. Baseline estimates and increased costs and benefits (by 50 percent) are contemplated for both suboptions for various discount rates.

Suboption A refers to construction of house and associated facilities, while suboption B refers to construction of only the house. It can be seen that for best estimate cases, suboptions A and B seem to be beneficial given the assumptions. Sub option B scores higher (i.e., higher B–C ratio), as costs for the project are reduced by the contribution made by residents. For example, the B–C ratio of suboption A is estimated as 1.4, while suboption B is estimated as 1.9 at a 12 percent discount rate, which is often used as a standard rate for the opportunity cost of public money in a developing country such as Bangladesh.

If more pessimistic assumptions about costs and benefits are used (e.g., 50 percent higher costs and 50 percent lower benefits), the suboptions eventually become inefficient with rising discount rates, as future benefits in terms of reduced losses are more strongly discounted and eventually reduced to zero earlier than they would be with lower discount rates (see figure 4.8). In such a case, the project (suboption) would no longer be economically viable. However, as well as creating flood protection and thereby avoiding huge flood damages, the adaptation measures (raising houses and dwellings) would generate employment and additional income for people in the disaster-prone and poverty-stricken Char areas. Raising the level of homesteads on a cluster basis might also lead to social gains, in terms of creation of community cohesion. These benefits are intangible but may be significant to the society. As the

TABLE 4.8 } B-C Ratio for Homestead Option for Option A

Discount rate	0%	5%	10%	12%	15%	20%
Baseline estimate	2.8	2.1	1.6	1.4	1.3	1.0
Costs + 50%	2.4	1.7	1.2	1.1	0.9[a]	0.7[a]
Costs + 50%, benefits—50%	1.2	0.9[a]	0.6[a]	0.6[a]	0.5[a]	0.4[a]

[a] Not economically efficient for the given discount rates and costs exceed benefits.

B-C Ratio for Homestead Option for Option B

Discount rate	0%	5%	10%	12%	15%	20%
Baseline estimate	3.2	2.6	2.1	1.9	1.7	1.4
Costs + 50%	2.9	2.2	1.7	1.5	1.3	1.1
Costs + 50%, benefits—50%	1.4	1.1	0.8[a]	0.8[a]	0.7[a]	0.5[a]

[a] Not efficient for the given discount rates, and costs exceed benefits.

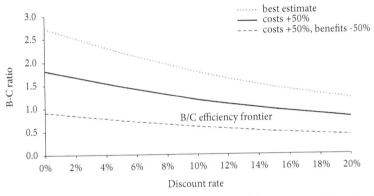

FIGURE 4.8 B ratios for homestead option A as function of discount rate and important assumptions

households concerned are extremely poor, the Option HS (A) (without participation from the community) may be more suitable. A side effect of Option HS (B), however, might be that the beneficiaries feel encouraged when contributing to the works.

Discussion and Conclusion

This chapter has discussed the appraisal of the economic efficiency of selected options for adaptation to extreme climate-related event risks in Bangladesh using a cost-benefit analysis. The methodology developed was tested for a selected intervention option in the Char area. The approach adopted provides information on the prioritization and implementation of cost-effective disaster risk management and climate adaptation ("no-regret") options that could help communities cope with current and future extreme events of possibly increasing intensity and/or frequency.

Economic risk and the economic efficiency of selected adaptation options is estimated by means of cost-benefit analysis, accounting for uncertainty and the dynamic driving forces of hazards, vulnerability, and exposure. A key concept employed in this analysis is the probabilistic representation of risks and of the benefits of risk reduction by loss-frequency functions. For valuing the benefits arising from public sector interventions, the expressed-preference approach was used, using available market prices for goods, such as would be used for reconstructing a damaged building. This involves adding up potential avoided impacts in terms of reconstruction costs. The revealed-preference approach is more common for disaster risk management due to the general availability of some data, while for the alternative expressed-preference method, specific surveys are recommended. A *risk-based* framework (forward-looking) was used, combining data on hazard, exposure, and vulnerability with an estimate of risk and risk reduced. Uncertainty around these estimates and the assumptions, while hard to quantify, is considerable and should be kept in mind. Accordingly, numbers should be understood with some caution.

The DRM option considered in this analysis involves the flood proofing of individual homesteads against a maximum of 20-year floods on riverine islands, known as Chars, in Bangladesh. The option, already being implemented as part of CLP, involves constructing earth platforms on beneficiaries' land covering the unit of a bari (homestead with four households). Monetary and economic losses and benefits considered were:

- structural loss to dwellings;
- inventory loss avoided;
- income loss; and
- other loss avoided, such as cleanup costs.

Results indicate that for the best estimate cases, the options studied seem to be economically beneficial with a range of 1.4 to 3.2 for the B–C, calculated using standard assumptions and data on costs and benefits. The CLP has already raised the homesteads of more than 90,000 Char. The CLP has recently also targeted the planting of Vetiver grass, Durba grass, and trees to protect slopes from erosion due to flooding.

Estimating extreme event risk and the benefits of risk reduction is fraught with substantial uncertainty, particularly so in this case, as disasters by definition are low-frequency, high-consequence events. Uncertainties relate in particular to:

- estimates of hazard and changes thereof (e.g., due to climate change);
- the exposure of assets and people;
- vulnerability (here defined as the degree of damage for a given level of hazard intensity);
- the benefits of risk reduction;
- the proper choice of the discount rate; and
- the cost concepts used for valuing impacts.

In this assessment, due to data limitations and the scope of the study, it was not possible to conduct a quantitative uncertainty analysis (e.g., using confidence intervals). Rather, sensitivity analysis was used to vary the costs and benefits of the options, as well as the discount rate. The sensitivity of results to assumptions of those parameters and variables (as often in CBAs) was found to be considerable: if more pessimistic assumptions about costs and benefits are made, and uncertainty is taken into account by means of sensitivity analysis, the options eventually become inefficient with increasing discount rates.

Extreme events, their potential impact, and the scope for adaptation are gaining in importance in the policy debate on climate change. This is also due to increasing empirical evidence and studies on climate-change-induced increases in the intensity and frequency of extremes events such as cyclones and flooding. The representation of extreme event risks and adaptation within modeling approaches is an emerging practice, but there is considerable scope for making better use of improved modeling of extremes in a risk-based, more geographically explicit manner, harnessing recent innovations and improvements in modeling techniques and data. In this vein, this assessment of the costs and benefits of adaptation to climate variability and change for Bangladesh should be understood as an exploration of these issues. With improvements in data and modeling techniques, similar approaches may contribute to helping hazard-prone societies better plan for, and adapt, to climate variability and change.

Acknowledgments

This research was supported by funding received from DFID for the ORCHID (Opportunities and Risks of Climate Change and Disasters) project. All opinions, *errors*, or omissions are the sole responsibility of the authors.

Notes

1. ORCHID, standing for Opportunities and Risks of Climate Change and Disasters, was commissioned by DFID, which saw that increased vulnerability to natural hazards and climate change posed a threat to its donor assistance portfolio in many places, and there had been few systematic assessments of vulnerability and risk and how to reduce and manage them. ORCHID's main objectives were to develop a climate risk screening approach for considering climate risk management in country assistance portfolios as a means of disaster risk reduction and adaptation to climate change. The ORCHID study process involved country-based portfolio screening of projects and programs, as well as a broader strategic assessment, aligning donor activities with national priorities and planning. Using profiles of current and future climate, hazards, exposure, and vulnerability, the process focused on key planned and ongoing development assistance activities in order to identify high-risk activities and valuable opportunities for integrating adaptation and risk reduction within current and planned development assistance. ORCHID also focused on raising awareness and interest among DFID staff and country partners, while acknowledging the complexity of decision making

in a context where information is often limited and uncertain. The process was also meant to critically assess possible limits to adaptive risk management responses (Tanner et al. 2007).

2. Generally, disaster statistics, as used in this case, list fatalities, people affected, and, less frequently, the direct economic (stock) losses in terms of impacts on physical structures such as roads, buildings, and other assets.

3. The general principle underlying CBA is the Kaldor-Hicks-Criterion, which holds that those benefiting from a specific project or policy should potentially be able to compensate those that are disadvantaged by it (Dasgupta and Pearce 1978). Whether compensation is actually given, however, is often not of importance. Also, methods to account for the distribution of costs and benefits have been proposed but are not used in practice (Little and Mirrlees 1990).

4. Also, no definite aggregation rule exists for aggregating individual preferences to a social welfare function. As Arrow (1963) has shown in the impossibility theorem, no such welfare function exists that allows the social ranking of alternative social states from individual preferences given that intuitively plausible criteria of social choice are satisfied. This is a serious restriction of CBA, as a main proposition contends that individual preferences should count in an assessment of social choice. The usual way out of this impasse is introduction of normative judgment by means of postulating a decision maker or observer that seeks to maximize social welfare. This can be the government, a project evaluator, or a representative agent (see Dasgupta and Pearce 1978).

5. Willingness to pay (WTP) denotes the maximum monetary amount an individual is willing to pay for receiving a good or service. A related metric is willingness to accept (WTA), which is the minimum amount an individual would demand to give up a good or service.

6. The literature often does not clearly distinguish between damages and losses. We refer to damage here as the physical impact, and losses as the monetized effect, whether direct or indirect.

7. Insurance and other risk-financing mechanisms are based on the law of large numbers, which states that with an increasing number of observations the probability distribution can be estimated more precisely and the variance around the mean decreases.

8. In most circumstances, the three methods are equivalent (see Zerbe and Dively 1994; Dasgupta and Pearce 1978; Brent 1998), and each metric has its limitations. For the NPV, there is some uncertainty regarding the choice of an appropriate discount rate. The main shortcoming with the IRR is that it sometimes cannot be defined unambiguously. Several IRRs may be possible if the IRR is the solution to a polynomial equation. If the polynomial is of degree n there will be n roots to it and n IRRs to choose from. Then, it is not clear which IRR to select (Dasgupta and Pearce 1978). A major problem with the IRR and the C–B–R is that they should not be used for mutually exclusive projects, i.e., for projects that cannot be adopted in combination with others as, e.g., the decision whether to build a two- or three-lane highway. The IRR would discriminate against large-scale projects with high initial capital outlays. Also, projects with high IRR that only last a short time would be preferred to projects whose returns are smaller but longer lasting (Gramlich 1981).

9. Risk and uncertainty are closely related. A famous distinction by Frank Knight is to refer to risk as "measurable uncertainty," when uncertainty can be quantified and assessed probabilistically (Knight 1921). Often this is not possible, and sensitivity analysis is used to account for important uncertainties.

10. *Char* is Bengali for "island."

11. Also, the flood-proofing of the Bangladesh road and highway system was studied. This study is supported by DFID within the program "Roads and Highways Policy Management,

Budgetary and Technical Assistance Support." More detail on this can be found in Islam and Mechler 2007.

12. Appropriate deflators for the cost of building materials (for structural damage) and national income (for inventory damage) are used in the benefit assessments to convert into current prices.

13. The districts stretch from Kurigram in the north to Sirajganj districts in the south. The other three districts are Jamlpur, Gaibanda, and Bogra.

14. Although the option refers to Char areas, this could also be adopted in any areas vulnerable to flooding, including coastal areas.

15. The major sources of information used in this analysis are CLP secretariat, government of Bangladesh (2001), Islam (2005, 2006), and the potential beneficiaries themselves, through use of appropriate deflators as applicable.

16. For the income loss, we assumed that losses would be reduced by 50 percent as discussed above.

17. Correlation $r = 0.66$ with more than 99 percent significance level (Islam 2006, 1998).

18. For further details, see Islam and Mechler 2007.

References

Arrow, K. (1963). *Social Choice and Individual Values*. 2d ed. New York: Wiley.

Bangladesh Bureau of Statistics (BBS). (Various Yearly Issues). *Statistical Year Book of Bangladesh*. Dhaka: Bangladesh Bureau of Statistics.

Benson, C., and Twigg, J. (2004). *Measuring Mitigation: Methodologies for Assessing Natural Hazard Risks and the Net Benefits of Mitigation—A Scoping Study*. Geneva: International Federation of the Red Cross and Red Crescent Societies, ProVention Consortium.

Brent, R. J. (1998). *Cost-Benefit Analysis for Developing Countries*. Cheltenham, UK: Edward Elgar.

Burby, R., ed. (1991). *Sharing Environmental Risks: How to Control Governments' Losses in Natural Disasters*. Boulder, CO: Westview Press.

CRED (2007). EM-DAT: International Disaster Database. Centre for Research on the Epidemiology of Disasters, Université Catholique de Louvain, Brussels, Belgium. http://www.emdat.be.

Dasgupta, A. K., and Pearce, D. W. (1978). *Cost-Benefit Analysis: Theory and Practice*. London: Macmillan.

Dinwiddy, C., and Teal, F. (1996). *Principles of Cost-Benefit Analysis for Developing Countries*. Cambridge: Cambridge University Press.

ECLAC (2003). *Handbook for Estimating the Socio-economic and Environmental Effects of Disasters*. Mexico City: ECLAC.

Goodess, C. M., Hanson, C., Hulme, M., and Osborn, T. J. (2003). "Representing Climate and Extreme Weather Events in Integrated Assessment Models: A Review of Existing Methods and Options for Development." *Integrated Assessment* 4: 145–171.

Government of the People's Republic of Bangladesh. (2001). *National Water Management Plan*. Vol. 3, *Investment Portfolio*. Dhaka: Ministry of Water Resources.

Gowdy, J. (2007). "Toward an Experimental Foundation for Benefit-Cost Analysis." *Ecological Economics* 63: 649–655.

Gramlich, E. M. (1981). *Benefit-Cost Analysis of Government Programs.* Englewood Cliffs, N.J.: Prentice-Hall.

GTZ (2004). "Risk Analysis—a Basis for Disaster Risk Management." Guidelines, GTZ, Eschborn, Germany.

Hecker, G. (1995). "A Review of the Disaster-Related Activities of the Asian Development Bank: An Economic Perspective." Disaster Prevention for Sustainable Development: Economic and Policy Issues, World Bank, Washington, D.C.

Hochrainer-Stigler, S., Kunreuther, H., Linnerooth-Bayer, J., Mechler, R., Michel-Kerjan, E., Muir-Wood, R., Ranger, N., Vaziri, P., and Young, M. (2010). "The Costs and Benefits of Reducing Risk from Natural Hazards to Residential Structures in Developing Countries." Wharton Risk Management and Decision Processes Center Working Paper Series WP2010–12-0.

IDB (2000). "Facing the Challenge of Natural Disasters in Latin America and the Caribbean: An IDB Action Plan." Inter-American Development Bank, Washington, D.C.

IPCC (2011). "Summary for Policymakers." In Field, C. B., Barros, V., Stocker, T.F., et al., eds., *Intergovernmental Panel on Climate Change Special Report on Managing the Risks of Extreme Events and Disasters to Advance Climate Change Adaptation.* Cambridge: Cambridge University Press.

Islam, K. M. Nabiul (1997). "The Impacts of Flooding and Methods of Assessment in Urban Areas of Bangladesh." Ph.D. diss., Flood Hazard Research Centre, Middlesex University, London.

———. (1998). "Health Aspects of Flooding-Evidence from Macro-level Data on Incidence of Diseases in Bangladesh." Research Report No. 155, BIDS, Dhaka.

———. (2000). "Micro and Macro Level Impacts of Urban Floods in Bangladesh." In *Floods*, Vol. 1, edited by D. J. Parker. London and New York: Routledge.

———. (2005). *Flood Loss Potentials in Non-agricultural Sectors: Assessment Methods and Standard Loss Database for Bangladesh.* Dhaka: Palok Publishers.

Islam, K. M. Nabiul, and Mechler, R. (2006). *Impacts of Flood in Urban Bangladesh: Micro and Macro Level Analysis.* Dhaka: A H Development Publishing House and Community Development Library.

——— (2007). *ORCHID: Piloting Climate Risk Screening in DFID Bangladesh: An Economic and Cost Benefit Analysis of Adaptation Options.* Institute of Development Studies, University of Sussex, UK.

Knight, F. (1921). *Risk, Uncertainty, and Profit.* Boston and New York: Houghton Mifflin.

Kopp, R. J., Krupnick, A. J., et al. (1997). "Cost-Benefit Analysis and Regulatory Reform: An Assessment of the Science and the Art." Discussion Paper 97–19, Resources for the Future, Washington, D.C.

Little, I., and Mirrlees, J. (1990). "Project Appraisal and Planning Twenty Years On." *Proceedings of the World Bank Annual Conference on Development Economics*, S. Fischer, Washington, D.C.

Mechler, R. (2005). "Cost-Benefit Analysis of Natural Disaster Risk Management in Developing Countries." Disaster Risk Management in Development Cooperation, Working Paper, GTZ, Eschborn, Germany.

Ministry of Agriculture (2001). "Flood and Coastal Defence Project Appraisal Guidance." London.

Nakicenovic, N., Alcamo, J., Gruebler, A., Riahi, K., Roehrl, R. A., Rogner, H. H., Victor, N., et al. (2000). "Special Report on Emissions Scenarios (SRES)." Special Report of Working Group III of the Intergovernmental Panel on Climate Change, Cambridge University Press, Cambridge.

OAS (1991). *Primer on Natural Hazard Management in Integrated Regional Development Planning*. Washington, D.C.: Organization of American States.

Parker, D., Green, C., and Thompson, P. (1987). *Urban Flood Protection Benefits: A Project Appraisal Guide*. Aldershot, Hants, UK: Gower Publishing.

Penning-Rowsell, E., Green, C., Thompson, P., Coker, A., Tunstall, S., Richards, C., and Parker, D. (1992). *The Economics of Coastal Management—A Manual of Benefit Assessment Techniques (The Yellow Manual)*. London.

Rahman, F. A. K. M. (2006). "The Impact of Floods on Major Highways and Mitigation Options." In *Options for Flood Risk and Damage Reduction in Bangladesh*, edited by K. U. Siddiqui and A. N. H. A. Hossain. Dhaka: University Press Limited.

Siddiqui, K. U., and Hossain, A. N. H. A. (eds.) (2006). *Options for Flood Risk and Damage Reduction in Bangladesh*. Dhaka: University Press Limited.

Sperling, F., and Szekely, F. (2005). "Disaster Risk Management in a Changing Climate." Informal discussion paper prepared for the World Conference on Disaster Reduction on behalf of the Vulnerability and Adaptation Resource Group (VARG), Washington, D.C.

Stern, N. (2007). *The Stern Review on the Economics of Climate Change*. Cambridge: Cambridge University Press.

Tanner, T. M., Hassan, A., Islam, K. M. N., Conway, D., Mechler, R., Ahmed, A. U., and Alam, M. (2007). "ORCHID: Piloting Climate Risk Screening in DFID Bangladesh." Summary Research Report, Institute of Development Studies, University of Sussex, UK.

Wenz, P. (1988). *Environmental Justice*. Albany: State University of New York Press.

World Bank (1989). *Bangladesh Action Plan for Flood Control*. Main Report, Dhaka.

———. (2006). *World Development Indicators*. Washington, D.C.: World Bank.

World Bank and United Nations (2010). *Natural Hazards, Unnatural Disasters: The Economics of Effective Prevention*. Washington, D.C.: World Bank.

Zerbe, R. O., and Dively D. D. (1994). *Benefit-Cost Analysis in Theory and Practice*. New York: Harper Collins.

5 }

Challenges Ahead
RISK MANAGEMENT AND COST-BENEFIT ANALYSIS
IN A CHANGING CLIMATE

Stéphane Hallegatte

Introduction

Climate change has become an important policy issue in the international debate. In particular, concerns have been raised about the influence of climate change on natural hazards and natural disasters. Climate change, indeed, will modify all meteorological and environmental variables, from temperatures and precipitation levels, to river runoff and sea levels. These modifications are particularly likely to affect these variables at the extremes.

These probable modifications in hazards are important because social and economic vulnerability to disasters has significantly increased in the recent past. Even the richest modern societies are vulnerable to natural hazards. The continuous increase since 1950 in insured and noninsured disaster losses at global scale makes this problem impossible to disregard.

In the first section, this chapter reviews the existing literature on climate change and extreme events, using the recent literature assessment carried out by the Intergovernmental Panel on Climate Change (IPCC 2007), and investigates the consequences for natural hazards. The next section discusses the link between hazards and natural disasters and suggests that an increase in hazards does not have to translate into more disasters, if adequate adaptation and risk management strategies are implemented. Comparing risk management in New Orleans and the Netherlands, the fourth section highlights the obstacles that make it difficult to implement efficient adaptation strategies and proposes policies to cope with these obstacles. Finally, the last section illustrates these difficulties and puts forward tentative solutions in the specific case of the protection of New Orleans against hurricanes.

Climate Change and Extreme Events

The IPCC's fourth assessment report was published in 2007. It summarizes current knowledge about climate change and its potential impacts. In particular, this report reviews the literature on the links between climate change and so-called "extreme events." Its findings are summarized below.

FROM SOCIOECONOMIC SCENARIOS TO LARGE-SCALE CLIMATE CHANGE

Investigating climate change requires forecasts of how man-made greenhouse gas (GHG) emissions will evolve. Of course, this evolution depends on many drivers, including demographic change, economic growth, technological change, and cultural choices. The IPCC bases its assessment on the use of a set of scenarios that describe the future evolution of these drivers. Such scenarios have been developed by the IPCC in the "Special Report on Emission Scenarios" (SRES) (Nakicenovic and Swart 2000). The numerous SRES scenarios aim at encompassing the various possible ways in which the world could evolve, using simple assumptions about, for instance, how the world might become more globalized, or remain regionalized, or the extent to which economic development will focus on industrial production. Depending on the scenario adopted, carbon-dioxide emissions in 2100 will, according to SRES, vary from 11 billion tons ($GtCO_2$) per year to 136 billion tons $GtCO_2$/ year, highlighting the wide range of possible futures in terms of GHG emissions.

From each of these GHG emission scenarios, carbon cycle and climate models (or General Circulation Models, GCMs) can produce climate scenarios, that is, possible evolutions of all meteorological variables (temperature, precipitation, wind, etc.). According to these models, global temperatures will increase during this century by between 1°C and 6°C , depending both on future emission levels and on the climate model used.

Different models, indeed, lead to very different projections. But all models show roughly the same pattern of warming. In the A1B scenario, a medium-range scenario that assumes a world where emissions peak in 2050 and reach 50 $GtCO_2$/yr in 2100, the increase in global temperature is 2.8°C in 2090–2099 compared with 1960–1999. But this warming is greater for continents than for oceans, and greater in higher latitudes than in the tropics. It is important to note that a + 2.8°C increase in global temperature leads to temperature increases of up to 6°C in polar regions. These differences show that climate change, and thus its impacts, will be very heterogeneous.

Of course, climate change is not only about temperature. Precipitation patterns will also be modified, even though there is much less certainty about precipitation changes than temperature changes. The main pattern is an increase in precipitation in high latitudes and in the tropics, and a decrease in precipitation in mid-latitudes, and especially in Central America, the Mediterranean region, South Africa, and Australia.

Climate change will also cause a rise in the global sea level. This rise is caused by two processes:

- the increase in sea water temperature, which leads to water dilatation and increased sea volumes;
- the melting of continental icecaps in mountain regions and at high latitudes (especially the Greenland ice sheet). According to the IPCC, sea

levels will, by 2100, rise by between 18cm and 59cm. The most recent IPCC report, however, makes it very clear that important processes are not taken into account in these estimates, and that the models that have been used underestimate the current pace of icecap disappearance. First attempts to take these processes into account suggest that sea levels could in fact rise by up to 140cm by 2100 (Rahmstorf 2007).

CONSEQUENCES IN TERMS OF EXTREMES

The large-scale changes in temperature, precipitation, and other meteorological variables forecast by the models suggest that all extreme events related to these variables (droughts, floods, heat waves, cold spells, etc.) will be affected. The IPCC conclusions are as follows, for some categories of extreme events.

Heat Waves

It is virtually certain that heat waves will become more frequent and more intense in the future. In most climate models and in most emission scenarios, a summer like 2003, during which heat waves caused more than 70,000 deaths, will become an "average" summer in Europe. This means that, in this region, every other summer will be warmer than 2003.

Droughts

The evolution of droughts will vary depending on location. It is likely, however, that many locations already afflicted by droughts will see annual precipitation decrease in the future. Examples of such locations are the Mediterranean basin, southeastern Europe, South Africa, Australia, and Central America. The increase in water scarcity will be caused by:

- changes in the annual amount of precipitation;
- the deepening of the precipitation seasonal cycle, as more precipitation is projected in winter and less in summer;
- the reduction of the buffering role of snow in mountain areas, since mountain winter precipitation is stored in the form of a snow pack that melts slowly in spring and summer;
- increased evaporation due to higher temperatures.

High Winds and Storms

With higher temperatures, atmospheric circulation will be modified, influencing winds and storms everywhere. To assess how wind hazards will change in the future, however, it is useful to distinguish between tropical storms and extratropical storms:

- Tropical storms are present in tropical regions and are particularly destructive. The strongest of them are referred to as hurricanes in the North Atlantic and typhoons in the Pacific. Their evolution in a changing climate is still hotly debated, and no consensus has been reached so far (e.g., Webster et al. 2005; Emanuel 2005; Landsea 2005; Hallegatte 2007a). A best guess today is that the number of tropical storms may decrease in the future, but that the number of the most intense storms may increase, especially in the North Atlantic.

- Extratropical storms cause significant losses in mid to high-latitude regions. Examples of such storms are those that struck Europe in December 1999, Lothar and Martin. There is no agreement about the evolution of extratropical storms in the future among climate models, with some models projecting a small increase in maximum wind speeds, while others project a small decrease. Models also suggest the possibility of a shift of the mean trajectory of these storms toward higher latitudes.

River Floods

As precipitation changes, river runoff will change too. This change may have significant consequences for flood risks. In some regions, it is possible that flood risks will decrease. In others, however, flood risks will increase. Importantly, annual precipitation and runoffs may decrease while extreme runoffs increase. In this case, therefore, annual runoffs are not good indictors of flood risks. One important issue is the fact that many river banks are now strongly anthropogenized, with river flows influenced or managed by infrastructure elements such as dykes, bridges, or reservoirs. This infrastructure has been designed in accordance with run-off dynamics that will change in the future, and the infrastructure is therefore likely to be revealed as poorly adaptable. This unsuitability of infrastructure may amplify runoff changes due to climate change, especially for the most extreme runoffs.

Coastal Floods

Climate change will cause sea-level rises, which will increase the flood risk from storm surges, that is, high-frequency high-water levels due to low pressure and high winds created by storms. In fact, it is likely that the largest losses from sea-level rise will not result from the rise in mean sea level but from short-duration extremes in sea levels. These risks are already substantial, as illustrated by the disastrous consequences of the tropical cyclone Sidr in Bangladesh in 2007, or the destruction caused by Hurricane Katrina in New Orleans in 2005. Large cities are particularly vulnerable. Nicholls et al. (2007) investigated the coastal flood risk for all world cities with more than one million inhabitants. The population of these cities that is exposed to the 100-year storm surge—that is, a storm surge that has an annual probability of occurrence of 1 percent—has already reached 40 million people and is expected to reach 140 million people with the 50cm sea-level rise and the urban development that one can expect by 2070.

Cold Spells

Fortunately, climate change will not make all extremes increase. Cold spells have very large negative consequences and are expected to decrease both in frequency and intensity.

Periods of High Local Pollution

An indirect impact of climate change is a possible increase in the frequency of periods of high local pollution. Ozone concentration, for instance, depends largely on climate conditions, especially temperature, insulation, and wind. Climate change is likely to increase the recurrence of large-scale conditions that lead to high concentration of many pollutants.

LOSSES FROM EXTREME EVENTS

In recent decades, insured and noninsured losses from these extreme events have increased significantly (Munich Re 2007) and the role of climate change in this evolution has been widely discussed. Moreover, many weather-related disasters have had huge socioeconomic consequences (e.g., Hurricane Mitch in 1998 in Honduras and Nicaragua, the Central European floods of 2002, the European heat wave of 2003, Cyclones Sidr and Nargis in 2007 and 2008 in Bangladesh and Myanmar), amplifying concerns about the influence of global warming on natural hazards. Overall, however, it seems that the current increase in disaster losses is entirely driven by socioeconomic factors, especially by population increase in coastal areas, the increasing wealth of at-risk areas, and the reduction in risk-mitigating behaviors.

Moreover, it is important to stress that all the dramatic events of recent years would have been possible in a climate with no human influence, even though the likelihood of some of them could have been increased by climate change. For instance, Stott, Stone, and Allen (2004) claim that the probability of the occurrence of the 2003 European heat wave is doubled by the human influence on climate, but it is impossible to claim that this heat wave is due to climate change. Generally, climate change should be considered as leading to a change in the frequency of weather events: no single event can be considered as a consequence of climate change, only the repetition of some types of event can be attributed to climate change.

DISCUSSION OF THE UNCERTAINTY ABOUT FUTURE CLIMATES

It is essential to be aware of the significant uncertainty that surrounds climate change forecasts. This uncertainty is caused by various factors. First, as previously explained, future GHG emissions are uncertain and depend on demography, economy, technology, and the preferences of future generations. Obviously, climate change will be less rapid and intense if emissions are controlled and grow less rapidly than predicted.

Second, climate models still disagree on how the same change in GHG concentration would translate into changes in climate variables (temperature, precipitation, etc.). These models disagree on values at the global scale (e.g., the increase in global mean temperature in response to an increase in GHG concentration), but they disagree even more on local changes. This problem is even more critical when focusing on extreme events. So, the future evolution of extremes is particularly hard to predict, making it difficult to manage future risks and to make decisions on risks with long-term consequences. The fourth section describes the consequences of these uncertainties.

The Link between Extreme Events and Natural Disasters and the Role of Adaptation

One conclusion that can be drawn from the preceding section is that climate change is very likely to reinforce the impacts of natural hazards in many regions. This is particularly the case because environmental infrastructure designed for the current distribution of natural hazards is likely to be ill-adapted to the new distribution of hazards. This increase of hazards is particularly worrying because of:

- the already large human toll of natural disasters;
- the impact a natural disaster can have on economic systems (see an analysis of the impact of Hurricane Andrew in West and Lenze 1994, and of Hurricane Katrina on Louisiana in Hallegatte 2008); and
- the impact a series of natural disasters can have on economic growth and development (see analyses of potential "poverty trap" effects of natural disasters in Benson and Clay 2004, and Hallegatte, Hourcade, and Dumas 2007).

But increased hazards do not necessarily translate into more disasters. Risk management policies and infrastructure are key to determining the future evolution of the impact of disasters. The role appropriate risk management can play can be illustrated using examples of places where the incidence of hazards has already increased, for reasons other than climate change.

The Netherlands and the US city of New Orleans are two regions where hazards are and have been increasing because of local soil subsidence and local sea level rise. Because of expected global sea level rise, many parts of the world can expect during the next hundred years to experience what these two regions have experienced in the last century. Investigating how these regions managed and adapted to this increasing hazard may provide interesting insights into relevant adaptation strategies.[1]

NEW ORLEANS

During the twentieth century, the New Orleans region subsided by 5 cm per decade. This subsidence is thus equivalent to a 50 cm local sea level rise in a century, which is of the same order of magnitude as the sea level rise expected from climate change in the twenty-first century. The management of this increasing hazard in New Orleans, however, has been far from impressive, as described in detail by Muir-Wood and Grossi (2006) or Burby, Nelson, and Sanchez (2006).

New Orleans was founded in 1718 and became in the early nineteenth century the largest city in the South. Because the area protected by natural levees was very small, most of the city was built on natural marshland, artificially dried using pumps, drainage canals, and artificial levees. From the beginning of the twentieth century, the use of more reliable electric pumps and the development of the levees allowed the city to develop more rapidly. However, notwithstanding its protection system, New Orleans has been flooded four times, in 1915, 1947, 1965, and 2005. In 1915, a category four hurricane hit the city causing a failure of the protection system along the Lake Pontchartrain shoreline. Water levels reached 13 feet (4 meters) in some districts, and it took four days to pump the water out of the city. Following this event, pumping stations were upgraded and levees were raised along the drainage canals.

In 1947, however, a category three hurricane caused the Lake Pontchartrain levees to fail again. Floods spread across 30 square miles, water levels reached 6 feet (1.8 meters), and 15,000 people had to be evacuated. As in 1915, major improvements were made to the protection system in the immediate aftermath of the disaster, with the levees raised and extended. In 1965, however, Hurricane Betsy (category three) came ashore at New Orleans and flooded the city again. About 13,000 homes were flooded, leaving 60,000 homeless, and causing 53 deaths and more than $1 billion in losses. This event led the US Congress to pass the 1965 Flood Control Act and resulted in an ambitious plan to protect New Orleans. This plan was supposed to be fully implemented within 13 years. Facing difficulties, including environmental protection conflicts, the plan stalled, however, and was finally revised into the "high level plan," a slow implementation of which began in the mid-1980s and was considered to be between 60 and 90 percent complete when Hurricane Katrina struck in 2005. The complete failure of the protection system in 2005 demonstrated that neither construction nor maintenance had been adequately supervised and monitored. What is striking in this series of disasters is the systematic implementation of ambitious protection upgrades after each disaster, but the absence of long-term risk management action.

THE NETHERLANDS

In the Netherlands also, subsidence caused sea level rises of about 2 cm per decade during the twentieth century. The Netherlands suffered a large flood in 1953, which caused more than 1,800 deaths and extensive damage. But the response to this event was not only concerned with engineering; a commission, the Delta committee, was created to manage the response from an institutional and technical point of view. This committee published in 1960 the Delta Plan, which included an engineering part, the Delta Works. But the Delta committee also introduced a completely new approach to determining the required level of protection against flooding. Using cost-benefit analyses, the Delta committee determined an acceptable level of flood risk and, from it, derived an optimum level of protection (see figure 5.1).

The Dutch Law on Water Defenses also requires that water levels and wave heights used in risk analyses and the design of protective measures should be updated every five years, and that water defenses should be evaluated for these new conditions. Of course, this response did not lead to the disappearance of the risk, and the Netherlands was flooded again in the 1990s as a result of river flooding, which had been underestimated. But risk management in the Netherlands does not exhibit the same cycle as New Orleans, where defense improvements are only made when a disaster has demonstrated the weakness of protection.

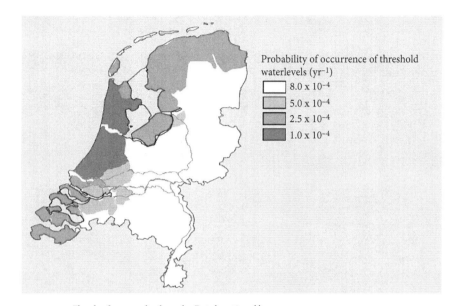

FIGURE 5.1 Flood safety standards under Dutch national law

Source: Netherlands Environmental Assessment Agency, National Institute for Public Health and the Environment.

The main difference in the responses of New Orleans and the Netherlands is that the Netherlands created institutions to manage the risk (i.e., to measure the risk on a regular basis, to update standards and methods, and to develop response strategies), while New Orleans focused on physical protection, which was implemented in the years following each event and then neglected until a new disaster occurred. The impact of these different approaches on flood risks is illustrated by figure 5.2, which shows how risk has evolved over time in the two cases. With a reactive risk management strategy, as observed in New Orleans, flood risks can increase very significantly. A proactive strategy, as that of the Netherlands, does not make disasters impossible, but keeps the risk within known boundaries.

Interestingly, the effect of climate change on natural risk is naturally taken into account in the Netherlands, thanks to the water-level revision every five years. This makes it much less likely that this country will suffer large losses from climate change, even though it is vulnerable. Of course, this methodology requires the maximum acceptable risk level to be defined. A methodology to do this, using a cost-benefit analysis based on protection costs and avoided flood losses, is proposed later in this chapter.

Obstacles to Adaptation

It is very likely that many societies, like the New Orleans community, have not adapted to the climate they are currently experiencing. If these societies are ill-adapted, it is because there are many obstacles to the implementation of adaptation measures. This section will review these obstacles.

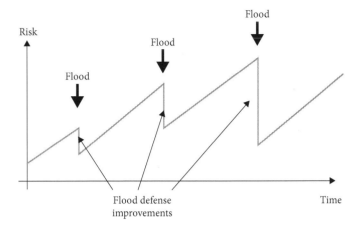

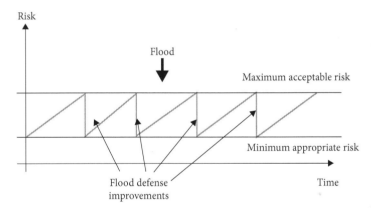

FIGURE 5.2 Two risk management strategies

Source: P. Grossi and R. Muir-Wood (2006). "Flood Risk in New Orleans: Implications for Future Management and Insurability." Accessed on January 26, 2009. http://www.rms.com/Publications/NO_FloodRisk.pdf.

FINANCIAL AND INSTITUTIONAL OBSTACLES

Many poor countries are very vulnerable to natural hazards but cannot implement the measures that could reduce this vulnerability for financial reasons or because of lack of technical know-how. It is striking, for instance, to see the lack of basic infrastructure in most mega-cities in developing countries. Correcting this lack of infrastructure (e.g., implementing sanitization networks) would reduce by a significant amount the impacts of many natural hazards (e.g., urban floods), both currently and in the future warmer world. Doing this, however, would require very large amounts of funding (Satterthwaite et al. 2007), which are not always available. The World Bank, the United Nations Development Programme, and the United Nations Framework Convention on Climate Change UNFCCC estimated the financial needs for adaptation as between $9 billion and $166 billion per year, up to 2030. Even though the methodologies that have been used are very questionable, the orders of magnitude are large enough to support the idea that funding will be a significant obstacle to adaptation in the future.

Another obstacle will be availability of technical know-how and appropriate technologies. An example of this is the introduction of water reuse technologies, which have been developed in a few countries (e.g., Israel), and which could bring great improvements in drought management, if they could be adopted by many developing and developed countries.

But money and technology are not enough to implement efficient adaptation strategies. Institutional and legal environments, as well as political will, are also very important, as illustrated by the difference in risk management in Louisiana and the Netherlands. The difference between the two regions is not explained by a difference in affordability; it is rather a difference in institutional organization. Another—even more striking—example of the importance of these factors is the flood protection levels of New York and Shanghai, which have both extremely high exposures to coastal floods. The former is not protected against a once-in-a-hundred-years' event; while the latter has a level of protection even good enough for a once-in-a-thousand-years' event, despite the much more limited financial resources (Nicholls et al. 2007).

THE ROLE OF UNCERTAINTY

Another issue arises from the difficulty in "measuring" the long-term climate and corresponding risks, in order to inform risk analysis and risk management strategies (Hallegatte 2009). A common example is the increase in population and assets at risk from hurricanes in Florida in recent decades. This increase took place during a period of exceptionally low hurricane activity, during which economic actors "forgot" the normal level of hurricane risks in the region. This change made Florida excessively vulnerable in phases of normal activity. In the future, climate change will greatly increase the uncertainty about climate and extreme events, meaning that the risk of underpreparedness will be even more significant. For instance, in many regions climate models do not agree, even on indicators of future changes in precipitation.

These uncertainties make it difficult to implement optimal risk management strategies, especially because many such strategies require a significant ability to anticipate events. For instance, in the case of the Thames barrier to protect London against storm surges, more than 30 years passed between the decision to construct the barrier and the barrier becoming fully operational: managing natural risks requires anticipation of how natural hazards will change over the next decades, but uncertainty about climate change is a significant obstacle to such anticipation.

HOW CAN WE DEAL WITH THESE OBSTACLES?

To limit future impacts from climate change as much as possible it is necessary to promote the best adaptation practices. Doing so can be done using special funds to help cope with financial obstacles (e.g., the UNFCCC Adaptation Fund, the Green

Climate Fund that is being created). Technology transfers can also be extremely useful—for example to share the most efficient water treatment solutions—and climate negotiations have included this dimension in the discussion. Good practices identification and exchange can also help design adaptation plans, even though local circumstances and context always need to be accounted for. The identification of best practices is likely to be one major role of the Adaptation Committee, created at the Durban conference of the UNFCCC in 2011. This international committee is supposed to provide insights and support for the development of national adaptation plans, using the available international experience.

This exchange of best practice can also be informal. In Europe, for instance, many countries are in the process of changing their systems of insurance for major disasters (e.g., Denmark, Italy, France) and are comparing the various systems that exist in Europe to inform their decisions. One can expect that this process will lead to the generalization of the most efficient systems, adjusted to take into account local needs and constraints.

Managing Uncertainty

It is not possible to wait for uncertainty about the future climate to be reduced or eliminated before making any decision involving adaptation or long-lasting infrastructure. Instead, adaptation decision-making frameworks should be amended so that they can take uncertainty into account. This means, for example, designing infrastructure so that:

- it can cope with a larger range of climate conditions than before; and
- this range is and will remain highly uncertain.

In such a context, optimizing infrastructure design for a given climate may not be the best strategy. A better approach might be to develop new strategies, especially those created to cope with the inherent uncertainties of climate change (e.g., Lempert and Schlesinger 2000; Hallegatte 2009). Examples of such new strategies are the selection of no-regret actions, which yield benefits for all possible climate changes (e.g., improving health-care systems), and the inclusion of "safety margins" in infrastructure design.

It is important to mention that adaptation to climate change may also provide a welcome opportunity to improve the way risks are managed in many contexts and places. Because current practices are likely to be unsustainable in a warming world, more robust risk management strategies will have to be implemented. Climate change awareness may be the trigger for their implementation, but these strategies are probably desirable even in the absence of climate change.

The Protection of New Orleans against Hurricanes: An Illustration

New Orleans provides an interesting illustration of the obstacles to efficient climate change adaptation (and to efficient risk management). This section describes these obstacles and solutions in this specific context, using cost-benefit analysis.

In this analysis, we will assume that New Orleans will be fully reconstructed and return to its pre-storm condition, even though some have proposed not to do so because of doubts about the possibility of protecting the city over the long term (see Giegengack and Foster 2006).

UNCERTAINTIES IN COST-BENEFIT ANALYSIS

The design of natural disaster protection systems is often based on cost-benefit analysis (CBA) (see, e.g., Arrow et al. 1996), even though other decision-making frameworks have been proposed (e.g., the precautionary principle). In a CBA framework, New Orleans would only benefit from a flood protection system able to cope with category five hurricanes, compared to a system able to cope with category four hurricanes, if the additional cost of the upgraded protection was lower than the expected additional benefits from reduced flood damage. Protecting New Orleans against a category five hurricane is not certain to be demonstrably beneficial, surprising as this might seem given Katrina's devastating impact.

To carry out a CBA of a category five flood protection system in New Orleans, one needs to assess the cost, C, of such a system, and its expected benefits, B. In the very early stages of rebuilding New Orleans, state officials evaluated the cost of category five protection at about \$32 billion, compared with about \$5 billion to provide a category four protection. The additional cost of category five protection is, therefore, about \$27 billion. The difference is substantial, because the storm surge created by category five hurricanes can be much higher than the highest surge caused by a category four hurricanes. There is great uncertainty about this cost, but this chapter will nevertheless assume that it is known with certainty in order to focus on the less common sources of uncertainty.

Protection benefits can be defined as the net present value of the expected amount of damages that can be avoided thanks to the protection system upgrade. These benefits can, therefore, be calculated as the discounted sum, for each year from now throughout the lifetime of the protection system, of the annual probability that a category five hurricane hits New Orleans, multiplied by the difference between the damage done by such a hurricane on a category four versus a category five protection system. This difference is discounted to take into account the fact that the same benefit is valued at a higher value when it occurs in the near future rather than further into the future. The values of three parameters are thus necessary: the discount rate (δ), the probability of occurrence (p), and the amount of avoidable damages in the year n (d_n). From them, expected benefits, B, are easy to calculate:[2]

$$B = \sum_{0}^{+\infty} p \left(\frac{1}{1+\delta} \right)^n d_n \qquad (5.1)$$

Assuming that damages are increasing over time at the same rate as economic growth, g, which is a conservative hypothesis considering the current growth of economic losses due to natural disasters (Mills, Roth, and Lecomte 2004; Munich Re 2007), expected benefits read:

$$B = \sum_{0}^{+\infty} p\left(\frac{1}{1+\delta}\right)^{n} d_{0}\left(1+g\right)^{n} \approx \frac{pd_{0}}{\delta - g},\qquad(5.2)$$

where d_0 is the avoidable damages if a category five hurricane hits New Orleans today. If the cost C of the flood protection system is lower than the expected benefits, B, then the system should be implemented.

From historical experience (i.e., by observing hurricane frequencies over the last century), one can evaluate the annual probability that a category five hurricane hits New Orleans at about $p = 1/500$ (H. Saffir, quoted in Schwartz 2005). The Office of Management and Budget (OMB), which carries out CBAs of federal regulations in the United States, uses two different discount rates to analyze policy decisions: 3 and 7 percent. These two discount rates are used to assess the robustness of findings to the choice of discount rate.

Assuming that category four protection does not reduce the damages caused by category five hurricanes, which is likely since there is little difference between no levees and broken levees, the flood caused by a category five hurricane coming ashore at an unprotected New Orleans would be close to the flood provoked by Katrina. The losses of the latter flood, therefore, can be used as a proxy for future avoidable losses thanks to an adequate protection system. The cost of the New Orleans flood, excluding all wind damage in New Orleans and the rest of Louisiana, were around $50 billion (i.e., 50 to 75 percent of the total Katrina direct losses according to the Louisiana Recovery Authority).

Taking casualties into account (about 1,000 people died in the flooding) raises the difficult issue of attributing a cost to a lost life. Because the expression *"value of the human life"* problematically suggests a market in which one could buy or sell human lives, it is preferable to use the expression *"society willingness to pay to reduce risk,"* which is much more acceptable wording. Even though the value depends on the type of risk and the probability of occurrence of the event under consideration, most estimates lie between $1 million and $10 million in the United States. Nevertheless, in the present analysis, we assume that a better evacuation program would probably be able to minimize the human losses, even in the absence of hard protection. The willingness to pay associated with the human toll will, therefore, be disregarded here.

The expected present benefit of a category five flood protection system in New Orleans can be calculated with equation (5.2) at $2 billion with a 7 percent discount rate and $10 billion with a 3 percent discount rate. Both are much lower than the building cost of such a system. This rough estimate clearly rules out a category five protection system: it suggests that it is more rational from an economic viewpoint to live the Katrina nightmare again in a more or less remote future.[3]

This estimate is, however, not very solidly grounded, as it does not take into account important processes whose impacts could be significant. In line with OMB requirements when uncertainty is large and economic implications are in excess of $1 billion (OMB 2003), we will now review the parameters of the CBA,[4] and propose alternative estimates.

New Estimates of the Probability of Occurrence

In the first CBA, historical evidence was used to assess the probability of an occurrence of a category five hurricane landfall on New Orleans. This assessment cannot, however, be considered robust. Indeed, a flood protection system has a very long lifetime. Such a long lifetime arises, of course, from the long lifetime of infrastructures (dykes, sea walls, bridges). But, above all, it comes from the fact that the flood protection system will shape the city's development over an even longer time horizon. The decisions that are taken on the protection system will constrain the flood protection of New Orleans for at least the next century. During this period, two mechanisms will influence hurricane risks, in addition to socioeconomic parameters like population change and asset vulnerability and value: local soil subsidence and climate change.

Climate change will influence hurricane risks through two channels: sea-level rise and changes in hurricane activity. Indeed, a rising sea level makes the consequences of any storm surge more destructive, in the same way that soil subsidence does. Thus, the probability of floods that are currently caused only by category five hurricanes might increase, as less powerful hurricanes could also cause them. A second way in which climate change modifies hurricane risks is, directly, through the probability of landfall. As already stated, there is great uncertainty about the effect of climate change on hurricane activity. Emanuel (2006) predicts that a 10 percent increase in potential intensity, which is expected to happen within this century, would cause a 15 percent increase in maximum wind speeds. Hallegatte (2007a) shows that such a change would then translate into a tripling for the United States of the annual landfall probability of category five hurricanes. For New Orleans, the probability of a category five hurricane landfall in the present climate can be estimated at once every 1,000 years; while it is once every 100 years in a climate in which potential intensity has been increased by 10 percent. Other models and researchers have produced more optimistic results (see Landsea 2005), and this assessment will be considered in the following as the worst-case scenario.

New Estimates of Avoidable Losses

Another major difficulty lies in the assessment of the actual damages that could be avoided through an upgrade of the protection system. We use the direct losses from the Katrina landfall as a proxy for the damages a future flood may cause. Several authors have suggested, however, that direct costs, evaluated by insurance companies, may be poor proxies of overall costs, especially concerning large-scale events (e.g., Tierney 1995; Lindell and Prater 2003; Hallegatte 2008). Indeed, direct costs can be amplified:

- by spatial or sectoral propagation into the rest of the economic system over the short term (e.g., through disruptions of lifeline services) and over the longer term (e.g., sectoral inflation due to demand surges, energy costs, insurance company bankruptcies, larger public deficits, housing prices);
- by responses to the shock (e.g., loss of confidence, change in expectations, indirect consequences of inequality deepening);

- by financial constraints impairing reconstruction (e.g., low-income families cannot easily finance the reconstruction of their home); and
- by technical constraints that slow down reconstruction (e.g., availability of skilled workers, difficulties in equipment and material transportation, difficulties in accommodating workers).

To measure the impact of these effects, Hallegatte, Hourcade, and Dumas (2007) introduced the *Economic Amplification Ratio* (EAR), which measures the ratio between the overall economic cost and the direct loss due to a disaster. While this ratio is less than one for small-scale disasters, the EAR is found, using a simple model, to increase dramatically for large-scale disasters like the New Orleans floods. This increase arises mainly from the addition to the capital replacement cost of the production losses during the reconstruction phase. For example, if a $1 million factory is destroyed and immediately rebuilt, the loss would be $1 million; if its reconstruction is delayed by one year, the total loss is the sum of the replacement cost and of the value of one year of production. For housing, the destruction of a house with a one-year delay in reconstruction has a total cost equal to the replacement cost of the house plus the value attributed to inhabiting the house during one year. The value of such production losses, in a broad sense, can be very high in some sectors, especially when basic needs are at stake (housing, health, employment, etc.). For Katrina over New Orleans, Hallegatte (2008) estimates the EAR at 1.44, meaning that the $50 billion of direct losses can be translated into $72 billion. Other types of losses are not included in this estimate (e.g., the cost of social network disruption or psychological trauma); they are indeed so difficult to assess that we will disregard them here.

We assume here that New Orleans will be rebuilt with the same structure it had before Katrina and that all previous inhabitants of New Orleans will return to the city, even if no improvement of the flood protection system is undertaken. This assumption is at odds with what has been observed and what is expected in reality. If the new population is much lower than the pre-Katrina one, the costs of a new flood would, of course, be greatly reduced, making our assessment of avoidable damages an overestimate. But it must be remembered that the flood protection system will protect New Orleans for at least a century. The pertinent variable is thus the population over the long term, not over the next decade. It is difficult to guess what will be the New Orleans population over this century. In the following, we will assume that the population will rapidly come back to its initial level, for two reasons: first, we assume that New Orleans inhabitants lived in this city for a reason, and that they want to come back; second, New Orleans' location makes it the perfect spot to have an important port, which creates activities and jobs and attracts population.

Using the new values of event probability ($p = 1/1000$ today, increasing linearly to stabilize at $1/100$ from 2100) and potential damages ($d_0 = \$72$ billion), the expected benefit of an upgraded protection system would be $4.5 billion with a 7 percent discount rate and $54 billion with a 3 percent discount rate. It is often considered that, for long-term projects, the smallest (3 percent) discount rate should be used. With this rate, the category five protection system is profitable, with a net present value of $27 billion, that is, a 100 percent return on investment and a benefit-cost-ratio equal to two.

Countervailing Risks, Risk Aversion, Inequality Aversion

Other factors must be taken into account in our analysis, in spite of the difficulty of doing so. First, one cannot assess a flood protection system without taking into account moral hazard and equity issues. A flood protection system funded through national taxes, like a uniform insurance premium, can constitute an incentive for people to settle in at-risk areas, as they do not pay for the risk their location choice creates. This problem, referred to as *countervailing risks* by Wiener (1998), reduces the benefits derived from protection.

Second, the discount rate is an important parameter of this analysis, and other governments (e.g., the UK) favor a decreasing discount rate over time, justified by uncertainty over future economic situations or other reasons (e.g., The Green Book, UK Treasury, see OXERA 2002; Hallegatte 2008). Using such a discount rate would increase the benefits derived from protection.

Third, a society that would use our method to assess a protection system is called *risk-neutral*. A risk-neutral agent is indifferent to risk, that is, it does not see any difference between losing \$1 with certainty and having a 10 percent chance of losing \$10, because the expected loss is the same in both cases. Theoretically, such an agent would never pay for insurance. Regarding protection against large-scale floods, however, there are good reasons to justify *risk-averse* behavior: people might indeed prefer to pay an additional amount of money (a *risk premium*) to avoid the risk of costly and deadly floods.

Fourth, a substantial part of the damage affects only a small fraction of the population, and it is often the poorest that are the most affected. On the other hand, the protection system is built with taxpayers' money, and the distribution among social categories can be decided in a fairer way. The *aversion to inequality*, therefore, has an impact on the benefits from protection, through the respective impact of protection and disasters on inequality. The two last factors—aversion to risk and aversion to inequality—increase the benefits derived from protection.

It is difficult to measure the impact of these four additional factors (see an attempt to do so in Hallegatte 2006), but their combined effect is likely to be in favor of protection.

Regardless, the main conclusion of this CBA is that fundamental uncertainty over the appropriate discount rate, over the amount of indirect losses, and over how climate change will influence natural hazards, means the analysis is unable to provide a definitive answer about the desirability of category five protection. With various parameters, the CBA even provides an assessment of protection benefits ranging from \$2 billion to \$54 billion.

Two important conclusions can be drawn from this disappointing result. First, because of these uncertainties, climate-change-adaptation and risk management decision making can only be done through a political process, and experts cannot provide a definitive assessment of the optimal protection level. Second, specific strategies must be developed to cope with this unprecedented level of uncertainty. Several authors have proposed such strategies (e.g., Nicholls and Leatherman 1996; Fankhauser, Smith, and Tol 1999; Hallegatte 2009). The next section describes some of these strategies in the New Orleans context.

STRATEGIES FOR COPING WITH UNCERTAINTY: LOOKING FOR ROBUSTNESS

In an uncertain context, easy-to-upgrade, reversible, and flexible strategies must be favored. If local authorities commit themselves to protect New Orleans against category five hurricanes, inhabitants and investments are likely to increase in the protected area. It will then be essential to maintain risk at the level that has been announced to investors and citizens. Because of sea-level rise and subsidence, defenses will have to be upgraded regularly. As a consequence, the design of defenses must take into account the need for future upgrades. There are strategies to make future upgrades easier and cheaper, for instance, through the oversizing of water-management long-term infrastructure (water canals, drainage pipes, etc.).

Also, there are limits to the protection dykes and sea walls can provide. If it is impossible to upgrade protection in case of strong climate change, that is, in particularly vulnerable areas, it is better to abandon protection immediately, rather than provide protection that will become ineffective in the future, putting more people and assets at risk. In case of uncertainty, therefore, it is better to give up areas before they are urbanized, rather than retreating from densely urbanized zones in a few decades. The protection system design phase must therefore identify the areas that may be impossible to protect in the future if hurricane activity or sea-level rise is greater than expected. If possible, additional urbanization is these areas must be avoided.

Also, hard protection using dykes and sea walls is not the only available strategy. Soft protection, based on warning systems, evacuation schemes, and insurance mechanisms, can also be efficient. Soft strategies have the advantage of being easy to adjust when new information becomes available: if hurricane activity increases more than expected, a warning system or an insurance scheme can be modified rapidly. This is not the case for a levee and sea-wall system.

Most importantly, hard and soft strategies are complementary and have to be designed together. In New Orleans, for instance, if the population can be evacuated when a hurricane is approaching and if properties are well-insured, the acceptable level of protection can be lowered. If insurance is unavailable and evacuation technically impossible, then it is essential to provide the highest possible level of hard protection.

FINANCIAL, TECHNICAL, AND INSTITUTIONAL OBSTACLES

When an adequate level of protection is defined by a political process and when a protection system has been designed, additional obstacles appear. If the Netherlands seems better protected than New Orleans, it is not because of uncertainties on the adequate level of protection or because of design flaws. It is because of implementation and maintenance issues that are described below.

First, protecting New Orleans is thought to cost about $30 billion. With an annual GDP per capita of $32,923 in Louisiana, and a New Orleans population of 400,000 inhabitants, protecting New Orleans would cost more than two years of the population's income. Even with aid from the federal government, financing such investments is not easy in a state that already has economic difficulties. So, protection against coastal floods is a very significant financial burden, which may explain insufficient investments in some cases.

Second, protecting New Orleans is not easy from a technical point of view, and earlier defenses failed during the Katrina landfall. If it is decided to build defenses, one has to make sure that it is actually possible to provide the required level of protection.

Third, protecting New Orleans would require strong political commitment. In particular, huge negative consequences would certainly result from the implementation of an ambitious flood protection system if it were not followed by a careful long-term maintenance program and by regular upgrades as climate change and subsidence increase the flood risk. In a worst case scenario, the existence of the protection system would lead to increased investment and population in the so-called protected area, which after a few decades of negligence would no longer be protected, making the risk even larger than if no protection was implemented in the first place. As a consequence, the implementation of a protection system must be considered as a long-term commitment.

Also, avoiding negative outcomes from the future flood protection system requires careful design and implementation, in order to protect already urbanized areas without steering additional urbanization toward nonprotected flood-prone locations. This makes rigorous application of risk-oriented land-use plans essential, in turn requiring strong institutions and political will.

Solving the design issues raised by climate change and other uncertainties will be of little help if these three other obstacles are not overcome. More particularly, research on risk management and climate-change adaptation should not look only at the technical components of these problems. Financial and institutional problems must also be investigated. Effective risk management can only be provided to New Orleans if all components of the problem are considered.

Conclusion: The Consequences of a Global Increase in Natural Hazards

Climate change will modify the statistics of all weather variables, and their extreme distributions in particular. These changes will affect natural risks in many different ways: cold-spell fatalities are very likely to decrease significantly, while damages caused by heat waves will soar. Floods risks will increase in some locations, especially coastal areas, and decrease in others. Storms and hurricanes may become more intense and the affected regions may change. High pollution events are likely to become more frequent. Most importantly, many risk management infrastructures (e.g., dykes and sea walls, buildings) will be made obsolete by these new conditions, meaning hazards will be more likely to translate into disasters.

These changes do not need to lead to soaring loss of life and property, however, if relevant adaptation measures are implemented, from changes in land-use management and investments in water infrastructures to improvements in insurance systems. Nevertheless, many obstacles to the implementation of optimal adaptation strategies exist, and past experience shows that places where risks are well managed are the exception at the global scale. This chapter has highlighted four main obstacles, namely financial constraints, technical problems, institutional issues, and the uncertainty linked to climate change and other long-term changes. It has also proposed strategies to cope with these obstacles: international adaptation and risk management funds, technology transfers, good practice exchanges, and robust investment strategies able to cope with climate uncertainty.

Depending on how adaptation measures are designed and implemented, the economic cost of climate change could vary widely (see, e.g., Hallegatte 2007b). In particular, the negative influence of natural disasters on economic growth and inequalities (Benson and Clay 2004) makes the potential impact of climate change worrisome, especially in developing countries (see, e.g., Adger et al. 2003; Hallegatte, Hourcade, and Dumas 2007; Lecocq and Shalizi 2007; Satterthwaite et al. 2007). Climate change and adaptation needs, therefore, will make it even more necessary to promote risk management as part of development strategies and infrastructure design. Doing so will also require more research and collaboration between risk managers and climate scientists.

Notes

1. Burby, Nelson, and Sanchez (2006) provides a comparison of risk management practices in Florida and Louisiana. Their analysis shows that, even within the United States, risk management practices differ widely and lead to greater or fewer losses over the long term.

2. It is assumed that protection systems have an infinite lifetime, after having checked that results were only weakly sensitive to the protection system lifetime, chosen in a reasonable range, for the selected values of the parameters. Indeed, if $\delta \approx g$, where g is the economic growth rate (see below), the system lifetime becomes an important variable.

3. An annual probability of $1/500$ means that there is a 20 percent chance of having a category five hurricane hitting New Orleans in the next 100 years, and a 33 percent chance in the next 200 years.

4. Among the necessary assumptions in the CBA, it is often useful to distinguish between the political choices that must arise from a political process (e.g., discounting scheme), and the scientific uncertainties that can be—at least theoretically—solved through additional research (e.g., future probability of occurrence).

References

Adger, W. N., Huq, S., Brown, K., Conwaya, D., and Hulme, M. (2003). "Adaptation to Climate Change in the Developing World." *Progress in Development Studies* 3(3): 179–195.

Arrow, K. J., Cropper, M. L., Eads, G. C., Hahn, R. W., Lave, L. B., Noll, R. G., Portney, P. R., Russel, M., Schmalensee, R. L., Smith, V. K., and Stavins, R. N. (1996). *Benefit-Cost Analysis in Environmental, Health, and Safety Regulation.* Washington, D.C.: American Enterprise Institute Press.

Benson, C., and Clay, E. (2004). *Understanding the Economic and Financial Impact of Natural Disasters.* Washington, D.C.: World Bank.

Burby, R. J., Nelson, A. C., and Sanchez, T. W. (2006). "The Problem of Containment and the Promise of Planning." In *Rebuilding Urban Places after Disaster: Lessons from Hurricane Katrina*, edited by E. L. Birch and S. M. Wachter. Philadelphia: University of Pennsylvania Press.

Emanuel, K. (2005). "Increasing Destructiveness of Tropical Cyclones over the Past 30 Years." *Nature* 436: 686–688.

———. (2006). "Climate and Tropical Cyclone Activity: A New Model Downscaling Approach." *Journal of Climate* 19: 4797–4802.

Fankhauser, S., Smith, J. B., and Tol, R. S. J. (1999). "Weathering Climate Change: Some Simple Rules to Guide Adaptation Decisions." *Ecological Economics* 30(1): 67–78.

Giegengack, R., and Foster, K. R. (2006). "Physical Constraints on Reconstructing New Orleans." In *Rebuilding Urban Places after Disaster: Lessons from Hurricane Katrina*, edited by E. L. Birch and S. M. Wachter. Philadelphia: University of Pennsylvania Press.

Hallegatte, S. (2006). "A Cost-Benefit Analysis of the New Orleans Flood Protection System." *AEI-Brookings Joint Center. Regulatory Analysis* 06–02.

———. (2007a). "The Use of Synthetic Hurricane Tracks in Risk Analysis and Climate Change Damage Assessment." *Journal of Applied Meteorology and Climatology* 46(11): 1956–1966.

———. (2007b). "Do Current Assessments Underestimate Future Damages from Climate Change?" *World Economics* 8(3): 131–146.

———. (2008). "An Adaptive Regional Input-Output Model and Its Application to the Assessment of the Economic Cost of Katrina." *Risk Analysis* 28(3): 779–799. DOI: 10.1111/j.1539-6924.2008.01046.

———. (2009). "Strategies to Adapt to an Uncertain Climate Change." *Global Environmental Change* 19: 240–247.

Hallegatte, S., Hourcade, J. C., and Dumas, P. (2007). "Why Economic Dynamics Matter in Assessing Climate Change Damages: Illustration on Extreme Events." *Ecological Economics* 62(2): 330–340.

IPCC (2007). *Climate Change 2007: The Physical Science Basis. Contribution of Working Group I to the Fourth Assessment Report of the Intergovernmental Panel on Climate Change*, edited by S. Solomon, D. Qin, M. Manning, Z. Chen, M. Marquis, K. B. Averyt, M. Tignor, and H. L. Miller. Cambridge and New York: Cambridge University Press.

Landsea, C. W. (2005). "Meteorology: Hurricanes and Global Warming." *Nature* 438: E11–E13.

Lecocq, F., and Shalizi, Z. (2007). "How Might Climate Change Affect Economic Growth in Developing Countries? A Review of the Growth Literature with a Climate Lens." Policy Research Working Paper 4315. Washington, D.C.: World Bank.

Lempert, R. J., and Schlesinger, M. E. (2000). "Robust Strategies for Abating Climate Change." *Climatic Change* 45(3/4): 387–401.

Lindell, M. K., and Prater, C. S. (2003). "Assessing Community Impacts of Natural Disasters." *Natural Hazards Review* 4: 176–185.

Mills, E., Roth, R. J., and Lecomte, E. (2004). "Availability and Affordability of Insurance under Climate Change: A Growing Challenge for the U.S." Accessed on December 28, 2011. http://www.pewclimate.org/docUploads/Ceres%20--%20Insurance%20&%20Climate%20Change%202005.pdf.

Grossi, P., and Muir-Wood, R. (2006). "Flood Risk in New Orleans: Implications for Future Management and Insurability." Accessed on January 26, 2009. http://www.rms.com/Publications/NO_FloodRisk.pdf.

Munich Re (2007). "Topics Geo Natural Catastrophes 2006." Munich Reinsurance Company, Munich.

Nakicenovic, N., and Swart, R. J. (2000). *Emissions Scenarios 2000—Special Report of the Intergovernmental Panel on Climate Change*. Cambridge: Cambridge University Press.

Nicholls, R., and Leatherman, S. (1996). "Adapting to Sea-Level Rise: Relative Sea-Level Trends to 2100 for the United States." *Coastal Management* 24(4): 301–324.

Nicholls, R. J., Hanson, S., Herweijer, C., Patmore, N., Hallegatte, S., Corfee-Morlot, J., Chateau, J., and Muir-Wood, R. (2007). "Screening Study: Ranking Port Cities with High Exposure and Vulnerability to Climate Extremes." OECD Environment Working Papers. Paris.

Office of Management and Budget (2003). Informing Regulatory Decisions: Report to Congress on the Costs and Benefits of Federal Regulations and Unfunded Mandates on State, Local, and Tribal Entities.

OXERA (2002). A Social Time Preference Rate for Use in Long-Term Discounting: A Report for ODPM, DFT and DEFRA.

Rahmstorf, S. (2007). "A Semi-Empirical Approach to Projecting Future Sea-Level Rise." *Science* 315: 368–370.

Satterthwaite, D., Huq, S., Pelling, M., Reid, H., and Lankao-Romero, P. (2007). "Building Climate Change Resilience in Urban Areas and among Urban Populations in Low- and Middle-Income Nations." Background paper prepared for the Rockefeller Foundation, IIED. London.

Schwartz, J. (2005). "Full Flood Safety in New Orleans Could Take Billions and Decades." *New York Times*, November 29.

Stott, P. A., Stone, D. A., and Allen, M. R. (2004). "Human Contribution to the European Heatwave of 2003." *Nature* 432: 610–614.

Tierney, K. J. (1995). *Impacts of Recent U.S. Disasters on Businesses: The 1993 Midwest Floods and the 1994 Northridge Earthquake*. Disaster Research Center, University of Delaware.

Webster, P. J., Holland, G. J., Curry, J. A., and Chang, H.-R. (2005). "Changes in Tropical Cyclone Number, Duration, and Intensity in a Warming Environment." *Science* 309: 1844–1846.

West, C. T., and Lenze, D. G. (1994). "Modeling The Regional Impact of Natural Disasters and Recovery: A General Framework and an Application to Hurricane Andrew." *International Regional Science Review* 17: 121–150.

Wiener, J. B. (1998). "Managing the Iatrogenic Risks of Risk Management." *Risk: Health, Safety and Environment* 9(39): 40–82.

6 }

Natural Disasters and the Insurance Industry
Angelika Wirtz

Introduction

Losses caused by natural disasters, both overall and insured, have dramatically increased since 1950 (figure 6.1). This increase is driven by population growth and rising population density, and by increasing asset values in urban areas, the development of highly exposed coastal and valley regions, the complexity of modern societies and technologies, and by the emerging consequences of global warming (Munich Re 1999). As these factors will not change in the near future, a further increase in losses is inevitable. At the same time, there are countless millions of people without adequate insurance cover to protect themselves against the financial risks associated with such disasters.

This chapter presents the issues related to the insurance market and the challenges related to specific risks in different countries. The history of insurance, the principles of modern insurance and reinsurance, as well as current insurance penetration, is given. Analyses of worldwide losses triggered by natural disasters in different insurance markets and different economies show the need for public–private partnership solutions. The chapter explains the role of microinsurance, gives successful examples of public–private partnership solutions, and discusses the challenge of transferring natural disaster risk to the capital market.

The History of Natural Catastrophe Insurance

The fundamental principle of insurance is based on a solidarity network of policyholders who pay contributions into a pool and in return receive compensation if a loss occurs, usually for the amount of this loss, sometimes minus a pre-agreed amount of "retained risk" typically known as a deductible.

We all wish to protect our assets from unwanted surprises and catastrophes. This need for material security is thousands of years old. Before professional insurers, people relied on help from family members to cope with crises. Subsequently, this principle of mutual assistance was extended to include tribes, villages, or other groups.

For example, we know that thousands of years ago on the ancient caravan routes in Mesopotamia any losses suffered by fellow travelers were shared among the whole

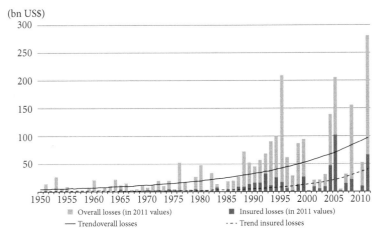

FIGURE 6.1 Great natural catastrophes, 1950–2011, overall and insured losses

Note: The chart presents overall losses and insured losses, adjusted to present values. The trend curves verify the increase in catastrophe losses since 1950.

Source: Munich Re, NatCatSERVICE.

caravan (Museum für Versicherungsgeschichte Gotha 2005). One might even regard this as the earliest form of today's marine or travel insurance.

Another example is burial insurance. As the name suggests, this provides funds for a decent burial, and it has long played an important role and still does in many societies and regions (Churchill 2006). Documents have even been found containing the complete statutes of a Roman burial fund from the year A.D. 130. These funds were popular with the lower classes and the military at that time.

The idea of mutual assistance—within the family, community, or other groups—evolved into contractual agreements as trade spread and the risks of transport and storage grew. A document from Genoa drawn up in 1347 is believed to be the oldest marine insurance contract. If the ship or its cargo were lost, a previously agreed amount of money would be paid out in reimbursement. The terms "insurance" and "policy" were born. From Italy, the idea of insurance then spread to Spain, France, England, the Netherlands, and Germany (Museum für Versicherungsgeschichte Gotha 2005).

The growth of manufacturing and industrialization in Europe in the seventeenth and eighteenth centuries, especially in England, led to the introduction of fire insurance. This guaranteed financial recompense for buildings, machines, and stored goods damaged by fire. As these "fire and contents" policies were usually based on private initiative, premiums and insurability were calculated very precisely: the premiums charged were graded according to the degree of exposure and were based on past loss experience. Indeed, until a few years ago this was still the standard method used for calculating premiums (retrospective underwriting). It was mainly because of the extremely loss-heavy years of 2004 and 2005, coupled with further scientific evidence of climate change and the resulting risks of change, that a shift took place toward prospective underwriting, that is, the inclusion of changing risks in premium calculations.

In past centuries, in Europe and North America, fire was the most feared hazard. Fear of losing all possessions as a result of fire was heightened by the great fires of London in 1666, Lisbon in 1755, Hamburg in 1842, San Francisco in 1850, and Chicago in 1871. These fires also highlighted the vulnerability of large cities: concentrations of large numbers of people in mainly wooden structures in small areas. In such circumstances, fires could spread very quickly and entire towns could be razed in no time. To combat this risk, trade guilds decided to develop mutual agreements. The first of these fire guilds was founded in north Germany in 1537.

In larger towns, so-called fire contracts emerged—a sort of private association of house owners. These societies undertook to pay financial recompense to members who lost their homes as a result of fire. The funds were paid solely for the purpose of rebuilding the property. It was from such fire contracts that the "Hamburger Feuerkasse" (Hamburg Fire Fund) came into being in 1676. This company is generally regarded as the oldest professional insurance firm in the world (Hamburger Feuerkasse 2008). In 1688, Edward Lloyd's coffeehouse, the precursor of Lloyds of London, became the central meeting place for shipowners seeking insurance for a voyage. In 1769, Lloyds of London formed and began its legendary role in English marine insurance (Insurance Information Institute 2008).

The first recorded insurer against the forces of nature was "Deutsche Hagelversicherungs-Gesellschaft" (German Hailstorm Insurance), established in 1797 in the north German province of Mecklenburg. In the United States, it was not until the late 1800s that insurers began to offer cover for weather-related risks (Mills, Lecomte, and Peara 2001). In its earliest form, policy contracts provided natural hazard insurance against loss by fire and storm, although until 1880 this type of insurance was confined to the eastern United States.

When Munich Re was founded in 1880, most losses caused by natural catastrophes were initially covered by fire policies. The first major challenge the new company faced came in the early morning of 18 April 1906. An earthquake struck San Francisco, destroying one-fifth of the city—28,000 buildings in all, most of which fell victim to a fire that burned for four days and nights. More than 3,000 people died in the earthquake. The overall loss came to $524 million, of which some $200 million was insured. Munich Re paid out claims totaling $11 million (original value) which was approximately 11 percent of its net premium income at the time. It represents for Munich Re the biggest single loss event to date from a natural disaster relative to its premium income (figure 6.2).

While there was a relatively short interval between the San Francisco earthquake of 1906 and the Tokyo earthquake of 1923 (with insured losses of $590 million), almost 40 years passed before the next natural catastrophe on a similar scale occurred. This was Hurricane Betsy, with an insured loss of $500 million. The first billion dollar loss was Hurricane Alicia, USA, 1983 where the insured loss was $1.5 billion. Since then, however, there has been no letup in the growing pace of ever-increasing losses. This trend began with the 2004 hurricane season in the North Atlantic, during which four hurricanes (Charley, Frances, Ivan, and Jeanne) caused a total of $32 billion in insured losses. That record was shattered just a year later by Hurricane Katrina, which resulted in a loss of $62 billion.

FIGURE 6.2 San Francisco Earthquake, USA, 1906
Source: Munich Re archive.

TABLE 6.1 } Costliest Natural Disasters for the Insurance Industry 1980–2008

Date	Loss event	Region	Insured losses (US$ millions, original values)
2005	Hurricane Katrina	USA	61,600
2008	Hurricane Ike	USA, Caribbean	18,500
1992	Hurricane Andrew	USA	17,000
1994	Earthquake	USA, Northridge	15,300
2004	Hurricane Ivan	USA, Caribbean	13,800
2005	Hurricane Wilma	Mexico, USA, Caribbean	12,400
2005	Hurricane Rita	USA	12,000
2004	Hurricane Charley	USA, Caribbean	8,000
1991	Typhoon Mireille	Japan	7,000
1999	Winter storm Lothar	Europe	5,900
2007	Winter storm Kyrill	Europe	5,800
2004	Hurricane Frances	USA, Caribbean	5,500
1990	Winter storm Daria	Europa	5,100
2008	Hurricane Gustav	USA, Caribbean	5,000
2004	Hurricane Jeanne	USA, Caribbean	5,000
1989	Hurricane Hugo	USA, Caribbean	5,000
2004	Typhoon Songda	Japan, South Korea	4,700
1998	Hurricane Georges	USA, Caribbean	4,200
2001	Tropical Storm Allison	USA	3,500
1999	Typhoon Bart	Japan	3,500

Source: Munich Re, NatCatSERVICE.

The list of the insurance industry's 20 most costly natural catastrophes (table 6.1) shows that 16 catastrophes were weather-related with the exception of 4 geological events. The global insurance industry is aware of the challenge that climate change poses. Munich Re drew attention to the possibility of climate change and its inherent risks in a study published as early as 1973 (Munich Re 1973).

It would be impossible for individual local insurance companies to bear losses of these magnitudes. Reinsurance came into existence in the mid-nineteenth century to render risks insurable by spreading them between a number of companies worldwide: Cologne Re was founded in 1846, Swiss Re in 1863, and Munich Re in 1888.

The Role of Reinsurance

As reinsurance is conducted worldwide and across all lines of insurance, it provides an optimal distribution of risk. It helps primary insurers to increase their underwriting capacities and protects them against extreme financial losses. It also enables them to insure risks they would otherwise lack the financial capacity to assume because it would be too risky and too costly for insurers to bear.

It is common practice for primary insurers—very often local insurers—to assume a larger share of a risk than they can safely retain, and thus reinsurance is acquired as a means to transfer part of the risk to others, thereby increasing the pool of capital available to support the risk (figure 6.3). In effect, the primary insurer takes a deductible equal to the difference between the customer's personal deductible and the level of loss beyond which the reinsurer(s) begins to pay. Additional reinsurance-type

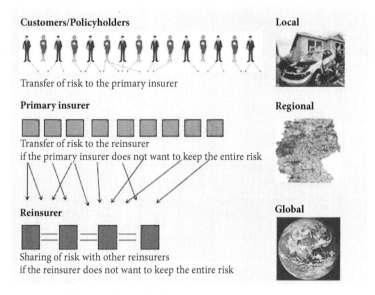

FIGURE 6.3 Scheme of risk transfer from customer to reinsurance

Source: Munich Re.

support can be obtained through retrocession, which is essentially reinsurance bought and sold among reinsurers. Reinsurance is typically bought in "layers," each of which covers a certain band of costs above what the primary insurer can pay. The higher layers of cover are used only if the losses are sufficiently large. This practice helps distribute the risk among many reinsurers (i.e., the sellers of each layer of coverage).[1]

The principle of reinsurance enables local insurers to assume only a small portion of a risk while the bulk of the risk and possible loss is transferred to the international market. The example of Hurricane Gilbert in 1988 illustrates this. When Hurricane Gilbert hit the Caribbean islands in September 1988, Jamaica was seriously affected. Gusts of up to 320 km/h and high waves up to 8 meters were reported. Serious damage was suffered by 50 percent of all houses. The banana crops were totally destroyed. The total insured loss at that time was $720 million. However, the majority—$690 million—was paid out by global reinsurers. Only $30 million was borne by local insurers.

Further examples are the 2001 earthquake in El Salvador and the 2002 floods in the Czech Republic. In both events 95 percent of the insured losses were borne by the reinsurance industry (Munich Re 2003).

Thus, keeping only a small portion of the loss in the country concerned, while the remainder is shared among international groups and markets, permits economies affected by catastrophes to recover much more quickly from major loss events.

However, many people simply cannot afford the "luxury" of insurance, and unfortunately these are frequently the very people that live in countries plagued by natural catastrophes. For example, the Sichuan earthquake in China in May 2008, which hit a rural and relatively poor region, led to claims of around $300 million, whereas the direct loss was more than $80,000 million.

The Insured and Noninsured World

There is an uneven insurance penetration rate around the globe. The most obvious reason for this inequality is that many people in developing countries cannot afford insurance. They need their money for basic needs. Also there are countries where—due to the political situation—insurance is not available or almost nonexistent. Myanmar is one example. When Cyclone Nargis devastated huge areas in May 2008, there was no insurance coverage for the affected people. This problem was intensively discussed at the Microinsurance Conference 2008 in Catagena (Columbia). Now, NGOs and microinsurance organizations are trying to create feasible microinsurance solutions.

There are various ways of calculating insurance coverage. One is to take the total insurance premium per country—though this leads to considerable distortions in particularly highly populated and large countries. A better approximation for the percentage of insured people or households is obtained using insurance premiums per capita. However, even in rich countries with sufficient insurance premiums on average, there will be large numbers of people who cannot afford cover and remain uninsured. In the United States, for instance, the average insurance premium per capita is $2,000. Around a quarter of the population is uninsured, however, as far

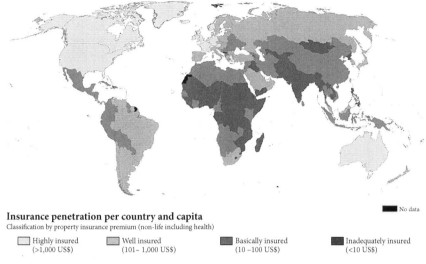

Insurance penetration per country and capita
Classification by property insurance premium (non-life including health)

No data

☐ Highly insured
(>1,000 US$)

▨ Well insured
(101– 1,000 US$)

▩ Basically insured
(10 –100 US$)

■ Inadequately insured
(<10 US$)

FIGURE 6.4 Global distribution of insurance premiums per capita
Source: Munich Re, Economic Outlook.

as homeowners' and renters' insurance is concerned. The map (figure 6.4) shows the global distribution in 2012 of property insurance premiums per capita in US$, including government pool solutions in some countries. The light countries are those with the highest insurance penetration, such as the United States and some European countries.

Four groups of countries can be distinguished:

1. Inadequately insured (property insurance premiums US$ < 10 per person and year): material assets not or inadequately insured.
2. Basically insured (property insurance premiums from $10 to $100 a year): most vital basic insurance just about provided.
3. Well insured (property insurance premiums from $101 to $1,000 a year): material assets (households) adequately to very well insured.
4. Highly insured (property insurance premiums exceed $1,001 a year): this group is to be considered to be extremely well insured; households take out several insurance policies.

The breakdown into the insured and uninsured world shows:

- In Africa there is only one country with annual property insurance premiums exceeding $5 per person. Of these, South Africa is the only country with a well-developed insurance market ($200).
- The largest and most highly populated countries (i.e., China, India, Russia, United States) are in different groups (China; India; Russia; USA). Nevertheless, it must be borne in mind that the picture will be distorted by the considerable sums insured for industrial plants and international construction projects or businesses (e.g., international hotel chains).

Also, size and distribution of populations lead to extreme regional differences, for example, between urban and rural populations. And some emerging markets are developing so rapidly that the insurance penetration may look very different in just a few years.

- In South America the average property insurance premium in all countries is above $10 a year, that is, in the basically insured group. This means that—at least in purely statistical terms—there is "basic protection" for the population's assets.
- In the wealthy industrial countries of North America, western Europe, and in Japan, South Korea, Australia, and New Zealand, a sum far exceeding $500 per person per year is spent on average for property insurance protection. As a rule, each household takes out several insurance policies, the people are considered to be well to highly insured.
- The countries with the highest annual property insurance premiums are Luxembourg ($2,900), Switzerland ($2,100), and the United States ($2,000).

To investigate the impact of natural disasters on the country groups as described above, the loss database NatCatSERVICE from Munich Reinsurance has been used.

Data Sources

The NatCatSERVICE database differentiates seven catastrophe categories (figure 6.5). This seven-level scale—from 0, natural extreme event, to 6, great catastrophe— makes it possible to assign each loss event to a particular category, even if the exact extent of the losses is not known or cannot be determined. The following analyses cover all events from categories 1–6 from 1980 to 2011. The loss data have been converted from original currency into US$ at the end-of-the-month exchange rate of the month in which the event occurred. The monetary thresholds for the categories have been adjusted for inflation (Consumer Price Index) each year. Figure 6.5 shows the mean values of the 1980s and 1990s, 2000 and 2010.[2]

The breakdown (figure 6.6) of natural hazard losses into categories reveals a clear increase in the number of moderate loss events (category 2) and severe natural catastrophes (categories 3 + 4 and 5 + 6). There is a downward trend since 2000 as far as small-scale loss events (category 1) are concerned.

Impacts of Natural Disasters

ANALYSIS OF IMPACTS IN THE INSURED AND NONINSURED WORLD

While the distribution of all natural catastrophes from 1980 to 2011 was more or less even geographically (figure 6.7), 60 percent of all fatalities (more than 1.3 million people) were in the underinsured group. The deadliest event was the tsunami of 26 December 2004, and nearly all tsunami-affected countries are in this group.

0 Natural event	No property damage					
1 Small-scale loss event	1-9 fatalities and/or small scale damage					
2 Moderate loss event	10-19 fatalities and/or damage to buildings and other property damage					
3 Severe catastrophe			2010	2000s	1990s	1980s
	20+ fatalities	Overall losses US$	> 61m	54m	42m	29m
4 Major catastrophe	100+ fatalities	Overall losses US$	> 239m	212m	164m	114m
5 Devastating catatrophe	500+ fatalities	Overall losses US$	> 636m	564m	437m	305m
6 Great natural catastrophe "GREAT disaster"	Region's ability to help itself clearly overtaxed, interregional/international assistance necessary, thousands of facilities and or/ hundreds of thousands homeless, substantial economic losses (UN definition). Insured losses reach exceptional orders of magnitude.					

FIGURE 6.5 Natural catastrophes, breakdown into seven catastrophe categories
Source: Munich Re NatCatSERVICE.

The well and highly insured countries are spared from catastrophic events as far as fatalities are concerned. The exceptions are the 2011 earthquake in Japan with 15,840 fatalities and the 2003 heat wave in Europe with a death toll of 70,000 (Robine et al. 2007). All countries affected by this extreme event are in the group of well and highly insured countries.

Roughly a third of all economic losses resulting from earthquakes, volcanic eruptions, storms, floods, and catastrophes related to extreme temperatures in the period 1980 to 2011—$1,000 billion—occurred in the inadequately and basically insured groups. Almost half of losses—$1,500 billion—were incurred in wealthy industrialized countries, in part due to the high degree of industrialization and comparatively high living standards.

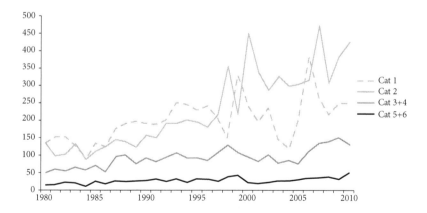

FIGURE 6.6 Number of natural catastrophes per year, 1980–2011, broken down into catastrophe categories
Source: Munich Re NatCatSERVICE.

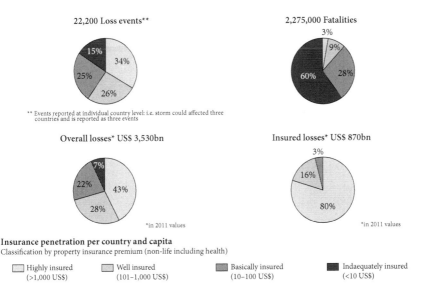

FIGURE 6.7 Natural catastrophes, 1980–2011, percentage distribution among insurance markets at various stages of development

Source: Munich Re, NatCatSERVICE, World Bank.

The overwhelming majority of insured losses resulting from natural disasters between 1980 and 2011 (80 percent) was inevitably paid out in the countries with high insurance penetration; a sum of more than $700 Billion. No major changes are expected in this distribution of insured losses within the different country groups in the near future. But in the longer term the share of premiums from emerging countries will increase. In India, for example, forecasts suggest that the country's insurance market will increase to some $150 billion, five times its current value, over the next 10 years (Munich Re 2008). This growth will be driven above all by rising demand from India's middle class, currently numbering some 300 million people. From 2001 to 2006, the annual increase in premiums in India averaged roughly 24 percent in life insurance and 11 percent in property insurance. Based on total population, market penetration is still comparatively low in what is the second most populous country in the world. The average premium, as a percentage of GDP, is about 0.6 percent for property insurance and 4 percent for life insurance. It is estimated that 90 percent of the Indian population has no property insurance. In terms of absolute premium volume, however, the country already ranks fifth in Asia after Japan, South Korea, China, and Taiwan, and fifteenth in the world (as at 2006). Experts agree that the speed of expansion will continue to be high in the years to come.

WILL THESE LOSSES CONTINUE TO BE INSURABLE IN THE FUTURE?

In the light of the increasing number of natural disasters and the growth in related losses, what are the limits of insurability of frequently affected markets or regions? There is no generally valid answer. In the long term, it could be that the insurance industry will have to limit its exposure in regions and zones that are regularly and almost predictably affected by natural catastrophes; this means the criteria of insurability—an unpredictable event—would no longer be met (Farny 2006). This could apply in particular to concentrated flood-prone areas so that the basic premise of the "sudden and unforeseen occurrence of an event" is no longer valid. However large regions or countries are in a different situation. Here the instruments available to the insurance industry will suffice for years to come, insofar as at least some conditions continue to be met, such as risk-adequate premiums and prospective insurance underwriters taking changing risks into account. There needs to be an effective accumulation control mechanism to identify and quantify concentrations of risks. Ultimately, action to increase risk awareness and to motivate risk-reduction efforts is vital. Implementation of these measures will enable the insurance industry to cope with even huge loss potentials.

ANALYSIS OF IMPACTS IN ECONOMIES AT DIFFERENT LEVELS OF DEVELOPMENT

The number of natural catastrophes is growing continually with no apparent letup in sight. For example, in the 1980s the average number of natural catastrophes was around 400 per year; in the 1990s it was 630 a year and, in the last 10 years (2002–2011), 800 a year. In 2011, experts recorded and analyzed 820 natural hazard events. How are economies at different stages of development affected differently by natural catastrophes, both in terms of the number of victims and monetary losses? In order to compare the different economies, countries were categorized into four groups according to the World Bank's per capita income groups (World Bank 2011):

- Income group 1: Per capita income US$ > 12,275;
- Income group 2: Per capita income US$3,976–12,275;
- Income group 3: Per capita income US$1,006–3,975; and
- Income group 4: Per capita income US$ < 1,006

The following tables show the natural catastrophes generating the highest costs and claiming the largest numbers of victims in each of the income groups:

TABLE 6.2 } Costliest Natural Catastrophes 1980–2008 (Criteria: Economic Losses), by Income Group

Group	Year	Event	Location	Losses, US$ millions[a]
IG 1	2005	Hurricane Katrina	USA	125,000
IG 2	1999	Earthquakes	Turkey	12,000
IG 3	1996	Floods	China	24,000
	2008	Earthquake	China	> 20,000
IG 4	1995	Floods	North Korea	15,000
	2008	Cyclone Nargis	Myanmar	10,000

[a] original losses.

TABLE 6.3 } Costliest Natural Catastrophes 1980–2008 (Criteria: Insured Losses), by Income Group

Group	Year	Event	Location	Losses, US$ millions[a]
IG 1	2005	Hurricane Katrina	USA	61,600
IG 2	2005	Hurricane Wilma	Mexico	1,800
IG 3	1998	Hurricane Gilbert	Jamaica	800
IG 4	2005	Floods	India	770

Source: Munich Re, NatCatSERVICE.

[a] original losses.

TABLE 6.4 } Deadliest Natural Catastrophes 1980–2008, by Income Group

Group	Year	Event	Location	Fatalities
IG 1	2003	Heat wave	Italy	19,300
IG 2	1999	Landslides	Venezuela	30,000
IG 3s	2004	Tsunami	Indonesia	160,000
IG 4	1989	Drought	Sudan	150,000

Source: Munich Re, NatCatSERVICE.

Figure 6.8 shows the percentage distribution of natural catastrophes in the four income groups. The wealthiest countries are the most frequently hit by natural catastrophes; 10,400 of the total of 22,100 events were recorded in this category. The most catastrophe-affected country is the United States with 3,220 events. For the second group, 5,770 events were recorded, with Russia, Chine, Mexico, and Turkey particularly afflicted. The third group of lower middle income countries accounted for 4,000 events and the fourth group of low-income countries, for 2,000 events.

In terms of fatalities, the situation is the opposite. The worst-hit countries are found in group four with 1,092,000 fatalities. These are mainly due to drought, windstorms, and floods and the earthquake in Haiti in 2010, which caused 222,570 deaths . The number of victims roughly reflects the stage of development reached in the regions affected. Many industrialized countries already have relatively advanced building and safety codes, efficient disaster-management systems, and early warning facilities, which have a major bearing on whether countermeasures can be adopted in time so that fewer people are exposed to immediate danger. However, even in the high-income countries, the lives of more than 100,000 people have been claimed, the 2003 heat wave in Europe alone being responsible for 70,000 fatalities. Hurricane Katrina caused more than 1,300 deaths, and the 2011 earthquake in Japan 15,840.

Insured losses are dominated by economies with high per capita incomes, as this is where insurance penetration and asset values are highest. Examples show, however, that losses in markets considered to be in the uninsured category or in the low-income group of countries have also increased. The floods in Mumbai,

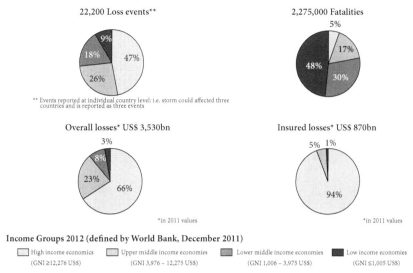

FIGURE 6.8 Natural catastrophes, 1980–2011, percentage distribution in economies at different stages of development

Source: Munich Re NatCatSERVICE, World Bank.

India, in July 2005 produced insured losses amounting to $700 million and made the floods the costliest natural catastrophe in the history of the Indian insurance market. The main reason was that, unlike the rest of the country, Mumbai has a high penetration of property insurance. The average insurance premium per person in Maharashtra state (which includes Mumbai) in 2005 was $12, compared to about $4 in India as a whole.

In terms of economic losses, it is again the wealthy countries that carry the heaviest burden, accounting for two third of the global losses of $3,530 billion. The relative burden on countries and the economic losses in relation to GDP present a quite different picture. The impact on the country groups with low per capita income is disproportionately high (figure 6.9).

The preceding analyses showed that it is vital for people in developing and emerging countries to have access to financial compensation after natural disasters. Affordable solutions should be implemented.

Public–Private Partnerships: From Postdisaster Relief to Predisaster Financing

In a public–private partnership, the insurance market, the government, and private-sector companies take measures together to cover people at risk who may not be able to afford premiums in a purely private insurance market.

Several public–private initiatives exist to mitigate the adverse consequences of natural catastrophes, especially in developing countries.

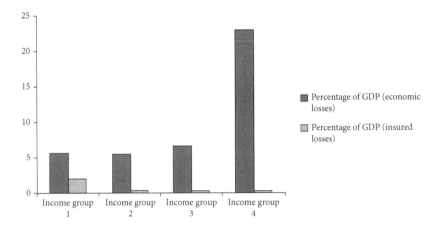

FIGURE 6.9 Overall and insured losses as a share of GDP

Note: Income group 1 is the richest; income group 4 is the poorest.

Source: Munich Re, NatCatSERVICE, World Bank.

THE CARIBBEAN CATASTROPHE RISK INSURANCE FACILITY

Every year hurricanes sweep through the Caribbean leaving a trail of death and destruction. On average, there is a destructive hurricane in the Caribbean every two years. The map of the tracks of tropical cyclones in the Atlantic clearly shows the exposure involved (figure 6.10). However, many of the islands are in the uninsured

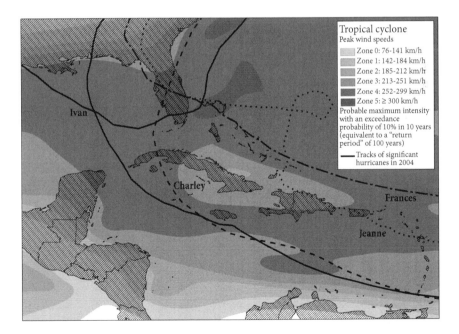

FIGURE 6.10 Tropical storm hazard zones and major Atlantic hurricanes

Source: Munich Re, 2007.

group of countries and/or in the group of low-income countries according to the World Bank classification. Natural catastrophes of this kind can put back the economic development of these countries by several years.

The map shows the tropical storm hazard zones and the tracks of some major hurricanes in the Caribbean and on the US Gulf coastin 2004. Major hurricanes are category 3–5 hurricanes on the Saffir Simpson Scale having wind speeds of more than 178 km/h (NOAA 2008).

In 2004, the Caribbean islands were hit particularly hard by natural disasters, especially hurricanes. For instance, in May 2004, record rainfall in Haiti and the Dominican Republic caused large-scale devastation, killing more than 2,000 people. Devastating floods and mudslides destroyed many peoples' possessions, as well as important infrastructure. The same year, in August, Hurricane Charley swept across Cuba, Jamaica, and the Cayman Islands. Infrastructure and agriculture suffered heavy losses, thousands of houses were destroyed, and 36 people died. Then, in September, Hurricane Frances left a trail of destruction across the Bahamas and the Turks and Caicos Islands. In the same month, Hurricane Jeanne caused record rainfall in Haiti and the Dominican Republic; 2,000 people were killed in the resulting floods and torrents of mud. In the same month, Hurricane Ivan surged across the Caribbean, reaching Grenada on September 7, where it became the worst storm to hit the island in 50 years. There were 39 fatalities and 90 percent of the buildings were damaged or destroyed. Economic losses were estimated at $900 million—amounting, in a nation with a population of just 100,000 people, to 200 percent of GDP.

Following this year of devastation, the Caribbean Catastrophe Risk Insurance Facility (CCRIF) was founded, starting operations on June 1, 2007 (Munich Re 2007; CCRIF 2008). The CCRIF offers 16 Caribbean countries financial assistance in the event of hurricanes and earthquakes. So far, the following states have subscribed to the CCRIF: Anguilla, Antigua and Barbuda, Bahamas, Barbados, Belize, Bermuda, the Cayman Islands, Dominica, Grenada, Haiti, Jamaica, St. Kitts and Nevis, St. Lucia, St. Vincent and the Grenadines, Trinidad and Tobago, and the Turks and Caicos Islands.

The Purpose and Concept of the CCRIF

The CCRIF is a type of reconstruction aid program. Its purpose is to provide governments with index-based insurance against losses caused by hurricanes and earthquakes. It allows governments to purchase insurance coverage at the lowest possible cost—approximately half the price they would have to pay if they had to purchase the same insurance coverage individually.

The use of parametric triggers (i.e., payment is triggered on the basis of a measured parameter of the hazard event and not on the damage caused) allows very rapid payment to the treasury of the affected country. For hurricanes, the parameter is wind speed; for earthquakes, it is ground acceleration.

The CCRIF carries losses up to $10 million itself and obtains additional capacity of $110 million on the international reinsurance market, including a natural catastrophe swap that has been devised with the participation of the World Bank.[3] This means that emerging countries will use the capital market for the first time to cover natural catastrophe risks using derivative products. However, can $110 million help a country to recover after a catastrophe? When hurricane Jeanne hit Haiti in 2004, it destroyed thousands of houses, caused infrastructure damage and killed 1,800 people. The overall loss was estimated at $100 million. Money from the CCRIF could have helped the country to recover sooner.

No hurricanes activated the parametric trigger in 2007. Although Hurricane Dean in September 2007 caused significant losses in the Caribbean, its wind speeds and index values were not sufficient to activate the trigger. The first event to activate the trigger was an earthquake with a magnitude of 7.4 in November 2007. The St Lucian government received $418,976 while the government of Dominica received $528,021. The money will go toward post-earthquake recovery efforts in both these nations.

On September 3, 2008, the CCRIF won the "Re/Insurance initiative of the year" award at The Review Worldwide Reinsurance Awards. This award cemented its reputation as a valuable and innovative form of catastrophe cover on the global stage and could help to export the CCRIF concept to other regions.

The CCRIF shows the effectiveness of an insurance solution in developing and emerging countries. The scheme is already being discussed for other regions, such as the Pacific Rim.

THE TURKISH CATASTROPHE INSURANCE POOL

Another example of an insurance instrument based on public–private partnership is the Turkish Catastrophe Insurance Pool (TCIP). Turkey is located in one of the most active earthquake regions in the world, with a majority of the population living in earthquake-prone areas. Table 6.5 shows the five largest earthquakes in Turkey since 1980 and illustrates the enormous losses involved.

The persistent potential for large-scale natural disasters and the very low level of catastrophe insurance penetration among households have become a fiscal and social issue for the Turkish government. This issue led to the establishment of the TCIP in 1999. The scheme was established with the assistance of the World Bank before the

TABLE 6.5 } Largest Earthquakes in Turkey since 1980

Year	Region	Fatalities	Overal losses US$m[a]
2003	Bingöl	176	400
1999	Izmit	17,000	12,000
1999	Düzce	845	500
1998	Adana, Ceyhan	144	550
1992	Erzinan	650	750
1983	Horasan	1,350	800

Source: Munich Re, NatCatSERVICE, 2008.

[a] original values.

Izmit earthquake of August 1999 (Gurenko et al. 2007). The Management Board of the pool has seven members from academia and the public and the private sectors. To keep down administrative costs and to create an efficient operational structure, most TCIP functions and operations are outsourced to the insurance and reinsurance industry, using their existing infrastructure. Currently, 32 insurance companies are entitled to distribute TCIP policies. The treasury undersecretary is responsible for supervising the program and auditing all TCIP operations and accounts. TCIP and its revenues are exempt from all taxes, levies, and charges.

The program has four principal objectives. Above all it provides earthquake insurance at affordable but actuarially sound rates for all registered urban dwellings. It also aims to limit the government's financial exposure, to build long-term reserves to finance future earthquake losses, and to encourage risk reduction and mitigation practices in residential construction.

Since the program began in 1999, insurance penetration for catastrophe coverage has more than tripled. The TCIP now provides coverage to more than two million Turkish homeowners. In the aftermath of several small and medium-scale earthquakes in the last few years, it has demonstrated its ability to pay claims quickly and fairly. Because of its low-cost structure, it makes catastrophe insurance affordable for middle-income homeowners. The insurance density is currently 18 percent country-wide.

MUNICH CLIMATE INSURANCE INITIATIVE

The third example of a public–private initiative focuses on the risk of climate change. The Munich Climate Insurance Initiative (MCII) was started in April 2005 by Munich Re together with other organizations, including insurers, climate experts, economists, and independent organizations (Munich Climate Insurance Initiative 2008).[4]

The main objectives of the MCII are to develop insurance-related solutions to help manage the impacts of climate change, especially in developing countries. It will conduct and support pilot projects for the application of insurance-related solutions, in partnerships and through existing organizations. Furthermore, it will promote insurance approaches in cooperation with other organizations and initiatives within existing frameworks such as the United Nations system, international financial institutions, international donors, and the private sector. Finally, the aim is to identify and promote loss-reduction measures for climate-related events. One major objective of the MCII is to introduce climate insurance concepts in the post-Kyoto negotiations in line with the commitments in the Bali roadmap.

The above three examples of public–private partnership—the CCRIF, the TCIP, and the MCII—are different approaches for financing losses from natural catastrophes. But they have the common aim of giving governments and victims quick access to funds needed for reconstruction measures. Such solutions are very helpful for governments trying to cope with the financial impact of a natural catastrophe. However, insurance mechanisms do not directly minimize the degree to which a disaster affects the population. Therefore, besides such international or national insurance systems, further solutions for people in need have to be implemented. In recent years, regional microinsurance has emerged to help those individuals who cannot afford traditional insurance.

Microinsurance

In essence, microinsurance is not different from other insurance: losses suffered by individuals are borne by the overall community. The only difference is that the clients for microinsurance are people who have not had access to financial instruments before and that levels of premiums and payouts are relatively low.

During his opening speech at the 2007 Microinsurance Conference in Mumbai, the Indian Finance Minister Shri P. Chidambaram said:

> While growth is the best antidote to poverty, governments must now turn their attention to those who are at the bottom of the income pyramid. It is obvious that wealth does not percolate down to society's poor. More than half of the Indian population has no access to banking, let alone insurance products. Addressing these concerns is as important as focusing on growth. (Munich Re Foundation 2007)

According to UN figures, there are some 2.6 billion people in the world living on less than $2 a day (UN 2000). Among those people only one in 10 has access to formal financial services, such as loans, insurance, wire transfers, or savings accounts. The war on poverty is one of the biggest challenges we face in the twenty-first century and natural catastrophes and disease are a very real threat to people in developing countries. Providing access to insurance for people on low and irregular incomes is an important part of development policy, as it allows families to protect themselves against financial hardship.

Since the first microcredits were issued in Bangladesh in the late 1970s, such schemes have repeatedly proven their worth as an effective instrument helping people to improve their economic situation and to overcome poverty. Over half a billion people now benefit from microloans and other microfinance products (Reinhard 2008).

Microinsurance is an important addition to microfinance products. Despite the fact that the number of schemes and insured persons has increased significantly in the last few years, microinsurance still has very low penetration. Even the most rudimentary of financial services are still out of reach of many people in developing countries. The Microinsurance Centre's "landscape study" (Roth et al. 2007) found that only 3 percent of the poor in the world's 100 poorest countries have access to insurance products, that is, fewer than 80 million people.

That is clearly not enough, especially since it is expected that the intensity of natural catastrophes will further increase because of climate change. The UNDP's 2007 report on human development (UNDP Human Development Report 2007/2008) explicitly states that little or no insurance cover, low incomes, and negligible to nonexistent financial reserves are high risk factors leading to the ruin of families when natural catastrophes occur (figure 6.11).

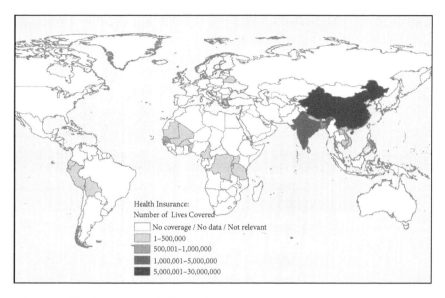

FIGURE 6.11 Microinsurance penetration

Source: The Microinsurance Centre (2007). "The Landscape of Microinsurance."

HOW DOES MICROINSURANCE WORK? CHALLENGES AND OPPORTUNITIES

For low-income households the greatest threat arising from a natural disaster is the loss of the breadwinner, if he or she becomes ill or dies. However, even if breadwinners are not directly affected by a catastrophe, they may still find themselves without the chance to earn money if they can no longer reach their place of work after a flood, or lose the basis of their business, such as a boat for a fisherman destroyed by a storm. A natural catastrophe therefore constitutes one of the greatest risks faced by poor families in risky environments.

Information and awareness programs are needed if microinsurance is to succeed. Policies must be designed in a very simple and easy-to-follow way. Premium payment has to be very flexible as well, otherwise insured persons will forfeit their cover as soon as they fall behind on their premium payments because they cannot work. The lack of a suitable financial infrastructure means that new sales channels have to be developed. At the same time, however, administration needs to be highly efficient to prevent rising costs, especially in light of the low premiums involved.

Given the enormous threat from natural catastrophes, microinsurance should be complemented by specially developed catastrophe bonds or weather derivatives and by tailored reinsurance, so that schemes are not put at risk by the accumulated losses of a single extreme event.

FOR WHOM IS MICROINSURANCE DESIGNED?

Several analyses have shown that it is not the poorest of the poor who are the potential buyers of microinsurance. Other solutions will have to be found to help this group. Microinsurance is intended more for people that are currently in the process of freeing themselves from poverty—the so-called working-poor—for example, after a microloan has helped them establish a business. Without suitable cover they would probably be plunged back into poverty at the first economic setback, triggered for example by a natural catastrophe.

According to the Indian insurance regulator, there are 250 million potential microinsurance clients in India alone. Reaching them would bring many families the sustained economic progress they need to cope with their daily lives and extreme risks (Munich Re Foundation 2007). Case studies carried out by the Consultative Group to Assist the Poorest/Microfinance Gateway Working Group (CGAP) on microinsurance have shown that the poor are more than ready to pay for cover as long as they know they will receive something for their money (CGAP 2003). After all, in the long term they will "pay" far more if they do not have suitable cover, for example, if they have to sell their livestock to pay a medical bill.

WHY MICROINSURANCE? OTHER OPTIONS FOR MANAGING RISKS

Microinsurance is just one of several instruments with which the poor can manage and control the risks they face. Savings, taking out loans, or the traditional method of mutual assistance in the village or family are obvious alternatives. However, such ideas can soon reach their limits if several loss events occur at the same time or in quick succession. Moreover, the precautionary and preventive concept of insurance and the detailed risk evaluation it involves offer enormous potential for preventing losses and the human suffering they bring. Unlike state support or emergency aid by third parties, insurance is an extremely reliable instrument for people to find their own way out of catastrophes and crises. Past experience has shown that the amount of aid provided in the wake of catastrophes depends to a great extent on the media's reaction to the disaster, which region is affected and the prevailing political situation at the time (Reinhard 2008).

HOW CAN MICROINSURANCE BE IMPLEMENTED?

Aid organizations, local NGOs, government representatives, and the insurance industry must work closely together. The supervisory authorities also need to create the right legal framework to facilitate the development of microinsurance. Sufficient financial resources need to be made available.

Microinsurance is already on the right track to becoming an established aspect of risk minimization. Table 6.6 shows some projects that have been established and organizations that support the successful implementation of microfinance and microinsurance solutions.

Commercial insurers are taking a growing interest in providing microinsurance solutions: they are starting to explore this potential growth market. The International Microinsurance Conference in November 2008 in Cartagena (Colombia) underlined this tendency: every second participant was a representative from an insurance

TABLE 6.6 } Examples of Microinsurance Funding and Projects

Organization		Activities/Projects	Next activities
The Bill & Melinda Gates Foundation	Sponsors and supports The Microinsurance Agency and Microinsurance Innovation Facility		
Microinsurance Agency	Funded by The Bill & Melinda Gates Foundation	> 3 million lives insured Started to work on index-based weather insurance	Expand into 11 new nations and provide life, health, and crop insurance to 21 million people by 2012
Microinsurance Innovation Facility	Funded by The Bill & Melinda Gates Foundation	Provides grants and technical assistance of organizations serving the poor	Issue of biannual requests for proposals and provide funding to pilot new insurance products Training of technical specialists to help replicate successful models
Microbank "Women's World Banking," Munich Re, Suramericana, Worldbank		Project in Bucaramanga, Columbia: Cover against the consequences of death, severe illness, natural hazards, burglary, theft, robbery, and fire, thus cushioning the impact of serious losses of earnings	
Munich Re		Pilot project in Jakarta, Indonesia: People buy a "Flood Protection Card" (US$ 5) and get a single payment (US 27) if the water on the Manggari Gates reaches 9.5 m	

Source: Munich Re Foundation 2008.

company. To summarize, the business field of microinsurance is an ideal combination of market-economic thinking and social responsibility.

Transferring Risk to the Capital Market

The steady increase in losses from natural catastrophes has prompted the insurance industry to look for alternative methods of risk transfer (ART). This type of alternative risk transfer must be seen as a supplement to reinsurance rather than competition for it. The principle behind ART is to transfer (financial) catastrophe risk into the capital markets instead of taking out traditional reinsurance. The main function is to provide additional capacity for top-rank, very large losses.

LINKING REINSURANCE AND THE CAPITAL MARKETS

The idea of transferring risks to the capital markets through bonds and derivatives came about in the mid-1990s. The global financial markets offered an additional source of capacity to supplement traditional reinsurance. It also gave investors the opportunity to diversify their investments. One of the first steps in implementing financial markets as supplementary instruments for dealing with insurance risks was taken by the Chicago Board of Trade (CBOT) with the development of insurance derivatives such as futures and options for natural catastrophe risks in the United States. At the same time, the first bonds securitizing insurance risks came into the market. After early attempts were made with smaller volumes, it became possible to also place larger volumes, from $100 million to $500 million, on the capital market as from 1997 to 1998 (Munich Re 2001).

A feature of most of the transfers of risks to the capital markets is that payments are triggered by indices; these may be market-loss indices or parametric triggers. A market loss index reflects the insured loss incurred after a natural catastrophe. A parametric trigger has precisely defined and transparent criteria in terms of the severity of a natural catastrophe, for example, magnitude of earthquakes, wind velocity, or minimum air pressure for windstorms.

SECURITIZATION VIA INSURANCE DERIVATIVES

Insurance derivatives can be structured as swaps or options. They can be based on a market-loss index or on a parametric trigger. In the case of a swap, different catastrophe risks are exchanged between insurers or reinsurers. For instance, in August 2003, Swiss Reinsurance and Mitsui Sumitomo Insurance Company arranged a $100 million catastrophe risk swap. Swiss Re exchanged a part of its North Atlantic hurricane and European windstorm risk for Mitsui Sumitomo's Japanese typhoon exposure. These are peak risks for both parties. By swapping segments of the risk both companies were able to improve the diversification of their risk portfolios (Swiss Re 2003).

With insurance options the cedant (the insurer or reinsurer) is the buyer and the investor is the seller of the option. If catastrophe losses meet or exceed the index or trigger, the investor must pay the insurer an amount based on the terms of the contract.

INDUSTRY LOSS WARRANTIES

Industry loss warranties (ILWs) are a type of reinsurance cover for insurers and are usually agreed for rare occurrences. They are triggered according to an industry-loss index. The industry loss can vary by amount or geographic scope. For example, an ILW may promise to pay when one of the following preconditions are fulfilled:

- a hurricane with industry-wide insured losses in Florida of over $15 billion;
- a winter storm with industry-wide insured losses in Europe of more than $20 billion;
- an earthquake with industry-wide insured losses of $35 billion anywhere in the world.

WEATHER INDEX INSURANCE

Weather index insurance is closer to a derivative than to traditional insurance. Typically, the insured (very often a farmer) is free to purchase as much cover as he wishes, and when the index is calculated, the payment received is a function of the index value and the amount of cover purchased rather the actual loss suffered. This makes claims payment very easy, as it does not require any claims validation beyond ensuring that the measurement of the index is correct. In effect, farmers do not need even to submit claims. At the end of the term, if the trigger has been met or exceeded, they receive a payment.

CAT BOND/BOND ISSUES

Catastrophe bonds are risk-linked securities that transfer a specified set of natural catastrophe risks from the issuer—normally insurers or reinsurers—to the capital market (investors). The investor subscribes for shares in a special-purpose entity. If a defined natural catastrophe does not occur, he receives a return that includes a premium for the risk in addition to the principal on its maturity date.

But if the pre-defined event occurs and triggers the CAT bond, then the principal or parts of the principal initially paid by the investors is lost and is instead used by the issuer (insurer or reinsurer) to pay policyholders' claims.

OUTLOOK

Alternative risk transfer is a growing market: the annual growth rates for insurance-linked securities are over 35 percent. However, it is still the case that only a small portion of the international reinsurance market's capacity is placed on the capital market. Most business conducted on the capital markets is in the field of natural catastrophes, with North America, Japan, and Europe accounting for most of this. The transaction and risk transfer costs are still very high. Nevertheless, this market looks set to develop further. This is borne out by the founding of the company PERIL, which was established in 2008 by the insurance companies Allianz, Axa, Munich Re, Swiss Re, and Zurich. The objective of PERIL is to provide speedy estimates of insured losses from European natural catastrophes. For the United States, it is Property Claims Services (PCS), a member of Insurance Service Offices, that provides the market loss estimates shortly after the event. This information can be used to serve as a market-loss index for catastrophe bonds or for catastrophe swaps. Market-loss indices are expected to play an increasingly important role in the transfer of insurance risks to the capital market.

Summary

Countless measures will have to be taken worldwide in order to ameliorate the impact of a persistent trend toward ever-larger and more catastrophic natural events. Knowledge must be imparted and awareness sharpened. For the people at risk it is vital to know what to do in advance of an imminent catastrophe, and how to react when it strikes. Insurance cover remains the most effective way of protecting property and belongings. People in the poorest countries have the chance to acquire microinsurance. This offers them a great opportunity to protect themselves against natural catastrophes, helps them to cope with emergencies and prevents them from sliding further into poverty. In addition, the UNFCCC negotiation processes will discuss whether premiums for coverage against weather catastrophes should be paid by the parties responsible for climate change, and not only by poor people in developing countries. Furthermore, governments can reduce the financial impact of large natural catastrophes via insurance in cooperation with the World Bank, development banks and the international insurance industry, which will facilitate quick reconstruction processes. Finally, assessing and reinsuring the risks of today and tomorrow is the business of international reinsurers. However, the losses specifically generated by major catastrophes are becoming increasingly complex. The reinsurers' task is not only to identify risks and develop insurance solutions but also to make their knowledge and potential prevention measures available to the public at large.

Notes

1. Literature recommendation: R. Philippe Bellrose, *Reinsurance for beginners*, 5th ed. (Witherby & Co., 2003), ISBN 13:9781856092395.

2. Data Sources: For the analyses of the global impact of natural disasters, the data are taken from the Munich Re NatCatSERVICE. This database on global natural catastrophes is the central element of Munich Re's Geo Risks Research. It was founded in 1974 and has currently more than 26,000 entries. It contains data on the major catastrophes of the last 2000 years and all post-1980 loss events. The systematic and accurate documentation allows precise analyses and hazard assessments. Analyses and statistics on current and historic natural disasters can be downloaded at http://www.munichre.com/geo.

3. The World Bank accepts 28.6 percent of the top layer of the Aggregate XL for the CCRIF in the form of a catastrophe swap. As the World Bank does not want to keep the risk on its balance sheet, the risk is transferred to Munich Re via a catastrophe swap agreement (in reinsurance language, an Aggregate XL). The wording uses capital-market language instead of reinsurance language. The World Bank fronts the risk without retaining it. Munich Re gets 100 percent ex 71.4 percent of the 'traditional' top layer and a leading share in the lower layers. The World Bank pays a fixed premium of $430,000, which is 2.15 percent of $20 million. The RoL (Rate on Line) for the traditional top layer is also 2.15 percent. RoL: a percentage derived by dividing reinsurance premium by reinsurance limit; the inverse is known as the payback or amortization period. For example, a $10 million catastrophe cover with a premium of $2 million would have a rate on line of 20 percent and a payback period of five years.

4. Representatives of a number of different organizations cooperate in the MCII, such as the European Climate Forum, Germanwatch, the International Institute for Applied Systems Analysis, the Munich Re Company and Munich Re Foundation, the Potsdam Institute for Climate Impact Research, UNFCCC, the UN University, the World Bank, the World Meteorological Organization, and other renowned institutions, companies, and experts.

References

Caribbean Catastrophe Risk and Insurance Facility (CCRIF). (2008). Accessed September 4, 2008. http://www.ccrif.org.

Churchill, C. (2006). "Protecting the Poor: A Microinsurance Compendium," International Labour Organization and Munich Re Foundation. Accessed February 20, 2009. http://www.munichre-foundation.org/StiftungsWebsite/Projects/Microinsurance/2006Microinsurance/Microinsurance_Compendium.htm.

Consultative Group to Assist the Poorest/Microfinance Gateway (CGAP). (2003). "Case Studies." Accessed February 20, 2009. http://www.cgap.org/p/site/c/template.rc/1.26.1436.

Farny, D. (2006). *Versicherungsbetriebslehre*. Karlsruhe, Germany: Verlag Versicherungswirtschaft.

Gurenko, N., Lester R., and Mahul, O. (2007). *Earthquake Insurance in Turkey: History of the Turkish Catastrophe Insurance Pool*. Washington, D.C.: World Bank.

Hamburger Feuerkasse. (2008). "Geschichte der Hamburger Feuerkasse, Zeittafel zur Geschichte." Accessed June 1, 2008. http://www.hamburger-feuerkasse.de/?direkt=http://www.hamburger-feuerkasse.de/owx_1_52_1_13_1_fac4990600708a.html.

Insurance Information Institute. (2008). *Fact Book 2007*, 161–163.

Mills, E., Lecomte, E., and Peara, A. (2001). "US Insurance Industry Perspectives on Global Climate Change." Lawrence Berkeley National Laboratory 45185, US Department of Energy, Berkeley, Calif.

Munich Climate Insurance Initiative. (2008). Accessed June 1, 2008. http://www.climate-insurance.org.

Munich Re. (1973). *Floods*, 7–8. Munich, Germany.

———. (1999). *Topics 2000: Natural Catastrophes*, 70–112. Munich, Germany.

———. (2001). "Risk Transfer to the Capital Markets—Using the Capital Market in Insurance Risk Management." Document No. 302–03011. Accessed February 20, 2009. http://www.munichre.com/publications.

———. (2003). *Topics: Annual Review of Natural Catastrophes 2002*. Munich, Germany.

———. (2007). "Insurance Cover for Countries in the Caribbean in Place for Hurricane Season 2007." Press release, June 1. Accessed February 20, 2009. http://www.lifepr.de/attachment/3078/07_06_01_Munich_Re_press_release.pdf.

———. (2008a). NatCatSERVICE Download-Center—Annual Statistics. Accessed February 20, 2009. http://www.munichre.com/publications.

———. (2008b). *Topics Geo: Natural Catastrophes 2007, Analyses, Assessments, Positions*. Munich, Germany.

Munich Re Foundation. (2007a). "Microinsurance Conference India." Press release, November 14. Accessed February 20, 2009. http://www.munichre-foundation.org/StiftungsWebsite/Projects/Microinsurance/2007Microinsurance/MIC2007_PressRelease.htm.

———. (2007b). "Report 2007," 18. Accessed February 20, 2009. http://www.munichre-foundation.org/StiftungsWebsite/Publications/Overview/de/2007report_Publication_summary.htm.

Museum für Versicherungsgeschichte Gotha. (2005). "Historische Entwicklung des Versicherungswesens." Gotha, Germany.

National Oceanic and Atmospheric Administration (NOAA). (2008). "The Saffir Simpson Hurricane Scale." Accessed December 15, 2008. http://www.nhc.noaa.gov/aboutsshs.shtml.

Reinhard, D. (2008). "Abgesichert aus der Armut." In *Klimwandel und Armut: Eine Heraus-forderung für gerechte Weltpolitik*, Welt-sichten. Accessed February 20, 2009. http://www.pik-potsdam.de/infothek/broschueren/klimawandel-und-armut.pdf.

Robine, J., Cheung, S., Le Roy, S., Van Oyen, H., and Herrmann, F. (2007). "Report on Excess Mortality in Europe during Summer 2003." EU Community Action Programme for Public Health, Grant Agreement 2005114. Accessed December 15, 2008. http://www.ec.europa.eu/health/ph_projects/2005/action1/docs/action1_2005_a2_15_en.pdf.

Roth, J., McCord, M., and Liber, D. (2007). "The Landscape of Microinsurance in the World's 100 Poorest Countries." Accessed February 20, 2009. http://www.microinsurancecentre.org/UI/DocAbstractDetails.aspx?DocID=634.

Swiss Re. (2003). "Swiss Re and Mitsui Sumitomo Arrange US$100 Million Catastrophe Risk Swap." Press release, August 4. Accessed December 15, 2008. http://www.swissre.com/pws/media%20centre/news/news%20releases%202003/swiss%20re%20and%20mitsui%20sumitomo%20arrange%20usd%20100%20million%20catastrophe%20risk%20swap.html.

United Nations. (2000). "Message of the United Nations Secretary General, Kofi Annan on the International Day for the Eradication of Poverty." Accessed February 20, 2009. http://www.un.org/events/poverty2000/messages.htm.

United Nations Development Programme (UNDP). (2007). "Human Development Report 2007/2008—Fighting Climate Change: Human Solidarity in a Divided World," 89–95, New York. Accessed February 20, 2009. http://www.hdr.undp.org/en/reports.

World Bank. (2011). "Data & Statistics, Country Classification." Accessed March 19, 2011. http://web.worldbank.org/WBSITE/EXTERNAL/DATASTATISTICS/0,,contentMDK:20420458~menuPK:64133156~pagePK:64133150~piPK:64133175~theSitePK:239419,00.html.

7 }

Natural Disaster Mitigation Policies
Ricardo Zapata-Marti

Introduction

This chapter takes a look at a range of disaster mitigation policies, both in terms of ongoing practice in a number of countries of which the author has personal and professional experience, and those policies that are considered relevant to a reduction in risk. The discussion first touches on the identification of vulnerability factors these policies ought to consider, then moves on to consider what type of public- and private-sector policies the author considers appropriate. Specifically, mitigation policies ought to take into account the need for effective information systems (national/regional), hazard reduction rules and norms, and insurance and governmental funds. The author concludes, based on his experience and knowledge of recent practice, that there is a distinct need for a revision of existing systems, rules, norms, and funds in these strategic areas.

Identification of the Vulnerability Factors

The concept of vulnerability in connection with disasters has been defined under the International Strategy for Disaster Reduction (ISDR), but its origins lie in many other disciplines, namely in medicine, engineering, and economics.[1] The specific definition of vulnerability in the different fields naturally varies, but common to all is the consideration of those conditions that make possible resilience or defense in the face of a specific factor.

Vulnerability factors are mostly of human construction and are linked to the development paradigm. In order to advance policies that can mitigate natural disasters, the concrete identification of the potential socioeconomic impact of vulnerability factors is essential. In economic literature, vulnerability is mostly seen as linked to financial and economic performance.[2] From this literature there has stemmed a growing body of research covering an assessment of vulnerability factors associated with exposure to natural events.[3]

Opinions expressed are the author's and do not necessarily reflect those of the UN Economic Commission for Latin America and the Caribbean (ECLAC).

The increased recognition, by both social and economic planners and first-line responders after disasters, of vulnerability as key to reducing exposure to risk (see figure 7.1) is fully acknowledged internationally in the context of the International Strategy for Disaster Risk Reduction.[4]

Risk results from the interaction between hazards and vulnerability, with the latter arising from internal processes related to the interaction between social-human systems and the environment.

The basic element to be considered is the capacity of those social and economic human systems to respond to external hazards. This sensibility traditionally has been seen as involving preparedness, response, and mitigation, leaving aside the reciprocal element related to the impact that those socioeconomic human systems have on natural processes. This has led to the notion that risk reduction can mainly be seen as interventions in order to reduce vulnerability by increasing response capacity and mitigation through reinforcement of physical structures, under the general consideration that the level, recurrence, and characteristics of hazards are outside human influence.

Hazards are traditionally seen as the result of external processes, that is, outside human influence in terms of their probability of occurrence, magnitude, intensity, speed, velocity, and persistence. In climatic events though, the mounting evidence is that human intervention can alter hazards, as is the case of the changing rainfall and decreased humidity associated with deforestation; "heat islands" as a consequence of urban concentrations; and the alteration of seasonality in terms of drought and extreme precipitation.

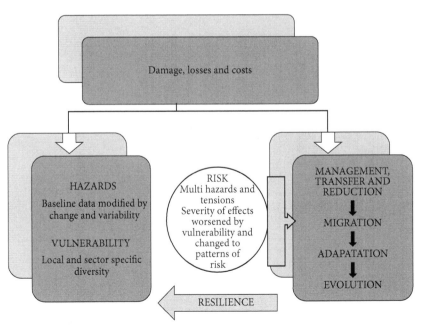

FIGURE 7.1 Risk management and adaptation (to changes associated with climate, socioeconomic and cultural factors)

Source: ECLAC.

TABLE 7.1 } Distribution of Natural Disasters, by Origin, 1900–2008, by Decade

Disaster subgroup	1900–1909	1910–1919	1920–1929	1930–1939	1940–1949	1950–1959	1960–1969	1970–1979	1980–1989	1990–1999	2000–2008	Total
Biological	5	7	10	3	4	2	37	64	170	394	559	1,255
Climatological	4	12	6	5	17	9	69	102	224	335	477	1,260
Geophysical	42	30	33	38	52	61	89	126	245	338	329	1,383
Hydrological	7	4	13	16	15	101	179	316	626	1,007	1,735	4,019
Meteorological	14	18	33	38	53	120	212	291	559	899	956	3,193
Total	72	71	95	100	141	293	586	899	1,824	2,973	4,056	11,110

Source: EM-DAT: OFDA/CRED International Disaster Database.

Given the mounting evidence of climate variability and climate change,[5] it is clear that risk can be also increased by human intervention, leading to different levels of hazards in terms of recurrence, force, and characteristics when we are considering climatic hazards. It is not only that hydrometeorological disasters have increased significantly (see table 7.1 and figure 7.2), but that their cumulative impact and increasingly reduced return periods reduce the capacity of households and authorities to cope and the resilience of societies and human activities. In the face of this, risk reduction requires not only mitigating measures for historical patterns of hazards but also adaptation to the new climatic trends and changes.

Box 7.1 lists a number of the vulnerability factors that are generally considered to play a major role in disasters and highlights how they have evolved over time.

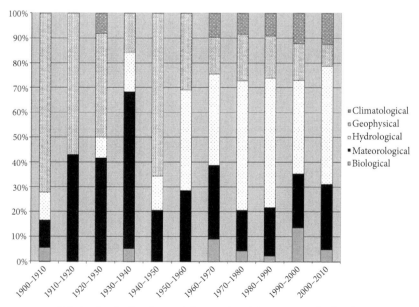

FIGURE 7.2 Relative distribution of natural disasters, by origin, 1900–2008, by decade
Source: EM-DAT: OFDA/CRED International Disaster Database.

BOX 7.1 } Reasons for the Increase in Natural Catastrophes and Natural Catastrophe Losses

- World population has experienced exponential growth. In 1800, for example, there were 1 billion people living on the planet. Today there are 6.9 billion.
- The rising standard of living in nearly all countries produces growing accumulations of wealth that are hit in the event of a catastrophe.
- Concentration of populations and value in conurbations: the emergence of numerous mega-cities—even in exposed regions, e.g., Tokyo and its surrounding area has 30 million inhabitants.
- Settlement and industrialization of very exposed regions, especially coasts and river basins, and tourism in danger zones enhance unmitigated risks, e.g., Florida.
- Vulnerability of modern societies and technologies, structural engineering, devices, equipment, and networks requires a revision of the current standards and norms to reduce risks.
- Increasing insurance penetration throughout the world, i.e., the proportion of insured goods is mounting globally. Consequently, insured losses are escalating even faster.
- Global changes in environmental conditions, climate change, water scarcity, and loss of biodiversity.

Source: Munich Re Group. Accessed February 20, 2009.

There has been an advance in the analysis of exposure to hazards and the concretion of hazards into social, economic, and environmental losses. However, the economic quantification of vulnerability needs to be developed further. In spite of the efforts to try to systematize the socioeconomic impact of disasters, available data (see table 7.2, compiled by ISDR based on the CRED database) remain not very trustworthy, since no standard quantification is applied systematically across industrialized and developing countries. So far, information comes mostly from case studies, such as those conducted by means of the damage and loss assessment methodology developed over the years by ECLAC, and through the development of indicators, with the support of the Inter-American Development Bank (IADB), and some advances being made by the United Nations Development Programme (UNDP).

The usefulness of these efforts lies in providing a quantified, sound, base for decision makers and advancing the development of policies. Reciprocally, it can be said that the lack or insufficiency of such quantification has led to uneven and insufficient development of disaster mitigation and risk reduction policies. The consequences of such inadequate policy development are evident in both developed and developing countries, as illustrated by the measured impacts of natural disasters in both sets of countries (table 7.2).

Although the link between the UN-approved Millennium Development Goals (MDGs) and disaster impact has not yet been quantified systematically, the ISDR proposes a methodological framework for the compilation of risk reduction indicators, to monitor whether interventions to attain MDGs are in fact reducing disaster risk (see ISDR 2008, for more details).[6]

TABLE 7.2 } Total Amount of Reported Economic Damage by Level of Development and Type of Disaster (2005 US$ Billion), 1991–2005

	Flood	Wind storm	Drought[a]	Slide	Earthquake and tsunami	Volcanic eruption	Insect infestation	Total
OECD	103.27	358.49	53.77	0.31	198.61	0.02	0.14	714.61
CEE + CIS	42.86	1.08	3.08	0.13	3.21	0.00	0.00	50.35
Developing countries	204.22	71.78	48.82	2.62	50.70	0.88	0.14	379.15
Least developed countries	14.99	4.98	0.08	0.00	2.55	0.01	0.00	22.61
Countries not classified	1.09	7.28	0.95	0.00	16.90	0.00	0.00	26.22
Total	366.43	443.61	106.69	3.06	271.98	0.91	0.28	1,192.95

Source: EM-DAT: OFDA/CRED International Disaster Database.

[a] Drought-related disasters category includes extreme temperatures.

Given the rising cost of disasters (figures 7.3 and 7.4),[7] it is not surprising that the insurance industry and reinsurers are increasingly concerned about the economic cost of disasters and links between this developing trend, climate change, and human-built vulnerabilities.

However, this just confirms the notion that when the economic impact of disaster losses and damage are felt, policies and instruments will be developed to reduce them, to better cope with risk, and to find means to cover them financially, institutionally, and structurally.

What Type of Public- and Private-Sector Policies?

Risk-reducing policies ought to be linked to the appropriation of risk by society, and not perceived as a public good to be provided by the state. The state does, nevertheless, have a social responsibility to promote risk reduction. This entails in many countries the need for regulatory and institutional changes where institutional competencies and responsibilities are confused and there is no subsidiarity principle, leading to redundancy, duplication, conflict among institutions, and, eventually, inaction.

In the crafting of policies geared toward risk reduction, markets are to be used and can be seen as clearinghouses where unattended risk is penalized and risk reduction is priced, leading to instruments, funds, and facilities that will spread the risk to areas wider than the traditional insurance instruments. In developing countries, risk is aggravated by a lack of insurance penetration and by the fact that disasters tend to widen the gap in the fulfillment of basic social needs by generating a demand for compensation mechanisms for the needy, promotion packages to rekindle economic activity, and solidarity with the affected.

On the other hand, especially as evidence and statistics point to an increased cost from and recurrence of disasters, policies must move toward making risk management into an investment and a business opportunity. But this requires norms and

Great natural disasters 1950–2007
Overall and insured losses

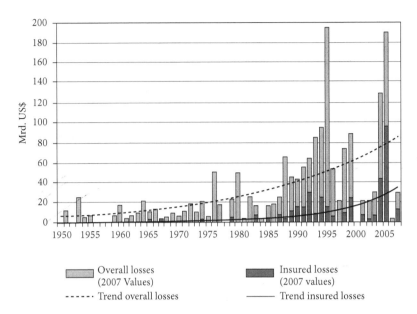

Great weather disasters 1950–2007
Overall and insured losses

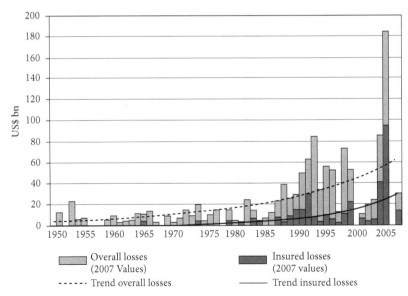

FIGURE 7.3 Overall and insured disaster losses, 1950–2007

Source: Natcat Service, Munich Re, data updated to April 2008.

in USD bn,
indexed to 2007

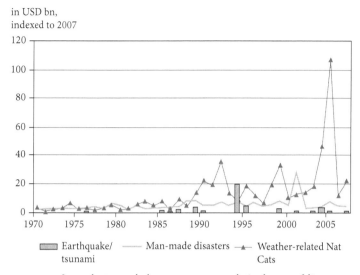

FIGURE 7.4 Insured catastrophe losses, 1970–2007, evolution by type of disaster

Source: Swiss Re. Accessed February 20, 2009. http://www.swissre.com/pws/research%20publications/sigma%20 ins.%20research/facts%20and%20figures/sigma_1_2008_ins_losses.html.

regulations that generate the appropriate market signals and mechanisms. In essence, since the cost of unattended risk is not appropriately valued—and hence priced—we are in the presence of imperfect markets that require governmental intervention.

In the private sector, it is the insurance industry, namely the major reinsurers, that seem to be at the forefront of risk reduction strategies, promoting not only the increased penetration of insurance but also developing new tools and taking a greater share of the market's new and innovative products, such as derivative, para-metric, and catastrophic bonds. Both Munich Re and Swiss Re are major advocates of increasing general recognition that

> current and expected changes in the natural environment are causing the business and political environments to react and change—even more so because climate change is intertwined with numerous other challenging issues such as water avail-ability and energy security.[8]

From a private-sector perspective, it is primarily through financial services that risk can be reduced substantially and generate an effective response. This leads directly to the need for public policies and changes in the regulatory and legislative frameworks so they will set the right incentives for risk management, appropriate risk transfer, and the linkage to disaster risk reduction, in combination with regu-lations that will have an reducing impact on greenhouse gases emissions and will encourage the appropriate financing of climate adaptation on a global scale.

The Stern Review on the Economics of Climate Change (2007),[9] the Global Roundtable,[10] and insurance loss analyses, as well as the gradual but potentially more dynamic changes in the near future to U.S. climate regulations,[11] show that the economic sector is taking climate change seriously. Such a movement can be seen clearly by the fact that the capital markets have had to cope with the consequences of increasingly frequent and violent natural catastrophes, while economic results and the share prices of major companies are affected by resulting raw material shortfalls, damage to production sites, and business interruption. In addition to the capital markets, sectors such as agriculture, tourism, and healthcare—being more vulnerable to climate extremes and variations—are also starting to feel the gradual effects of climate change. Ultimately, economic performance as a whole suffers.

From a public-sector perspective, on the other hand, the real groundbreaking work has yet to materialize. Again, in this respect, Stern (2007) and the IPCC Fourth Assessment report (2007, 2008) have coincided with a growing urgency in facing the costs of adaptation and mitigation and establishing a link to major disasters and their effects, generating a clear line of action in terms of risk reduction, which is a move in the right direction. The ISDR platform's[12] conclusions add a synergistic force to the potential change in policies. In the United States, a significant senatorial proposal was made in 2006 to set up market-based mechanisms for the regulation of emissions and President Barack Obama has backed the establishment of an emissions trading scheme.[13] In Europe, this market, the EU Emissions Trading Scheme, has been in existence since January 2005 and is worth US$59.2 billion as of 2007.

An additional development that points in the direction of what should be on the policy agenda, even if it is still at the declaration level, is the Hyogo Framework, adopted by 168 governments at the World Conference for Disaster Reduction in Kobe, Japan, in January 2005. This framework outlines an agenda for policy changes that should achieve a substantial reduction of disaster losses in terms of lives and social, economic, and environmental assets. It identifies five priorities for action:

(1) ensuring that disaster risk reduction is a national and a local priority with a strong institutional basis for implementation;
(2) identification, assessment, and monitoring of disaster risks and enhancement of early warning systems;
(3) use of knowledge, innovation, and education to build a culture of safety and resilience at all levels;
(4) reduction of the underlying risk factors; and
(5) strengthening of disaster preparedness for effective response at all levels.

In spite of this, in most developing countries, disaster risk reduction—as with climate change—is mostly a matter of coping, and the subject is not yet part of the development agenda. Disaster risk reduction mostly takes a back seat to a government's policy priorities that are more closely associated with economic growth and competitiveness: the trade agenda, and, on the social side, poverty alleviation, uneven income distribution, and social marginalization and exclusion. The clear synergies between sound environmental policies, sustainable development, and the attainment of the MDGs has not been clearly established, just as the link between a social policy agenda and national security is beginning to assert itself.

Even though the appropriate policies are known and there is consensus around them (see box 7.2), actual national, state, or even local governmental policies are moving at a slow pace.

1. Participants expressed considerable concern about the growing risk of disasters, especially in highly vulnerable regions, and about the relatively slow progress being made to address the problem and to implement the Hyogo Framework for Action. We are not on track to achieve the Hyogo Framework's sought-after outcome of a substantial reduction in disaster losses by 2015. The need for action is more urgent than ever.

2. Many countries face a steep learning curve in terms of building their basic institutional capacities, the development or revision of legislation and policy frameworks, the provision of budgets, and the implementation of national platforms and action plans. Some countries, however, have made considerable progress and have gained a wealth of experience. They are encouraged to help significantly by sharing their knowledge and best practices, particularly concerning legislation and institution building, and by donating expertise and funds. The ISDR system should support the achievement of a target for the number of national platforms for disaster risk reduction.

3. Investment in risk reduction needs to be substantially increased. National and local government budgets should adopt specific targets for expenditures, for instance, a certain percentage of sector budgets. International funding should be better coordinated and tracked to ensure that development projects do not inadvertently increase risks. In addition there should be monitoring of the volume of investment in risk reduction and measuring of the performance of those investments that have been made in actually reducing risks. Governments and donors should give consideration to establishing funding targets for community-level implementation and special mechanisms to channel funding directly to at-risk poor communities and local authorities. Donors should develop common standards of good donor practice for risk reduction, including making long-term commitments such as investing target percentages of humanitarian budgets.

4. Countries need to quickly establish systems to monitor and report on their risk profiles and on the implementation of the Hyogo Framework for Action, including best practice codes, verifiable indicators, benchmarks, and targets, in order to guide action and improve accountability for results. In one example, some nations have committed to achieving zero mortality in schools by 2015. Stakeholders at regional and international levels should similarly establish systems of accountability for their activities.

5. The private sector should recognize its key role in the creation and reduction of disaster risks, and should be engaged and challenged by governments and civil society to provide better financial tools to manage disaster risks, and to contribute to risk reduction through participation in public policy debate and in public–private partnerships.

6. Some progress is being made to integrate disaster risk reduction with sustainable development and poverty reduction frameworks and mechanisms and into environmental management tools. This is a long-term task. ISDR system partners should seek innovative ways to increase the involvement and commitment of development and environmental stakeholders, including

civil society and community actors. They should also develop practical tools, for example, the screening of high-risk factors and the implementation of multihazard approaches.

Source: Excerpt from the proceedings of the first session of the Global Platform for Disaster Risk Reduction Geneva, June 5–7, 2007.

This is, again, a matter of not having compelling arguments for the costs and benefits of such policies. On the one hand, the costs are clearly identifiable in terms of institutional arrangements, funding needs, and personnel capacity building, while the benefits of risk reduction tend to be seen only as a probabilistic figure based on potential recurrence and not clearly assessed damages and losses of such potential scenarios, and insufficient quantification of the total actual impact of disasters. The macroeconomic effects have long been under discussion and most of the discussion is centered on the questioning of the validity of data used in most research.

The Need for Effective Information Systems (National/Regional)

The fact that not enough systematized and generalized assessments take place—which, as indicated, leads to a certain level of skepticism in investing in risk reduction and not prioritizing it as a development policy issue—leads to inappropriate disaster impact information systems. Those that exist are either based on nonvalidated information from a number of scattered sources, or built on secondhand information and double-checking and verification by indirect means. Just as truly reliable data on fatalities and affected populations has advanced to a certain extent, data on economic impacts tends not to be as reliable. This is due to the lack of a standardized and widely used methodology for assessment.

Even though such a methodology has been under development for over 30 years in Latin America through the efforts of the ECLAC, there is still no consistency of disaster data in the region. As an illustration of the application of this tool, table 7.3 shows the cumulative negative impact of extreme events as illustrated by ECLAC's disaster assessments over the years—which tends to be more consistent over time and attempts to quantify both damage and losses.

Even though this tool is increasingly being used in other parts of the world, economic assessment overall is still not consistent, comparable, and reliable. In most cases, damage is quantified in terms of infrastructure reconstruction needs (houses, roads, and other public infrastructure) and expressed through the valuation of repairing or rebuilding costs. The assessment of losses, that is, the economic flows altered as a consequence of the disaster, is even more elusive and hardly considered in rapid assessments or even in case studies.

This means that, on the one hand, the cost from damages mostly reflects alternative reconstruction costs (which can be quite different from the actual value of the assets and capital losses), leading to a variable level (not easily established or distinguishable) of overvaluation or overestimation. On the other hand, most estimates

TABLE 7.3 } Disaster Assessment in Latin America and the Caribbean, 1972–2005

Period	AFFECTED POPULATION		TOTAL DAMAGE AND LOSSES
	Deaths	Primary affected population	(millions of US$, at 2004 value)
1972–1980	38,042	4,229,260	78,085
1980–1990	34,202	5,442,500	101,251
1990–1999	32,648	2,518,508	31,367
2000–2010 (estimated)	18,032	35,478,470	50,050
1972–2005	122,924	47,668,738	260,753
Yearly average	3,725	1,444,507	7,902
Of which are of a meteoro-logical or climatic nature	50,067	22,929,198	127,923

Source: ECLAC led assessments since 1973.

are done for public damage, while the private sector tends not to be transparent. These damages (and sometimes the resulting losses) may be indirectly obtained through the value of insurance claims.

In the case of developing countries, where insurance coverage and penetration is limited (mostly to less than 10 percent and concentrated in certain items with almost no coverage of low-income households and small enterprises and almost no presence in agricultural and small commerce—see figure 7.5 and table 7.4), this leads to a significant underestimation. Nevertheless, it is on these figures that the major international reinsurers base their estimate of the global cost of major disasters, using their own techniques and methodologies (table 7.5 shows how data are presented by Munich Re and Swiss Re and the CRED database).

According to the CRED database, in 2007, 414 natural disasters were recorded in the EM-DAT database, killing more than 16,000 people, affecting over 234 million and producing a bill of almost US$75 billion in economic damages—a figure quite different from the one estimated by Swiss Re. The relevance of this comparison is not to emphasize that available national and regional data are sometimes contradictory,

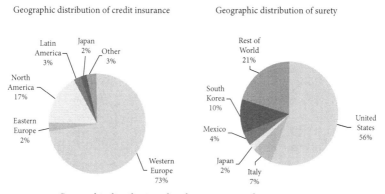

FIGURE 7.5 Geographic distribution of credit insurance and surety, 2006

Source: Swiss Re, Economic Research & Consulting, sigma No. 4/2007.

TABLE 7.4 } Total Insurance Growth, Penetration, and Density by Region

Region	Premiums (in US$m)	Real growth (in %)	Share of the world market (in %)
America	1,329,729	2.7	35.71
North America	1,258,301	2.2	33.79
Latin America and the Caribbean	71,428	11.6	1.92
Europe	1,484,881	7.5	39.88
Western Europe	1,428,806	7.3	38.37
Central and Eastern Europe	56,075	11.4	1.51
Asia	800,819	3.8	21.51
Japan and newly industrialized Asian economies	643,621	0.9	17.29
South and East Asia	138,297	20.8	3.71
Middle East and Central Asia	18,901	5.6	0.51
Africa	49,667	17.5	1.33
Oceania	58,316	2.2	1.57
World	**3,723,412**	**5.0**	**100.0**
Industrialized countries	3,390,180	4.0	91.05
Emerging markets	333,231	16.3	8.95
OECD	3,338,160	3.9	89.65
G7	2,731,315	4.1	73.36
EU, 15 countries	1,357,328	7.6	36.45
NAFTA	1,273,373	2.4	34.20
ASEAN	32,977	1.3	0.89

Source: Swiss Re, Economic Research & Consulting, sigma No. 4/2007.

TABLE 7.5 } Natural Catastrophes in 2007

Ranking by overall losses according to Munich Re

Date	Country/Region	Event	Fatalities	Overall losses (US$m)	Insured losses (US$m)
July 16	Japan	Earthquake	11	12,500	300
January 18–20	Europe	Winter Storm Kyrill	49	10,000	5,800
June–August	China	Floods	650	6,800	
June	UK	Floods	4	4,000	3,000
July	UK	Floods	1	4,000	3,000
June 4–8	Oman	Cyclone Gonu	70	3,900	650
October 28–November 6	Mexico (Tabasco and Chiapas)	Floods	22	3,000	700
October	US	Wildfires	8	2,500	1,900
November 15–17	Bangladesh, India	Cyclone Sidr	3,300	2,300	
April 13–17	US	Winter storm	23	2,000	1,566
			4,138	51,000	16,916

Source: © 2007 NatCatSERVICE, Munich Re.

(continued)

TABLE 7.5 } continued

Catastrophes in 2007 by region, according to Swiss Re

Region	Number	Victims	Insured losses (US $m)
North America	47	983	8,767
Europe	35	1,088	12,431
Asia	146	13,748	3,533
South America	19	1,216	2,228
Oceania/Australia	7	303	1,283
Africa	32	2,215	46
Oceans/Space	49	2,000	1,276
World Total	335	21,533	27,564

Source: Natural catastrophes and man-made disasters in 2007, sigma No.1, 2008, Swiss Reinsurance Company (Swiss Re), Economic Research & Consulting.

Natural disasters in 2007: summary of EM-DAT (CRED)

	2007	2000–2006 yearly average
No. of country-level disasters	414	394.7
No. of countries affected	133	116.3
No. of people killed	16,847	73,946
No. of people affected	211 million	234 million
Economic damages (US$)	74.99 billion	81.86 billion

Source: CRED Crunch newsletter, issue 12, April 2008.

but that this is the result of having neither effective information systems (national/ regional), nor an agreed set of assessment tools and methodologies.

Such information systems are not technically difficult to put together and, with the current state of information technology, their interlinkage is something that could be agreed upon at the technical level. Difficulties arise not because of technical complications but mostly because basic, commonly agreed definitions are not established, starting from the definition of a casualty or a fatality "directly" resulting from the event, to the definition of victims or affected population, identification of the disaster itself, and how to value the impact.

Hazard Reduction Rules and Norms

There are a number of policies that need to be considered, linking adaptation, mitigation, and risk reduction in the face of increased recurrence of extreme climate events, and which would include measures to help communities cope with climate risks. In the special case of developing countries, focusing on the following areas can produce significant results:

- Better housing for poor people located outside hazardous zones such as floodplains, adapting construction techniques to local climatic conditions, local culture and traditions, better use of local materials and reducing dependence on imported techniques, models, and resources.

- Improved sanitation and greater access to clean water in poor neighborhoods and more efficient use of water in key areas, reducing not only the pollution of water sources but generating new sources of income for the population. One of the most common problems in urban areas is the disposal of waste, for which the potential for economic use—instead of posing an increasing public cost—is only rarely being considered. The challenge in this area seems to move beyond successful pilot experiments in waste disposal, which convert waste into energy, recycle materials for economic benefit, and reduce pollution of soil, air, and water. There is already much good practice and experience in this realm, but scaling up these pilot exercises into larger scale activities has so far suffered from a lack of technological proposals and has been dependent on government funding. The lack of appropriate regulatory measures, as well as leaving these issues to local authorities, has also meant a fragmentation of the process and an unclear division of responsibilities between the different levels of government.

- Early warning systems combined with public education about potential hazards have also been very limited and dependent more on technology than on community participation. This has meant little adaptation to local conditions, scant adoption and appropriation from society, and insufficient education as to what to do in the face of warning messages. Such warning and monitoring mechanisms could also be a crucial source of knowledge of climate indicators and their evolution over time. The lack of sufficient solid, historically consistent, and registered meteorological and climate information on a local scale, however, is a common limitation in developing countries.

- Orchestrating preventative actions prior to a warning and appropriate responses when a warning is issued would allow prevention to move away from simply being emergency response preparation, to a more structural perspective in which community organization, social networks, and community design—including land-use zoning and construction techniques—cohere with local conditions and cultures. The role of social groups, including women, should be a part of this process in order to ensure local involvement and acceptance.

- Better building codes and strict enforcement thereof thus are not to be seen as externally imposed but internally generated.

- Better management of resources during emergencies should also be seen as part of an adaptation process, providing an opportunity to use local providers in advance to have the necessary stockpiles that are required for an emergency. This would also provide opportunities for intra-regional trade and cooperation, and would reduce dependency on external resources.

- Public education programs ought to be expanded from existing ones covering preparations and alertness in the face of sudden events. These should specifically target agricultural producers in terms of the necessary preparations for slow-onset hazards such as drought and changing rain patterns, which can cause seasonal dryness that in turn can lead to wildfires. Such targeted programs would also address the need to alter traditional planting practices that often employ pre-planting burning (which increases greenhouse gas emissions) and to promote more organic and energy-efficient agriculture. Education must also consider adaptation to changing seasonal patterns, as with the increased intensity and recurrence of El Niño/La Niña events in Latin America, for instance, which produce flooding in some areas, extended drought and dryness in others, and, overall, aggravate climate extremes.

- Improved weather and climate forecasting from short-term to seasonal time horizons should be seen as part not only of the education and public awareness programs but as an institutional strengthening of climate agencies, most of them governmental and chronically underfunded. These institutions should also have their technological base strengthened, particularly in terms of modernization of monitoring equipment and stations. In some countries, there is an overlap of institutional responsibility that leads to duplication of efforts in some areas (where large irrigation programs or hydroelectricity generation and river basin commissions exist, for example), leaving unattended and scantily monitored large swathes of national territories—usually those that are highly remote, least developed, and most vulnerable.

- Partnerships are needed among forecasters, intermediary organizations, and users to facilitate delivery, interpretation, and application of forecasts to manage climate risks. Here, there is great potential for intraregional cooperation and reducing dependency on external sources of information which, although crucial, such as the international monitoring of hurricanes, are insufficient for local forecasting or prevention of flash flooding and to avoid preventable damage from landslides and avalanches, for example.

- Better coastal zone planning guidelines, especially those that recognize the flood mitigation potential of mangroves and natural wetlands, are to be seen not only as desirable environmental conservation practice but as a risk prevention tool, increasing resilience against sea surges. One common thread linking a number of recent disasters has been the increased losses in those coastal areas where native vegetation cover has been reduced, or mangroves uprooted, in order to expand beach surfaces for tourists, plant non-native 'tropical' gardens, and build golf courses.

- Watershed management and river basin monitoring control and restoration is also an increased concern given the recent disasters that have been associated with siltation and the reduced ability of watersheds to contain floods. This phenomenon is often a result of the lack of integrated management for a whole basin system that suffers at its source from the impact of deforestation, which not only depletes natural sources but also makes a region more vulnerable to sudden unseasonably high rainfall when the increased volume of water leads to landslides, debris moving downstream, and major flooding. All of this is aggravated when the normal flow to the sea is diminished either by changes in a river's natural course or incursions into the natural coastal environment by activities such as fish ponds, tourism developments, inappropriately built marinas and sea walls in port structures. Additionally, when these courses head toward the sea, water flow can be slowed by storm surges, rises in sea level, and changes in climate patterns.

A further two issues call out for specific attention: the use of clean production techniques and the trend toward promoting biofuels. They are both potentially useful in reducing the region's carbon footprint, but raise questions of equity and competition for the use of resources.

Many countries have established general institutional legal frameworks. In some cases these were carved out of or combined with reorganized existing institutions, tending to either separate emergency response functions or unify risk management under a single institution. For the most part, this has led to administrative complications, institutional rivalry, and confusion as to ownership of competencies and respective roles. Risk management policies cut across different issues—environmental management, the actual implementation of strategies, policies, programs, and projects—and have generated confusing institutional and administrative procedures that tend to be more attuned to the institutional culture or tradition of countries than to a conceptual framework that clearly distinguishes the competencies, skills, and authority to manage disasters from the ones associated with risk management. The first set requires means and ways more linked to first-line responders, equipment, and logistics, while the second set deals mostly with strategic planning, financial resource management, and coordination of multisectorial and actual multi-institutional delivery.

Even in developed countries, these functions tend to be confused. In developing countries, given the resource limitations, they tend to excessively tax the first-line responders. The ISDR Hyogo Plan of Action and the institutional platform it promotes have in many cases complicated institutional relationships and generated rivalries among institutions. For the most part, the crucial actors involved in risk reduction—planning, finance, and budget offices—tend not to prioritize risk reduction. This is because, as mentioned before, the economic burden of disasters is not taken as seriously as other economic and financial considerations—overall economic growth, financial gaps, external deficits, price fluctuations, or employment—ignoring, to the peril of the attainment of other goals, the fact that these macroeconomic variables will be affected by major disasters or bogged down by the repeated occurrence of minor disasters that have cumulative, slow-developing effects.

Insufficient resources for monitoring, uneven institutional practices, and a number of political obstacles have all plagued the effectiveness of any broadening of the legal framework for disaster mitigation, which to some extent has developed since the inception of the first International Decade for Disaster Reduction in the 1990s.

Insurance and Governmental Funds

For all the reasons earlier discussed, there is undoubtedly a need for financial protection instruments to reduce these risks, which seem to be ever-increasing. Moreover, even were there a static level of risk, insurance and other risk-transfer mechanisms remain insufficiently used. Limited risk markets and the predominance of traditional insurance mechanisms imply inappropriate pricing of risk in the market.[14]

This situation prevails as insurers have control of the market and, as has been the case in some regions, in the wake of major catastrophic events, premiums are raised, insurance is denied and coverage becomes either scarce or prohibitively expensive. Government intervention and regulation has tended to be absent, with the dominant perception that "public goods" (the state's responsibility to protect lives and property) become public calamities. Instead, a virtuous circle should be promoted: transparent assessment of risk, pricing, and valuation, leading to risk reduction investment and risk aversion financial strategies that then reduce dependence on credit, subsidies, and direct reconstruction compensation from the state.

A growing number of available instruments are starting to be developed. They are mostly privately operated and generated, although there are a few official, governmentally sponsored pilot mechanisms. These instruments include catastrophic (CAT)[15] bonds, parametric measurement, and financial derivatives and other innovative tools currently in the process of being brought to market. Advances such as the development of parametric insurance policies have also expanded the availability of coverage for countries and households.[16]

In the face of risk and its costs, there are different levels of response. First, there is a level of risk that societies and governments can face, and which can be considered "acceptable" or accepted risk. This refers to recovery and reconstruction needs from recurrent, periodic, or seasonal events of minor magnitude (which can vary in terms of economic implications for different countries and the capacity of the local economy). Above this level, this is a more severe level of risk that nonetheless remains within the bounds of what has been historically observed, with a known recurrence of hazard. Although few countries have special funds or multiannual disaster response and recovery funds, any financing gap at this level tends to be covered by resource transfers within national budgets or through credit and donations. But there is a still higher level of risk, associated with events of such extreme nature and with a long return period that they not only exceed a country's or region's capacity to pay for response and recovery, but also have a negative cost-benefit function. The sources of monies for financing these different levels of risk are diverse (see figure 7.6).

Events with an acceptable level of risk for facing recurrent multihazard events (two to three or slightly more return periods that derive from appropriate and

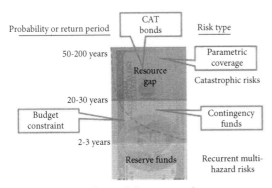

FIGURE 7.6 Establishing risk-financing needs

Source: World Bank presentation on the Caribbean Catastrophe Risk Insurance Facility.

BOX 7.3 } Caribbean Catastrophe Risk Insurance Facility

The Caribbean Catastrophe Risk Insurance Facility (CCRIF), a Caribbean-owned regional institution, is the first regional disaster insurance facility in the world and aims to provide participating governments from the Caribbean with immediate liquidity if hit by a hurricane or earthquake. The CCRIF essentially allows Caribbean countries exposed to adverse natural events to pool their risk together and thus reduce their individual insurance premium by some 40 percent.

A total of 18 CARICOM members and associate member governments have confirmed their participation in the CCRIF. This high level of enrolment will allow the CCRIF to efficiently diversify its portfolio and access reinsurance on better terms.

Following the devastation caused by natural disasters in the Caribbean in 2004, CARICOM heads of government requested the World Bank's assistance in establishing a risk insurance facility for the region. In January 2006, with grant funding from the government of Japan, the World Bank initiated the preparatory studies for the establishment of the CCRIF.

The insured countries are to pay an annual premium proportionate to their own specific risk exposure. For example, annual premiums may vary from US$200,000 to US$2,000,000 for pay-outs that range from US$10 million to US$50 million.

The facility is to act as a risk aggregator and allow participating countries to pool their country-specific risks into a single, better diversified portfolio. Claims payments will depend on the type of natural disaster in a specific area over a certain time period. The parameters for coverage will be determined ahead of time and then triggered automatically after the occurrence of an earthquake or hurricane. The location and severity of the disaster will be confirmed by an independent agency.

Source: IDB Brief for Journalists, February 22, 2007.

updated hazard and vulnerability analyses, charts, and maps) tend to be covered by reserve funds. For events with return periods from this level to 20–30 years, there are two possible sources: (1) budget transfers and reallocations or (2) predisaster established contingency funds (some of which may include some level of insurance or reinsurance but are mostly of the self-insurance type). For events with higher return periods—the really extreme scenarios—budgeting involving current resources is improbable and would introduce rigidity or generate a large "pot" that would be a tempting source of funds in times of budget constraints or downturns in the economic cycle. It is in the face of these extreme events and scenarios that it is recommended that the resource gap be covered through parametric coverage, derivative mechanisms, and CAT bonds.

These new instruments may help overcome political reluctance to engage in insurance purchase, which derives from the minimal benefit for political leaders that enter into insurance contracts. Especially in the absence of concrete quantification of potential impacts, insurance premiums are perceived as costs today with a possible but not certain payoff at some time in the future, when the government may have changed. And because disasters are still also seen as natural phenomena, citizens and politicians cannot be blamed for their occurrence. All of this results in weak incentives for taking relatively complex measures such as purchasing market insurance to offset some of the costs.

Through the development of these instruments, there is a growing convergence between the insurance industry and capital markets. Insurance-linked securities are dramatically changing the market. For example, in the case of the European insurance and reinsurance markets, the CAT bond market has experienced significant growth—between 2005 and 2006 alone it grew from $1.99 billion to $4.69 billion. This growth has been further promoted since the European Commission unveiled the first draft Solvency II directive, which, according to traders and experts, could encourage more risks to be securitized by allowing one to reduce capital requirements.

Disaster contingency funds are a source for multiannual funding and recurrent operational budgets, which is much more attractive than insurance and reinsurance, since it can offer access to resources to be used in preventative, reinforcement, re-engineering, and adaptation projects. For smaller developing countries, these instruments are very attractive, but given their exposure and limited economic size, they may face reduced levels of coverage and ratios of insurance cost to liability as a result of their geographic location. In the Caribbean recently, a reduction of operational costs, transfers and risk sharing by resource pooling, microfinancing and microinsurance mechanisms has been achieved through the Caribbean Catastrophe Risk Insurance Facility (see chapter 6 for a detailed profile).

One recent experience of parametric insurance bought by a government is the Mexican earthquake bond (box 7.4).

These mechanisms additionally provide government funding for support to those segments of society affected, particularly those that cannot access the markets through normal financial institutions as their assets are characterized by undocumented tenure, informality, and a lack of financial access.

The size of these bonds and the amount insured by means of these instruments is a mathematical calculation that requires economic modeling.[17] As indicated several times, it is only through the use of actual assessments that the modeling exercise can offer monetary values associated with the events that are to be protected or insured.

BOX 7.4 } Mexican CAT Bond

In May 2006, the Mexican government placed on financial markets a bond that would ensure compensation in case an earthquake should occur in one of three specific risk areas of the country's Pacific coast, affecting the vicinity of Mexico City. This is the first CAT bond launched by a Latin American country. It is expected to be the first step by the Mexican government in its strategy of increasing its protection against disasters, particularly hurricanes.

The operation comprises two instruments: direct parametric insurance that would provide payment in the case of Mexico suffering an earthquake of a certain magnitude over the next three years in the defined areas. The second is a set of two bonds to cover the principal, which mature in three years or are cancelled if the disaster occurs. The nominal value of the two bonds, US$160 million, adds to the monetary compensation provided in the insurance contracts and brings the total insurance to US$450 million as compensation (US$150 million to be received in case of an earthquake hitting one of the three regions). The cost to Mexico is also divided in two parts: a yearly difference of 230 base points in the CAT bonds and the direct insurance premium of around US$14 million.

This type of operation illustrates the economic benefits of using market insurance to obtain protection against potential shocks associated with natural disasters. The market insurance is more expensive that self-insurance. It is also an instrument that is less subject to political manipulation or distortion, which is an added advantage.

Even though a small, relatively modest operation, Mexico's system took three years to put together, in part due to the intricate process of internal budget approval.

Revision of Systems, Rules, Norms, and Funds

The argument for the revision of current risk management processes at all levels has been made in many instances, with the author moreover providing a range of supplementary elements in this chapter. The crucial and moral imperative to save lives, property, and infrastructure has been firmly established and reiterated—at the international level by the International Disaster Decade in the 1990s and the Hyogo Framework for Action in 2005. The relevance of preserving macroeconomic equilibriums is less evident for policy makers. As was stated, this has to do with the difficulty policy makers have in understanding probability analysis, and the actual economic costs are in many cases based on insufficient and not very reliable data.

There are at present new elements (mostly associated with the certainty of climate change and the already visible implications in terms of the increasing costs of damage and losses) already being faced. Additionally, the capacity to cope and face these increased costs from such hazards, given the vulnerability of smaller, nondiversified, and less developed economies, leads to the search for financial instruments and resources that are not available to regular budgets or via traditional cooperation or development assistance mechanisms.

These new funds are also crucial for affected nations because they allow governments to access resources that provide compensation for the social consequences of disasters, protecting the livelihoods of the more vulnerable social segments of the population. Disaster response, recovery, and reconstruction strategies have also to be expanded from the infrastructural aspects to include the preservation and restoration of economic activity.

The need to review systems, rules, norms, and funds stems from the observation that many of the prevailing rules of risk management and the characteristics of existing disaster funds and compensation mechanisms do not fully address critical strategic questions: not rebuilding vulnerability, reconstruction for livelihood rather than damage needs, the preservation of habitat sustainability over human settlements, and all in a context of sustainable risk-reducing land planning and zoning.

The direct relationship between urban and land planning and risk reduction implies legal modifications and capacity building, since mostly these responsibilities lie with local authorities. From observations in many concrete cases, inadequate zoning, planning, and building and land development permits are not transparent or directly linked to risk analysis, hazard and vulnerability maps, or environmental sustainability. Moving beyond this entails changing regulations to increase transparency and improving the technical competence of officials involved in these processes, as well as reducing their powers of discretion—which tends to be a prevailing situation.

There is also the need to modify or introduce legislation, norms, and regulations for the establishment of financial and economic instruments. Current financial and banking rules, as well as insurance regulations and supervision mechanisms, do not explicitly include these types of instruments and the internal implication of establishing internationally marketed instruments is lacking. Even more importantly, risk appropriation is lacking, meaning the inappropriate transfer, or externalizing, of risk from the individual (be it at the personal or the enterprise and corporate level) to the state, which is then faced with sovereign moral hazard. Thus, there is an uneven burden placed on government. Most crucially, there is little incentive for private (individual, entrepreneurial, or community) appropriation of risk, either through insurance, by the inclusion of risk management as part of the financial viability and profitability formulas of businesses, or through communities' appropriate management of risk in terms of planning, zoning, and building codes' application.

This last issue leads to some crucial social considerations: risk management must be internalized by the community and the population. In multicultural and diverse communities, risk management should not to be seen as an imposition by central government or as merely a technical requirement. In many instances, current risks come from a disregard of local practices and uses, and insufficient consideration of cultural and ethnic diversity, including an adequate gender perspective. The revaluation of these factors seems to be a crucial absent element in current decision-making processes.

These conclusions in terms of policy changes also point out those economic research areas that require analysis and further in-depth study. A crucial issue, as this chapter has indicated, is that the economic costs in terms of damages and losses of actual disasters and projections of what those costs will be when they occur is still elusive. Additional case studies of specific disasters, further development and application of existing assessment methodologies (namely the Damage and Loss Assessment methodology developed by the ECLAC), and further research on modeling disasters from an economic perspective (what kind of economic impact is to be associated with a specific parametric event) are crucial, beyond the need that insurers may have for these figures. Additionally, the relationship (and potential correlation) between the recurrence of disasters and climate change needs enhanced multidisciplinary research.

Notes

1. For a review of existing concepts, practice, and applications, see Bankoff, Frerks, G., and Hilhorst (2004).

2. See http://www.imf.org/external/np/exr/facts/vul.htm.

3. See http://www3.cepal.org.mx/iadb-eclac-project/.

4. See http://www.unisdr.org.

5. See http://www.ipcc.ch/ipccreports/ar4-syr.htm.

6. These indicators are based on the measures laid out in the road map to implementation of the United Nations Millennium Declaration (Secretary-General Report to GA A/56/326), but have been modified to capture the risk reduction element.

7. See http://www.unisdr.org/disaster-statistics/introduction.htm.

8. Jacques Aigrain, CEO, Swiss Re, quoted in http://www.swissre.com/pws/about%20us/knowledge_expertise/top%20topics/our%20position%20and%20objectives.html?contentI DR=c21767004561734fb900fb2ee2bd2155&useDefaultText=0&useDefaultDesc=0. Accessed February 20, 2009.

9. Can be found at http://www.hm-treasury.gov.uk/stern_review_report.htm. Accessed February 20, 2009.

10. The fifth meeting of the *Global Roundtable on Climate Change* convened February 12–13, 2008 at Columbia University. See http://www.earth.columbia.edu/grocc/. Accessed February 20, 2009.

11. See United States *Climate Change Fact Sheet*, released by the White House, Office of the Press Secretary, Washington, DC, June 30, 2005, at http://georgewbush-whitehouse.archives.gov/news/releases/2005/06/20050630-16.html. Accessed February 20, 2009.

12. See http://www.preventionweb.net/globalplatform/. Accessed February 20, 2009.

13. See Senator Pete V. Domenici and Sen. Jeff Bingaman, *Design Elements of a Mandatory Market-Based Greenhouse Gas Regulatory System* (February 2006), at http://energy.senate.gov/public/_files/ClimateChangeWhitePaper.doc. Accessed February 20, 2009.

14. For a very recent discussion on the role of financial instruments in reducing risk and insecurity in the face of natural hazards, economic instability, and other aspects such as social unrest and conflict, see United Nations (DESA), *World Economic and Social Survey 2008, Overcoming Economic Insecurity*, Department of Economic Affairs, New York, 2008 (E/2008/50/Rev.1, ST/ESA/317).

15. A catastrophic bond is a high-yield debt instrument that is usually insurance-linked and meant to raise money in case of a catastrophe such as a hurricane or earthquake. It has a special condition that states that if the issuer (insurance or reinsurance company) suffers a loss from a particular predefined catastrophe, then the issuer's obligation to pay interest and/or repay the principal is either deferred or completely forgiven. CAT bonds are not closely linked with the stock market or economic conditions and offer significant attractions to investors. For example, for the same level of risk, investors can usually obtain a higher yield with CAT bonds relative to alternative investments. Another benefit is that the insurance risk securitization of CATs shows no correlation with equities or corporate bonds, meaning they would

provide a good diversification of risks. Investopedia, http://www.investopedia.com/terms/c/catastrophebond.asp. Accessed February 20, 2009).

16. Instead of basing payments on an estimate of the damage suffered, parametric insurance contracts establish the pay-out as a function of the occurrence or intensity of certain natural phenomena, as determined by a specialized agency such as the US National Hurricane Center or the US National Earthquake Information Center. In this way, the transaction costs and uncertainty associated with insurance payments are considerably reduced. There is no need to verify and estimate damages, and no potential disagreement or litigation about the pay-outs. Moreover, the country has immediate access to the resources when the disaster takes place. See Eduardo Borensztein, Eduardo Cavallo, and Patricio Valenzuela, *Debt Sustainability under Catastrophic Risk: The Case for Government Budget Insurance*, IMF/IDB, June 2007.

17. See Mechler et al. (2005).

References

Bankoff, G., Frerks, G., and Hilhorst, D. (2004). *Mapping Vulnerability: Disasters, Development and People*. London: Earthscan.

Bingaman, J., and Domenici, P. V. (2006). "Design Elements of a Mandatory Market-Based Greenhouse Gas Regulatory System." Accessed February 20, 2009. http://energy.senate.gov/public/_files/ClimateChangeWhitePaper.doc.

Borensztein, E., Cavallo, E., and Valenzuela, P. (2007). "Debt Sustainability under Catastrophic Risk: The Case for Government Budget Insurance." Inter-American Development Bank Working Paper WP 607, Washington, D.C.

EM-DAT. The OFDA/CRED International Disaster Database, Université Catholique de Louvain, Brussels. http:// www.em-dat.net.

Intergovernmental Panel on Climate Change (IPCC). (2007, 2008). "Climate Change 2007." Fourth Assessment Report, Cambridge: Cambridge University Press. Accessed February 20, 2009. http://www.ipcc.ch/#.

ISDR (2008). *Indicators of Progress: Guidance on Measuring the Reduction of Disaster Risks and the Implementation of the Hyogo Framework for Action*. Geneva: United Nations, International Strategy for Disaster Risk Reduction.

Mechler, R., Hochrainer, S., Pflug, G., and Linnerooth-Bayer, J. (2005). "Modeling Financial Disaster Risk Management in Developing Countries." American Geophysical Union, Fall Meeting, San Francisco, Calif.

Munich Re Group. NatCatSERVICE statistical database. Accessed February 20, 2009. http:// www.munichre.com/en/ts/geo_risks/natcatservice/default.aspx,

Stern, N. (2007). *The Economics of Climate Change*. The Stern Review. Cambridge: Cambridge University Press.

United Nations (2008). *World Economic and Social Survey 2008: Overcoming Economic Insecurity*. Department of Economic Affairs, New York (E/2008/50/Rev.1, ST/ESA/317).

Zapata-Marti, Ricardo. (2011). "Strategies for Coping with Climate Change in Latin America. In H. G. Brauch, U. O. Spring, C. Mesjasz, et al., eds., *Coping with Global Environmental Change, Disasters and Security Threats, Challenges, Vulnerabilities and Risks*, pp. 1341–1355. New York: Springer.

Zapata-Marti, Ricardo, and Saldaña, Sergio. (2011). "Cambio Climatico y Desastres." In Simone Lucatello and Daniel Rodríguez Velázquez, coordinators, *Las dimensiones sociales del cambio climático: Un panorama desde México. ¿Cambio social o crisis ambiental?* Cuauhtémoc, Mexico: Colección Cooperación Internacional.

PART II

Case Studies of Natural Disasters

8 }

Natural Disasters in Vietnam
A SYNTHESIS FROM A SOCIOECONOMIC PERSPECTIVE
Tran Huu Tuan and Bui Dung The

Introduction

Lying in the tropical monsoon area of the northwestern Pacific, Vietnam is one of the most disaster-prone countries in the world. It is affected by many kinds of disasters (in this chapter, "disasters" generally refers to natural disasters), such as floods, storms, tropical depressions, storm surges, whirlwinds, flash floods, coastline erosion, hail, rains, droughts, and landslides. Disasters occur in every part of the country and in every season of the year, causing huge losses in terms of lives and assets, and destroying socioeconomic and cultural infrastructures, as well as the natural environment. Disasters are the main obstacle to economic development because they result in environmental degradation and they widen the poverty gap and increase the poverty rate in the population, especially in disaster-prone areas. In the last 10 years, extreme events have killed more than 7,500 people, and have seriously damaged assets, with losses estimated to be equivalent to about 1.5 percent of the country's GDP. The disasters afflicting Vietnam have increased in terms of severity, as well as frequency (CCFSC 2005; SRV 2007).

This chapter sets out to reach a better understanding of disasters in Vietnam through a review of relevant case studies, policies, plans, and strategies. The focus is on the socioeconomic aspects of disasters such as socioeconomic and poverty impacts, adaptation strategies, and institutional arrangements from national to local levels. This chapter includes:

- a brief introduction to the geography, climate, and socioeconomic situation of Vietnam, as well as its disaster profile;
- an analytical review of the socioeconomic, health, and environmental impacts of disasters in Vietnam;
- a discussion of the country's strategies for mitigating disasters at national, meso (i.e., provincial, district, and communal), and household levels; and
- a conclusion and discussion of future research in the field.

The authors would like to acknowledge the Centre for Research on the Epidemiology of Disasters for financial support in the writing of this chapter.

179

This synthesis was prepared using documentary research methods. Secondary data and previous studies were gathered from national and local authorities, academic and research institutes, related projects, and websites. Among the constraints and challenges was the limited availability of research reports on disasters in Vietnam: disaster research in Vietnam is at an early stage. Most studies done so far are descriptive in nature and cover only a small study area. Second, there are even fewer studies concerned with the socioeconomic aspects of disasters in particular. Third, there may be case studies of disasters in Vietnam that were unknowingly omitted.

Background

VIETNAM'S GEOGRAPHY, CLIMATE, AND SOCIOECONOMIC STATUS

Geographical Location and Topography

Vietnam, located in southeast Asia, has a coastal line of 3,260 km, from the Chinese border in the north to the frontier with Cambodia in the Gulf of Thailand (SRV 2007).

The country's topography is rather diverse, including mountains, hills, rivers, plains, coastlines, and islands. Three fourths of the country is covered by mountains and hills. Vietnam has a rather dense river network with 2,360 rivers. Plains are usually situated in the lower reaches of rivers and only account for a quarter of the territorial area. The Red River Delta in the north and Mekong River Delta in the south are the country's two biggest plains. Vietnam is divided into seven economic regions based on its topography: the Northern Mountains, the Red River Delta, the North Central Coast, the South Central Coast, the Central Highlands, the Eastern South, and the Mekong River Delta (MoNRE 2003; SRV 2007).

Climate

Vietnam has a monsoon tropical climate with high temperature and humidity. There is significant variation in climate between regions. The north is affected by the northeast monsoon and has two typical seasons: the hot season from May to October and the cold season from November to April. The south is mainly affected by the southeast monsoon with heat and wetness year round. Both parts of the country have different climate subregions depending on geographical features and topographic position.

Temperature varies slightly between regions; mean temperature in the summer varies from 25 to 30°C. There are large variations, however, in average monthly temperatures—about 10 to 15°C in the north and 2 to 3°C in the south. There are about 100 rainy days with a total rainfall amount of 1,500 to 2,000 mm per year. About 80–90 percent of rainfall is concentrated into the rainy season. Annual rainfall also varies in different regions, ranging from 600 to 5,000 mm. Floods and inundation usually occur during the rainy season, while drought happens in the dry season because rainfall is distributed unevenly during the year. Every year there are 6 to 10 storms and tropical depressions directly affecting Vietnam and causing heavy rains and floods. Storms and tropical depressions often occur from June to November but mainly in September and October. Most of them occur in central and northern coastal provinces of the country, with very few in the southern part (MoNRE 2003). Given such climate conditions, the country is exposed to a regular threat of storms, tropical low pressures, floods, and other disasters.

Socioeconomic Conditions

In 2007, the population of Vietnam was 85.2 million, of which females make up 50.9 percent. Twenty-seven percent live in urban areas. The population growth rate is 1.21 percent. The poverty rate for the whole country is 14.8 percent, though this varies across localities. Average life expectancy is 71 years. The GDP structure of the country is 20.3 percent for agriculture, forestry, and fishery; 41.6 percent for industry and construction; and about 38 percent for services (GSO 2008). Although the agriculture, forestry, and fishery sector occupies the smallest share of the country's GDP, it plays an important social security role, especially for the population that lives in rural areas.

The Vietnamese economy has grown at more than 7 percent annually in the last two decades. This trend is expected to continue for the next decade. The high economic growth rate and high speed of urbanization place heavy pressure on the environment and natural resources. Overexploitation of natural resources, deforestation, and environmental pollution also increase the risk of natural hazards and disasters (SRV 2007; Chaudhry and Ruysschaert 2007).

PROFILE OF NATURAL DISASTERS IN VIETNAM

Vietnam's geographic location and topographical conditions generate particular climate characteristics that result in severe and diversified natural disasters in Vietnam. The country suffers from many types of disasters: floods, storms, tropical depressions, storm surges, inundations, whirlwinds, flash floods, river bank and coastline erosion, drought, landslides, and forest fires. Disasters occur all year round in Vietnam, but there are typical disasters in each season and particular characteristics in each area.

As shown in figure 8.1, the frequency of disasters in Vietnam has increased. The greatest threat to Vietnam is flooding. During the flood season, heavy rainfall upstream causes high discharges and large-scale flooding. There are different flood patterns in different regions of the country. In North Vietnam, flooding normally occurs from May to September, earlier than in other regions. On average, there are three to five floods in the region every year. River floods in the South Central Coast area occur from September to December. This region is characterized by short and steep river systems with rapid flows. Dyke systems in this region are inadequate or incomplete. Floods also spread across the floodplains, causing huge losses. Floods in the Mekong River Delta are caused by upstream floods and are also directly influenced by tides and the capacity of upstream reservoirs to hold waters. Floods in the Mekong River Delta usually last for a long time (four to five months), causing

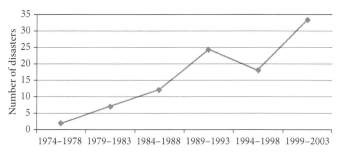

FIGURE 8.1 Number of natural disasters in Vietnam

Source: D. Guha-Sapir, D. Hargitt, and P. Hoyois (2004). *Thirty Years of Natural Disasters 1974–2003: The Numbers.*
Louvain, Belgium: UCL Press, Louvain Catholic University.

inundation in almost all areas of the delta. Floods occur in other regions of the country as well, but less severely (SRV 2007; Ninh 2008).

Typhoons are also one of the major disaster types afflicting Vietnam. Typhoons raise
sea levels and cause storm surges and inundation. They destroy houses, buildings, and
infrastructure in affected areas and generate waves that can damage sea dykes protecting coastal areas. The torrential rains that accompany typhoons can cause flash floods
and submerge low-lying areas, causing losses to agriculture and fisheries. The runoff
from typhoon rains, added to rivers that are already full because of monsoon rains,
creates floods that endanger river dykes and threaten to destroy millions of households
and other assets. On average, Vietnam suffers directly from four to six typhoons per
year, which cause heavy rainfall and extensive flooding. Between 1954 and 2006, there
were 380 typhoons and tropical depressions affecting Vietnam, of which 31 percent hit
the North, 36 percent the Northern Central and Middle Central regions, and 33 percent the South Central and the South. It is estimated that 80 to 90 percent of Vietnam's
population can be affected by typhoons (SRV 2007; CCFSC 2008).

Flash and mud floods, meanwhile, often occur in mountainous and hilly areas.
In recent years, flash floods have become more frequent in Vietnam with two to four
events per year. Flash floods usually occur suddenly and on a small scale but can be
very severe and cause major human and asset losses (SRV 2007).

Drought is considered the third source of major risk, after typhoons and floods. In
recent years, drought has recurred in many regions of the country. The most affected
areas were central provinces, particularly in 1997, 1998, 2000, 2002, and early 2004.
In 1998, severe drought destroyed tens of thousands of hectares of rice and other
crops, and caused numerous forest fires. This drought caused severe water shortages
for nearly three million people in the Central and Central Highlands provinces, and
drained small reservoirs throughout the region (CCFSC 2005).

Other types of disasters such as inundation, salinity intrusion, landslides, erosion, whirlwinds, cyclones, earthquakes, tsunamis, and sea surges happen in different regions and at different times in Vietnam. There is an increasing trend toward
extremes of precipitation and temperature, while extreme events such as floods,
storms, and other disasters have become more frequent in recent decades. In particular, devastating floods and heavy storms have increased in frequency, intensity,

and severity as global warming has increased (Viner et al. 2006; SRV 2007; CCFSC 2008; Ninh 2008; Tran et al. 2008).

Socioeconomic Impacts of Natural Disasters in Vietnam

Vietnam has suffered from a number of extremely destructive disasters. In 1997, Typhoon Linda killed nearly 3,000 people in the Mekong Delta provinces; Linda was considered as the most devastating disaster for Vietnam in the twentieth century. In 1999, the Central Vietnam region was inundated by a record-breaking flood that killed 715 people, inundated nearly one million houses, swept away thousands of houses, and caused economic losses of nearly 5,000 billion dong ($287 million). This represented one of the greatest disaster-related damage losses in Vietnam during the twentieth century (CCFSC 2005). In November 2008, floods in the 20 northern provinces and the capital city Hanoi led to at least 85 deaths, destroyed or damaged more than 100,000 houses, and significantly affected infrastructure and agricultural crops. The US Embassy in Hanoi reported total economic losses of more than $440 million (USAID 2008).

According to Guha-Sapir, Hargitt, and Hoyois (2004), between 1974 and 2003, the total number of victims (people killed and affected) by natural disasters in Vietnam was 69,847,607 (or 2,328,254 per year, on average). Over the period 1989 to 2003, total economic losses reported were $3,064 million, or $204 million per year on average.

According to SRV (2007), disasters in Vietnam have caused tremendous loss of life and property. Disasters are considered an obstacle to economic growth and sustainable development. They increase poverty and are a big impediment to the achievement of the Millennium Development Goals. They have led to considerable damage with severe economic consequences. For example, in 2005, disasters in Vietnam killed 272 people, affected more than 856,000 people, and caused more than $295 million in damage (table 8.1). As a consequence, people's living standards decreased, and the process of hunger alleviation and poverty reduction was obstructed and delayed, especially in regions suffering a high frequency of disasters. Disasters affect the development of education, destroy educational infrastructure, and interrupt school time, especially in mountainous areas and the Mekong River Delta. Disasters also cause great problems for vulnerable people such as the elderly, disabled, women, and children.

TABLE 8.1 } Natural Disasters in Vietnam (2005)

Disaster type	Number of disasters	People killed	People affected	Sum of damage US$ (000)
Drought	1		410,000	42,120
Flood	5	184	101,893	34,000
Windstorm	4	88	344,160	219,250
Total	10	272	856,053	295,370

Source: Guha-Sapir, Hargitt, and Hoyois 2004.

ECONOMIC IMPACTS

Natural disasters in Vietnam have a significant impact on people's lives. The most affected sectors include agriculture, aquaculture, infrastructure, and animal husbandry.

The Impact on Agriculture

Vietnam is heavily dependent on its natural resources, particularly agriculture and fisheries with almost three quarters of the population living in rural areas (Viner et al. 2006). As pointed out by Chaudhry and Ruysschaert (2007), the long duration of floods, storms, typhoons, salt water intrusion, and droughts affect agriculture in terms of growing periods, crop calendars and crop distribution, pest increases, and virus activity. These changes cause the reduction in yields of the main crops. However, aggregate damage was not estimated.

Adger (1998) shows that typhoons have a great impact on rice cultivation in Nam Dinh province, though salt production and other agricultural activities tend not to be impacted. Storms disrupt the harvest and damage the rice seedlings being prepared for the second crop. Viner et al. (2006) find that the annual cycle of flooding, tropical storms, and cyclones that bring high winds, very intense rainfall, flash flooding, and storm surges affect the Red River Delta region several times a year, causing extensive and repeated agricultural losses. Chinh (2008) investigates the impact of storms and floods on households and communities, and finds that floods and storms have a major impact on agricultural production. For instance, surveyed households outside the sea dyke area suffered a 38 to 45 percent production loss, compared to a 36 to 39 percent loss for those families located inside the dykes.

Ninh, Trung, and Niem (2007), in a study of the Mekong River Delta, found that devastating floods and long-lasting inundation had an impact on the rice crop, causing low yields and crop losses. Floods with strong currents aggravated by high winds and sea surges are a danger to irrigation systems. Floods that are less violent but inundate large areas over long periods have major economic impacts. Floods and inundation cause losses of food stocks, as well as crops in the field. Drought and salt water intrusion during the dry season affect the summer rice crop.

A number of studies have investigated disaster impacts in Central Vietnam. Malin (2005) examines the resilience and vulnerability of people in two districts in Quang Tri and Thua Thien Hue provinces who experienced the 1999 flood. The study finds that some poor people in the flood areas lost almost all crops and part of their land.

Lap, Oanh, and Hirai (2005), in a study of coastal lagoons in Thua Thien Hue province in central Vietnam, finds that saltwater intrusion makes agricultural land unsuitable for rice cultivation; farmers have to switch to fish farming but ultimately abandon it. The study also finds that as most of the land is flat and badly drained floodwater does not drain away, adversely affecting daily life and the economic activity of local households. Inundation and salinization badly affect local socioeconomic development.

In a study of coastal communities in Quang Tri province, Huy (2007) found that due to saltwater intrusion, households in coastal communities have less cultivated land and land has become too degraded for agricultural production. Households lack the financial resources needed to buy farming inputs, while their crops cannot cope with disasters and reduced land quality.

Suu and My (2008) assessed livelihoods and the vulnerability to disasters in the Huong River basin in Thua Thien Hue province. The study found that long-lasting and consecutive flooding prevents planting of crops in affected areas. Tran et al. (2008) investigated the impacts of floods on the economy, environment, and society in Thua Thien Hue. The study found that floods have an impact on most sources of income because of the way that they destroy crops in the rice field. Tran et al. (2009) observe that, in the dry season, low rainfall and saltwater intrusion around river estuaries in Thua Thien Hue province badly affect agriculture and aquatic resources.

Most of the studies reviewed above illustrate that agriculture as a climate-sensitive sector is significantly affected by natural disasters. More needs to be done, however, to calculate the losses caused by natural disasters.

Impacts on Aquaculture and Fisheries

Vietnam started a reform program in 1986, aiming to transform itself from a centrally planned economy to a market-based economy. As a consequence, thousands of hectares of agricultural land and wetlands were converted into aquaculture ponds in coastal areas (e.g., see Tuan et al. 2009; Tran et al. 2008). Aquaculture helped to generate employment, bring in income, and improve the livelihood of local people. However, aquaculture is highly vulnerable to flooding. Hong (2002) reported that the 1999 flood destroyed more than 1,000 hectares of pond area and damaged 2,500 hectares of net enclosures in the lagoon area in Thua Thien Hue province. Floods swept away aquaculture products and destroyed fish and shrimp ponds in Central Vietnam (Tran et al. 2008). This study found that about 25 percent of surveyed households working in aquaculture are affected each year by floods. Floods and storms overcome the dyke systems and breakwaters built to protect aquaculture in the Red River Delta, causing losses to aquaculture production (Chinh 2008). For example, Chinh observed that storms numbered six and seven in 2005 led to the breakdown of all breakwaters in the study area; unharvested aquaculture products were entirely lost due to the sea tide flowing over breakwaters. Damage to aquaculture affects the livelihood of local people, especially in areas where disasters occur frequently (Suu and My 2008). Viner et al. (2006) found that annual floods, tropical storms, and cyclones in the Red River Delta caused extensive losses to fisheries.

Impacts on Animal Husbandry

Most households in rural Vietnam have investments in animal husbandry, which, at the household level, not only helps farmers to increase income and diversify income sources but also provides organic fertilizer for agricultural production.

When disasters hit rural households, almost everything in the households can be destroyed or lost, including livestock (Malin 2005). Ninh, Trung, and Niem (2007) observe that in the Mekong River Delta livestock was drowned or washed away in floods. Further, any livestock surviving a flood may succumb to epidemics in the aftermath. This suggests that losses of animals represent for many rural households a significant proportion of the losses they suffer because of flooding.

Impacts on Infrastructure

Natural disasters have had a widespread impact on infrastructure in Vietnam. For example, the 1999 flood had enormous effects on infrastructure in Thua Thien Hue province. Floodwater broke through floodgates, inundating areas near the lagoon with sea water (PCFSC 2000). The flood caused the collapse of 1,027 schools and 25,056 houses, and destroyed many roads, bridges, and telecommunication systems (Nam 2008).

Infrastructure such as sea dykes, roads between villages, and main roads in coastal communities in Central Vietnam has been damaged by floods and erosion brought about by storms. Houses built on sandy ground, houses constructed with simple materials and electricity poles collapsed or were destroyed by storms and floods (Huy 2007). During the rainy season, crops, infrastructure, and the inhabitants of river basins suffer huge losses due to disastrous floods and storms. Floods isolate villages, prevent access to services, and lead to the suspension of business activities. Thus, many economic opportunities are lost because floods and inundations lead to communities becoming isolated (Tran et al. 2008); their research shows that 41 percent of surveyed households experienced serious damage to community roads in the study area.

Floods, storms, and cyclones frequently damage buildings and infrastructure in the Red River Delta (Chinh 2008; Viner et al. 2006). Storms often bring in heavy rains that cause high-level floods in the area. For example, storm number five in October 2007 caused floods in many places in the Red River Delta. More than 67 people died, thousands of dwellings and many bridges and roads were damaged, and thousands of hectares of paddy rice, maize, and vegetables were destroyed.

Ninh, Trung, and Niem (2007) found that severe floods destroyed infrastructure such as roads, houses, embankments, and canals in the Mekong River Delta. Floods that are less violent but inundate large areas over long periods cause damage to property and houses, which might be under floodwater for a long time, weakening building structures and rendering possessions unusable.

POVERTY IMPACTS

The poor have fewer options for coping with disasters. They have fewer assets, almost no insurance, and less diversified sources of income. A disaster can push them into a downward spiral of *destitution* (World Bank 2001). When resources have been depleted by crop losses, debts, and high medical costs, a severe flood can push a household further into debt and can lead to out-migration or the further erosion of their livelihood base by forcing them to sell vital assets (Miller 2003). The poor often experienced relatively more damage to their houses because of poor quality construction. The study of the 1999 flood in Central Vietnam by Malin (2005) reports that the better-off lost more in absolute terms, while the losses of the poor, though not as heavy, had a relatively greater impact on their livelihoods. This implies that poverty can increase vulnerability in terms of increased exposure and/ or decreased capacity to cope and to recover. In other words, there is a two-way relationship between poverty and vulnerability to natural disasters.

Poverty and vulnerability to floods are integrally linked and mutually reinforcing in a vicious circle (Tran et al. 2008). The poor in coastal communities suffer from disasters more often than those that are better-off because they have little or no savings, little income or production options, and limited resources to mitigate the *ex-post* impact of disasters. They are also more vulnerable and recover more slowly (Huy 2007). The 1999 flood in Thua Thien Hue province was extremely traumatic for villagers, particularly for those living in temporary or poorly constructed houses. Poor households have the ground floor set at a lower level than better-off households, and thus the poor are more exposed to floodwater (Tran et al. 2008). Consistent with Malin (2005), this study concluded that, in absolute terms, the flood caused more economic impact and damages to the better-off and medium households, but for the poor, the losses represented a larger proportion of their income and assets. Furthermore, because damage to assets and livelihoods by one disaster often make households more vulnerable to future impacts, vulnerability to disaster risks is cyclical.

Tran et al. (2008) found that local households tend to lose their houses, assets, and livelihoods after flooding, thus they are forced to heavily exploit natural resources for survival. The pressure of high population growth and high population density in the region also causes overexploitation of aquatic resources in vulnerable areas. For example, runoff of fertilizers and pesticides is caused by intensive agricultural practices, and organic effluent from towns and villages in the surrounding areas is discharged directly into coastal lagoons. These practices cause degradation or decline of lagoon resources. As a result, poor households, whose livelihoods depend mainly on these resources, are the most affected.

Malin (2005) concludes that the poor are most at risk of sinking deeper into poverty because of floods. For most of the vulnerable households, increased poverty is a gradual process, to which floods contribute but are not the only factor. Insufficient paddy fields, poor health, frequent crop losses, and animal husbandry losses make the situation in rural areas very difficult even without disasters. The lack of resources that has led to their poverty before a disaster continues to be a constraint to their recovery from disaster losses.

SOCIAL IMPACTS

Natural disasters have negative effects not only for individual households but also for the community as a whole. Tran et al. (2008) found that community cohesion was stronger and people tended to help each other more after the severe 1999 flood. The study also observed that community cohesion was stronger at first, but then weakened due to the stress of the flooding and the recovery process. During the flood season, the laborers in the affected coastal area of Thua Thien Hue migrated to cities to find jobs (IMOLA 2006). This had the effect of increasing the risk for the people left behind, especially the infirm and elderly, because communities were left without adequate human resources for flood response and recovery. Further, the study observed that a large number of children could not go to school during the flood season, and a large proportion of these children may permanently drop out of school (IMOLA 2006). Similar problems were also reported by Ninh, Trung, and Niem (2007). Elderly and disabled people may face serious health problems during flood periods; school time can be disrupted for long periods, especially when buildings require repairs. Malin (2005) observed that the communities in Central Vietnam had great capacity to respond to the 1999 flood and that a large proportion of the population received support from the government, civil societies, and NGOs. This enabled them to gradually recover. Local organizations with the authority and credibility to organize collective action, an active local government with strong linkages to the villages, and a relatively equitable distribution of resources are important factors helping communities and households cope with and recover from this sort of exogenous shock. The homogeneity of the community is also an important factor for resilience. In line with Adger and Kelly (1999), Malin argues that vulnerability to shocks is not just related to individually controlled resources but also to the overall resilience of the community.

Social networks are very relevant for access to resources, when disaster relief supplies are provided. People without a family network in the area face many difficulties. State authorities, the cooperatives, community organizations (Women's Union, Youth Union, veterans' organizations, farmers' associations, etc.), professional organizations, and religious bodies have played important roles in helping communities to cope with and recover from floods. For example, cooperatives in affected communities in Central Vietnam are key institutions for giving the poor access to resources. Access to irrigation and drainage via the cooperatives is institutionalized and collectively organized for all members of the community. After the 1999 flood, there were shortages of piglets and seedlings. Households had to wait until the local authorities and community organizations provided seedlings before they could reinvest in agricultural production. The Buddhist societies played a major role in mobilizing and distributing relief supplies to meet basic needs. In some communities there are Christian groups, which were also active in the relief work (Malin 2005).

Ninh, Trung, and Niem (2007) showed that, after disasters, community organizations, cooperatives, the Red Cross, and other local organizations in the Mekong River Delta take part in organizing the repair of houses and infrastructure, and clean up the environment. People organize labor teams to help each other to restore agricultural fields that were filled with sand and wastes. The study concludes that when there is a major impact from a disaster, local government, community organizations, and community groups take action together to handle the immediate aftermath.

Suu and My (2008) found that community organizations helped households obtain loans, buy health insurance, and access agricultural extension services. When a disaster occurs, local people help each other to rebuild destroyed houses.

Huy (2007) found that people in coastal communities at his study site have strong family and kinship relationships that help them cope with disasters. The study also revealed that in the area examined, however, disaster response and mitigation were compromised by weak leadership, weak community organizations, weak organizational structures, and weak collaboration with government and administrative structures. Decision-making processes were sometimes ineffective because poor groups in the community could be excluded; participation in community affairs and disaster mitigation plans may be unequal.

ENVIRONMENTAL IMPACTS

Rapid population growth and overuse of natural resources have led to environmental destruction. Human activities such as the conversion of wetlands and agricultural lands to shrimp ponds, and the construction of roads and infrastructure without taking into account their environmental impacts have adverse effects on the environment (Tuan et al. 2009). These practices, combined with inappropriate management of natural resources, lead to the deterioration and degradation of the environment, and make some areas more vulnerable to the effects of disasters.

Natural disasters also contribute to environmental degradation. The 1999 floods in Quang Tri and Thua Thien Hue provinces, for example, uprooted many hectares of trees and caused many landslides despite extended forest cover (Malin 2005).

HEALTH IMPACTS

An indirect impact of disasters is the generation and spreading of enormous quantities of waste including hazardous waste, vegetation, soil, sediment, waste from dumpsites and septic tanks, healthcare waste, demolition debris from destroyed buildings, and waste generated by relief operations. This waste poses risks to human health. Sanitation facilities are often destroyed. The displacement of families from severely affected places to safer locations puts a further strain on local sanitation systems. Sanitation facilities at relief camps are difficult to manage adequately, causing additional wastewater. Disasters reduce already limited access to safe drinking water and sanitation facilities in communities at risk. Floodwater increases the risk of water-borne diseases (Tran et al. 2008). The study found that 55 percent of respondents claimed that annual floods caused serious damage to sanitation systems.

There are only a few studies focusing on the health risk associated with climate hazards in Vietnam. The incidence of diarrhea is known to increase after typhoons and floods; skin disease and conjunctivitis increase because of water contamination. Respiratory diseases and dengue also are associated with floods (see, e.g., Few, Tran, and Hong 2004; Few and Tran 2007; Few, Ha, and Chinh 2007). It should be noted that these studies did not include any quantitative measurements of the health effects.

Long-lasting inundation caused serious problems to individuals' health in the Mekong River Delta, particularly to elderly and disabled persons living in poor conditions with limited food stocks, unclean water sources, and poor sanitation. Epidemic diseases such as marsh fever, dengue fever, and diarrhea, among many others, also spread after flooding (Ninh, Trung, and Niem 2007; Few and Tran 2007).

Kien, Shaw, and Ninh (2008) review the current and potential impacts of climate change and disasters on human health, vulnerability, and adaptation capacity in Vietnam. Their study reveals that people living in coastal communities are extremely vulnerable to health impacts caused by floods and storms. The study addresses a number of challenges and shortcomings of the public health system in Vietnam. For example, the impact of socioeconomic reforms on the health system have not been considered properly; health-related policies are made in a conventional top-down and centralized manner; and the risks of dengue, malaria, pneumonia, and water-related diseases remain high due to poor public health environment and sanitation. The study also suggests that it is necessary to include explicitly health-related issues in an integrated assessment of disaster impacts and vulnerability. Such an initiative would assist key institutions and personnel in building the capacity needed for handling the integration of disasters into the health sector.

A review of the existing literature shows that the economic, social, environmental, and health impact of natural disasters in Vietnam is documented by a limited number of studies. The data are incomplete, however, and few reliable quantitative estimates exist of the effects of natural disasters on the country. Most evidence for the impact of disasters on economic sectors is available for agriculture, aquaculture and fisheries, infrastructure, and livestock. However, the impact on other sectors such as tourism and recreation, forestry, and biodiversity are little touched upon. Those studies and papers that do report the economic costs of disasters provide, however, only tentative numbers. Furthermore, no attempt has been made to distinguish between the short- and long-term effects, or the direct and indirect effects of disasters.

Disaster Prevention, Response, and Mitigation in Vietnam

To effectively prevent and mitigate natural disasters, especially floods and storms, agencies have been established at different administrative levels, and in different sectors and localities. The responsibilities of the agencies at each level are briefly discussed below.

At the national level, the Central Committee for Flood and Storm Control (CCFSC) is responsible for assisting the government in observing and investigating the establishment and implementation of the annual flood and storm preparedness solutions and plans. The CCFSC also issues mandates mobilizing labor forces and equipment, so that pressing situations can be responded to. The CCFSC has authority over local administrations and can instruct them to act in the face of the consequences of floods and storms. In addition, the CCFSC organizes workshops on disaster preparedness and mitigation as a way of sharing experience, lessons, and technologies for disaster preparedness and mitigation.

In the provinces, districts, and communes, People's Committees establish local Committees for Flood and Storm Control (CFSC). These are responsible for helping the respective People's Committee to build and implement flood and storm protection measures in the relevant area, by, for example, organizing dyke protection, encouraging flood and storm preparedness and mitigation, and dealing with the flood aftermath.

Line ministries and central authorities also establish Sector Committees for Flood and Storm Control. The main responsibilities of these committees include implementing flood and storm preparedness and mitigation measures; protecting people, physical, and technical materials under the Sector Committee's management; managing materials and equipment to be used in contingencies; timely supply of materials and equipment to affected areas in emergency situations and providing support in the aftermath of a flood or storm.

NATIONAL STRATEGIES

Flood and storm prevention, response, and mitigation have been considered important measures for socioeconomic development in Vietnam, especially since 1986. The Vietnamese state has put forward a strategy to deal with natural disasters through the Ordinance on Dykes (1989), the Ordinance on Flood and Storm Control (1993), the Strategy for Water Disaster (1994), the Law on Dykes (2006), and multiple decrees guiding the implementation of these laws and ordinances. In 2007, the National Strategy for Natural Disaster Prevention, Response and Mitigation to 2020 was approved by the prime minister (SRV 2007).

This National Strategy addresses both general and region-specific measures for disaster preparedness, response, and mitigation. General measures include:

- consolidation of the system of law, policy making, and organizational structures;
- development of human resources and social mobilization;
- increasing financial resources;
- raising community awareness;
- research related to disaster prevention, response, and mitigation;
- ensuring the effectiveness of dyke, reservoir, and dam systems;
- enhancing search and rescue capacities; and
- promoting international cooperation and integration. Specific measures are proposed for different regions (see table 8.2).

In recent years, the government has made considerable efforts to prevent and mitigate disasters. Physical and technical infrastructures for disaster preparedness have been improved, and substantial progress has been made in coordinating disaster response, central to local levels. Important policies and decisions have been put in place, for example, policies for the "living with floods" areas (Mekong River Delta), flood diversion and retarding areas (Northern region) and "avoidance and adaptation" areas (Central region). Much structural work has been done such as reservoir building, dyke upgrading, boat and ship shelter building, and so on. Nonstructural solutions have also been put in place including forest rehabilitation, renovation of communication systems, improvement of forecasting, international cooperation, community awareness raising, and consolidation of organizational mechanisms for flood and storm control and for search and rescue (SRV 2007).

There have been some recent achievements in disaster prevention, response, and mitigation in Vietnam. For example, a particular success was recorded in response to the Damrey Storm in 2005. To cope with the storm, authorities at all levels, armed forces, and community associations were involved in the mobilization of substantial

TABLE 8.2 } Region-Specific Measures for Disaster Preparedness, Response, and Mitigation

Regions	Main approach	Specific measures
The Red River Delta and the North Central	Prevent floods, take initiatives to respond to droughts and storms	– Enhance the flood-prevention capacity of river dyke systems – Build new reservoirs, regulate water levels for downstream areas – Improve the flood discharge capacity of river channels – Implement programmes to restore sea dykes, build embankments in coastal provinces
The Central Coast, the Eastern South and Islands	Pro-activeness in disaster prevention and adaptation for development	– Prepare residential, industrial, and tourism areas for possible disasters – Modify crops and animal husbandry infrastructure to suit regional disaster characteristics – Strengthen dykes, build reservoirs, dredge river channels – Build storm shelters for boats and ships; establish coastal typhoon and tsunami warning stations – Promote research into solutions to prevent river mouth deposition
The Mekong River Delta	Living with floods	– Establish flood control plans, be proactive in flood prevention – Build residential clusters above flood levels, improve flood discharge, construct sea dykes and other structures for salinity prevention and fresh water preservation – Enhance cooperation with countries in the Mekong river basin to reasonably use and protect water resources
Mountainous areas and Central Highlands	Proactively prevent natural disasters	– Map areas that are highly prone to flash floods, landslides – Establish local warning and communication systems – Build structures to prevent landslides and flash floods – Expand flood discharge systems – Build reservoirs for both flood and drought control – Strengthen cooperation with bordering countries on disaster forecasting, warning, search, and rescue
Sea areas	Proactive prevention and response	– Establish a management system for vehicles and boats operating at sea – Establish communication systems, deliver disaster forecasts and warnings to sea-going vessels – Establish professional search and rescue forces – Strengthen cooperation with other countries in disaster forecasting, warning, communication, search, and rescue

Source: SRV 2007.

state and private resources in order to evacuate residents and boats fishing at sea to safe places (Phuong 2007).

The above review suggests that the government has paid much attention to prevention, response, and mitigation of disasters. However, there are a number of constraints and challenges in disaster mitigation and management in Vietnam. Constraints and limitations include forecasting and warning systems that are insufficient to meet requirements, especially in the case of flash floods, landslides, and whirlwinds. Prevention activities in local areas have been insufficient. Communities in mountainous areas have not received timely warnings about disasters, especially for flash floods and landslides. The infrastructure for disaster preparedness and mitigation remains poor, and investment in disaster prevention and response infrastructure remains limited. Emergency relief, damage recovery, and rehabilitation are limited and sometimes affected by poor coordination and lack of cooperation. Search and rescue activities are limited due to lack of equipment and facilities. The awareness of the relationship between disasters and environmental protection remains low (CCFSC 2005; Phuong 2007; SRV 2007).

Particular challenges for disaster prevention, response, and mitigation in Vietnam are the increasing frequency and severity of disasters; the high speed of socioeconomic development and population growth, and the high rate of urbanization and industrialization, which have contributed to the increase in the frequency of disasters. This has included construction work related to tourism, as well as building of industrial and residential areas without considering the impact of possible disasters. The combination of different types of disasters in particular localities hinders the setting up of disaster preparedness and mitigation strategies and action plans for that locality (CCFSC 2005; Phuong 2007).

PROVINCIAL, DISTRICT, AND COMMUNAL LEVEL STRATEGIES

As discussed earlier in provinces, districts, and communes, local CFSCs are responsible for helping the equivalent People's Committee in planning, monitoring, coordinating, and implementing the disaster prevention, response, and mitigation efforts.

Each province and district is responsible for implementation of national disaster prevention and mitigation policies. Local authorities at provincial, district, and communal levels participate to different extents in formulating legal documents, and in planning, managing, and monitoring the implementation of programs and projects related to disaster prevention, response, and mitigation. For example, local authorities in Nam Dinh province have identified and implemented structural measures (e.g., build reservoirs, clear floodways, strengthen dyke management and protection works, etc.) and nonstructural measures (forecasting, awareness, education) that will contribute to disaster prevention, response, and mitigation (Viner et al. 2006). Communes and districts in the Red River Delta have been responsible for the construction of sea dykes. Communes officially employ a variety of strategies for use of the revenue they raise for storm protection (Adger 1998).

Nam (2008) reveals that, in preparing for and mitigating disaster impacts, the province of Thua Thien Hue has implemented a range of actions including:

- rearrangement of aquaculture farms and lagoons used for fish-breeding;
- building of dams for preventing saltwater intrusion upstream;

- preventing coastal erosion by closing off a channel to the sea that was opened by the 1999 flood;
- construction of upstream reservoirs for reducing flood peaks; and
- setting up resettlement programs for sampan people (who live on boats on lagoons).

In addition, the local authorities have organized resettlement projects to protect the lives of people from vulnerable areas by moving them to safer locations in order to mitigate disasters risks.

Local governments have worked with farmers in the Mekong River Delta to construct and maintain dyke systems around rice fields in an attempt to control flooding and protect crops. Local authorities and local organizations play a key role in encouraging households to actively engage in many activities (e.g., repairing homes, reinforcing infrastructure, etc.) at least a month before the storm and flood season (Ninh, Trung, and Niem 2007). Communal authorities organize annual disaster impact reduction training sessions (e.g., on emergency rescue) before the flood and storm season. Through the mass media, warnings, guidance, and advice are broadcast to people and communities at risk.

HOUSEHOLD LEVEL

Various measures related to natural disaster prevention, response, and mitigation have been adopted by households in different regions in Vietnam. These measures are often based on local experiences, perceptions, and economic capacity.

People in the Red River Delta respond to flood and storm impacts in various ways including changing their economic structure by reducing their investments in agriculture and investing more in aquaculture and fisheries. Other measures include establishing irrigation systems to reduce saltwater intrusion and building better, more solid infrastructure (Chinh 2008).

Farmers in Central Vietnam stabilize agricultural production by adjusting their farming practices, changing their crop calendars, the type of seeds used, the crops planted, rotating crops, employing early harvests, and moving crops to higher ground (Malin 2005; Huy 2007; Suu and My 2008). Hill farmers diversify agricultural production (e.g., groundnuts, cassava, forest plantation, and animal husbandry) to minimize vulnerability, because this reduces dependence on paddy rice as the main source of income and food security (Malin 2005). Households sustain their income levels by diversifying supplementary nonfarm income sources through migration (IMOLA 2006). People in coastal communities use various ways to cope with disasters, for example, building houses on higher ground or with high foundations to avoid floods, protecting houses with sandbags, reinforcing pillars and roofs before a storm, and so on (Huy 2007; Tran et al. 2008). Some households use steel wire to tie thatched roofs to the frame. Some protect their corrugated iron roofs with sand bags. Some fetch bamboo to make rafts; sometimes banana trunks are put aside for the same purpose. Others build small huts to protect their livestock. Households that own small boats keep them ready for use when there is a flood (Huy 2007). People store necessities for emergencies and are involved in flood mapping and evacuation routing for their areas (Phuong 2007). People take steps to try to avoid disease risk in the aftermath of a storm and flood, and during long-term inundations by participating in cleanups of the environment (removing solid waste, dead animals, etc.), by trying to ensure that water and food is safe, and by using bed nets against mosquitoes (Few, Ha, and Chinh 2007).

Farmers in the Mekong River Delta construct and maintain dyke system around their agricultural fields in an attempt to control floods and protect crops. Farmers adopt adaptive measures against floods such as consolidation of rice field embankments, elevated storage for harvested paddy, moving animals to safer ground, and stocking emergency food, firewood and medicine. People accommodate flooding via flood-based livelihoods; diversify plantations by cultivating additional vegetable crops; diversify livelihoods by growing mushrooms, expanding fish ponds, increasing the area of fruit tree plantations, and so on. Some farmers seasonally migrate to work in cities or farms as physical laborers, or work locally as day laborers (Few, Tran, and Hong 2004; Ninh, Trung, and Niem 2007; Few and Tran 2007).

Conclusions and the Way Forward

A number of studies have been carried out in Vietnam dealing with the different impacts of disasters. While data about these impacts are incomplete, the existing evidence indicates that disasters in Vietnam cause grave impacts to economic sectors, increase poverty, adversely impact individual households and the community as large, cause environmental degradation, and induce serious health problems.

There is a need for more accurate, comprehensive, and systematic information on disaster impacts, in order to increase support for disaster management among policy makers, government officials, and international donors. Such data would illustrate the vulnerability of sectors and localities. This can be useful for policy makers and donors by helping them better target financial resources for enhanced adaptation to climate disasters in Vietnam. This would also help governments to develop appropriate national and sectoral policies, particularly for reconstruction, preparedness, and mitigation.

However, most of the existing studies are descriptive in nature. This may be due, among other things, to the lack of expertise, data, facilities, and tools needed for rigorous studies. Moreover, the existing studies rarely touch upon impacts on other economic sectors such as tourism, recreation, forestry; long-term impacts on the flows of goods and services; macroeconomic impacts; and nonmarket impacts such as biodiversity damage. The ability to understand systematically and comprehensively the socioeconomic impacts of disasters in Vietnam is, therefore, limited. This opens up space for future economic research. For example, tourism is an important economic activity in many coastal provinces such as Quang Ninh, Thua Thien Hue, and Quang Nam, where disasters are frequent. The possible impacts of disasters on tourism could be an important area for research. The potential loss of biodiversity, in terms of its economic value, caused by disasters is another research area where economic tools can be applied.

The review of disaster prevention, response, and mitigation measures in Vietnam points to the importance of public education and community awareness about disasters and of enforcement of legislation and policies on disasters. This chapter also suggests that in designing programs and policies on disaster prevention, response, and mitigation, there is a need to mainstream them into socioeconomic development strategy for every region, sector, and for the country as a whole.

References

Adger, W. N. (1998). "Indicators of Social and Economic Vulnerability to Climate Change in Vietnam." CSERGE Working Paper, GEC 98–02, University of East Anglia, Norwich, UK.

Adger, W. N., and Kelly, M. (1999). "Social Vulnerability to Climate Change and the Architecture of Entitlements." *Mitigation and Adaptation Strategies for Global Change* 4: 253–266.

CCFSC (Central Committee for Flood and Storm Control). (2005). "National Report on Disasters in Vietnam." Working paper for the World Conference on Disaster Reduction, January 18–22, Kobe-Hyogo, Japan.

———. (2008). "Introduction about Disasters in Vietnam." Accessed July 20, 2008. http://www.ccfsc.org.vn/DMU_En/Disaster+M-anagement/Charaterictics/General+information +on+natural+disasters+in+Viet+Nam.htm.

Chaudhry, P., and Ruysschaert, G. (2007). "Climate Change and Human Development in Vietnam." Human Development Report 2007/2008, Human Development Report Office, Occasional Paper, 2007, New York.

Chinh, N. Q. (2008). "Household and Commune Adaptation Experience and Strategies for Sea Level Rise in Nam Dinh Province, Red River Delta." Paper presented at the EEPSEA Climate Change Conference, February 13–15, 2008, Bali, Indonesia.

Few, R., Ha, N. H., and Chinh, N. C. (2007). "Climatic Hazards, Health Risk and Response. Case Study 1: Central Vietnam." Research report, University of East Anglia, Norwich, UK.

Few, R., and Tran, P. G. (2007). "Climatic Hazards, Health Risk and Response. Case Study 2: Mekong Delta, Vietnam." Research report, University of East Anglia, Norwich, UK.

Few, R., Tran, P. G., and Hong, B. T. T. (2004). "Living with Floods: Health Risks and Coping Strategies of the Urban Poor in Vietnam." Research project funded by British Academy (Committee for South East Asian studies), research report, May.

GSO (General Statistics Office). (2008). *Statistical Yearbook of Vietnam—2007*. Ha Noi, Vietnam: Statistical Publishing House.

Guha-Sapir, D., Hargitt, D., and Hoyois, P. (2004). *Thirty Years of Natural Disasters 1974– 2003: The Numbers.* Louvain, Belgium: UCL Press, Louvain Catholic University.

Hong, V. T. (2002). "Impacts of the Historical Flood 1999 on Aquaculture in Phu Tan." In *Lessons in Resource Management from the Tam Giang Lagoon,* edited by V. J. Brzeski and G. F. Newkirk. Halifax, Nova Scotia, Canada: Dalhousie University.

Huy, H. T. (2007). "Early Warning System for Storm Management in a Coastal Community Role of Information and Local Institutions." Paper presented at the 28th EEPSEA Biannual Workshop, November 2007, Kuala Lumpur, Malaysia.

IMOLA (Integrated Management of Lagoon Activities). (2006). "Socio-economic Baseline Survey of Hue Lagoon Report—Part I." Accessed February 2, 2007.http://www.imolahue. org/pdf/SE-survey-I-en.pdf.

Kien, T. M., Shaw, R., and Ninh, N. H. (2008). "Vulnerability and Adaptation to Climate Change: A View from Human Health and Policy Perspectives in Vietnam." Paper presented at the EEPSEA Climate Change Conference, February 13–15, Bali, Indonesia.

Lap, N. V., Oanh, T. T. K., and Hirai, Y. (2005). "Assessment of Impacts of Sea Level Rise on TT Hue Lagoon Area." *Proceedings of National Workshop on TT Hue Lagoons*, Department of Science and Technology of TT Hue province (Hue), December: 302–305.

Malin, B. (2005). "Resilient Society, Vulnerable People: A Study of Disaster Response and Recovery from Floods in Central Vietnam." Doctoral thesis, Swedish University of Agricultural Sciences, Uppsala, Sweden.

Miller, F. (2003). "Society-Water Relations in the Mekong Delta: A Political Ecology of Risk." Ph.D. diss., Division of Geography, University of Sydney, Australia.

MoNRE (Ministry of Natural Resources and Environment). (2003). "Vietnam: Initial National Communication, under the United Nations Framework Convention on Climate Change." Hanoi, Vietnam.

Nam, D. (2008). "Impacts of Sea-Level Rise on Coastal Lagoon: A Case Study of Tam Giang—Cau Hai Lagoons in Central Vietnam." Paper presented at the EEPSEA Climate Change Conference, February 13–15, Bali, Indonesia.

Ninh, N. H. (2008). "Vulnerability, Adaptation and Resilience to Climate Change: Experiences and Implications in Vietnam." Paper presented at the EEPSEA Climate Change Conference, February 13–15, Bali, Indonesia.

Ninh, N. H., Trung, V. K., and Niem, N. X. (2007). "Flooding in Mekong River Delta, Vietnam." Human Development Report 2007/2008, Human Development Report Office, Occasional Paper, New York.

PCFSC (Provincial Committee of Floods and Storms Control of Thua Thien Hue). (2000). "Report on Disasters in Thua Thien Hue Province in 2000." Hue, Vietnam.

Phuong, N. T. (2007). "Vietnam Country Perspective." Paper presented at the ADB small group workshop on Large-Scale Emergencies, July 5–6. Manila, Philippines.

SRV (Socialist Republic of Vietnam). (2007). *National Strategy for Natural Disaster Prevention, Response and Mitigation to 2020.* November 16. Hanoi, Vietnam.

Suu, L. T. T., and My, P. T. H. (2008). "Livelihood Vulnerability and Local Adaptation Strategies to Natural Disasters in Huong River Basin: Case Study in Thuan An Town, Phu Vang District, Thua Thien—Hue Province." Paper presented at the EEPSEA Climate Change Conference, February 13–15, Bali, Indonesia.

Tran, P., Marincioni, F., Shaw, R., Sarti, M., and An, L. V. (2008). "Flood Risk Management in Central Vietnam: Challenges and Potentials." *Natural Hazards* 46(1): 119–138.

Tran, P., Shaw, R., Chantry, G., and Norton, J. (2009). "GIS and Local Knowledge in Disaster Management: A Case Study of Vietnam." *Journal of Disasters Studies, Policy and Management* 33(1) (January): 152–169.

Tuan, T. H., Xuan, M. V., Nam, D., and Navrud, S. (2009). "Valuing Direct Use Values of Wetlands: A Case Study of Tam Giang—Cau Hai Lagoon Wetland in Vietnam." *Ocean & Coastal Management* 52: 102–112.

USAID (2008). "Most Recent Disaster Declaration: Floods, 11 March 2008." Accessed December 1, 2008. http://www.usaid.gov/our_work/humanitarian_assistance/disaster_assistance/countries/vietnam/template/index.html.

Viner, D., Bouwer, L. M., Ninh, N. H., and Thanh, N. C. (2006). "Linking Climate Change Adaptation and Disaster Risk Management for Sustainable Poverty Reduction." Vietnam country study, Ref MWH 475000177.001–6 rev.1. November. Available at http://ec.europa.eu/development/icenter/repository/env_cc_varg_adaptation_en.pdf.

World Bank (2001). "World Development Report 2000/01." Washington, D.C.

9 }

Natural Disaster Mitigation in West Bengal

Debesh Chakraborty, Sabari Bandyopadhyay, Ivy Das Gupta, Sayanti Sen, and Debabrata Mitra

Introduction

India frequently suffers from a range of natural disasters—floods, cyclones, earthquakes, and droughts—that cause massive loss of both life and property. This is evident from table 9.1, which shows the type, number, and impact of natural disasters in the country over the decade of 1998 to 2007. The proportion of people affected by floods is higher than that affected by cyclones or earthquakes. Floods caused damage totaling US$14.22 billion (representing 68.16 percent of all damage caused by natural disasters), whereas cyclones and earthquakes combined were responsible for damages of US$6.64 billion (representing 31.83 percent of all damage).

Further insight can be gathered from the studies documented in table 9.2, which describes extreme events in India, where they have taken place and the devastating effects they have had.

Of all natural disasters, floods are the most consistently recurring. India has suffered from the aftermath of floods since the early days of its civilization. Some of the earliest evidence for this dates back to the floods of the Indus Valley civilization (Joshi et al. 2007). Much more recently, a serious effort was launched to study the economic, health, and social impact of these disasters on several Asian and European countries. The present study is an outcome of this research, known as MICRODIS.[1]

Most of the existing studies on natural disasters in India, as evidenced in table 9.2, are descriptive in nature, based on secondary data and do not address the issue of disaster mitigation measures and government policies.. Thus this chapter has unique features compared to other studies: it provides detailed information on the nature and effect of floods on the basis of a micro-study and develops a clear conceptual framework based on vulnerability. Moreover, the chapter includes a discussion of the government measures and policies in the field of natural disasters.

The authors express their sincere thanks to Panchayat Pradhan and other members of Debhog Gram Panchayat, Sabang block, Paschim Medinipur, West Bengal, Professor Shyamapada Manna, the local insurance agent and also the villagers of the area for their kind cooperation. We acknowledge the useful discussions we had with the officials of the Disaster Management Department, Government of West Bengal, who also provided us with several government documents.

199

TABLE 9.1 } Natural Disasters in India, 1998–2007

		Deaths		Affected people		Damages	
	Number of events	No	% of total from natural disasters	Million	% of total from natural disasters	Million USD	% of total from natural disasters
Floods	86	11,130	25.75	255.21	92.42	14,223.75	68.16
Cyclones	14	10,689	24.72	13.98	5.06	3,018.42	14.46
Earthquakes	4	21,416	49.53	6.96	2.52	3,625	17.37
Total	104	43,235	100.00	276.15	100.00	20,867.17	100.00

Source: EM-DAT, CRED.

The objective of this chapter is to analyze the nature and extent of flooding as a devastating disaster, its magnitude and the extent of damage in India, using a case study from West Bengal. In addition, this chapter documents and assesses the policies that have been adopted to tackle flooding in the state.

The chapter has been divided into five sections. First, we introduce our measure of flood vulnerability and apply it to states in India. Then we present the flood profile of West Bengal and describe the magnitude and extent of damages due to floods. This is followed by a case study of Debhog Gram Panchayat in West Bengal. In the next section, we discuss the public policies adopted to tackle flood disasters in the region, before summarizing and concluding the chapter.

Flood Vulnerability Index for India

India has several regions that are particularly vulnerable to floods and, for successful disaster planning, it is of the utmost importance to identify the most vulnerable areas. Here, vulnerability is defined by the International Strategy for Disaster Reduction (ISDR) as: "The conditions determined by physical, social, economic and environmental factors or processes that increase the susceptibility of a community to the impact of hazards" (UN/ISDR 2004).

In this chapter, we have formulated a "Vulnerability Index" that identifies these vulnerable regions in India. The index tries to capture a more comprehensive scale of vulnerability than has previously been considered and employs a variety of indicators as proxies to look at different aspects of vulnerability. The variables chosen for the construction of this index depend broadly on the ideas of ISDR. Our different sources of vulnerability include climatic, demographic, agricultural, occupational, and infrastructural factors (figure 9.1).

The methodology used to construct our vulnerability index is discussed in box 9.1.

VULNERABLE REGIONS IN INDIA

The flood vulnerability indices calculated for all the states of India are shown in table 9.3. The values of the index lie between zero and one, where a ranking of one

TABLE 9.2 } Literature Review on the Impact of Natural Disaster in India

Author and year of publication	Region affected	Type and date of disaster	Main findings
Majhi et al. (2005)	Murshidabad District, West Bengal	Millennium Flood, September 2000	4 million people marooned, 255 villages, 7 municipalities, 672 primary schools, and 375 secondary schools were swept away. Millions of homeless and displaced were forced to settle temporarily on roads and railway lines.
Chapman and Rudra (2007)	Murshidabad District, West Bengal	Millennium Flood, September 2000	The onset of the flood was extremely rapid and from unexpected directions. 1,366 km of railway tracks, 9 bridges, and 2,763 km road were damaged.
Victoria (2002)	Orissa	Successive disasters within 1999, flooding in August, cyclone on October 17–18, and Super Cyclone on October 29–30	A local disaster management (preparedness and mitigation) system has been installed within the 10 blocks.
Panigrahi (2003)	Orissa	Super Cyclone, 1999	10,000 fishermen died. NGO's assistance, rather than government relief, has a positive impact on fishermen communities.
Thomalla and Schmuck (2004)	Orissa	Super Cyclone, 1999	Failure of warning systems and lack of awareness can result in large human loss.
Sarangi and Penthoi (2005)	Orissa	Various occurrences of naturals calamities, 1971–1991	Loss of property of Rs. 4,640 million ($1,066 million).
Lahiri et al. (2001)	Gujarat	Earthquake, 2001	15.8 million of the population affected. Total number of deaths was around 19,000. 166,000 people were injured. Annual loss of gross state domestic product, Rs. 23,040 million ($493.3 million).
Singh (2003)	Gurdaspur District, Punjab	Recurrent flooding	20% of net cropped area damaged.
Srivastava et al. (2000)	Assam	Flood, 1998	An area of 915 km² was inundated, and 51,068 ha of agricultural area was damaged. During two weeks of inundation, 28,028 ha of crop area and other infrastructure such as road network and settlements were affected.
O'Hare (2001)	Godavari Delta region, Andhra Pradesh	Tropical hurricane 07B, on November 6-7, 1996	The largest impact occurred near the coast. Two districts, 7.1 million population were affected, 64,600 houses damaged, 236,000 ha of crop area damaged, 1,059 persons died, livestock loss was 6,845. Estimated loss was Rs. 61,264.7 million ($1,556.1 million). Poverty and social ordering in Indian society puts differential limits on the risk reduction abilities of individuals and social groups in the face of cyclone hazards.
Roy, Mruthyunjaya, and Selvarajan (2002)	Kendrapara district, Orissa	All kinds, 2002	About 22% of rural households of Kendrapara district, Orissa, seasonally migrate to other areas in search of jobs or earning due to natural calamities.

Source: Authors.

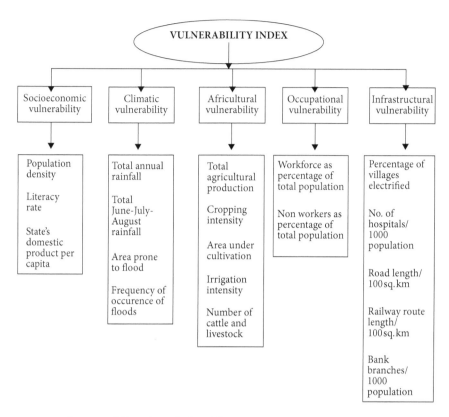

FIGURE 9.1 Sources and dimensions of vulnerability

Source: I. Das Gupta (2007). "Development of Field Protocol." Presented in the Economic Working Group Meeting, MICRODIS, Jadavpur University, November 2–4, Kolkata, India.

indicates maximum vulnerability and zero no vulnerability. The state of Bihar, with a ranking of 0.223 is the most vulnerable overall, followed by West Bengal, with a ranking of 0.216. At the other end of the scale, Tamil Nadu, ranking 0.109, comes thirteenth, with the least flood vulnerability. If we divide India using a different regional breakdown, however, it can be observed from figure 9.2 that in the northeastern region of India, Assam is the most vulnerable state. In the east, Bihar, West Bengal, and Orissa, and in the central region, Uttar Pradesh and Madhya Pradesh are the more vulnerable states. Rajasthan, Haryana, and Punjab are in turn the most vulnerable in the northwest. Elsewhere, Maharastra in the west, and Andhra Pradesh and Kerala in the south are the most flood-prone areas.

According to the vulnerability indices, Bihar, West Bengal, Orissa, and Assam are the four most flood-prone states in the eastern and northeastern regions. The Ganges-Brahmaputra-Meghna (GBM) river system flows through this area, presenting a huge challenge in terms of both the water potential and its destructive reality. The Ganges-Brahmaputra-Meghna system delta is popularly known as "GBM." Taken as a whole, it comprises an area of 1.75 million km^2 and drains, on average, an annual volume of about 1,276 m^3 billion into the sea (Ghani 2001). The GBM basin is

BOX 9.1 } Vulnerability Index: Methodology

___

The methodology used to calculate the vulnerability index follows the basic approach developed by the UN Development Programme (UNDP) to compute the Human Development Index.

Step 1: A dimension index of each of the indicators for a region or subregion (Xi) is calculated by using the formula:

(Actual Xi - Minimum Xi)/(Maximum Xi - Minimum Xi)

For literacy rates, state domestic product (SDP) per capita and infrastructure, the dimension index is calculated by using the formula (Maximum Xi – Actual Xi)/(Maximum Xi – Minimum Xi), as the higher the literacy rate and SDP per capita, the lower the vulnerability will be.

Step 2: An average index is calculated for each of the five sources of vulnerability (socioeconomic, climatic, agricultural, occupational, and infrastructural). This is done by taking a simple average of the indicators in each category.

Average Index i = [Indicator 1 +.........+ Indicator I]/I

Step 3: All the sources of vulnerability are aggregated by the following formula.

$$\text{Vulnerability Index} = \left[\sum_{i=1}^{n} (\text{Average Index } i)\, \alpha \right] 1/\alpha\ /n$$

where,

i = number of indicators in each source of vulnerability
n = number of sources of vulnerability (in the present case $n = \alpha = 5$).

The vulnerability index is the generalized mean. The values of the index will lie between zero and one. After the values of the index are calculated both for states/regions and districts/subregions, a ranking of the various regions and subregions is possible for identifying the most vulnerable area in terms of indicators.
Source: Das Gupta 2007.

___

the largest and the most dynamic on earth, with floods a regular feature. Within the basin, Bihar, West Bengal, Orissa, and Assam are the most flood-prone states. In the analysis that follows, we focus on West Bengal.

The Case of West Bengal

The geography of West Bengal is diverse, from the high peaks of the Himalayas in its northern extremes to coastal regions in the south, with plateaux and the Ganges delta in between. West Bengal covers a total area of 88,752 km², with 19 districts and three divisions (figure 9.3).

West Bengal's climate meanwhile varies from tropical savannah in its southern portions to humid subtropical in the north. It has a summer, a rainy season,

TABLE 9.3 } Vulnerability Index of Floods in Indian States

States	Vulnerability						
	Socioeconomic	Climatic	Agricultural	Occupational	Infrastructural	Overall	Rank
Punjab	0.367	0.368	0.508	0.455	0.000	0.116	12
Uttar Pradesh	0.828	0.386	0.821	0.692	0.702	0.204	3
Haryana	0.345	0.273	0.498	0.522	0.455	0.125	11
Rajasthan	0.489	0.043	0.464	0.155	0.993	0.201	5
Bihar	0.991	0.237	0.286	0.464	0.945	0.223	1
Assam	0.563	0.526	0.244	0.331	0.792	0.168	7
West Bengal	0.639	0.298	0.543	0.988	0.819	0.216	2
Orissa	0.531	0.269	0.304	0.244	0.827	0.169	6
Madhya Pradesh	0.503	0.155	0.465	0.195	1.000	0.202	4
Gujarat	0.292	0.131	0.258	0.241	0.781	0.157	9
Maharastra	0.226	0.670	0.488	0.312	0.764	0.169	6
Andhra Pradesh	0.458	0.141	0.475	0.284	0.797	0.164	8
Karnataka	0.396	0.214	0.360	0.279	0.772	0.156	10
Kerala	0.381	0.281	0.168	0.777	0.111	0.156	10
Tamil Nadu	0.401	0.117	0.243	0.511	0.308	0.109	13

Source: Das Gupta 2007.

Note: Data for other states are not available.

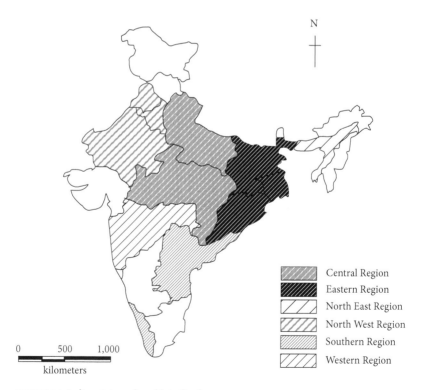

FIGURE 9.2 Indian states vulnerable to floods

Source: Map prepared by Sayanti Sen.

1. Darjeeling
2. Jalpaiguri
3. Cooch Behar
4. Uttar Dinajpur
5. Dakshin Dinajpur
6. Malda
7. Birbhum
8. Murshidabad
9. Bardhaman
10. Nadia
11. Purulia
12. Bankura
13. Hooghly
14. North 24 Parganas
15. Paschim Medinipur
16. Howrah
17. Kolkata
18. South 24 Parganas
19. Purba Medinipur

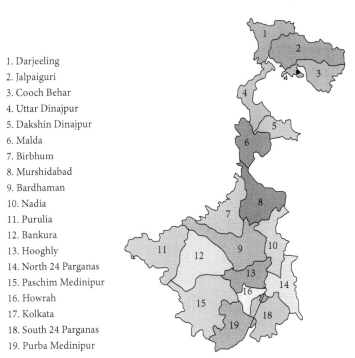

FIGURE 9.3 Districts of West Bengal
Source: http://en.wikipedia.org/wiki/Geography_of_West_Bengal.

a short autumn, and a winter. West Bengal, a part of the Bengal Delta, has been subject to floods throughout its history, as the landmass of the state is formed by the Ganga-Padma system of rivers through the delta building process of which flooding is a necessary adjunct, being the main carrier of sediment—the bulk of fluvial deposits—and in huge volumes.

FLOODS IN WEST BENGAL

In West Bengal, only five years were flood-free between 1960 and 2007—that is years when less than 500 km^2 was inundated. In 1978, a particularly devastating flood severely affected several parts of the state. More recently, the state suffered three consecutive years of horrendous floods, in 1998, 1999, and 2000.

In late September 2000, a devastating flood called the "Millennium Flood" struck Gangetic West Bengal. It destroyed most of the assets of approximately 20 million poor rural people in West Bengal and three million in an adjacent part of Bangladesh. Seventy-two hours of continuous and concentrated rainfall over the western river basin areas of the River Bhagirathi from the Pagla-Bansloi to the Ajoy generated such huge flood volumes that almost all embankments on the eastern side of the Bhagirathi were washed away and the whole of Nadia and large parts of Murshidabad and northern areas of North 24 Parganas were flooded and remained underwater for an extended period (Chapman and Rudra 2007).

Table 9.4 shows the cross-district scenario of West Bengal for the year 2000. Of all the districts affected in the 2000 flooding, Murshidabad was one of the most severely affected. Chapman, and Rudra (2007) have provided some estimates on the subject, noting that nearly 1,366 km of railway tracks were damaged, with 236 breaches, requiring some 800,000 man-days for their repair. For roads, the figures amounted to 2,763 km and four million man-days required for the renovation. Together, these estimates show that a total of almost five million man-days were required for repairs and renovations due to the Millennium Flood. This expenditure not only funded the rebuilding of the damaged area but also produced a positive effect on the Murshidabad district domestic product through a multiplier effect, thus resulting in an increase of 11.14 percent that year.[2]

RECENT FLOOD EXPERIENCE IN WEST BENGAL

Due to heavy rainfall in the state, according to Ministry of Home Affairs Disaster Management Division sources, about 10.8 million people in 10,173 villages were affected by floods in 2007. The magnitude of the damage suffered by the most-affected districts in West Bengal is shown in table 9.5.]

SELECTION OF FLOOD-PRONE DISTRICTS IN WEST BENGAL

West Bengal, as identified by our vulnerability index, is one of the most flood-prone states of eastern India. Table 9.6 shows the estimated indices and ranking of West Bengal districts.[3]

According to the vulnerability index, Medinipur ranks as the most flood-affected district of West Bengal. This led us to carry out pretesting of a questionnaire prepared as part of the MICRODIS project in one of the most flood-affected areas of this district to gain insight into the economic impacts of flooding. The next section reports this case study.

Impacts of Disaster in West Bengal: A Case Study

For our study, we selected the Debhog Gram Panchayat, part of the Sabang block[4] of Paschim[5] Medinipur, which was the worst affected area by floods in 2007 (Dan Church Aid 2007).

The study was done via focus group discussions and personal interviews of households in the flood-affected area on the basis of a questionnaire to find out their sociodemographic and economic background, disaster preparedness, how well the warning system worked, how they managed to survive, what losses they suffered, and how rehabilitation has proceeded following the floods. Different contexts were tested in the focus group discussions along with one-to-one interviews in order to compare the different aspects and draw conclusions. Two focus group discussions were organized on January 18–19, 2008. The first focus group consisted of 12 male members and the second group of 10 female members. The age of participants ranged

TABLE 9.4 } Flood Disaster in West Bengal for the Year 2000, by District

District affected	Blocks affected	Municipalities affected	Area damaged		House affected		Crop area affected		Death and missing live stock			Health infrastructure	
			Hectares	%	Number	%	Hectares	%	Cattles	Goats & sheep	Poultry	Health centers affected	Hospitals affected
Murshidabad	26	7	522,600	22	490,313	25.98	450,600	23.38	7,000	55,000	14,000	98	6
Bardhaman	25	9	359,796	15.2	215,695	11.43	300,400	15.59	14,341	9,949	2,351	80	4
Birbhum	19	5	282,500	11.9	457,947	24.27	246,300	12.78	7,341	3,138	4,579	56	4
Hooghly	18	10	290,000	12.2	152,209	8.07	240,100	12.46	56	48	21	27	1
North 24 Parganas	22	18	210,400	8.9	174,580	9.25	155,600	8.08	10	9	20	9	3
Nadia	17	10	370,000	15.6	320,463	16.98	335,000	17.39	38	49	640	66	7
Medinipur	24	5	180,600	7.6	72,610	3.85	99,900	5.18	43	30	25	12	2
Malda	9	1	39,740	1.7	0	0.00	22,000	1.14	0	0	0	0	0
Howrah	11	3	120,000	5.1	3,162	0.17	77,000	4.00	0	0	0	9	3
TOTAL	171	68	2,375,636	100	1,886,979	100	1,926,900	100	28,829	68,223	21,636	357	30

Source: Ghosh 2005.

TABLE 9.5 } Extent of Damage Due to Floods in Different Districts of West Bengal in 2007

Name of districts	Population affected (million)	%	Villages affected Number	%	Relief camps opened	People accommodated	Crop area damaged	Houses damaged Fully	Partially
Howrah	0.259	6.37	492	5.13	112	39,220	3,213 ha	8,797	25,925
Bardhaman	0.512	12.59	2,402	25.06	190	53,890	92,661 ha	5,264	27,710
Murshidabad	0.185	4.55	241	2.51	15	n.a.	20,000 ha	2,347	6,034
South 24 Parganas	0.335	8.24	585	6.10	01	202	8,640 ha	4,691	13,923
North 24 Parganas	1.139	28.01	963	10.05	353	37,375	65,166 ha	17,000	–
Paschim Medinipur	0.370	9.10	385	4.02	83	18,523	0.3 million ha	40,000	–
Poorva Medinipur	0.929	22.84	1904	19.86	65	4,600	64,229	11,432	2,356
Birbhum	0.175	4.30	931	9.71	n.a..	n.a.	19,594 ha	11,000	38,000
Bankura	0.163	4.0	1683	17.56	28	4,650	5,560 ha	3,325	13,550
Total	4.067	100	9586	100	847	158,460	279,063.3	103,856	127,498

Source: Government of India 2007.

n.a.: not available.

TABLE 9.6 } Vulnerability Index of Floods in West Bengal, by District

Districts	Vulnerability						
	Socioeconomic	Climatic	Agricultural	Occupational	Infrastructural	Index	Rank
Darjeeling	0.373	0.444	0.036	0.019	0.249	0.096	9
Jalpaiguri	0.232	0.589	0.251	0.172	0.079	0.118	5
Koch Bihar	0.291	0.642	0.252	0.136	0.127	0.129	4
Uttar Dinajpur	0.008	n.a.	0.329	0.148	n.a.	0.053 +	14
Dakshin Dina-jpur	0.248	0.396	0.181	0.058	0.135	0.081	11
Maldah	0.042	0.319	0.302	0.322	0.110	0.078	12
Murshidabad	0.113	0.263	0.540	0.627	0.174	0.136	2
Birbhum	0.212	0.177	0.408	0.216	0.200	0.083	10
Bardhaman	0.354	0.164	0.603	0.544	0.244	0.134	3
Nadia	0.290	0.341	0.564	0.371	0.211	0.118	5
North 24 Parganas	0.493	0.263	0.367	0.599	n.a.	0.145 +	n.a.
Hooghly	0.437	0.291	0.430	0.360	0.469	0.114	6
Bankura	0.234	n.a	0.337	0.259	0.194	0.070 +	13
Purulia	0.115	n.a	0.162	0.198	0.202	0.042 +	15
Medinipur	0.412	0.643	0.865	0.912	0.380	0.209	1
Howrah	0.495	0.405	0.336	0.290	0.266	0.109	8
Kolkata	1.000	n.a	n.a.	0.211	n.a.	n.a.	n.a
South 24 Parganas	0.335	0.414	0.296	0.517	0.273	0.113	7

Source: Das Gupta 2007.

n.a.: not available.

from 18 to 65 years old. The data from the focus group discussions were captured by manual note taking and audio recording, with no individual interviews performed during the focus group discussion.

In addition, personal interviews of households were conducted, in which 15 households were randomly selected from among 4,000 households, based on variable economic status and occupational backgrounds in different locations in the Debhog Gram Panchayat. The purpose of the personal interview was pretesting of the MICRODIS questionnaire. Thus, the sample size was quite small and results should be considered with caution.

Paschim Medinipur is located on the southwestern side of West Bengal. The study area is in the southeastern part of the district, some 200 km from Kolkata. Sabang block has 13 Gram Panchayats,[6] among which, the most flood-affected was Debhog Gram Panchayat, which has 16 Gram Sansads.[7] In this Gram Panchayat, Julkapur, Badalpur, Benadighi, and Gumai are mostly affected by the floods in 2007. The affected Gram Sansads are situated along the river Kopaleshwari and the Sati Khal (a canal). These water channels later merge with the River Keleghai. The rivers are not perennial in nature and the levees are not well maintained. The water channels have not been de-silted in the last 25 years. As a result, the carrying capacity of these water channels has decreased, causing overflows of the water channels during the monsoon and the postmonsoon phase.

During the monsoon season, from mid-June to September 2007, heavy rainfall resulted in floods in this region. About 16 km^2 were affected. Some 2,990 families were affected because of the floods, with 30 houses heavily damaged, 425 houses partially damaged, and a death toll in Paschim Medinipur district of 38. There were also considerable crop and livestock losses and Sabang block was particularly adversely affected in the district. During the monsoon and the postmonsoon phase, rains caused an overflow of the river basin and, as a result, the agricultural lands along the riverside were flooded, destroying about 900 ha of crops, whose monetary value was estimated to be approximately 10 million rupees (US$254,000).[8] Although no human lives or cattle were reported lost, public utilities were damaged. Around 28 km of morum road[9] and 38 km of kancha road[10] were damaged, 95 tube wells were put out of service, and one wooden bridge and a concrete one were also affected. The value of the disrupted public utilities was also estimated to be 10 million rupees (US$254,000). As a percentage of the district's Gross Domestic Product, however, this amounted to only 0.011 percent.[11]

Next, we will describe the major findings from the pretesting of the questionnaire.

SOCIODEMOGRAPHIC FEATURES

The sociodemographic features of the surveyed area are presented in table 9.7. Most of the respondents were male, Hindu by religion, and spoke Bengali. Close to 40 percent of the population belongs to the backward class.[12]

A look at the education level shows a literacy rate of 68.5 percent, less than the West Bengal state average rate of 69.22 percent (Census of India, 2001), with few of the villagers having more than a secondary level of education. The age distribution reveals a dependency ratio in the area of 36 percent, lower than the state average (40 percent) according to the Census of India (2001).

Generally, houses are made of mud, with thatched roofs. Only 6.67 percent of the respondents had cemented walls and tiled roofs. The pattern of houses indicates the financial status of the respondents and also the risk of being subject to damage due to flooding.

ECONOMIC SITUATION

The income distribution pattern of the households in the area reveals that most households are not well off and are thus likely to be more vulnerable to the effects of flooding (table 9.8a). The major source of income for locals comes from agriculture, while consumption patterns show that households spend a high proportion of their budget on foodstuffs.

In terms of insurance, a worrying picture emerged. None of the respondents had life or crop insurance. Some 60 percent of people do, however, have loans from banks or self-help groups for diverse reasons.

TABLE 9.7 } Sociodemographic Features of Debhog

Indicators	Percentage of surveyed households
Respondent's gender	
Male	73.33
Female	26.67
Religion	
Hindu	100
Respondent's mother tongue	
Bengali	93.33
Thare	6.67
Respondent's caste	
Schedule Caste	20
Schedule Tribe	6.67
Other Backward Class	13.33
General	53.33
Others	6.67
Respondent's educational status	
Literacy rate	68.5
Up to primary	23.91
Primary–secondary	31.52
Secondary and above	8.69
Others	0
Family size and age distribution	
0–4	26.08
14–60	64.13
60–above	9.78
Average family size	6
Housing	
Kancha (mud houses)	93.33
Pucca (concrete houses)	6.67
Rented	0

Source: Authors.

The average size of land holdings is about 0.174 ha (table 9.8b). Focus group discussions also indicated a small size of landholdings. Agricultural production and loss of production due to flooding depend on the location of the agricultural land. The findings indicate that 60 percent of land is located along the riverbanks. In the summer, these lands along the rivers can be irrigated, whereas during floods they are the first to be impacted. Approximately 50 percent of the lands are under irrigation, with the source of irrigation being shallow tube wells and at times river water. Focus group participants informed us that in the lands along the riverbanks, irrigation is not practiced due to a lack of canals and only perennial water facilities.

The main agricultural production comes from paddies, where 80 percent of farmers cultivate their crops during both Kharif and Rabi seasons.[13] In a normal

TABLE 9.8A } Economic Situation in Debhog

Indicators	Percentage of households
Income	
Rs. 0–6000 ($0–152.4)	20
Rs. 6000–12000 ($152.4–304.8)	33.33
Rs. 12000–60000 ($304.8–1524)	40
Rs. 60000–above ($1,524–above)	6.67
Income composition by source	
Agricultural product	34.76
Wages and salaries	12
Horticulture	11.38
Others	41.86
Expenditure pattern	
Expenditures in food	76.4
Expenditures in clothing	5.1
Expenditures in medical services	4.35
Expenditures in transport	6.71
Expenditures in others	7.44
Insurance	
Life insurance	0
Premium paid for life insurance	–
Crop insurance	0
Premium paid for crop insurance	–
Loan	
Households[a]	60

Source: Authors.

[a] The loan was taken out by the households in 2007 not for redressing flood damage but for other proposes over the course of the year.

year, the average value per household of agricultural production amounts to 16,712 rupees (US$424), with a cost of production amounting to approximately 7,595 rupees (US$19). When floods affect this production, villagers become worse off.

Livestock are also a source of income for the villagers, while bullocks are employed for cultivation. Animal products are mainly used for self-consumption and the excess is sold on the local market. Normally, each household owns three or four head of livestock. A few households responded that they owned a pond with an average size of 0.022 ha. Use of the ponds is confined to fishing, irrigation, and, at times, household work. This was also confirmed by the focus group discussions.

Mat-making is also an important small-scale industry in this area. The focus group participants informed us that mats are sold to agents in the local markets and even outside the district and the country. Standard size mats fetch around 100 rupees (US$2.54).

TABLE 9.8B } Economic Activities in Debhog

Indicators	Percentage of households	Average per household
Land holding patterns		
Agriculture land holding	60	
Size of own agricultural land (in ha)		0.174
Value of own land		Rs. 44,422.28 ($1,128.33)
Land held by share cropper (in ha)	33.33	0.076
Location of land		
Riverside land	60	
Others	40	
Irrigation facility		
Household having irrigation facility	46.67	
Household not having irrigation facility	53.33	
Agricultural production		
Paddy farmer	80	
Value of production (yearly)		Rs. 16,712 ($424.5)
Cost of production		Rs. 7,595 ($192.9)
Animal resources		
Number of livestock		3
Cost of rearing		Rs. 163 ($4.14)
Value of livestock		Rs. 742.60 ($18.86)
Pond holdings		
Percentage of households	53.33	
Size of pond (in ha)		0.022
Value of pond		Rs. 11,232.55 ($285.31)
Income from pond (yearly)		Rs. 2,016.67 ($51.22)
Small-scale industrial activities		
Value of average production (yearly)		Rs. 44,178 ($1,122.12)
Cost of production (yearly)		Rs. 33,690 ($855.73)

Source: Authors.

ECONOMIC IMPACTS OF FLOODING

Table 9.9 reports the economic impact of the 2007 flood.

The expenditure of each household in this region changes after floods, with a 39.94 percent increase in average expenditure levels from pre- to postdisaster phases in 2007. Flooding in this area reduces the supply of foodstuffs and increases prices, which results in a 38 percent increase in expenditure level on foodstuffs. Again, the respondents of this area usually use renewable energy resources such as agricultural waste, cow dung, or leaves from trees as fuel. However, floods almost completely destroy these sources of renewable energy. Affected households then have to buy nonrenewable fuel resources such as kerosene or coal from the market, resulting in

TABLE 9.9 } Economic Impacts of Flood in Debhog, 2007

Indicators	Percentage of households	Average
Increase in expenditure due to flood		
Food	38	
Fuel	54.6	
Average expenditure levels	39.94	
Loss due to flood		
Loss of agricultural production		Rs. 4,789.31 ($121.65)
Loss per livestock		Rs. 120 ($3.04)
Loss of income from pond		Rs. 1,946.67 ($49.45)
Loss of production from small-scale industries		Rs. 17,333 ($440.26)
Repairing or replacement cost of household property		
Repaired house last year	73.33	
Cost of repair		Rs. 1,817.5 ($46.16)
Cost of household assets		Rs. 1,600 ($40.64)
Drinking water		
Households affected	60	
Disruption of services of drinking water (in days)		18–20
Disrupted road services (days)		15–20

Source: Authors.

an enormous rise in fuel expenditure—approximately 58 percent in the immediate post-flood period. Some of the more well-to-do families have gas facilities for cooking. In normal times, they primarily use renewable energy sources, but after floods, they have to use LPG gas due to the nonavailability of renewable sources. This results in an increase in their fuel expenses as well.

Due to floods, the average loss of agricultural production per household amounted to about 4,789.31 rupees (US$121.65) for the 2007 last monsoon or approximately 22 percent of the average income. In 2007, the entire Kharif production was damaged. Households also suffered losses to livestock, as villagers were not able to provide fodder for the cattle. Ponds can also be severely affected, as contamination by overflow from polluted waters damages fish stocks.

The impact of natural disasters on trade, however, has been less researched. Natural hazards reduce the availability of particular goods and services for export either directly or via disruptions to transport and communication networks (Benson and Clay 2003). The Sabang area—well known for its mat industry, recorded an average loss per household of 17,333 rupees (US$440.26) in 2007 from lost production in small-scale industries.

As most of the houses are kancha—made of mud with a thatched roof—a good proportion of the houses were damaged from flooding in 2007. Even if the damage is minimal, an average of 1,817.5 rupees (US$46.16) per household is still spent on repairs. Household assets, such as clothing, utensils, furniture, agricultural instruments, radios, and televisions are also damaged or lost. As a result, households have to repair or replace these items, on average costing approximately 1,600 rupees (US$40.64). As the source of drinking water in the area is not piped water, villagers are rather dependent on government-made tube wells and also own their own tube wells. In 2007, households faced disruption of water services and contamination of drinking water for about 18 to 19 days. Moreover, waterlogging damaged the roads, disrupting transportation for 15 to 20 days during the flooding period, causing significant inconvenience to public life. Transport disruption was also a key issue raised by members of the focus group.

DISASTER-INDUCED DISPLACEMENT

Migration has been adopted by people as an important means of survival in dealing with floods. Our case study shows that floods resulted in the displacement of 40 percent of households in this region (table 9.10), commonly moving to a school building or a public office and staying there for approximately six to seven days.

While staying in rescue centers, displaced families have little access to public amenities and depend on food and support from the government and NGOs. Because of the distress, it can take people considerable time to return to their home and resume their normal course of work. In addition, crowding can also facilitate the transmission of infectious diseases.

DISASTER PREPAREDNESS

Disaster preparedness is defined as the process of ensuring preventive measures and a readiness to contain the effects of a forecast extreme event. Such preparedness attempts to minimize loss of life, injury, and damage to property, and to provide rescue, relief, rehabilitation, and other services in the aftermath of the disaster.

From our focus group discussions and interviews of households, we only managed to get a glimpse of disaster preparedness and mitigation efforts in the area. Table 9.11 nevertheless throws some light on this. We observed that only a small proportion of the affected households (14.28 percent) were willing to move to a safer place and leave behind their home and land. Those who were not willing to move out reported financial constraints as the main reason for staying, while others said that they did not want to leave their ancestral home. A total of 8 percent of the respondents also stated that they did not want to move to alternative locations due to difficulties in adjusting to the new environment, workplace, and culture. Our findings

TABLE 9.10 } Disaster-Induced Displacement in Debhog, 2007

Household displacement during flood (%)	40
Duration of displacement (Average days)	6–7
Time taken to return home in the postdisaster phase, among displaced	
Within 1 month (%)	50

Source: Authors.

TABLE 9.11 } Flood Preparedness in Debhog, 2007

Indicators	Percentage of households	Average per household
Willing to move to a safer place	14.28	
Reasons for not moving to other safer places[a]		
For economic reasons	66.67	
To ancestral place	33.33	
Others	8.33	
Amount willing to spend on better protection		
For house		Rs. 62,500 ($1,587.5)
For crop		Rs. 25,000 ($635)
For cattle		Rs. 8,250 ($209.55)
Incentives for better protection		
Low interest rate loan	37.5	
Government subsidy	50	
Others	12.5	
Early warning system	20	
Warning from government source		
Warning from radio source		
Warning from TV source		
Personal Experience		
Willingness to pay	80	Rs. 414.55 ($10.53)
Man-days	73.33	5 to 6 days
Materials	6.67	Rs. 150 ($3.81)
Willingness to accept		
Willingness to accept	33.33	Rs. 25,200 ($640.1)

Source: Authors.

[a] Reasons mentioned by the households are not mutually exclusive. The households interviewed have provided several answers and thus the figures add up to more than 100 percent.

more or less corroborate the findings of other studies. For example, Matsuda (1993) found that Bangladeshi farmers living in the flood plains have adapted to normal floods and are not willing to shift. They think that "Almighty God knows everything" and appear not to be interested in leaving their community for a safer place.

When asked if they would like to protect their property from natural disasters, respondents cited that they would like to make their home more resistant to natural disasters and were willing to pay more than 62,500 rupees (US$1,587.50) to do so. Similarly, to protect crops, their willingness to pay is 25,000 rupees (US$635), while they would spend 8,250 rupees (US$209.55) toward safeguarding their livestock. This amount of money is significantly higher than their annual income and higher than the losses suffered, demonstrating the villagers' strong willingness to pay[14] to protect themselves from natural disasters.

It is clear that the people of this region need external support for better protection from flooding. The majority of the respondents would like to receive help from the government in the form of loans and subsidies. Close to 37.5 percent were keen on low-interest-rate loans to fund protection measures, while 50 percent of respondents would prefer government subsidies. Some of the respondents asked for cattle/livestock vaccination.

A warning system plays an important role in disaster preparedness. This may take different forms, such as warnings from the local government, radio, or television. In our case study, when asked about the accuracy of the warning system, only 20 percent of respondents said they had received early warning information. Instead, they depend on personal experience of increasing water levels during floods.

The respondents were also asked about the maximum amount they would be willing to pay to restrict the increasing devastation each year caused by floods. A total of 80 percent reported that they are willing to pay, not in cash but in the form of man-days,[15] for about five to six man-days per household. The focus group members also informed us that they would be willing to pay to save their families from flooding but here too, not by paying in cash but in the form of man-days. Few of the respondents said they would wish to share construction materials, which on an average cost not more than 150 rupees (US$3.81). The willingness to pay for the residents can be assigned an average figure of 414.55 rupees (US$10.53) per household. However, the question of willingness to pay was not asked to each household member. Assuming the wage rate is 70 rupees (US$1.77) per day, this amounts to approximately 400 rupees (US$10.16).

In a developing country such as India, the percentage of respondents who are willing to accept[16] aid should have been more in line with their willingness to pay but in our case study area, only 33.33 percent of people would be willing to accept monetary help up to 25,200 rupees (US$640.08), a figure higher than their income and losses. It is interesting to point out that people at the same time wanted the government to take the initiative to improve the irrigation facilities and generate employment in their locality. The focus group members also said that they wanted the government to carry out a de-siltation process to improve the carrying capacity of the river.

An Overview of Measures and Policies to Tackle Flooding in West Bengal

India has never had a disaster management policy. Instead, the approach to disaster management has been reactive and relief-centric. However, a paradigm shift has now taken place at the national level from this relief-centric perspective to a more holistic and integrated approach, with emphasis on prevention, mitigation, and preparedness (Kumar 2008).

After the unexpectedly heavy floods of 1954, the government of India took several steps to study the phenomenon and suggested measures to address some of the issues, notably:

- a policy statement (1954);
- a high-level committee on floods (1957);
- another policy statement (1958);

- a ministerial committee on flood control (1964);
- a ministers' committee on floods and flood relief (1972);
- working groups on flood control producing five-year plans;
- a National Food Commission (1980);
- a national water policy (1987);
- a national commission on an integrated water resource development plan (1996);
- regional task forces (1996) and
- the Disaster Management Act (2005).

These commissions on flooding and natural hazards have offered valuable recommendations covering different aspects of disaster management. Of all the above-mentioned moves, the Disaster Management Act (2005) has assumed the most importance.

The present institutional framework following the Act's introduction can be illustrated by a flowchart (figure 9.4). Specifically, mitigation, preparedness, and response are multidisciplinary functions involving a number of ministries and departments. The Act proposes the creation of Disaster Management Authorities, both at national and state levels, with representatives from the relevant ministries and departments.

The states have also been asked to set up Disaster Management Authorities under the chief minister, with ministers of relevant departments (Water Resources, Agriculture, Drinking Water Supply, Environment & Forests, Urban Development, Home, Rural Development, etc.) as members.

Following the guidelines, the West Bengal government has taken the initiative for disaster management, especially flooding, renaming the Department of Relief, formed in 1992, the Department of Disaster Management on June 29, 2006.

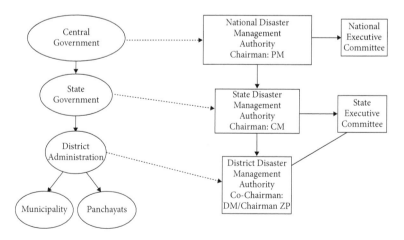

FIGURE 9.4 Institutional framework for disaster management

Source: P. G. Dhar Chakrabarti, National Institute of Disaster Management, presentation at the World Bank, February 2007. Accessed February 20, 2009.
http://siteresources.worldbank.org/INTDISMGMT/Resources/339456–1158594430052/2950719–1172610358251/chakrabarti.pdf.

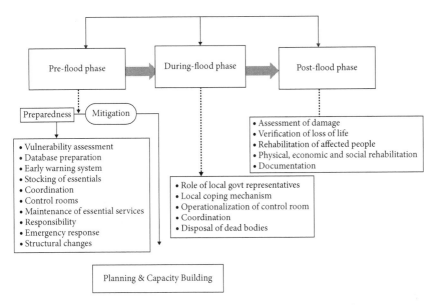

FIGURE 9.5 Standard operating procedure for a flood management in West Bengal

Source: Government of West Bengal (2006). *Monograph on Flood Management*. Kolkata, India: Department of Disaster Management.

This now constitutes a holistic approach toward flood management, with emphasis not only on the traditional postdisaster response but also on predisaster preventive/ mitigation preparedness as well. The standard operating procedure (SOP), which is formulated for the person supervising flood management, consists of three phases: pre-flooding, during-flooding, and post-flooding. The structure of the approach can be explained with the help of a flow chart (figure 9.5). Below, the different aspects of the flow chart are briefly explained.[17]

Activities during the pre-flood phase are essentially aimed at preparedness and mitigation.

Preparedness refers to the protective measures that enable an individual, the community, and the government to respond appropriately to a flood situation by minimizing the loss of lives, disruption of critical services and damage to properties when the flood actually occurs. It includes:

- a vulnerability assessment,
- database preparation,
- an early warning dissemination system,
- stocking of essential commodities,
- maintenance of essential services,
- preparedness for emergency response,
- arrangement of boats, and other equipment
- structural verification and changes.

Mitigation, on the other hand, refers to those measures that help to reduce both the impact of flood and the vulnerability of the area. These include the construction or improvement of drainage channels, the strengthening of embankments, the de-silting of riverbeds, and the removal of human encroachment along riverbanks.

It is also important to train the community affected by natural hazards in tackling floods. The disaster managers are to perform these activities as a part of the SOP for the pre-flood phase.

During the flooding phase, the different steps that can be taken refer to the involvement of local government representatives, local coping mechanisms,[18] and the operation of the control room, as well as the disposal of carcasses and dead bodies.

Finally, the post-flood phase consists of an assessment of damages, the verification of loss of life, the rehabilitation of the affected people, animal care, physical, economic, and social rehabilitation, and the documentation of the events.

The discussion clearly reflects a paradigm shift in the attitude of the government from its earlier relief-centric perspective to a more holistic and integrated approach, with an emphasis on prevention, mitigation, and preparedness. Instead of crisis management the government is now playing a proactive role.

ACTIVITIES OF THE WEST BENGAL GOVERNMENT[19]

The Department of Disaster Management as the designated nodal agency of the West Bengal state government for disaster management activities has undertaken the following activities since 2006/07:

- Ten flood shelters were constructed, costing six million rupees (US$152,000), as well as 10 relief stores at a cost of 1.6 million rupees (US$140,000).
- Emergency relief/financial assistance from the District Magistrates was established. Special Gratuitous Relief is paid to flood victims in kind (rice/wheat) at a rate of 12 kg per adult. The amount of wheat distributed, 1,065 megatons, cost 697,500 rupees (US$180,000), while the rice distributed, 19,055 megatons, cost 167,684,000 rupees (US$4.26 million).
- Relief materials such as tarpaulins, clothing, blankets, dry food, and baby food were also distributed.
- Indigent families, having no financial resources to rebuild or repair their dwellings, were given 4,000 rupees (US$101.60) per family for heavily damaged houses and 2,000 rupees (US$50.80) for partly damaged houses.
- Relief contingency funds were used for the purchase of dry food, the functioning of a soup kitchen, the hiring of boats for rescue operations, preparation of temporary shelters, and transportation of food and other relief and rescue materials.

ASSESSMENT

Due to the programs relative infancy, it is difficult to make an in-depth assessment of its effectiveness and results. By considering the opinions of different stakeholders however, such as the local Panchayat Pradhan (head of the elected rural local bodies), the secretary of a local NGO and an insurance agent, as well as from the focus group discussions and household interviews, a modest assessment can nonetheless be attempted.

The local Panchayat Pradhan of Debhog Gram, reported that three million rupees (US$76,200) had been spent on road and school repairs. The Gram Panchayat has allotted 50,000 rupees (US$1,270) for clothing and food items.

The government of West Bengal, with the help of the UN Development Programme, adopted a Disaster Risk Management program in 2003 to be implemented in different districts of West Bengal. The Panchayat Pradhan said that, as part of an early warning system for disaster preparedness, the residents receive information through announcements from the local Gram Panchayat office. However, when asked about the accuracy of the warning system, only a few households said they had received such early warning information. Rather, they estimate the timing of floods based on past experience. The Gram Panchayat also organized awareness camps for flood protection, spending 2,000 rupees (US$50.8) for this purpose. Although the Gram Panchayat wants a permanent solution, it says it cannot do anything except provide information to the upper tier of the government.

The former principal of Sabang College reported that to mitigate the impacts of natural disasters, government/nongovernment organizations supplied food and clothing, medicine and medical services, and materials for shelter at the appropriate time and in sufficient quantities. Distribution, however, was inadequate. Removal of debris and restoration of water supply was also performed in a timely fashion, while restoration of communication services was delayed. Additionally, there exists no drainage system in the area, so flood water can only recede via a natural process.

The local insurance agent informed us that there exists no policy for affected people. Two years ago, however, nonlife general insurance for disasters was available from an Indian company, Housing Development and Finance Corporation (HDFC). However, people were unable to make claims until the government announced that 80 percent of the block had been affected by the flood. The HDFC is now no longer interested in covering the area with this type of insurance, as the area is too prone to flooding and they risk huge losses.

The analysis shows that most of the steps taken are relief-oriented and are thus short term in nature. Some structural measures such as construction of flood centers and relief stores, though undertaken, are inadequate. The government has not taken sufficient initiative in promoting flood-resistant housing, as well as providing an adequate number of shelters for affected households.

The main problem is the unplanned development of transport facilities such as roads and railways, as well as the siltation of the rivers, which results in greater frequency of flooding and stagnation of flood water for many days. For long-term flood management, flood control measures, especially structural measures, should be given more attention.

Summary and Conclusion

This chapter has dealt with vulnerable flood-prone regions, the extent of damages caused due to major floods in the past, and related policies and measures adopted in West Bengal. Flood problems in India have been described, dividing the country into vulnerable regions via the application of a vulnerability index. West Bengal remains one of the most flood-vulnerable states in India and a flood disaster profile of West Bengal has been put forward, showcasing the nature and extent of flood and the damage caused by floods in recent years.

The results of the case study conducted in one of the flood-affected areas, Debhog Gram Panchayat, in Paschim Medinipur, West Bengal, shows that floods severely affect the poor people of these regions. The floods of 2007 caused a range of different types of damage, such as reductions in agricultural production, loss of livestock, harm to small-scale industry, destruction of household property, contamination of drinking water, and disruption of utilities. The case study revealed that rural households are willing to give five to six man-days for the development of public infrastructure in the flood-affected rural areas. Thus, a successful mix of willingness to pay and schemes such as the Employment Guarantee Scheme (EGS),[20] implemented first in Maharastra, may work well to support the reconstruction process. The case study also demonstrates that most respondents are not willing to accept compensation. Rather, people want the government to engage in preventative initiatives.

Thus, the case study enhances our knowledge by enlightening us to how the residents of a disaster affected area have locally adopted various measures to develop disaster prevention, response, and mitigation. These measures are often based on local experiences, perceptions, and economic capacity.

An overview of the measures and the policies adopted by the government of West Bengal reflects a paradigm shift from a relief-centric perspective to a holistic and integrated approach toward management of floods with emphasis not only on the traditional postdisaster response, but also on predisaster preventive/mitigation preparedness, as well as the standard operating procedure (SOP), which is formulated for a disaster manager for flood management.

Various measures for flood management have been presented. Short-term, as well as long-term, strategies are required for combating floods and to minimize their detrimental effects on society. There is a need to improve cooperation and coordination between scientific communities and the appropriate local government and civil defense agencies for developing effective, workable response plans for flood disasters.

Managing floods in any tropical or developing country is difficult for any single agency or organization. Community participation in preparedness, flood fighting, and disaster response is required. Voluntary organizations can act as an interface between the government and community. The media can also play an important role in flood mitigation by disseminating official safety information before and after a disaster, for example.

Flood insurance has several advantages as a means of alleviating the loss burden. It enables property owners to spread an uncertain but potentially large loss uniformly over a long period of time. Flood insurance has yet to be implemented, but sincere efforts have to be made for its introduction.

An assessment of the recent performance of the government in prevention, mitigation and preparedness in light of our case study does not paint a very hopeful picture. People are willing to participate in this effort, although their dependence on the government persists.

In conclusion, it is important that flood management programs be integrated with the overall development effort of the state. We have to live with floods, but it would be easier if the quality of life improves. We still have a long way to go.

Notes

1. MICRODIS is an integrated project funded under the European Union's Sixth Framework Programme—Thematic Priority 6.3—Global Change and Ecosystems. The overall goal of the project is to strengthen preparedness, mitigation, and prevention strategies in order to reduce the health, social, and economic impacts of extreme events on communities (CRED 2006)

2. Estimated from the data on district domestic product of West Bengal (Government of West Bengal, State Domestic Product and District Domestic Product 2007b).

3. See box 9.1 for the methodology.

4. A "block" consists of group of Gram Panchayats, the grassroots-level tier of the Panchayati Raj system in West Bengal. The Panchayat Raj system consists of elected bodies at the Gram, Block, and District levels.

5. Paschim means west.

6. Local government: A Gram Panchayat is the grassroots-level tier of the Panchayati Raj system in West Bengal. The Panchayat Raj system consists of elected bodies at the Gram, Block, and District levels.

7. Grouping of those individuals registered at any time in the electoral rolls pertaining to a constituency of a Gram Panchayat.

8. Exchange rate ($1 = 39.37 rupees) as of December 2007 (http://www.x-rates.com).

9. Made of pebbles.

10. Made of mud.

11. See note 2.

12. The "backward class" is a term used by the Government of India for castes that are economically and socially disadvantaged. They typically include the Dalits, the Scheduled castes and tribes, and the Other Backward Classes.

13. The Kharif crop is the autumn harvest, but better known as the monsoon crop in the Indian subcontinent (India, Pakistan Sri Lanka, Nepal). The Rabi crop is the spring harvest (also known as the "winter crop") in the Indian subcontinent.

14. The question that was asked for willingness to pay is as follows: "How much you are willing to pay to better protect your home, crop and other assets from floods?".

15. An industrial unit of production equal to the work one person can produce in a day.

16. The question that was asked for willingness to accept is as follows: "How much are you willing to accept as compensation from the government for recurring damage due to floods?" The concepts of Willingness to Pay (WTP) and Willingness to Accept (WTA) are normally applied to estimate the total economic value of natural resources through contingent valuation method. However, these concepts can also be applied to estimate flood losses.

17. This section draws heavily from Government of West Bengal 2006.

18. Some of the local coping mechanisms include:

- temporary levees made during the floods along the river banks,
- raising the height of the base foundation of residential houses,
- makeshift boats for temporary transportation,
- shelter in the highlands.

19. These activities are reported in Government of West Bengal Administrative Report 2007a.

20. The Employment Guarantee Scheme prevailing in Maharastra, India, is one of the largest public work programs in the developing world. This program mainly services poverty alleviation as it guarantees employment at a defined wage (Dev 2005).

References

Benson, C., and Clay, E. J. (2003). "Disaster, Vulnerability, and the Global Economy." In *Building Safer Cities: The Future of Disaster Risk*, edited by A. Kreimer, M. Arnold and A. Carlin. Disaster Management Series 3. Washington, D.C.: World Bank.

Census of India. (2001). Office of the Registrar General, New Delhi, India.

Chapman, G. P., and Rudra, K. (2007). "Water as Foe, Water as Friend: Lessons from Bengal's Millennium Flood." *Journal of South Asian Development* 2(1): 19–49.

CRED (2006). *Sixth Frame Work Programme, Sub-Priority 1.1.63, Global Change & Ecosystems, MICRODIS, Integrated Health Social and Economic Impacts of Extreme Events: Evidence, Methods and Tools*. Brussels, Belgium: Université catholique de Louvain.

Dan Church Aid. (2007). Accessed March 2008. http://www.danchurchaid.org/sider_paa_hjemmesiden/where_we_work/asia/india/what_we_do.

Das Gupta, I. (2007). "Development of Field Protocol." Presented in the Economic Working Group Meeting, MICRODIS, Jadavpur University, November 2–4, Kolkata, India.

Dev, S. M. (2005). "India's (Maharastra) Employment Guarantee Scheme: Lessons from Long Experience." In *Employment for Poverty Reduction and Food Security*, edited by J. von Braun. Washington, D.C.: International Food Policy Research Institute (IFPRI).

EM-DAT: The OFDA/CRED Emergency Disaster Database. Université catholique de Louvain, Brussels, Belgium. http://www.emdat.be.

Ghani, M. U. (2001). "Participatory Strategy for Flood Mitigation in East and Northeast India: Case Study of the Ganges-Brahmaputra-Meghna Basin." Accessed February 18, 2009. http://www.unescap.org/esd/water/disaster/2001/india.doc.

Ghosh, A. (2005). "Strategies in Flood Disaster Management: West Bengal." In *Combating Disaster: Perspective in the New Millennium*, edited by A. Banerjee, B. Mallick, D. Sarkar, and H. Datta. Kolkata, India: ACB Publication.

Government of India, Ministry of Home Affairs, Disaster Management Division. (2007). Accessed March 2008. http://www.ndmindia.nic.in/flood2007/floodMonth/SEPT2007/SITREPNO.120DTD28.09.2007.doc.

Government of West Bengal. (2006). *Monograph on Flood Management.* Kolkata, India: Department of Disaster Management.

———. (2007a). *Administrative Report 2005–06 & 2006–07.* Kolkata, India: Department of Disaster Management.

———. (2007b). *State Domestic Product and District Domestic Product of West Bengal.* Kolkata, India: Bureau of Applied Economics & Statistics.

Joshi, P. C., Khattri, P., Singh, M., Fordham, M., and Guha-Sapir, D. (2007). "Flood: Trends and Social Impacts in Indian Context." Accessed February 18, 2009. http://www.pik-potsdam. de/events/scenario/presentations/joshi.pdf.

Kumar, S. (2008). "National Institute of Disaster Management, Policy, Planning and Cross Cutting Issues Division." Presented in MICRODIS Annual Meeting, February 17–20, Delhi University, Delhi, India.

Lahiri, A., Sen, T. K., Rao, R. K., and Jena, P. R. (2001). "Economic Consequences of the Gujarat Earthquake." *Economic and Political Weekly* 36(16): 1319–1332.

Majhi, B., Dey, K., Ghosh, M., and Biswas, R. (2005). "Strategies in Flood Disaster Management: West Bengal." In *Combating Disaster: Perspective in the New Millennium,* edited by A. Banerjee, B. Mallick, D. Sarkar, and H. Datta. Kolkata, India: ACB Publication.

Matsuda, I. (1993). "Loss of Human Lives Induced by the Cyclone of 29–30 April, 1991 in Bangladesh." *GeoJournal* 31(4): 319–325.

O'Hare, G. (2001). "Hurricane 07B in the Godavari Delta, Andhra Pradesh, India: Vulnerability, Mitigation and the Spatial Impact." *Geographical Journal* 167(1): 23–38.

Panigrahi, N. (2003). "Rehabilitation of Fisherfolk Communities: The Role of State and NGOs in Super Cyclone Affected District of Orissa." *Review of Development and Change* 8(1) (January–June): 71–94.

Roy, B., Mruthyunjaya, C., and Selvarajan, S. (2002). "Vulnerability to Climate Induced Natural Disasters with Special Emphasis on Coping Strategies of the Rural Poor in Coastal Orissa, India." Paper prepared for the UNFCCC COP8 Conference organized by the Government of India, United Nations Environment Programmes, and FICCI, October 23–November 1, Vigyan Bhaban, New Delhi, India.

Sarangi, P., and Penthoi, G. C. (2005). "Economic Implications of Natural Disasters in Orissa: A Retrospective View." *Orissa Review,* June.

Singh, O. (2003). "Floods in the Gurdaspur District of Punjab—Need for a Systematic Study of their Nature, Impact and Control." *Indian Journal of Public Administration* 49(3) (July–September): 463–467.

Srivastava, Y. K., Doley, B., Pal, D. K., Das, R. K., Sudhakar, S., Adiga, S., Venkatachary, K. V., and Srivastava, S. K. (2000). "High Resolution Remote Sensing Data & GIS Techniques in Updating of Infrastructure Details for Flood Damage Assessment—A Case Study." Proceedings ARCS 2000. Taipei, Taiwan.

Thomalla, F., and Hanna Schmuck, H. (2004). "We All Knew That a Cyclone was Coming: Disaster Preparedness and the Cyclone of 1999 in Orissa, India." *Disasters* 4: 373–387.

UNDP (Various issues). *Human Development Report.* New York: Oxford University Press.

UN/ISDR (2004). *Living with Risk: A Global Review of Disaster Reduction Initiatives.* Geneva: UN Publications.

Victoria, L. (2002). *Impact Assessment Study of the Orissa Disaster Management Project.* Bangkok, Thailand: Asian Disaster Preparedness Centre.

10 }

How Do Households Manage the Effects of Natural Disasters?
THE ROLE OF INTERHOUSEHOLD TRANSFERS IN NICARAGUA
Indhira Santos

Introduction

This chapter explores the role of interhousehold transfers in the recovery process in the aftermath of a natural disaster and how these transfers interact with public aid schemes. Three facts motivate this work. First, interhousehold transfers represent an important share of household income in developing countries, in an environment in which income tends to be highly volatile, in large part due to nature-related shocks. Second, our understanding of the effects of natural disasters at the household level, and the mechanisms through which they work, is surprisingly poor. Third, climate change, population growth, and environmental degradation are likely to intensify the frequency and destructive power of natural disasters, as well as the vulnerability of populations to these events.

Natural disasters can have substantial and long-lasting effects on the well-being of households, especially in poor countries. In the absence of formal insurance schemes, households in these settings are likely to use a variety of methods to deal with risk and its consequences. In this chapter, I explore the capacity of private transfers to act as insurance in the aftermath of a large storm, as well as the interaction between public aid and such informal assistance. Since both formal and informal safety nets only partially protect households from loss of income, I also analyse the extent to which households may resort to other measures.

I focus on the case of Hurricane Mitch in rural Nicaragua. Hurricane Mitch hit Central America in October 1998. This storm, with over 50 inches of rain in five days, was one of the most destructive natural phenomena ever experienced in the region, causing more than 10,000 deaths. In Nicaragua alone, there were more than 3,000 deaths and more than 45,000 households were affected.[1]

This chapter reflects the views of the author and does not necessarily represent the views of any organizations to which the author is affiliated.

Studying informal insurance schemes in rural Nicaragua is interesting for a number of reasons. First, Nicaragua is the second poorest country in Latin America and shocks to income and wealth can, therefore, have devastating consequences for household welfare. This is especially true in an economy where formal insurance arrangements are effectively nonexistent. In 1998 only 2 percent of rural households had savings, 10 percent had received loans in the previous 12 months, and only 6 percent had made any purchase on credit in the previous year. By contrast, interhousehold transfers are common: 22 percent of rural households participated in private transfers. For the median household, these represented 35 percent of nontransfer income.

Existing Evidence on Risk Sharing

There is a growing literature on the *ex-ante* and *ex-post* private mechanisms used by households in poor countries to deal with shocks. In general, there seems to be evidence of households being able to protect themselves from consumption fluctuations, at least partially. Townsend (1994), in his seminal paper on the topic, fails to find evidence of perfect risk-sharing among rural households in India, since household consumption depended on household income even after controlling for consumption at the village level (where risk-pooling is expected to happen). The author concludes, however, that there is an important degree of risk-sharing, since the coefficient on household income is small.

Studies have moved away from testing the existence of perfect risk-pooling toward analyzing the actual mechanisms used to smooth consumption. This line of work has focused on the sale and purchase of assets, suboptimal choices in production and employment, changes in living arrangements, informal borrowing, and interhousehold transfers, among other factors. Deaton (1990, 1992) and Rosenzweig and Wolpin (1993), for instance, have found evidence of risk being shared through asset markets. The covariance of asset values and income as a result of common shocks, however, reduces the usefulness of assets as a self-insurance mechanism; furthermore, assets are expensive so, even if effective in dealing with shocks, not very many households in poor countries have assets that can potentially be used as insurance.

Risk can also be reduced *ex-ante* by diversifying or by carrying out economic activities that are less risk-sensitive. This strategy could lead to inefficient diversification, however, causing household income to decrease. Using household data from India, Rosenzweig and Wolpin (1993) find evidence that absolute average losses for wealthier farmers are smaller than for less wealthy farmers in rainfall variable environments. They argue that farmers in riskier environments choose portfolios of assets that are less sensitive to weather variations but are less profitable. On the other hand, also using data from India, Kochar (1993) emphasizes the use of labor markets as a mechanism for dealing with idiosyncratic crop shocks.

Household structure may also change as a result of a shock. Foster and Rosenzweig (2002) argue that living arrangements are often wrongly considered a fixed characteristic of households in the literature on risk-sharing. The authors suggest a model where households balance the costs and benefits of staying in the household after a shock. The benefits refer to the economies of scale in agricultural production and cost of living, while the costs refer to a lesser ability to diversify away risk. In this model, there is nonsatiation of the public good, so a rise in income increases consumption of the public good by all members and decreases the probability of breakup in the household. A negative shock, on the other hand, increases the probability of division in the household. Deaton and Paxson (1998) present an alternative model where the public good has a fixed cost—like utilities, so a negative shock may increase the probability of cohabitation.

Informal credit has also been shown in the literature to be relevant for risk-sharing (Rosenzweig 1988; Udry 1990, 1994; Townsend 1995). In an environment where there is imperfect commitment, Kocherlakota (1996) argues that informal risk-sharing arrangements could be easier to achieve if transfers are combined with contingent credit. This is based on the assumption that credit creates more incentives to reciprocate. With this in mind, if households are self-interested, then informal credit should be the main mechanism through which risk is shared.

In this chapter, I look at the role of interhousehold transfers in dealing with the effects of Hurricane Mitch in rural Nicaragua. Interhousehold transfers of cash, clothing, and food are common in many countries. Cox and Jimenez (1998) report that the percentage of households receiving private transfers in a sample of six developing countries (El Salvador, Indonesia, Malaysia, Mexico, Peru, Philippines) ranged from 19 to 47 percent, and the median amounts transferred represented up to 30 percent of the median household income. Interhousehold transfers have been found to be relevant for informal insurance in studies carried out by Lucas and Stark (1985), Rosenzweig (1988), Rosenzweig and Stark (1989), Platteau (1991), and Fafchamps and Lund (2003), among others.

In particular, Lucas and Stark (1985) showed that, controlling for wealth, rural households in Botswana that were exposed to droughts received more transfers than households in nondrought regions. An important limitation of this study, however, is that it looks at households at one point in time, so it is not possible to know if the households in drought-blighted regions received more transfers because of the shock or because of some other characteristic that made them different from those in the nondrought areas. To show that interhousehold transfers are used as an informal insurance mechanism, it has to be the case that transfers increase the most for the households that suffer the greatest shocks, *ceteris paribus*.

Rosenzweig (1988) uses data from rural India and finds evidence that private transfers offset part of the impact of income fluctuations on household consumption. Moreover, the author finds some evidence that these interhousehold transfers are a better way to mitigate consumption variation than alternative methods like credit markets. In a related paper, Rosenzweig and Stark (1989) present findings suggesting that long-distance marriages in rural India are used to diversify risk, since ties with other families that do not face the same shocks are strengthened. These new ties create a new and reliable source of private transfers that help smooth consumption.

In short, the existing evidence seems to suggest that rural households in poor countries use a wide variety of mechanisms to deal with shocks. Among these mechanisms, interhousehold transfers have been widely explored in the literature and found to play a key role in risk-sharing. There is less evidence, however, on the insurance capacity of interhousehold transfers in the case of a large generalized shock like a natural disaster. Furthermore, using a weather-related shock provides a clear exogenous shock to the household, which strengthens any causal interpretation of the results.

Hurricane Mitch in Nicaragua

Hurricane Mitch hit Nicaragua during the last week of October 1998. With winds of up to 290 km per hour, it was one of the most destructive storms ever to hit Central America. It formed as a tropical front between October 19 and 20 and later developed as a low pressure zone and eventually as the thirteenth tropical depression of the hurricane season. On October 24, the storm was categorized as a hurricane.

Mitch followed a very irregular trajectory (figure 10.1). While initially Cuba and Jamaica had been alerted, Mitch later changed course toward the northwest, generating hurricane warnings in Mexico and Belize. On October 27, the storm unexpectedly moved into Central America, hitting Honduras first. Once inland, Mitch weakened, becoming a tropical storm by the time its rains arrived in Nicaragua. Nonetheless, in five days, Mitch generated more rain in Nicaragua than the country typically receives in an average year.

Nicaragua, with an area of 130,700 square km and a population of 4.8 million in 1998, was at the time the second poorest country in Latin America. It had a per capita income of US$741 (constant 2000 dollars). Seventy-nine percent of the population lived on less than US$2 a day and 45 percent lived on less than US$1 in extreme

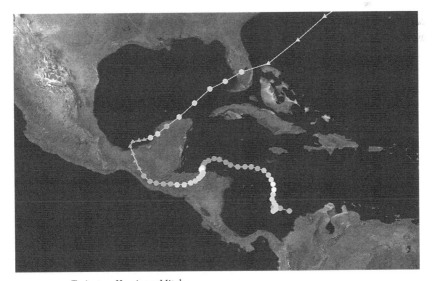

FIGURE 10.1 Trajectory Hurricane Mitch

Source: Wikipedia, WikiProject Tropical cyclones/Tracks. The background image is from NASA. Tracking data from the National Hurricane Center.

poverty. The main source of foreign exchange was the remittances sent home by Nicaraguans abroad. These transfers amounted to 17.8 percent of the country's GDP in 2004, the third largest in the region (World Bank 2008).

Nicaragua is divided into three main geopolitical regions, Pacific, Central, and Atlantic, and it is further divided into 15 departments and two autonomous subregions, which are, in turn, divided into 147 municipalities. Hurricane Mitch affected mainly the country's Central and Pacific regions. Over 3,000 people died and almost 300 were reported injured. The worst incident was the collapse of the Casitas volcano just northwest of Managua, where 505 housing units were destroyed and 2,887 people were killed. Overall, more than 867,000 people lost their homes due to landslides and floods, and over 500 schools and 140 health centers were damaged or destroyed. Mitch generated estimated losses of over US$1 billion or 51 percent of Nicaragua's 1997 GDP, and it is considered one of the top ten disasters in terms of costs as a proportion of the size of the country's economy (Guha-Sapir, Hargitt, and Hoyois 2004).

In response to the huge economic and human loss caused by Hurricane Mitch, significant help was provided to those affected. The Nicaraguan government put together an emergency fund of over US$1.1 million, drawing on resources from governments, financial institutions, and the private sector. In addition, food was distributed in affected areas. Moreover, the international aid received by November 23, 1998, added up to US$15.8 million, most of it in kind (ECLAC 1999).

The Data: Living Standards Measurement Studies

To carry out the empirical analysis, I use data from the Living Standards Measurement Studies (LSMS) carried out in Nicaragua in 1998 and 1999 with the support of the World Bank.[2] The 1998 nationally representative survey was completed between April and August of that year, with a total of 4,209 households being interviewed, 46 percent of which were in rural areas. Shortly after the completion of the 1998 questionnaires in late October, Hurricane Mitch hit Nicaragua. It was decided to conduct a follow-up survey in order to assess the damage caused by the storm. For the 1999 round, interviewers revisited only the households located in areas affected by the hurricane that had been surveyed one year earlier.[3] Hence, the 1999 and 1998 household surveys in Nicaragua constitute a panel. In 1999, 561 households—323 in rural areas—were reinterviewed. These 323 rural households interviewed in both 1998 and 1999 constitute the panel sample.

Nicaragua's LSMS surveys are ideal for answering questions on informal insurance mechanisms thanks to the number of detailed questions on private transfers and other insurance mechanisms, as well as information on the type and size of losses suffered and other characteristics of households.

I first consider the main characteristics of the rural households in the sample. Table 10.1 includes the sample means and the standard deviations of each variable, as well as the difference in the average values between 1999 and 1998. I use monthly information, unless otherwise noted. The areas of Nicaragua most affected by Mitch

TABLE 10.1 } Descriptive Statistics

Variable	1998		1999		
	Mean	Std. Dev.	Mean	Std. Dev.	Difference
Demographics					
Household size	6.11	0.17	6.79	0.19	0.68**
Region—proportion of households on each region					
Central	0.43	0.03	0.43	0.03	0.00
Pacific	0.46	0.03	0.45	0.03	0.01
Atlantic	0.11	0.02	0.11	0.02	0.00
Characteristics of the dwelling					
Floor material—proportion of households with each type					
Soil	0.72	0.03	0.72	0.02	0.00
Floor tile	0.13	0.02	0.13	0.02	0.00
Other	0.15	0.02	0.15	0.02	0.00
Wall material—proportion of households with each type					
Wood	0.27	0.02	0.31	0.03	0.04
Brick	0.17	0.02	0.15	0.02	0.01
Cement	0.11	0.02	0.13	0.02	0.02
Roof material—proportion of households with each type					
Zinc	0.47	0.03	0.52	0.03	0.04
Tile	0.38	0.03	0.38	0.03	0.00
Other	0.14	0.02	0.10	0.02	−0.04
Non-transfer monthly income (cordobas)					
Household income	1,049.18	110.61	1,172.12	121.20	122.93
Adjusted household income per capita	337.62	34.88	346.82	33.36	9.19
Public transfers	17.45	15.52	80.52	11.83	63.07**
Monthly private transfers (cordobas)					
Proportion households receiving private transfers	0.15	0.02	0.20	0.02	0.06**
Proportion households sending private transfers	0.01	0.01	0.02	0.01	0.01
Net private transfers	62.54	12.64	141.70	37.74	79.16**
Assets					
Proportion of households that own land	0.42	0.03	0.48	0.03	0.06
Land size (in "manzanas")	13.01	3.40	12.08	2.65	−0.93
Value land (cordobas)	32,831.90	18,749.46	12,197.39	2,117.68	20,634.51
Value nonland assets (cordobas)	48,669.59	18,880.08	20,513.29	1,762.10	28,156.30
Characteristics Head of Household					
Age (years)	46.72	0.91	47.48	0.89	0.46
Proportion that is female	0.15	0.02	0.15	0.02	−0.01
Proportion that has a partner	0.81	0.02	0.80	0.02	0.00
Proportion that is alphabetized	0.55	0.03	0.55	0.03	0.00
Years of education	3.68	0.22	3.91	0.22	0.23
Number of households	323		323		

were the northern and western parts of the country, which correspond to the Central and the Pacific regions. In fact, 43 percent of the households in the sample lived in the Central region, while 46 percent were in the Pacific region in 1998.

Table 10.1 includes the average monthly nontransfer income of the affected households. Total income is obtained by adding up self-reported income for all members of the household from the following sources: wages, net profits from self-employment, interest, insurance indemnification, lottery, compensation for work-related accidents, bequests, income from rental (of land, animals, or machinery), and other income.

Income in the affected areas is low. The average monthly household income for the affected households did not change significantly between the two years: it was 1,049.18 cordobas (US$87.43) in 1998 and 1,172.12 cordobas (US$97.68) in 1999.[4] In per capita terms, adjusting for economies of scale and child-adult equivalent, monthly income was 337.62 cordobas (US$28.13) in 1998 while it was 346.82 cordobas (US$28.90) the year after. If one looks at median income instead of averages, median per capita income was 173.85 cordobas (US$14.49) in 1998 and 194.45 cordobas (US$16.20) in 1999.

Private transfers are one of the main components of household income. In Nicaragua, these transfers are large and prevalent in the different regions and in households with very different characteristics. The 1998 and 1999 surveys include two main questions regarding private transfers. First, the household was asked whether it had received any transfer (monetary or in kind) from family outside the household or friends, and then it was asked how much. Private transfers significantly increased after Hurricane Mitch—15 percent of all households in the affected area received transfers from family or friends in 1998, rising to 20 percent by 1999. The average size of the monthly net private transfers received in 1998 was 62.54 cordobas (US$5.21), more than doubling in real terms by 1999. This increase in the flow of private gifts is also evident when one looks at the median net private transfers conditional on having received such transfers: 250 cordobas (US$20.83) before the shock and 278.40 cordobas (US$23.20) after. Furthermore, these interhousehold transfers represented an important source of income for the families. For the median family, conditional on having received transfers, they represented 43 percent of total nontransfer income in 1998.

The dataset does not contain information on who is sending the private transfers to whom, so one cannot know exactly how risk is being shared. Private transfers increased noticeably after Mitch, however; this could be an indication that private transfers might be coming from areas in Nicaragua not affected by the storm, or from abroad. This interpretation is reinforced by the fact that only 2 percent of the affected households sent any gifts in 1999 and that the average value of such transfers was significantly lower than the average value of the transfers received by such households. Moreover, using the nationally representative 1998 survey, one can see that only 1.26 percent of the households in Nicaragua were sending transfers to other households (while 21.45 percent of households received transfers). This may indicate that, as expected, most transfers came from abroad.

The 1998 and 1999 surveys also included two questions on public transfers. The household was asked whether it had received help from the government during the month preceding the interview in any of the following forms: scholarships, pensions, food, and transfers for widowhood or orphanhood. Members of the household were also asked about their social security benefits. In the definition of public transfers used here, however, social security benefits and pensions were excluded because they represent small amounts and depend on elements not related to aid in the aftermath of Mitch. The average size per household of the public transfers received was 17.45 cordobas (US$1.45) in 1998, while it was 80.52 cordobas (US$6.71) in 1999. This difference is statistically significant and reflects the large flow of aid that came to Nicaragua after Mitch, especially from international organizations and NGOs, and which was channelled through the Nicaraguan government.

Nicaragua is the second poorest country in Latin America. Of the rural households in the panel sample, 69 percent were poor in 1998–42 percent of which lived in extreme poverty.[5] The prevalent high poverty levels were reflected, no doubt, in the characteristics of dwellings and the value of assets owned. As table 10.1 shows, roofs were mainly made from zinc and walls from wood, making dwellings very vulnerable to the strong winds and rain brought by Mitch. There are no significant differences in the construction materials used in dwellings between the two years. In terms of physical assets, there are no significant differences in their average value between 1998 and 1999 either. Forty-two percent of the households in 1998 owned land and the median size of these plots was five *manzanas* in both years.[6] Similarly, the median value of nonland assets was 10,265 cordobas (US$855.42) in 1998 and 10,588 cordobas (US$882.33) in 1999. Nonland physical assets included business assets, household assets (such as appliances), houses, animals, agricultural equipment, and agricultural installations.

We now turn to the nonfinancial characteristics of the households in the sample. After the hurricane, the average household size increased from 6.11 to 6.79 members. As discussed in the next section, this increase in average household size could reflect the use of living arrangements as a mechanism to share risk after a shock (Foster and Rosenzweig 2002; Deaton and Paxson 1998). In terms of demographics, table 10.1 includes information on the average age of the head of the household, and the proportion of heads of households that were female, as well as their educational attainment. In particular, 15 percent of households were headed by women in both years. There was no change in either the average age or the educational attainment of the household head.

In short, average household characteristics, except for those related to public and private transfers and household size, did not change significantly over the selected period.

EFFECTS OF HURRICANE MITCH

Consumption per capita among households affected by Mitch fell from an average of 556.62 cordobas (US$46.39) in 1998 to 539.50 cordobas (US$44.96) in 1999. However, this difference is not statistically significant. The fall in consumption, however, was larger for the households mostly affected by Mitch as measured by their agricultural losses. It is interesting to note that the fall in consumption observed one year later is surprisingly small. One potential explanation is that households had found ways to smooth consumption one year after the disaster.

Alternatively, one could think that since most losses resulted from lost crops, this constitutes an income shock that by 1999 would not significantly affect that year's consumption since crops can be grown again. Partial evidence for this hypothesis is that income is actually higher in 1999. Another explanation could be that had Mitch not affected these households, consumption would have actually increased. Since I do not have information on a control group in 1999, this hypothesis cannot be tested.

As expected, due to the low quality of construction materials, dwellings in rural areas were significantly affected by Mitch. In particular, 39.63 percent of the households surveyed declared that their dwelling or basic services had suffered damage as a consequence of the hurricane. Similarly, 25.70 percent had to temporarily move out of their dwelling, while 12.4 percent had to permanently do so (to somewhere else in the same municipality).

Households were also asked if they had experienced losses related to their agricultural activity. 74.30 percent responded positively, with median losses of 2,115.84 cordobas (US$176.32), or more than twice the average household income. Table 10.2 includes the percentage of households that suffered losses in a series of categories, ranging from crops (73.6 percent of households) to agricultural equipment (0.01

TABLE 10.2 } Effects of Hurricane Mitch and Social Programs

Effect of Mitch	Percentage of households	Social programs	Percentage of households benefiting
Dwelling		Food donations	58.20
Temporarily moved to another dwelling	25.70		
Permanently moved to another dwelling	12.40	Health programs	40.25
Dwelling or basic services affected by Mitch	39.63		
		Reconstruction roads	34.98
Agricultural losses	74.30		
Crops	73.06	Clothing donations	25.08
Animals for work	2.40		
Agricultural property	7.40	Employment programs	21.36
Agricultural installations	5.00		
Agricultural equipment	0.01	Medicines/water donations	11.76
Other	2.20		
		Installation latrine	9.60
Other			
A member of the household died	0.00	Reconstruction schools	6.81
Own business suffered damages	38.22		
Own business had to close	5.10	Housing donations	1.90
Own business still open, but not at full capacity	26.11		
		Reconstruction health centers	1.55
Number of households	323	*Number of households*	323

percent). Figure 10.2 shows the distribution of losses over households' pre-shock income. Conditional on experiencing losses from the hurricane, the median household lost four times its monthly income, but there was significant variation in the ratios, with the household in the 75th percentile losing 14 times its income while the 90th percentile lost over 45 times its monthly budget. This measure of the impact of Hurricane Mitch on households is used in the empirical estimations as the main indicator of the shock.

Households' own businesses were also greatly affected by the storm. In particular, 38.22 percent of those households that had their own business reported that it suffered damages. Furthermore, 5.1 percent of households had to permanently close their business because of Mitch, while 26.11 percent reported that their business remained open but not at full capacity.

In the aftermath of a major shock like a natural disaster, however, large amounts of aid usually come into the afflicted country. Public transfers, as discussed above, increased significantly after the storm. But, in addition, a number of social programs were also put into place or expanded after October 1998. Table 10.2 includes information on the proportion of households that benefited from these programs. Food donations, health programs (such as vaccinations), and the reconstruction of roads are the three programs most often cited as having benefited the rural households in the sample hit by Mitch. As discussed in the next section, nevertheless, it is important to also look at other possible mechanisms that households might have used to deal with the adverse effects of Mitch.

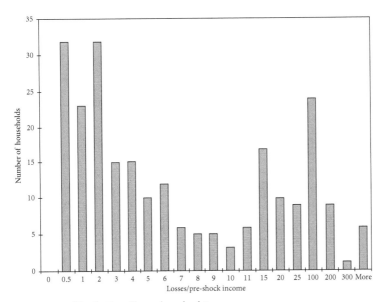

FIGURE 10.2 Distribution of losses/pre-shock income

Note: Only includes households that had losses. In the sample, over 30 percent of households had no losses. Data come from the LSMS 1999 survey.

Source: Own calculations based on Nicaragua LSMS household surveys.

Theoretical Model and Empirical Strategy

The objective of this chapter is to analyze the extent to which interhousehold transfers respond to a natural disaster. Here, I present a simple model of risk-sharing, following Fafchamps and Lund (2003) and Townsend (1994), defining the space of income-sharing as the whole world to account for the flow of international remittances.

The main idea of the model is that, if risk is efficiently shared among households, then the consumption of the household should be independent of idiosyncratic variations in income. In a closed exchange economy without storage, where at least some individuals are risk averse, Pareto efficiency means that the ratios of the households' marginal utilities will be equalized across the different states of nature. That is:

$$\frac{V'_{i}(c^{i}_{s,t},h^{i}_{s,t})}{V'_{i}(c^{i}_{s',t},h^{i}_{s',t})} = \frac{V'_{j}(c^{j}_{s,t},h^{j}_{s,t})}{V'_{j}(c^{j}_{s',t},h^{j}_{s',t})} \quad \text{for all } t, i, j, s_t \text{ and } s'_t, \tag{10.1}$$

where:

$i, j \in \{1,2,...N\}$ represent two households in the world, where N is very large;
$s_t \in S$ represents the state of nature;
$c^i_{s,t}$ is consumption of household i at time t in state s;
$h^i_{s,t}$ is a preference shock that refers to unexpected expenses.[7]

Assuming constant absolute risk aversion, one can obtain the following expression:

$$c^i_{st,t} = h^i_{st} - \frac{1}{N}\sum_{j=1}^{N}h^j_{st} + \frac{1}{N}\sum_{j=1}^{N}c^j_{st,t} + \frac{1}{\gamma}(\log\omega^i - \frac{1}{N}\sum_{j=1}^{N}\log\omega^j) \tag{10.2}$$

where:

ω^i is the implicit welfare weight of household i.

This equation is often used in the literature to test for risk-sharing. There would be perfect risk-sharing if the coefficient on household income is not significantly different from zero, and the coefficient on aggregate consumption is equal to $1/N$. This equation illustrates that the more households are able to share income with the rest of the world, the less will be the effect of shocks on households' consumption.

The literature is not clear on how one can determine the relevant risk-sharing pool. In the case of Nicaragua, I have assumed that the whole world is the relevant pool, as Nicaraguans abroad are an important source of income for households and are likely to respond with increased transfers in the face of shocks. The increase in private transfers registered in the aftermath of Hurricane Mitch suggests that risk-sharing does not happen in the immediate area of a household.

Following Fafchamps and Lund (2003), one can test for specific mechanisms of risk-sharing as, for instance, interhousehold transfers. Consumption is defined in the following way:

$$c^i_{s,t} = y^i_{st} + g^i_{s,t} + b^i_{s,t} + \Delta w^i_t \tag{10.3}$$

where:

$g^i_{s,t}$ is the net interhousehold transfers received by household i at time t in state s;
$b^i_{s,t}$ is the net informal borrowing of household i at time t in state s;
Δw^i_t is the change in assets of household i at time t.

Combining (10.2) and (10.3), one obtains:

$$g^i_{s,t} = -y^i_{s,t} + h^i_{st} - \frac{1}{N}\sum_{j=1}^{N} h^j_{st} + \frac{1}{N}\sum_{j=1}^{N} c^j_{st,t} + \frac{1}{\gamma}(\log \omega^i - \frac{1}{N}\sum_{j=1}^{N}\log \omega^j) - b^i_{s,t} - \Delta w^i_t$$

(10.4)

This is the base equation for the empirical estimations discussed in this chapter. One can divide income into a transitory component and a permanent one. Permanent income is a function of the characteristics of the household and their initial level of assets (X^i_t), while transitory income and the preference shock variable depend on the observable shocks to the household $(m^i_{s,t})$. Finally, unobserved aggregate variables, $1/N\sum_{j=1}^{N} h^j_s$ and $1/N\sum_{j=1}^{N} c^j_{s,t}$ can be replaced by regional dummies and the different countries where migrants live, as the areas within which risk is being shared.

The reduced-form equation used in the estimations is:

$$g^i_{s,t} = \beta_0 + \beta_1 m^i_{s,t} + \beta_2 X^i_t + \beta_3 b^i_{s,t} + \beta_4 \Delta w^i_t + a^i + u^i_t$$

(10.5)

One would expect that if risk is shared, then the coefficient on the shock variable should be significant and positive. Furthermore, if risk is efficiently shared, then the coefficient on the shock variable should also be of similar magnitude to the monetary loss caused by the shock.

In (10.5), a^i represents the household fixed effects. Due to the potential unobserved heterogeneity among households, related in particular to risk preferences, abilities, and social network of the households, I use fixed effects as suggested by the theoretical model presented. As discussed in Rosenzweig (1988), one worries in particular about the relationship between the risk preferences of the household and its use of *ex-ante* and *ex-post* mechanisms to cope with risks. To eliminate the biases that can arise from these unobserved characteristics of the households, and assuming that they are time-invariant, one can carry out fixed-effects estimations for private transfers. To this fixed-effect estimation, I add interaction terms to see if the effect of the shock on interhousehold transfers varies with any other characteristic, especially access to other *ex-post* insurance mechanisms.

Before discussing the insurance role of private transfers in the aftermath of Hurricane Mitch in Nicaragua, it is important to analyze the exogeneity of this shock. Although it is clear that the timing of the hurricane is exogenous to households, there would still be some endogeneity concerns if the households in the sample are particularly likely to be affected by hurricanes. However, all regions in Nicaragua have a positive probability of being hit by a storm (and by other natural disasters more generally). While Hurricane Mitch mostly affected the Central and Pacific regions of the country, the departments in the Atlantic have often been hit in the past. In particular, according to the Nicaraguan Institute of Terrestrial Studies (INETER), 42 tropical storms affected Nicaragua between 1892 and 1998. As all departments in the country have been affected several times by different storms, it is unlikely that households in different regions take systematically different preventive measures to deal with adverse shocks, once one accounts for initial characteristics.

As discussed before, the size and prevalence of interhousehold transfers increased markedly after Mitch. It is unlikely that, in the absence of the shock, there would have been such a large jump in transfers in just a matter of months. In this section, I investigate whether the amount of private transfers received responded to households' needs, following the model specified in the previous section. If this were the case, one could interpret this as evidence that transfers were used as an informal *ex-post* mechanism of insurance in the aftermath of Hurricane Mitch.

Mitch did not affect all households equally. From the LSMS 1999 survey, one can construct different indicators of the size of the shock at the household level. In this chapter, the main indicator of the severity of the Hurricane Mitch at the household level is the economic value of agricultural losses as a percentage of pre-shock household income. In particular, households were asked whether or not Hurricane Mitch had generated losses in any of seven categories—crops, tools, equipment, animals for work, facilities, agricultural property, and other, and the amount of the loss for every category. By adding up all losses, I construct the variable "losses." Agricultural losses were reported by 74.3 percent of households, and the median value of such losses was 2,115.84 cordobas (US$176.32) or 40 percent of pre-Mitch household income.

As discussed in relation to the theoretical model, one of the determinants of net private transfers received is the level of household income. There are two problems, however, that arise from using income in the specification of private transfers. First, there might be significant measurement error. Second, income might be endogenous if the amount of private transfers received influences labor supply decisions and, therefore, household income. To address this issue, I construct a measure of "full" income to be used as an instrument for income. This measure is independent of current labor supply decisions and only affects the outcome of interest—interhousehold transfers—through its impact on household income. Specifically, full income is constructed by multiplying the labor supply of each household—fixed at the 1998 level, before Hurricane Mitch—by the sectorial average national wage in 1998 and 1999, depending on the year. Average wages are calculated by the Central Bank of Nicaragua, according to the economic activity of each individual and include 10 categories—including agriculture, manufacturing, construction, and government. This measure of income incorporates the effects of the hurricane on wages, but isolates the *ex-post* changes in labor supply, which might be endogenous. Hence, I use full household income per capita as the main indicator of income. I adjust it to take into account economies of scale, as well as the number of children in the household.

In short, the preferred econometric specification includes as controls per capita full income, public transfers, household size, number of migrants, value of own land and other assets, construction materials of the dwelling, social programs that benefited the household, and if a member of the household is part of an organization such as the church, municipality association or "Pro-Mitch" organization. I also include interaction terms between the shock and the age, age squared, gender and years of schooling of the head of household, as well as with the pre-shock access to other forms of insurance. Finally, regressions also consider household, municipality, and year fixed effects.

OTHER INSURANCE MECHANISMS

In the aftermath of Hurricane Mitch, households may have adopted a variety of other strategies—in addition to public and private transfers—to cope with the consequences of the storm. These strategies may be correlated with the size of the shock experienced by each household. The impact of Mitch on the amount of inter-household transfers received could also be different depending on the degree to which these other risk-sharing mechanisms are used. This translates into interaction terms that are also included in the fixed effects estimations described above. In this subsection, I briefly discuss the likelihood that some of these alternative instruments could be used to cope with the risks arising from natural disasters in rural Nicaragua.

First, households could rely on savings to manage the impact of a shock. Households in rural Nicaragua have very low incomes and, as a result, most of them have no savings. In 1998, only 2.2 percent of the rural households in the sample reported having any savings.

Asset markets could also serve to share risk. The value of assets between 1998 and 1999 changed for two reasons. First, assets were lost because of Hurricane Mitch, and these changes in assets are part of the main indicator of the magnitude of the shock losses. Second, assets also changed because people may have sold assets as a way of smoothing consumption *ex-post*. However, as discussed above, households in Nicaragua are very poor, and they do not have many assets to sell even if they wanted to. The median value of own land and nonland assets in 1998 was 10,265 cordobas (US$855.42) or ten times the average monthly income. The 1999 survey also includes information on the productive assets bought and sold after Hurricane Mitch. Only a small proportion of households that owned land sold any agricultural installations or equipment in the ten months after Mitch (4.52 percent and 3.87 percent, respectively). In contrast, the proportion of households buying these assets was significantly higher, especially for equipment (37.42 percent). Because of major losses of agricultural equipment in the storm, many households needed to replace a large part of their equipment. Additionally, the government put in place special programs to sell agricultural tools at lower prices (ECLAC 1999).

Aside from using their savings and assets, households may borrow to deal with the effects of a natural disaster. In our sample, only 9.6 percent of households received a loan in the 10 months after Hurricane Mitch, while 4.7 percent had one in the 10 months preceding the storm. In fact, only 12.35 percent of households asked for a loan after Mitch. Of those that did not ask for credit, 24.47 percent said they did not have any collateral, while 26 percent responded that a loan would be too risky, or that they preferred to work with their own resources. A more detailed analysis would be needed to determine whether these households did not want a loan or were credit-constrained. It is clear, however, that borrowing, formal or informal, was not widespread in rural Nicaragua among the households surveyed. Moreover, for those households that did have access to credit, the amounts are rather small: an average of 100 cordobas (US$8.33) monthly in loans or 10 percent of the average nontransfer income.

In terms of labor supply, there is no statistically significant difference in the average number of hours worked by individuals between 18 and 60 years old before and after Mitch. The average weekly labor supply, conditional on working, was 47.08 hours in 1998 and 45.97 hours in 1999. For all working age individuals, regardless of whether they were part of the labor force, the average labor supply was 31 hours per week in both years. Aggregating at the household level, results are similar: there are no significant changes from one year to the next. Therefore, labor supply does not seem to have responded in the aftermath of the storm.

One way in which households did partially cope with the effects of Mitch was by moving in with other households to take advantage of economies of scale. In fact, table 10.1 shows that the average household size among affected households did increase from 1998 to 1999—going from 6.11 to 6.79 members. In the sample, 12 percent of the individuals are new to their households; however, only 9 percent of them report having moved in because of Mitch. Migration is another way in which living arrangements can change after a shock. Eight percent of household members in 1998 were part of another household by 1999, and 33.5 percent of these individuals moved to either another municipality or another country to look for a job after Mitch. That is, 2.72 percent of the individuals in the 1998 sample had migrated by 1999 and 12.23 percent of rural households in 1999 had at least one person who had migrated.

In what follows, I focus on interhousehold transfers and their relationship to the size of the shock experienced by individual households. I also discuss some of the factors that appear to influence this relationship.

Do Interhousehold Transfers Act as Insurance?

Table 10.3 presents the main empirical results. Here, I report the fixed effects and random effects estimates. Using fixed effects does not allow for estimating the effect on private transfers of time-invariant characteristics, but here the main focus is on how transfers respond to households' needs after a large shock. The alternative, random effects estimates that account for the existence of time-invariant and time-varying error components but ignore the correlation between the persistent error and the time-varying explanatory variables, are also obtained. However, these latter estimates are not consistent. Therefore, the analysis that follows focuses on the fixed effects specification.[8]

The most interesting coefficient is that of the ratio of losses and pre-shock household income. Results indicate that Hurricane Mitch had a strong positive effect on interhousehold transfers, and that the severity of the shock experienced by a particular household was positively correlated with the amount of informal resources

TABLE 10.3 } Estimates of the Impact of Hurricane Mitch on Net Interhousehold Transfers Received

Dependent variable: Net private transfers received

Variable	Fixed effects		Random effects	
	(i)	(ii)	(i)	(ii)
(Losses/Income 98)	0.565 ** [0.271]	32.456 *** [12.446]	0.636 *** [0.199]	26.83 *** [9.331]
Full income per capita	−0.046 [0.072]	0.030 [0.072]	−0.048 * [0.030]	−0.029 [0.030]
Public transfers	−0.259 ** [0.130]	−0.264 ** [0.128]	−0.172 ** [0.088]	−0.162 * [0.086]
Number of new migrants	135.83 * [72.765]	152.774 ** [72.270]	123.332 *** [53.200]	133.452 *** [53.912]
Full income*Shock	...	−0.002 ** [0.001]	...	−0.002 ** [0.001]
Female*Shock	...	5.173 *** [1.703]	...	5.019 *** [1.290]
HHsize* Shock	...	0.500 * [0.263]	...	0.536 *** [0.192]
Age*Shock	...	−1.302 *** [0.519]	...	−1.163 *** [0.387]
Age2*shock	...	0.011 [1.780]	...	0.011 *** [0.003]
Central Region* Shock	...	−3.98 *** [1.780]	...	−1.767 [1.336]
Atlantic region* Shock	...	−4.125 [3.284]	...	−1.270 [2.347]
Household demographics	yes	yes	yes	yes
Household's assets	yes	yes	yes	yes
Construction materials	yes	yes	yes	yes
Social programs	yes	yes	yes	yes
Affiliated to social organizations	yes	yes	yes	yes
Municipality	yes	yes	yes	yes
Year	yes	yes	yes	yes
Number of observations	646	646	646	646

received. On average, a household that experienced losses equivalent to one month of income due to Mitch received 57 cordobas (US$4.75) more per month in private transfers (equivalent to over 90 percent of pre-shock average transfers). For a household at mean income, whose losses amounted to one year of income, these new transfers offset 38 percent of the losses in the eight months after Mitch. Thus, interhousehold transfers do act as insurance, but only partially.

At first, for such a large shock, this estimate of the impact of the hurricane on net interhousehold transfers received may seem relatively small. After all, the proportion of households that received transfers increased from 15 percent before the hurricane to 20 percent by June 1999, and it took eight months for transfers to offset 38 percent of the losses. In addition to this estimate taking into account only *new* transfers after the shock, some other facts are important to keep in mind. First, these are estimates obtained after adjusting for geographic fixed effects, that is, after taking into consideration damages at the municipal level. One may think that, since families sending transfers do not have perfect information on the damages suffered by a particular household and/or how they relate to the family's wealth, they use regional damages as a proxy. If this is the case, I only account here for the idiosyncratic part of the shock, and interhousehold transfers may also be a response to local damages. Second, these results suggest that there are fixed costs involved in sending transfers. Rural areas may be far removed from financial centers, and getting access to money-transfer companies may be difficult. Actually, further inspection of the data reveals that all but one of the households that received transfers before the shock did so also after the event, so there are no big changes in the pool of affected households that received transfers. Similarly, over 90 percent of these households have family abroad, and presumably these expatriates are the ones sending money. Since there are costs to migration, changes to the proportion of households receiving transfers may not occur frequently or in a significant manner. Additionally, it is important to recognize that the "losses" variable does not fully capture all damages suffered by a household as a consequence of Mitch.

Other interesting coefficients are income per capita and number of migrants. Although the first is only significant under random effects, higher income seems to be associated with lower transfers. As expected, a larger number of migrants is associated with higher net private transfers. In fact, the coefficient is quite large. One more migrant in a household, *ceteris paribus*, is associated with an increase of 136 cordobas (US$11.33) in net private transfers received, more than twice the pre-shock average.

The second specification includes interaction effects. The coefficients for the explanatory variables considered in the first model remain more or less unchanged.[9] Included in table 10.3 are interactions between the shock indicator and pre-shock values for income, gender and age of the head of the household, household size, and the region where the dwelling was located. The results obtained are interesting. In particular, households headed by women receive 5 cordobas (US$0.42) more in transfers for a given shock and other characteristics. Similarly, one additional member of the household means 0.50 cordobas (US$0.04) more in transfers. There are also regional differences, with households located in the Central region receiving 4 cordobas (US$0.33) less than those located in the Pacific for a given severity of the shock. Finally, there is a nonlinear relationship between the impact of the shock on transfers received, depending on the age of the head of household, since the younger and the older households are the ones receiving more transfers (after adjusting for needs).

On the other hand, interaction effects with other insurance mechanisms, such as the number of migrants, if the household has savings, assets, and the value of loans, show up with the expected sign but are not statistically significant. That is, the impact of the shock on net transfers did not vary according to the other measures taken by the household to deal with the consequences of Mitch. In part, this result may be due to the fact that these other insurance mechanisms are not readily observable by the households that send transfers.

To verify the robustness of the results to alternative definitions of the shock, I use another indicator for the exposure to Mitch: if the household needed to move from its dwelling temporarily or permanently after the storm. Since this indicator is a dummy variable, one is not able to use it to test if private transfers increased with the size of the shock. Findings suggest that, on average, the monthly net private transfers received doubled from pre-shock levels—increasing by 126.50 cordobas (US$10.54)—for those households that needed to move from their dwelling.

In short, results indicate that interhousehold transfers allowed households to partially share the economic costs associated with Hurricane Mitch. As expected, households with more migrants, more losses, headed by women, and those that are part of community organizations received the largest transfers after the storm, once geographical location and economic and demographic characteristics are taken into account.

Crowding Out of Interhousehold Transfers

As is often the case after natural disasters, there was a significant influx of international aid into Nicaragua in the aftermath of Mitch. This aid was mostly administered by NGOs or by the Nicaraguan government. For simplicity, I refer to all nonprivate aid as public transfers.

These public transfers could reduce the amount of private transfers received by households, with considerable policy implications for the design and effectiveness of public programs. The nature of the interaction between private and public transfers can also reveal important information about household behavior and the motivations behind income-sharing arrangements across households. In particular, if there is crowding out, then public transfers aimed at helping the poor will be less effective than initially thought, and the gains from such public programs would actually be shared with better-off households who are the ones who usually give the transfers. In other words, if there is crowding out, government transfers will have a limited distributional effect, in addition to possibly having pervasive effects on existing informal risk-sharing arrangements.

As described by Cox (1987), there are several channels through which one could expect public transfers to affect private transfers, depending on the motivations behind private transfers and their relationship with pre-transfer income. From a theoretical point of view, there are four main models that try to explain private transfers: altruism, exchange, insurance, and "warm glow."

ALTRUISTIC MODEL

Altruism is often considered the main justification for private transfers. The main idea behind the altruistic model (Barro 1974; Becker 1974) is that one individual (or household in this case) cares about the utility of another, and therefore the utility of the second person (household) enters directly the utility function of the first one. This type of relationship is often assumed to exist, for instance, between parents and their children, where one can think of the parents as being altruistic toward their children: parents include their children's utility in their own utility function, so an increase in the children's well-being also makes parents better off. *Ceteris paribus,* an increase in the income of the donor household increases the amount transferred; on the other hand, an increase in the income of the receiving household will be associated with a decrease in the transfers received. Therefore, if the altruistic model holds, one would expect that an increase in public transfers crowds out private transfers as it represents an increase in the income of the receiving household.

EXCHANGE MODEL

The exchange model (Bernheim, Schleifer, and Summers 1985; Cox 1987) is based on the idea that transfers, implicitly or explicitly, are just part of an interhousehold informal exchange motivated by the provision of some kind of good or service that the recipient performs for the donor. For instance, parents may give transfers to their children expecting their children to do the same for them when they get old, or children may give transfers to their parents hoping to get an inheritance from them later (Bernheim, Schleifer, and Summers 1985). The literature usually assumes that the "price" a household charges for the service rendered is either independent of its income (Ward-Batts 2000) or increases with it (Cox 1987). Therefore, if demand for the household's service has not decreased, public transfers should have either no effect on the size of transfers or a positive one. Cox (1987), on the other hand, argues that under the exchange model, it is possible that private transfers are an outcome of a Nash bargaining situation and in such a case, the relationship between the size of the transfers and the recipient's income, conditional on receiving a transfer, will be non-monotonic.

HOUSEHOLD RISK-SHARING MODEL

In the household risk-sharing model (Lucas and Stark 1985; Rosenzweig 1988; Rosenzweig and Stark 1989), transfers are part of an insurance scheme through which participants share idiosyncratic risks. That is, when a household suffers a negative transitory shock not experienced by the other household, the latter will send transfers to the former, and vice versa. This model implies, like the altruistic model, that if the income of the receiving household increases due, for instance, to public transfers, the amount transferred will decrease.

"WARM GLOW" MODEL

The "warm glow" model (Andreoni 1989) assumes that a household directly derives utility from giving a transfer to another family, instead of from the utility of that household as in the altruistic model. The implication of this condition in its pure form is that the amount transferred is independent of the income of the receiving household, so there would be no change in private transfers as public transfers to the receiving household increase. If the true motive for transfers is a combination of warm glow (or good feeling) and altruism, then one would expect a smaller decrease in transfers compared to what the pure altruistic model predicts.

In short, an increase in the income of the receiving household will lead to a decline in the private transfers received under the altruistic and the insurance models, which implies a crowding out of private transfers when public transfers increase. On the other hand, when warm glow is the motivation for transfers, there should be no effect of public transfers on private transfers; while under the exchange model, public transfers might have no effect or a positive effect on private transfers.

In general, the evidence from developing countries on the relationship between public and private transfers has been mixed. Evidence for the altruistic model has been found in Vietnam (Cox 2002) and the Philippines (Cox and Jimenez 1995). Similarly, Murrugarra (2002) uses a difference in difference estimation technique, exploiting the increase in social assistance in Armenia, to find evidence of significant displacement of private transfers due to the increase in public transfers. On the other hand, Cox and Jimenez (1992, 1998) find that in Peru the exchange model seems to better reflect the motivation for private transfers. More recently, authors have tried to exploit the exogenous nature of some policy changes that have increased public transfers in order to resolve some of the deficiencies in previous work. Albarran and Attanasio (2002), when analyzing the effects of the Progresa Programme, find evidence of crowding out of private transfers, while Jensen (2004) finds that in South Africa each rand of public pension income that went to the elderly resulted in a 0.25–0.30 rand reduction in private transfers from the migrant children. On the other hand, Foster and Rosenzweig (2001) obtain results that support the insurance model in Bangladesh and Pakistan.

Here, I am interested in analyzing if the amount of public transfers that households received after Hurricane Mitch had an effect on the size of interhousehold transfers. For this, I focus on the coefficient on public transfers on table 10.3. Results from the fixed effects estimation indicate that private transfers decreased by 25 cents for every cordoba of public aid received by the household. What were the characteristics of households receiving these transfers in the aftermath of the storm? Households that suffered damages to their dwelling, and those affiliated to community organizations, received larger transfers from the government, after taking into account relevant locality and household characteristics. This crowding-out effect is greater when concentrating on the most visible components of public transfers such as housing.

Both an altruistic and an insurance motive for private transfers predict a negative relationship between private and public transfers. However, as explained by Lucas and Stark (1985), a possible test to differentiate both models would be to see if the increases in private transfers are larger for households that own assets that are particularly vulnerable to the shock being analyzed. In this study, the fact that increases in private transfers are larger for households that suffer higher losses due to Mitch seems to indicate that private transfers are, at least partially, part of an informal insurance scheme. However, since risk-sharing seems to be incomplete, the underlying motivation for private transfers could reflect a combination of both insurance and warm glow.

Main Lessons and Challenges

The evidence discussed in this chapter on the effects of Hurricane Mitch in Nicaragua strongly suggests that interhousehold transfers serve as insurance against exogenous shocks.

Conditional on experiencing losses from the hurricane, the median household lost four times its monthly income, but there were large variations in the ratios, with the household in the 75th percentile losing 14 times its income, while the 90th percentile lost over 45 times its monthly budget. Households that faced the largest economic losses from the storm (as a percentage of their pre-shock income) were those receiving the largest transfers, even after adjusting for community-wide effects. On average, a household that experienced losses equivalent to one month of income due to Mitch, received 57 cordobas (US$4.75) more per month in private transfers (equivalent to over 90 percent of pre-shock average monthly transfers). For a household at mean income, whose losses amounted to one year of income, these new transfers offset 38 percent of the losses in the eight months after Mitch.

Moreover, private transfers decreased by 25 cents for every cordoba of public transfers received. These results provide support for the altruistic or insurance models as a motivation for private transfers, and evidence of crowding out of private transfers due to public transfers.

Several lessons can be drawn from this study. First, the good news: although, as predicted by economic theory, informal insurance mechanisms only partially protect households against large shocks, they do respond substantially to households' needs. This insurance role of private transfers is further confirmed by evidence of public transfers crowding out these interhousehold donations. Now the bad news: in the face of a large shock and failing formal and informal insurance schemes, households turn to potentially harmful mechanisms to smooth consumption. Worryingly, evidence suggests that children's well-being may be highly affected after natural disasters and in ways that hamper their future prospects (Baez and Santos 2007).

The results discussed in this chapter have important implications for policy makers. They highlight that, even in the presence of a major natural disaster, informal mechanisms for risk-sharing can play a role—although incomplete—in insuring households against the effects of a shock. As a result, public and international aid programs in the aftermath of natural disasters need to account for the pervasive displacement effects these could have on informal risk-sharing mechanisms and, therefore, on households' welfare.

Results further highlight the need for policy makers to think hard about the effects of aid on the existing informal risk-sharing networks. While private transfers represent a significant source of income for those households that receive them, they only reach a small proportion of households. On the other hand, although public transfers are more widespread, they represent a smaller proportion of households' budgets. Among households that experienced losses between one and 14 times their monthly income (second and third quartiles), 21 percent received private transfers with a median value of 278 cordobas (US$23.17). On the other hand, among that same subset of households, 64 percent received public transfers, but with a median value of only 29 cordobas (US$2.42).

The existence of important informal risk-sharing mechanisms has two main implications for aid, both from national and international donors. On the one hand, risk-sharing reduces the need to target aid to particular households when it is possible to identify the groups within which risk is being shared. On the other hand, public aid could reduce the effectiveness of informal insurance mechanisms, such as interhousehold transfers, if there is crowding out.

One should be cautious, however, in extrapolating the results of this chapter's findings to other shocks. Even when interhousehold transfers constitute a mechanism to share income among households in the event of a natural disaster, they may not be so in the case of other types of shocks. Losses arising from a hurricane, for instance, are relatively easy to observe and are somewhat exogenous. So, even though it may be hard to monitor the exact losses, it is not difficult to know whether a family lives in an area highly affected by a storm. This is shown by the case of Nicaragua, as I find that private transfers are most sensitive to visible forms of public aid, such as housing.

Future research can focus on understanding the differences in the informal insurance mechanisms used by households when facing large shocks versus smaller and less generalized shocks. The availability of new datasets for different countries, like the one used in this chapter for Nicaragua, represents an excellent opportunity for research in this area. More work is also necessary to determine which forms of aid are to a greater or lesser extent prone to crowding out private transfers or other insurance mechanisms. Finally, understanding the channels through which natural disasters may have pervasive effects on children and other vulnerable segments of the population is also a fruitful avenue for research.

Notes

1. For more details on the effects of Mitch in Nicaragua, see World Bank (2001).

2. For more information on the methodology used for these household surveys, see World Bank (2001).

3. The interviewers followed the households they needed to survey even when they moved out of their 1998 dwelling as long as they stayed in the same municipality.

4. In 1999 the official exchange rate in Nicaragua was US$1 = 12 cordobas.

5. Poverty classification according to the Nicaraguan national poverty line, adjusted for local prices. See World Bank (1999) for the definition of the poverty line.

6. *Manzana* is the most used Central American unit of land area: 1 *manzana* = 0.708 hectares = 1.75 acres.

7. Notation in this model follows Fafchamps and Lund (2003).

8. Random effects Tobit estimates were also obtained, truncating the sample to positive net private transfers. These estimates are not included here, but the coefficient of interest on the shock is still statistically significant at the 5 percent level.

9. The coefficient on losses in this specification must be interpreted with care, since it only represents the effect of the shock on interhousehold transfers when all the other indicators interacted with the shock are zero.

Research

Albarran, P., and Attanasio, O. (2002). "Do Public Transfers Crowd Out Private Transfers? Evidence from a Randomized Experiment in Mexico." DP2002/06, World Institute for Development Economics Research, Helsinki.

Andreoni, J. (1989). "Giving with Impure Altruism: Applications to Charity and Ricardian Equivalence." *Journal of Political Economy* 97(6): 1447–1458.

Baez, J., and Santos, I. (2007). "Children's Vulnerability to Weather Shocks: A Natural Disaster as a Natural Experiment." Accessed January 7, 2012. http://siteresources.worldbank.org/INT-MIGDEV/Resources/2838212-1160686302996/Baez&SantosChildrenvulnerability.pdf.

Barro, R. (1974). "Are Government Bonds Net Wealth?" *Journal of Political Economy* 82(6): 1095–1117.

Becker, G. (1974). "A Theory of Social Interactions." *Journal of Political Economy* 82: 1063–1094.

Bernheim, D., Schleifer, A., and Summers, L. (1985). "The Strategic Bequest Motive." *Journal of Political Economy* 93(1): 45–76.

Cox, D. (1987). "Motives for Private Transfers." *Journal of Political Economy* 95: 508–546.

———. (2002). "Private Inter-Household Transfers in Vietnam in the Early and Late 1990s." Boston College Working Papers in Economics, No. 524, Boston College at Boston, Mass.

Cox, D., and Jimenez, E. (1992). "Social Security and Private Transfers in Developing Countries: The Case of Peru." *World Bank Economic Review* 6(1): 155–169.

———. (1995). "Private Transfers and the Effectiveness of Public Income Redistribution in the Philippines." In *Public Spending and the Poor; Theory and Evidence*, edited by D. van de Walle and K. Nead. Baltimore: Johns Hopkins University Press.

———. (1998). "Risk-Sharing and Private Transfers: What about Urban Households." *Economic Development and Cultural Change* 46(3): 621–637.

Deaton, A. (1990). "Saving in Developing Countries: Theory and Review." Proceedings of the World Bank Annual Conference on Development Economics 1989, Washington, D.C.

———. (1992). *Understanding Consumption*. Oxford: Clarendon Press.

Deaton, A., and Paxson, C. (1998). "Economies of Scale, Household Size, and the Demand for Food." *Journal of Political Economy*, 106(5): 897–930.

Economic Commission for Latin American and the Caribbean (ECLAC). (1999). "Nicaragua: Evaluación de los Daños Ocasionados por el Huracán Mitch, 1998. Sus Implicaciones para el Desarrollo Económico y Social y el Medio Ambiente." Accessed December 17, 2008. http://www.eclac.cl/cgi-bin/getprod.asp?xml=/publicaciones/xml/2/15502/P15502.xml&xsl=/mexico/tpl/p9f.xsl&base=/mexico/tpl/top-bottom.xsl.

Fafchamps, M., and Lund, S. (2003). "Risk-Sharing Networks in Rural Philippines." *Journal of Development Economics* 71: 261–287.

Foster, A., and Rosenzweig, M. (2001). "Imperfect Commitment, Altruism, and the Family: Evidence from Transfer Behaviour in Low-Income Rural Areas." *Review of Economics and Statistics* 83(3): 389–407.

———. (2002). "Household Division and Rural Economic Growth." *Review of Economic Studies* 69(4): 839–869.

Guha-Sapir, D., Hargitt, D., and Hoyois, P. (2004). *Thirty Years of Natural Disasters 1974–2003: The Numbers*. Brussels: UCL Presses Universitaires de Louvain.

Jensen, R. (2004) "Do Private Transfers 'Displace' the Benefits of Public Transfers? Evidence from South Africa." *Journal of Public Economics* 88(1–2): 89–112.

Kochar, A. (1993). "Labour Market Responses to Idiosyncratic Agricultural Shocks: Empirical Evidence from Rural India." Stanford University, Stanford, Calif. Mimeographed.

Kocherlakota, N. (1996). "Implications of Efficient Risk Sharing without Commitment." *Review of Economic Studies* 63(4): 595–609.

Lucas, R., and Stark, O. (1985). "Motivations to Remit: Evidence from Botswana." *Journal of Political Economy* 93: 901–918.

Murrugarra, E. (2002). "Public Transfers and Migrants' Remittances: Evidence of the Recent Armenian Experience." *World Bank Economist's Forum* 2: 25–47.

Platteau, J. (1991). "Traditional Systems of Social Security and Hunger Insurance: Past Achievements and Modern Challenges." In *Social Security in Developing Countries*, edited by E. Ahmad, J. Drèze, J. Hills, and A. Sen. Oxford: Clarendon Press.

Rosenzweig, M. (1988). "Risk, Implicit Contracts, and the Family in Rural Areas of Low-Income Countries." *Economic Journal* 98: 1148–1170.

Rosenzweig, M., and Stark, O. (1989). "Consumption Smoothing, Migration, and Marriage: Evidence from Rural India." *Journal of Political Economy* 97(4): 905–926.

Rosenzweig, M., and Wolpin, K. (1993). "Credit Market Constraints, Consumption Smoothing, and the Accumulation of Durable Production Assets in Low-Income Countries: Investment in Bullocks in India." *Journal of Political Economy* 101(2): 223–244.

Townsend, R. (1994). "Risk and Insurance in Village India." *Econometrica* 62: 539–592.

———. (1995). "Consumption Insurance: An Evaluation of Risk-Bearing Systems in Low-Income Economies." *Journal of Economic Perspectives* 9: 83–102.

Udry, C. (1990). "Credit Markets in Rural Nigeria: Credit as Insurance in a Rural Economy." *World Bank Economic Review* 4(3): 251–269.

———. (1994). "Risk and Insurance in a Rural Credit Market: An Empirical Investigation in Northern Nigeria." *Review of Economic Studies* 61: 495–526.

Ward-Batts, J. (2000). "Do Public Transfers Crowd Out Private Inter-Household Transfers? Responses among Lone-Mothers Families in the UK." Population Studies Center, University of Michigan, Report No. 01–465.

World Bank (2001). "Supplemental Information Document. Nicaragua Living Standards Measurement Study Survey. Post-Mitch Survey 1999, Poverty and Human Resources Development Research Group, Washington, D.C.

———. (2008). World Development Indicators. WDI Online. http://web.worldbank.org/WBSITE/EXTERNAL/DATASTATISTICS/0,,contentMDK:21725423~pagePK:64133150~piPK:64133175~theSitePK:239419,00.html.

11 }

The Economic Impact of Earthquakes on Households
EVIDENCE FROM JAPAN
Yasuyuki Sawada

Introduction

Japan is vulnerable to a wide variety of natural disasters such as earthquakes, tsunamis, volcanic eruptions, typhoons, floods, landslides, and avalanches. Of these natural disasters, earthquakes are the most serious and frequently occurring. The continuous earthquake activity is due to the country's location on a subduction zone, where four of the more than ten tectonic plates covering the globe are crushed against each other. Indeed, of the 912 earthquakes with magnitude of 6.0 or greater that occurred in the world between 1996 and 2005, 190 occurred around Japan (Cabinet Office 2007). This means that more than 20 percent of the world's large earthquakes have occurred around Japan.

Throughout the history of Japan, earthquakes have regularly hit the country: a total of 248 large earthquakes have occurred in Japan in the 1,300 years since the Hakuho earthquakes of 684—the oldest Japanese earthquakes to have been recorded in written form. Moreover, in the Nankai and Tokai areas, earthquakes occur regularly every 100 to 200 years (figure 11.1), winning the name "the twin earthquake" (Hayashi 2003).[1] In terms of human losses, the worst earthquake in the country's history was the Great Kanto earthquake of September 1, 1923, which had a magnitude of 7.9. Large parts of Tokyo and Kanagawa were destroyed, several hundred thousand homes and buildings were in ruins, and more than 140,000 people were killed or went missing. The fires that followed the quake spread rapidly as many houses and other buildings were made of wood. In Tokyo, 477,128 houses, or 70 percent of the total, burnt down, with the fire blazing for a full three days (ADRC 2008). Thus some 44 percent of Japan's GDP in 1922 was lost either directly as a result of the earthquakes, or indirectly due to the fires, aftershocks, and tsunamis (table 11.1).[2] Aiming never to forget the lessons of the Great Kanto earthquake, the Japanese government set September 1 as the annual date for a variety of earthquake disaster prevention exercises and related activities (ADRC 2008). Since this time, through the development of disaster management systems and enhanced disaster information communication systems, the death toll and number of missing persons from disasters, most particularly earthquakes, has declined ever since, with the two notable exceptions of the Great East Japan earthquake in 2011 and the Great Hanshin-Awaji (Kobe) earthquake in 1995 (figure 11.2). Particularly, we see vividly the 2011 devastating earthquake, tsunami, and nuclear radiation crisis in Japan that has killed tens of thousands people and resulted in damages of around 200 to 300 billion dollars. These two exceptions highlight the significance of natural disasters that can generate the most serious consequences ever known (Sawada and Kotera 2011).

How can people insure themselves against the devastating damages arising from earthquakes? What are the roles of markets and government in mitigating the negative impacts of earthquakes on households? This chapter will attempt to address these questions based on household-level microevidence from Japan. The country's long history of earthquakes has enabled us to obtain unusually rich information. By investigating this subject, we believe we can make a strong contribution to the existing literature: while it has been an important issue for households and firms to secure an effective insurance instrument against unexpected shocks such as earthquakes, micro-level studies on earthquakes using either household-level or firm-level data are largely absent. The existing economic studies on the earthquakes in Japan focus

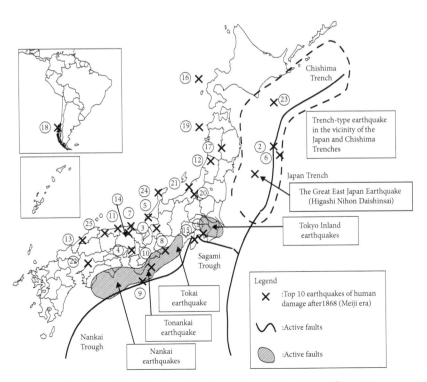

FIGURE 11.1 Locations of the 26 major earthquakes and tsunamis in Japan with seismic intensity of 6.0 or greater in the last 30 years, ranked by human losses

Note: For the names of the earthquakes and tsunamis, see Appendix table.

TABLE 11.1 } Estimated Damages from Natural Disasters

Event (Year)	Damages (USD billion)	Loss as percentage of GDP
Great East Japan Earthquake (2011)	200-300[k]	4.0 (approximately)
Hurricane Katrina (2005)	125[h]	1.7[j]
Tsunami in India (2004)	1.02[a]	0.17[e]
Tsunami in Indonesia (2004)	4.45[b]	2.14[e]
Tsunami in the Maldives (2004)	0.47[c]	2.58[e]
Tsunami in Sri Lanka (2004)	0.97–1.00[d]	4.4–4.6[e]
Chuetsu Earthquake in Japan (2004)	28.3[f]	0.6[g]
Hurricane Ivan in the United States (2004)	3[h]	0.04[h]
Earthquakes in Turkey (1999)	22[i]	5[i]
Hurricane Mitch in El Salvador (1998)	2.9[i]	14.6[i]
Great Hanshin-Awaji Earthquake in Japan (1995)	95–147[i]	2.5[i]
Hurricane Andrew in the United States (1992)	26.5[i]	0.5[i]
Cyclone/floods in Bangladesh (1991)	1[i]	5[i]
Great Kanto Earthquake (1923)	32.6[g] (based on 2003 price)	43.6[g]

Sources: (a) Asian Development Bank, United Nations, and World Bank (2005). "India: Post-Tsunami Recovery Programme—Preliminary Damage and Needs Assessment"; (b) BAPPENAS and the international donor community (2005). "Indonesia: Preliminary Damage and Loss Assessment: The December 26, 2004 Natural Disaster"; (c) World Bank, Asian Development Bank, and UN System (2005). "Tsunami: Impact and Recovery"; (d) Asian Development Bank, Japan Bank for International Cooperation, and World Bank (2005). "Sri Lanka 2005 Post-Tsunami Recovery Programme—Preliminary Damage And Needs Assessment"; (e) author's calculation based on the World Bank's World Development Indicators; (f) Niigata Prefecture, Japan; (g) author's estimates using information from the Cabinet Office and the Ministry of Finance of the government of Japan; (h) author's calculation based on information from Risk Management Solutions (RMS); (i) Table 1 in Freeman, Keen, and Mani (2003); (j) United Nations International Strategy for Disaster Reduction; (k) Cabinet Office, the Government of Japan.

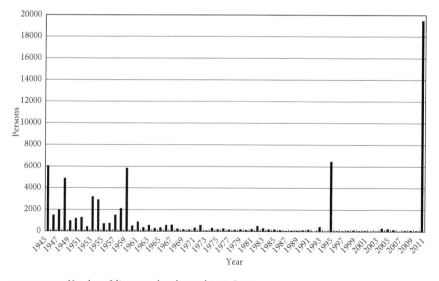

FIGURE 11.2 Number of disaster-related casualties in Japan

Source: Cabinet Office and Fire and Disaster Management Agency, Government of Japan.

exclusively on macroeconomic and financial aspects (Horwich 2000; Skidmore 2001), except for the household-level analysis of Kohara, Ohtake, and Saito (2006), and Sawada and Shimizutani (2007, 2008).

Since earthquakes are typically an aggregate event, there are two major constraints in designing formal insurance. First, it is known that people have a tendency to underestimate the risk of an earthquake. In other words, there will be a systematic gap between the objective and subjective probabilities of earthquakes (Camerer and Kunreuther 1989). This suggests that the demand for earthquake insurance is systematically lower than the optimal level. Second, earthquakes are characterized by a rare and unexpected event, which makes it difficult to design actuarially fair insurance with the appropriate insurance premiums. Moreover, since earthquakes are highly covariate, risks that affect large areas simultaneously often cannot be diversified well across a country. Accordingly, the insurers have the potential need to secure their financial position by using international reinsurance markets. It is known, however, that reinsurance markets and trade in catastrophe (CAT) bonds are still weak and with limited capacity.[3]

Interestingly, however, by using data on hurricane exposure, Yang (2008) found that the exposure of poor people to hurricanes leads to a substantial increase in migrant remittances, so that total financial inflows from all sources in the three years following hurricane exposure amount to roughly three quarters of the estimated damages. This suggests that the aggregated shock arising from natural disasters can be insured at least partially by household-level informal transfers. Therefore, it would be misleading to focus on the effectiveness of formal insurance markets only. It is, rather, indispensable to investigate the overall effectiveness of a wide variety of the informal insurance mechanisms, as well as the formal ones, available to households in order to mitigate damages arising from earthquakes. Moreover, in order to answer operational questions about the tools and timing of appropriate policies for earthquake victims, the micro-level household responses to various damages need to be investigated. To this aim, recent empirical research methodologies in microdevelopment economics should be adopted as an indispensable research strategy here because there has been remarkable progress in the theoretical and empirical literature on risk and household behavior (Fafchamps 2003; Dercon 2005).

In this chapter, we review selected studies on the impact of earthquakes on households' welfare in Japan. Specifically, we focus on two research questions: are people insured against earthquakes; and how do people cope with the negative shocks generated by earthquakes? After reviewing the two contrasting cases of the Kobe and Chuetsu earthquakes, we discuss the role of public policy in facilitating risk management at the household level in the case of natural disasters. In spite of the downward trend of the number of deaths and missing persons in disasters in Japan, the Great Hanshin-Awaji (Kobe) earthquake in 1995 caused more than 6,400 casualties mainly because the earthquake hit the Hanshin area, one of the most developed areas in Japan. Other examples on much smaller scales include the Chuetsu earthquake on October 23, 2004. The former and the latter earthquakes show a striking contrast. The Kobe earthquake hit the urban center, where industries and residence are densely located, while the Chuetsu earthquake occurred in mountainous and remote farming areas, where people aged 65 and older make up a significant proportion of the population. A comparison of Kobe and Chuetsu earthquakes shows differences in income, consumption, and other household level socioeconomic variables that help us to identify the effectiveness of formal and informal insurance mechanisms.

The chapter is organized as follows. First, we summarize the conceptual framework, then present case studies looking at the Great Hanshin-Awaji (Kobe) and the Chuetsu earthquakes. In the final section, we discuss the public policy implications of our review and draw lessons from these earthquakes in Japan.

Conceptual Framework

CONSUMPTION INSURANCE

In order to approach one of the main questions of this chapter, that is, whether people insure themselves against earthquakes, we can apply the framework of the full consumption insurance or consumption risk-sharing hypothesis of Cochrane (1991), Mace (1991), Hayashi, Altonji, and Kotlikoff (1996), and Townsend (1987, 1994). Under the full consumption insurance, we obtain the conditions by solving a benevolent social planner's problem to maximize the weighted sum of people's utilities (Cochrane 1991; Mace 1991):

$$\frac{u'(c_{it})}{u'(c_{it-1})} = \frac{u'(c_{jt})}{u'(c_{jt-1})},$$ (11.1)

where u (•) is the concave instantaneous utility of a household, c is household consumption, and i, j denotes i, j the household, respectively. Equation 11.1 shows that full consumption insurance necessitates that the intertemporal marginal rates of substitution are equalized across agents for all states. Supposing that the utility function takes the form of a constant absolute risk aversion function, that is, $u(c_{it}) = -(1/\alpha) \exp(-\alpha c_{it})$, we obtain:

$$\Delta c_{it} = \Delta\left(\frac{1}{N}\sum_{j=1}^{N} c_{jt}\right),$$ (11.2)

where Δ is a first-difference operator and N represents the number of households in an insurance network, including formal credit or insurance market transactions. Under full insurance, idiosyncratic household income changes should be absorbed by all other members in the same insurance network and these shocks should not affect changes in consumption. As a result, idiosyncratic income shocks should not affect consumption changes. However, a household's consumption level is affected by aggregate factors. This is the empirically testable implication of the full consumption insurance model.

While the above framework of the full consumption insurance may appear extremely unrealistic, *de facto* household-level insurance can be attained through a wide variety of real-world market and nonmarket mechanisms, through credit and security markets, the government's state-contingent transfers—such as unemployment insurance and disaster insurance schemes, and informal transfer networks among family members or close communities. Our intention in applying this framework as a benchmark is to test the overall effectiveness and efficiency of informal/formal networks and markets as a whole to achieve efficient resource allocation.

RISK MANAGEMENT STRATEGIES

As a second framework, we also discuss how people in the area used risk-coping measures to mitigate changes in consumption arising from the natural disaster. In response to the wide variety of shocks caused by natural disasters, including earthquakes, households have developed formal and informal mechanisms to deal with the consequences. In the more general context, such insurance mechanisms can be divided into *ex-ante* risk management and *ex-post* risk-coping behaviors (Alderman and Paxson 1992; Dercon 2005; Fafchamps 2003). Risk management strategies can be defined as activities for mitigating risk and reducing income instability before the resolution of uncertainties in order to smooth income (Walker and Jodha 1986; Alderman and Paxson 1992). Risk management methods include accumulation of precautionary savings, participation in formal earthquake insurance, and investments in earthquake-proof housing structures.

Precautionary savings can take the form of bank deposits, cash holdings, jewelry, and physical assets such as land and real estate. In Japan, a major proportion of household assets is commonly held in the form of cash and cash equivalents, including in bank accounts, as well as land and real estate (Allen and Gale 2000). Zhou (2003) observed that precautionary savings arising from earnings uncertainty comprises 5.56 percent of the total savings of salaried worker households and a remarkable 64.3 percent of the total savings of agricultural, forestry, fishery, and self-employed households. While Japan has been criticized for its excessive savings behavior in the 1980s and early 1990s, which created large current account surpluses, the frequency of geological and climatic disasters such as earthquakes, landslides, and typhoons was significantly correlated with household saving rates (Skidmore 2001). According to Skidmore's (2001) estimation results, of Japan's saving rate of 12.4 percent, 10.1 percent can be explained by the past damages caused by natural disasters. This illustrates the significance of precautionary saving against disasters in Japan.

In Japan, earthquake insurance is complementary to fire insurance (homeowner insurance), and the amount insured ranges from 30 percent to 50 percent of that insured by fire insurance, with a cap of 50 million yen ($550,000) for houses and 10 million yen ($110,000) for assets. While the Japanese government provides reinsurance schemes to the private insurance companies that sell earthquake insurance, the government strictly regulates earthquake insurance premiums and there are only four different insurance premium categories across Japan.[4] For example, as shown in figure 11.1, the Kinki region, which includes the Kobe area at its center, was rated as a "Tier 3" area in terms of earthquake insurance premiums, implying that the risk of earthquake damage was considered to be lower than in the "Tier 4" areas. Since premiums do not vary much across regions and serious limitations do exist

TABLE 11.2 } Earthquake Insurance Participation Rate in Japan, 1993–2003, percentage

Year	1993	1994	1995	1996	1997	1998	1999	2000	2001	2002	2003
Japan overall	7.0	9.0	11.6	13.1	14.2	14.8	15.4	16.0	16.2	16.4	17.2
Hyogo	2.9	4.8	8.4	10.2	11.2	11.5	12.0	12.3	12.4	12.4	12.9
Tokyo	16.1	17.9	20.7	22.6	23.7	24.2	24.7	24.9	24.6	24.2	24.8

Source: Non-Life-Insurance Rating Organization of Japan.

in private but highly regulated insurance markets for earthquakes in Japan (Saito 2002; Yamaguchi 1998),[5] it has been known that insurance participation is rather limited in Japan in spite of it having the world's highest earthquake risk (table 11.2). For instance, only a small fraction of households in Kobe had earthquake insurance at the time the earthquake hit. In December 1994, only 3 percent of the population in Hyogo Prefecture, where Kobe is located, was covered by such insurance. Another reason for this is likely to be that people have an inherent tendency to underestimate the probability of rare bad events (Camerer and Kunreuther 1989), and thus there seems to be a systematically lower earthquake insurance participation rate than the optimal level.

It has been argued that *ex-ante* investments in mitigating the risk of earthquakes are very cost-effective in providing *ex-post* compensations for losses. By their very nature, however, it is often difficult to elaborate proper risk management strategies against earthquakes as they are typically rare and unforeseen events.

RISK-COPING STRATEGIES

Accordingly, even if households adopt a variety of risk management strategies, an earthquake can happen unexpectedly, causing serious negative impacts on household welfare. Therefore, *ex-post* risk-coping strategies—those used to reduce consumption fluctuation—will be indispensable (Alderman and Paxson 1992). In general, the existing literature identified the following different types of risk-coping mechanisms against different risks.

First, households can reallocate or reduce luxury consumption expenditure (McKenzie 2006; Kang and Sawada 2008). Affected households changed their consumption behavior substantially after the Kobe and Chuetsu earthquakes (Sawada and Shimizutani 2005, 2007, 2008; Ichimura, Sawada, and Shimizutani 2007). For example, according to Sawada and Shimizutani (2005, 2007, 2008, 2011), who analyzed a household survey conducted among the Kobe earthquake victims, around 62.7 percent of respondents answered that their consumption behavior changed prior to and after the earthquake, suggesting a trend of consumption reallocation after facing an unexpected disaster.

Second, households can use credit market transactions to weather the shock and smooth out consumption by reallocating future resources to current consumption. The lack of *ex-ante* formal insurance is compensated for by easy access to credit markets. For various reasons, however, households often have limited access to credit markets, a fact that can be attributed to high information costs and/or lack of assets for collateral. Indeed, using a unique household dataset from the Great Hanshin-Awaji (Kobe) earthquake, Sawada and Shimizutani (2008) showed that households with a large amount of collateralizable assets before the catastrophe, that were free from a binding borrowing constraint, were able to maintain their consumption levels by borrowing. In contrast, households subject to a binding borrowing constraint before the disaster were unable to borrow to cope with the losses inflicted by the earthquake. While the existence of credit constraints limits the risk-coping abilities of households, Horioka and Kohara (1999), and Sawada, Ii, and Nawata (2011) observed that less than 10 percent of households face credit constraints in Japan and therefore the overall impact of credit constraints may not be very significant.

Third, households can accumulate financial and physical assets as a precautionary device against unexpected income shortfalls. In the event of such shocks, households can use their own financial and physical assets. In fact, using household panel data, Horioka, Murakami, and Kohara (2002) examine how Japanese households cope with risk in a usual nondisaster situation and find that when they encounter unforeseen contingencies, households rely mostly on their savings. Similarly, according to Sawada and Shimizutani's (2005) analysis of subjective questions of Kobe earthquake victims, among those respondents who faced an expenditure shock due to the earthquake, more than half said that they used their savings. Yet, after carefully controlling for other factors, Sawada and Shimizutani (2005) found that savings were used only to cope with smaller asset damage, not large damages. Along with the finding that savings were used to compensate for smaller losses while larger shocks were dealt with by borrowing, our empirical findings suggest the existence of a hierarchy of risk-coping measures, ranging from dissaving to borrowing.

Finally, private and public transfers can be used as an *ex-post* risk-coping mechanism. For private transfers, through informal arrangements of state-contingent mutual transfers among relatives, friends, or neighbors, a household can weather the shocks and achieve consumption smoothing (Cochrane 1991; Mace 1991; Townsend 1987; Kohara, Ohtake, and Saito 2002, 2006; Sawada and Shimizutani 2007). Public transfers meanwhile (whether direct cash or in-kind transfers)—through means-tested targeting, tagging, or geographical/group targeting such as unemployment insurance or workfare—can act as a formal safety net for households facing difficulties. Horioka, Murakami, and Kohara (2002), using a household panel data set, find that Japanese households also rely on supports from family members, relatives, friends, and the government. Using a unique household data set from the Great Hanshin-Awaji (Kobe) earthquake, Sawada and Shimizutani (2008) showed that households relied on private transfers to weather the losses caused by the earthquake, depending on the extent of the damage.

As for public support, there existed three formal frameworks at the time of the Kobe earthquake in 1995. First, the Disaster Countermeasures Basic Act, established in 1961, formulated a comprehensive and strategic disaster management system with clearly defined roles and responsibilities for the national and local governments (Cabinet Office 2007). Second, the Disaster Relief Act of 1947 defines a variety of disaster emergency supports, including the construction and provision of temporary shelters for victims. Third, there is the Payment of Compensation for Disasters Act through which the death of the head of the household, or another household member, were compensated for by payments of five million yen ($55,000) and 2.5 million yen ($27,500), respectively. For serious disabilities caused to the head of the household or another member, 2.5 million yen ($27,500) and 1.25 million yen ($13,800) is paid out.

However, these acts did not provide any government compensation for households' asset losses after the Kobe earthquake.[6] The low levels of official compensation for the reconstruction of houses in Kobe proved controversial. As a result, the government passed the Support for Livelihood Recovery of Disaster Victims Act in 1998. As a result of which, each household whose home collapses now receives compensation of up to 3 million yen ($33,000).

Government transfers include not only the above-mentioned benefits from publicly provided schemes for victims but also people's donations to a variety of nonprofit organizations. After a natural disaster in Japan, the allocation of collected donations to victims is usually centrally determined by a special semi-public committee, with transfers allocated to households based on the certified level of damages. In the case of the Kobe earthquake, while 80 billion yen ($0.88 billion) in private donations was collected, because of the large number of victims, a mere 100,000 yen ($1,100) was paid out to each household with a completely destroyed house by this special committee, *Hyogo-Ken Nanbu-Jishin Saigai Gienkin Kanri-Iinkai.*

Case Studies: The Great Hanshin-Awaji (Kobe) and the Chuetsu Earthquakes

In order to capture an overall picture of the impact of earthquakes on households' welfare in Japan, we review selected evidence from the two contrasting cases of the Kobe and Chuetsu earthquakes (figure 11.3). While the Kobe earthquake hit the urban center, with its dense concentration of industry and residential areas, the Chuetsu earthquake occurred in mountainous and remote farming areas, where people aged 65 and older make up a significant proportion of the population.

THE GREAT HANSHIN-AWAJI (KOBE) EARTHQUAKE

In the early hours of January 17, 1995, the Hanshin (Kobe) area in Japan was hit by a major earthquake of magnitude 7.2 on the Richter scale (figure 11.3). The epicenter was located on the nearby northern Awaji Island, with the movements of the active fault causing the earthquake. The area is densely populated—home to more than four million people—and part of the second largest industrial cluster in Japan. As a result of the earthquake, more than 6,400 people died, 43,792 were injured, and 104,906 houses were completely destroyed. The housing property loss amounted to more than $60 billion, while capital stock loss was calculated to be more than $100 billion, making the event one of the largest economic disasters ever recorded (Horwich 2000; Scawthorn, Lashkari, and Naseer 1997). Given the fact that, in 1994,

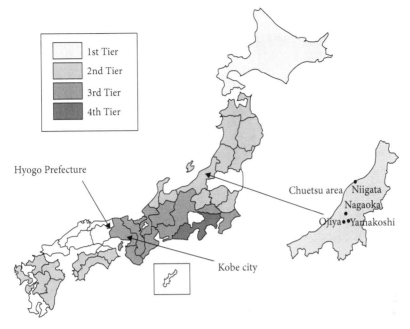

FIGURE 11.3 Two earthquakes
Source: Ministry of Finance.

only 4.8 percent of the property in Hyogo Prefecture, where Kobe is located, was covered by earthquake insurance, it is reasonable to assume that the earthquake was entirely unexpected in this area (table 11.2). In comparison, the insurance coverage for the Tokyo Metropolitan Area, which was hit by a massive earthquake in 1923, was 17.9 percent in 1994 (table 11.2). Stock prices dropped sharply after the quake (up to 20 percent), taking a year to recover to their pre-earthquake levels. Similarly, the value of yen against the US dollar dropped by 15 percent within three months.

There are several studies on the Kobe earthquake, notably Horwich (2000), Scawthorn, Lashkari, and Naseer (1997), Toyoda and Kawachi (1997), and Hagiwara and Jinushi (2004). Horwich (2000) conducted a useful calculation of the total damages caused by the Kobe earthquake. Taking Japan's capital stock to be three times its annual GDP of $5 trillion in 1995, the Kobe earthquake damage of $114 billion was only 0.8 percent of the capital stock of 3 × 5 = $15 trillion. Moreover, assuming that the value of human capital of an average Japanese person is $2 million, the total physical and human asset loss amounted to $127 billion ($114 million + 6,500 × $2 million). Considering that the total national wealth of Japan in 1995 was $167 trillion under a discount rate of 3 percent ($5 trillion/0.03 = $167 trillion), the physical and human asset loss of the Kobe earthquake was only 0.08 percent of the total wealth of Japan. While this back-of-the-envelope calculation from Horwich (2000) is very informative, capturing one of the core reasons why the Kobe earthquake barely affected the Japanese economy as a whole, these numbers should not be interpreted as a justification for ignoring individual micro-level impacts of the earthquake.

CONSUMPTION INSURANCE AND RISK-COPING STRATEGIES AGAINST THE GREAT HANSHI-AWAJI (KOBE) EARTHQUAKE

Most existing economic studies on the Kobe earthquake, including the above, focus on production, the macroeconomy, or rehabilitation policies, rather than on households, with the exception of Kohara, Ohtake, and Saito (2002, 2006), who tested the full consumption risk-sharing hypothesis shown by equation 11.2. Nevertheless, the latter's data set suffers from a serious attrition problem, as it retains only one quarter of the original households in the areas hit by the earthquake. To mitigate the estimation bias involved in Kohara, Ohtake, and Saito (2002, 2006), Sawada and Shimizutani (2005, 2007, 2008) used a unique micro data set from the victims of the Kobe earthquake—*Research report on changes in lifestyles and consumption behaviour following the disaster* (*Shinsai-go no Kurashi no Henka kara Mita Shouhi Kouzou ni Tsuite no Chousa Houkokusho*), collected by the Hyogo Prefecture in October 1996. The survey was completed by 1,589 women over the age of 30, and who were selected on the basis of a stratified random sampling scheme in the six areas seriously affected.[7]

Shortly after the earthquake, local governments conducted metrical surveys and issued formal certificates for damage to houses. The information on damage is objective and accurate. A total of 71.3 percent of the respondents suffered damage to their house and 78.6 percent suffered damage to their household assets (table 11.3).

By testing the implications of equation 11.2 with an econometric model applied to the above-mentioned data set, Sawada and Shimizutani (2007) found that households suffering larger nonincome shocks are more likely to change their consumption than those experiencing small nonincome shocks. Similar qualitative results can be verified by looking at numbers in table 4(b) of Sawada and Shimizutani (2008). The table shows the share of households reporting a substantial, slight, or no change in consumption behavior classified by the extent of damage they suffered. More than 80 percent of households that experienced major damage to their home changed their consumption behavior, while only half the households without any damage to their home changed their consumption behavior. The table thus shows that the share of households that changed their consumption behavior is positively correlated with the extent of housing asset damage, implying a rejection of efficient risk-sharing in

TABLE 11.3 } Household-Level Damages Caused by the Kobe Earthquake

Proportion of respondents who encountered	Percentage
Major housing damage caused by the earthquake	17.4%
Moderate housing damage caused by the earthquake	25.1%
Minor housing damage caused by the earthquake	43.1%
Major household asset damage caused by the earthquake	9.4%
Minor household asset damage caused by the earthquake	77.3%
Health-related shocks to the family caused by the earthquake	21.3%

Source: Sawada and Shimizutani 2005, 2007, 2008.

the entire area. A similar pattern can be found with regard to the change in consumption behavior in relation to the extent of damage to household assets.

To sum up, similar to the results from Kohara, Ohtake, and Saito (2006), the full consumption insurance hypothesis of equation 11.2 is rejected strongly, suggesting the overall ineffectiveness of the formal/informal insurance mechanisms against the earthquake. This finding suggests that the lack of insurance for real estate and physical assets is a particularly serious issue. These findings are consistent with the fact that very few properties in Kobe were covered by earthquake insurance in January 1995.

Even in the absence of full consumption insurance, households may be able to insure themselves against unexpected shocks through a wide variety of risk-coping behavior. Sawada and Shimizutani (2005, 2008) also investigate possible factors that inhibit consumption insurance by comparing the effectiveness of different risk-coping strategies, that is, dissaving, as well as borrowing and receiving private and/or public transfers. According to their descriptive statistics, among the respondents who faced an unexpected increase in their expenditure due to the earthquake, approximately 25 percent managed to cope by changing the constituents of consumption and more than half used their savings. Borrowing and receiving transfers were also considered as significant risk-coping strategies for approximately 10 percent and 12 percent of valid responses, respectively. Further careful econometric analyses by Sawada and Shimizutani (2005, 2008) reveal that the risk-coping means exploited by households are specific to the nature of the loss caused by the earthquake. For instance, households borrow extensively against housing damage, whereas savings are used to compensate for smaller damages caused to assets. This implies the existence of a hierarchy of risk-coping measures, starting from dissaving to borrowing. Also, Sawada and Shimizutani (2008) found that credit market accessibility plays an important role in weathering housing damage as credit-constrained households faced difficulties coping with such damage.

THE CHUETSU EARTHQUAKE

On the evening of Saturday, October 23, 2004, the Chuetsu earthquake struck the middle part of Niigata prefecture (figure 11.3), registering 6.8 on the Richter scale, with a hypocenter depth of 13 km—not very deep underground. The earthquake resulted in the deaths of 68 people, serious injuries to 632, and minor injuries to more than 4,000 in Niigata prefecture (Niigata Prefecture 2009). The housing property and capital stock losses were estimated to amount to more than $20 billion, making it one of the largest economic disasters in the new millennium.

We now examine Ichimura, Sawada, and Shimizutani (2007) to discuss the case of the village of Yamakoshi, which was located close to the epicenter and thus was one of the most heavily hit areas. It is fair to say that people in Yamakoshi did not expect a large earthquake. Since the most recent large landslides in the village took place in 1824 due to a thaw, the current villagers had never experienced such a disastrous catastrophe. Also, figure 11.3 shows that Niigata prefecture belongs to the area whose earthquake insurance premium is at the third tier level out of four different regions, in the ranking of the different risk of earthquakes (figure 11.3).

In Yamakoshi, five people died, 12 people were seriously injured, and an additional 13 people sustained minor injuries. In addition to the human losses, almost all the houses in the village were damaged, but the size of the losses was diverse, with 285 collapsed houses, 56 half-collapsed houses, 234 houses with moderate damage, and 106 houses with partial damage. Moreover, the resulting landslides forced the closure of highways and smaller roads, leaving most localities in Yamakoshi isolated. Since a continuous series of aftershocks increased the danger of further landslides, the government announced an evacuation order for the entire village, with all the villagers successfully evacuated two days after the earthquake. Two months later, around 80 percent of the villagers moved to temporary shelters (Kasetsu Jyutaku) provided by local governments in the neighboring city of Nagaoka.

Ichimura, Sawada, and Shimizutani (2007) designed a household survey exclusively for their study. The survey was conducted in April and May 2006 among the former residents of Yamakoshi. The sample is the registered Yamakoshi households at the time of the disaster. With strong cooperation from local governments, the survey covered 597 households out of the total of 663 registered households in the village.

In the village, more than half of all houses were seriously damaged: 43.2 percent of houses completely collapsed and 9.9 percent almost completely collapsed. In addition, 30.3 percent were classified as half-collapsed. According to Ichimura et al. (2007), unlike in the case of the Kobe data, the full consumption insurance hypothesis of equation 11.2 cannot be rejected.

In order to investigate possible factors behind the full consumption insurance, we can compare the important risk-coping strategies against unexpected costs caused by the earthquake. According to responses to subjective questions, approximately 70 percent of households managed to cope with the damages by drawing on their savings, while only 4 percent borrowed funds. Receiving insurance payments was also a significant risk-coping strategy for approximately half the households. Moreover, private and public transfers were used by 52 percent and 74 percent of the respondents, respectively.

Using parametric and nonparametric econometric models, Ichimura, Sawada, and Shimizutani (2007) compared the effectiveness of different risk-coping strategies, that is, dissaving, as well as borrowing and receiving public and private transfers. Similar to the case of the Kobe earthquake, borrowing played an effective role in coping with damage to houses, whereas dissaving played a minor role. Interestingly, households seem most likely to receive private transfers when they encounter health and unemployment shocks. Moreover, Ichimura, Sawada, and Shimizutani (2007) found that formal earthquake insurance, donation, and government transfers functioned effectively in Yamakoshi. Indeed, the earthquake insurance participation rate in Yamakoshi before the earthquake was more than 80 percent. This high participation rate may not be attributed to people's prior expectation of an earthquake. Rather, this is mainly because a majority of households participated in the housing insurance program provided by farmers' cooperatives, Japan Agriculture (JA), and the program automatically includes the earthquake insurance contract. Yet this was not the case for a much larger earthquake such as the Kobe earthquake in 1995 (Sawada and Shimizutani 2008), or disasters in developing countries (Sawada 2007).

Lessons from Earthquakes in Japan

The feature that distinguishes most sharply the Kobe and Chuetsu earthquakes is in the effectiveness of consumption insurance. While the full consumption insurance hypothesis was strongly rejected in the case of Kobe, the hypothesis seems to hold in Yamakoshi village. These results suggest that there is a serious lack of de facto insurance markets for damage to real estate and physical assets caused by the earthquake in Kobe. We may attribute this difference to two distinctive causes.

First, there is a significant difference in the total amount of private and public transfers. In Kobe, allocation of donations per victim was very limited—a mere $1,000 for a collapsed house, with no other government transfers provided mainly because the total number of the victims defined as those killed or injured in Kobe— 50,225 individuals—was more than 10 times as large as the total number of the victims of the Chuetsu earthquake—4,862 individuals. By contrast, there were two different additional public transfers made in the case of the Chuetsu earthquake: publicly distributed donations (*gienkin*) and Livelihood Recovery Transfers, that is, a government cash transfer program for the victims of the earthquake.

Second, in Yamakoshi, the earthquake insurance participation rate was very high mainly because of the JA's sales efforts in housing insurance products before the earthquake, compared to a participation rate of only 4.8 percent in Hyogo prefecture, where Kobe is located, in 1994.

Under these different conditions, it would be reasonable to find full consumption insurance in Yamakoshi, not in Kobe. These differences indicate the importance of further cross-disaster comparisons.

In both earthquakes, we observe that the means for coping are specific to the nature of shocks caused by the earthquake. For example, borrowing was extensively used to recover losses resulting from housing damage, while savings were used to compensate for the loss of smaller household assets. These findings suggest the existence of a hierarchy of risk-coping, ranging from dissaving to borrowing.

Our empirical results imply a serious lack of formal insurance markets for damage to real estate and physical assets in urban areas. Without effective *ex-ante* measures, the actual economic losses caused by an earthquake as strong as the Great Hanshin-Awaji earthquake prove to be too large for the government to compensate affected households effectively. After the Kobe earthquake, the central and local governments provided the largest financial support in the history of Japan to reconstruct the affected areas and to facilitate the economic recovery of the victims. However, despite the extensive support provided by the government, consumption insurance was not effectively achieved.

Regarding public and/or private provision of safety nets covering fallout from natural disasters, this review teaches two main lessons. First, it is imperative that *ex-ante* risk management policies be designed. For example, further development of markets for earthquake insurance would lead to the efficient pricing of insurance premiums and efficient land market prices reflective of the amount of risk involved (Saito 2002). This development would generate proper incentives to invest in mitigation, including investments in earthquake-proof construction. In Japan, housing rent is substantially lower in risky areas than in safer areas, while rent for apartments built prior to the Building Standard Law being amended is discounted more substantially in risky areas than those built after this date (Nakagawa, Saito, and Yamaga 2007). Similarly, Nakagawa, Saito, and Yamaga (2009) found that land prices were low in areas with substantial exposure to earthquake risk. Our review in this chapter suggests that more efficient resource allocation can be achieved effectively by price interventions as these *ex-ante* measures would significantly reduce the overall social loss caused by the earthquake.

Second, in its attempt to provide *ex-post* public support in the event of a natural disaster, the government may create a moral hazard problem by encouraging

APPENDIX TABLE } The Locations of the 25 Major Earthquakes and Tsunamis in Japan with Seismic Intensity of 6.0 or Greater in the Last 30 Years, Ranked by Human Losses

ID shown in fig. 11.1	Date	Magnitude	Name of earthquake	Total human losses (dead and missing)
1	1923. 9. 1	7.9	Great Kanto earthquake	142,807
2	1896. 6. 15	8.5	Meiji-Sanriku earthquake	21,959
	2011.3.11	9.0	Great East Japan earthquake	19,371
3	1891. 10. 28	8	Nobi earthquake	7,273
4	1995. 1. 17	7.3	Great Hanshin-Awaji earthquake	6,437
5	1948. 6. 28	7.1	Fukui earthquake	3,769
6	1933. 3. 3	8.1	Syowa-Sanriku earthquake	3,064
7	1927. 3. 7	7.3	North Tango earthquake	2,925
8	1945. 1. 13	6.8	Mikawa earthquake	2,306
9	1946. 12. 21	8	Nankai earthquake	1,330
10	1944. 12. 7	7.9	Tonankai earthquake	1,223
11	1943. 9. 10	7.2	Tottori earthquake	1,083
12	1894. 10. 22	7	Syonai earthquake	726
13	1872. 3. 14	7.1	Hamada earthquake	550
14	1925. 5. 23	6.8	North Tajima earthquake	428
15	1930. 11. 26	7.3	North Izu earthquake	272
16	1993. 7. 12	7.8	Hokkaido-Nansei-oki earthquake	230
17	1896. 8. 31	7.2	Rikuu earthquake	209
18	1960. 5. 23	9.5	Tsunami by Great Chilean earthquake	142
19	1983. 5. 26	7.7	Nihonkai-Chubu earthquake	104
20	2004. 10. 23	6.8	Chuetsu earthquake	68
21	2007. 7. 16	6.8	Chuetsu offshore earthquake	15
22	2001. 3. 24	6.7	Geyo earthquake	2
23	2003. 9. 26	8	Tokachi offshore earthquake	2
24	2007. 3. 25	6.9	Noto Peninsula earthquake	1
25	2000. 10. 6	7.3	Tottoriken-Seibu earthquake	0

Source: Cabinet Office Japan 2007; and Fire and Disaster Management Agency.

people to expose themselves to greater risks than they otherwise would if there were no expected support (Horwich 2000). Experiences of the two earthquakes suggest that providing subsidized loans, rather than direct transfers, to victims can be a good example of facilitating risk-coping behavior, and such interventions are less likely to create moral hazard problems. Issues such as these will be important research topics in the future. Moreover, since those who lost homes by the Great East Japan earthquake tend to be older than those who lost homes in the earlier Kobe earthquake, new complementary financing instruments such as reverse mortgage programs to victims are required to facilitate the asset recovery process.

Notes

1. According to Hayashi (2003), the Nankai earthquake occurred in 684, 790, 887, 1000, 1099, 1250, 1361, 1498, 1605, 1707, 1854, and 1946, and the Tokai earthquake happened in 1096, 1498, 1605, 1707, 1854, and 1944.

2. According to ADRC (2008), the damage was especially serious in Tokyo and Kanagawa Prefectures and the quake left 99,331 dead, 43,476 missing, 103,733 injured, 128,266 houses totally destroyed, and 126,233 partially destroyed.

3. Describing the overall effectiveness of mutual insurance across national borders, existing studies show that the extent of international risk-sharing remains surprisingly small (Obstfed and Rogoff 2001).

4. In each category, there are two premiums: one for nonwooden houses and another for wooden houses. In addition, there are four premium discount programs, depending on the quality of house, but these discounts do not vary much. Moreover, the government sets the overall cap on the total insurance payments for an earthquake—set at 5 trillion yen or $50 billion since April 2005.

5. Froot (2001) also observed that, in the United States, most insurers purchased relatively limited catastrophe reinsurance against natural disasters. He concluded that this is attributable to supply restrictions associated with capital market imperfections and market power exerted by traditional reinsurers. Nonetheless, Brookshire et al. (1985) showed that the housing market in the United States exhibits an effective response to the risk of damage caused by natural disasters.

6. Hayashi (2003) however pointed out that the total government compensation in the form of free meals in the initial stage, temporary shelters, public housing, etc. to the victims of the Kobe earthquake amounted to about 13 million yen ($143,000) per person.

7. Respondents were those who still lived there after the earthquake. Hayashi and Tatsuki (1999) found that the degree of damage to houses caused by the earthquake was on average larger for those who had moved outside the earthquake-hit areas than those who remained within the areas. This suggests that Sawada and Shimizutani's (2005, 2007, 2008) results can be interpreted as lower-bound estimates of the negative impact of the Kobe earthquake.

References

ADRC (Asian Disaster Reduction Centre). (2008). *Disaster Prevention in Japan*. Kobe, Japan: Asian Disaster Reduction Center.

Alderman, H., and Paxson, C. (1992). "Do the Poor Insure? A Synthesis of the Literature on Risk and Consumption in Developing Countries." Policy Research Working Paper 1008. Washington, D.C.: World Bank.

Allen, F., and Gale, D. (2000). *Comparing Financial Systems*. Cambridge, Mass.: MIT Press.

Brookshire, D., Thayer, M., Tschirhart, J., and Schulze, W. (1985). "A Test of the Expected Utility Model: Evidence from Earthquake Risks." *Journal of Political Economy* 93(2): 369–389.

Cabinet Office Japan. (2007). *Disaster Management in Japan*. Tokyo: Cabinet Office.

Camerer, C., and Kunreuther, H. (1989). "Decision Processes for Low Probability Events: Policy Implications." *Journal of Policy Analysis and Management* 8(4): 565–592.

Cochrane, J. (1991). "A Simple Test of Consumption Insurance." *Journal of Political Economy* 99(5): 957–976.

Dercon, S. (ed.) (2005). *Insurance against Poverty*. Oxford: Oxford University Press.

Fafchamps, M. (2003). *Rural Poverty, Risk and Development*. Cheltenham, UK: Edward Elgar Publishing, Inc.

Freeman, P., Keen, M., and Mani, M. (2003). "Dealing with Increased Risk of Natural Disasters: Challenges and Options." IMF Working Paper WP/03/197. Washington, D.C.

Froot, K. (2001). "The Market for Catastrophe Risk: A Clinical Examination." *Journal of Financial Economics* 60: 529–571.

Hagiwara, T., and Jinushi, T. (2004). "Which Area has been Recovered to What Extent?" (in Japanese). *Kobe University Memorial Symposium on the Hanshin-Awaji Earthquake*, November 5, 2004, Kobe, Japan.

Hayashi, H. (2003). *Earthquake Protection to Secure Lives* (in Japanese). Tokyo: Iwanami Shoten.

Hayashi, H., and Tatsuki, S. (1999). *A Report on Relocation and Living Condition of People after the Great Hanshin-Awaji Earthquake* (in Japanese). Research Center for Disaster Reduction Systems (DPRI), Kyoto University, Kyoto, Japan.

Hayashi, F., Altonji, J., and Kotlikoff, L. (1996). "Risk-Sharing between and within Families." *Econometrica* 64(2): 261–294.

Horioka, C., and Kohara, M. (1999). "Consumption Behaviour under Credit Constraints" (in Japanese). In *Analysis of Japanese Women's Behaviours by using Panel Data*, edited by Y. Higuchi and M. Iwata. Tokyo: Toyo-Keizai Shinpo-Sha.

Horioka, C., Murakami, A., and Kohara, M. (2002). "How Do the Japanese Cope with Risk?" *Seoul Journal of Economics* 15(1): 1–30.

Horwich, G. (2000). "Economic Lessons from Kobe Earthquake." *Economic Development and Cultural Change* 48: 521–542.

Ichimura, H., Sawada, Y., and Shimizutani, S. (2007). "Risk Coping against an Earthquake: The Case of Yamakoshi Village." Paper presented at the International Workshop on Consumption, March 19, 2007, at Hitotsubashi University, Kunitachi.

Kang, S., and Sawada, Y. (2008). "Credit Crunch and Household Welfare: The Korean Financial Crisis." *Japanese Economic Review* 59(4): 438–458.

Kohara, M., Ohtake, F., and Saito, M. (2002). "A Test of the Full Insurance Hypothesis: The Case of Japan." *Journal of the Japanese and International Economics* 16: 335–352.

———. (2006). "On [the] Effects of the Hyogo Earthquake on Household Consumption: A Note." *Hitotsubashi Journal of Economics* 47(2): 219–228.

Mace, B. (1991). "Full Insurance in the Presence of Aggregate Uncertainty." *Journal of Political Economy* 99(5): 928–996.

McKenzie, D. (2006). "The Consumer Response to the Mexican Peso Crisis." *Economic Development and Cultural Change* 55(1): 139–172.

Nakagawa, M., Saito, M., and Yamaga, H. (2007). "Earthquake Risk and Housing Rents: Evidence from the Tokyo Metropolitan Area." *Regional Science and Urban Economics* 37: 87–99.

——. (2009). "Earthquake Risk and Land Prices: Evidence from the Tokyo Metropolitan Area." *Japanese Economic Review* 60: 208–222.

Niigata Prefecture. (2009). "Damages Caused by the Chuetsu Earthquake." http://www.pref.niigata.lg.jp/kikitaisaku/1202058033358.html.

Obstfeld, M., and Rogoff, K. (2001). "The Six Major Puzzles in International Macroeconomics: Is There a Common Cause?" In *NBER Macroeconomics Annual 2000*, Vol. 15: 339–412. Boston: National Bureau of Economic Research.

Saito, M. (2002). "Natural Disaster Risks and Land Price Formations: Land Prices as a Signal of Risks" (in Japanese). In *Fudousan Shijyou No Keizai Bunseki*, edited by K. G. Nishimura. Tokyo: Nihon Keizai Shimbun Sha.

Sawada, Y. (2007). "The Impact of Natural and Manmade Disasters on Household Welfare." *Agricultural Economics* 37(1): 59–73.

Sawada, Y., and Kotera, T. (2011). "Disasters and Economies" (*Saigai To Keizai* in Japanese) *Sekai Keizai Hyoron* (*World Economic Review*) 55(4): 45–49,

Sawada, Y., and Shimizutani, S. (2005). "Are People Insured against Natural Disasters? Evidence from the Great Hanshin-Awaji (Kobe) Earthquake in 1995." CIRJE DP F-314, Faculty of Economics, University of Tokyo, Tokyo.

——. (2007). "Consumption Insurance against Natural Disasters: Evidence from the Great Hanshin-Awaji (Kobe) Earthquake." *Applied Economics Letters* 14(4): 303–306.

——. (2008). "How Do People Cope with Natural Disasters? Evidence from the Great Hanshin-Awaji (Kobe) Earthquake in 1995." *Journal of Money, Credit and Banking* 40(2–3): 463–488.

——. (2011). "Changes in Durable Stocks, Portfolio Allocation, and Consumption Expenditure in the Aftermath of the Kobe Earthquake." *Review of Economics of the Household* 9(4): 429–443.

Sawada, Y., Ii, M., and Nawata, K. (2011). "Did the Financial Crisis in Japan Affect Household Welfare Seriously?" *Journal of Money, Credit, and Banking* 43(2–3): 297–324.

Scawthorn, C., Lashkari, B., and Naseer, A. (1997). "What Happened in Kobe and What If It Happened Here." In *Economic Consequences of Earthquakes: Preparing for the Unexpected*, edited by B. Jones. Buffalo, N.Y.: National Centre for Earthquake Engineering Research.

Skidmore, M. (2001). "Risk, Natural Disasters and Household Saving in a Life Cycle Model." *Japan and the World Economy* 13: 15–34.

Townsend, R. (1987). "Arrow-Debreu Programmes as Microfoundations of Macroeconomics." In *Advanced in Economic Theory: Fifth World Congress*, edited by T. F. Bewley. Cambridge: Cambridge University Press.

——. (1994). "Risk and Insurance in Village India." *Econometrica* 62: 539–591.

Toyoda, T., and Kawachi, A. (1997). "Estimation of Industry Damages by the Hanshin-Awaji Earthquake" (in Japanese). *Kokumin Keizai Zasshi* 176(2): 1–16.

Walker, T., and Jodha, N. (1986). "How Small Farm Households Adapt to Risk." In *Crop Insurance for Agricultural Development: Issues and Experience*, edited by P. Hazell et al. Baltimore: Johns Hopkins University Press.

Yamaguchi, M. (1998). *Gendai No Risk To Hoken* (Modern Risk and Insurance). Tokyo: Iwanami-Shoten.

Yang, D. (2008). "Coping with Disaster: The Impact of Hurricanes on International Financial Flows, 1970–2002." *B. E. Journal of Economic Analysis & Policy* 8(1): 1–13.

Zhou, Y. (2003). "Precautionary Saving and Earnings Uncertainty in Japan: A Household-Level Analysis." *Journal of the Japanese and International Economies* 17(2): 192–212.

Urban and Nonagricultural Impacts of Flooding and Their Assessments

THE CASE OF BANGLADESH

K. M. Nabiul Islam

Introduction

Floods are one of the major sources of disaster in Bangladesh. A total of 29 major river floods in the past five decades and 11 major tidal surges in the past four decades have occurred.[1] Flat topography, heavy rainfalls, geographical location, transboundary flows, and global warming, in addition to Bangladesh's socioeconomic conditions, have added complications to the country's flood problem. Bangladesh is located in a region extremely vulnerable to floods. To the north of the country is located the world's highest mountain range, the Himalayas, and to the south, the Bay of Bengal, which has some of the longest coastlines in the world. Upstream of Bangladesh is India. About 92 percent of the total catchment area (1.8 million km²) of the three international rivers is located outside of Bangladesh, mostly in India. With all the major rivers originating in India, Bangladesh tends to suffer from upstream externalities, such as actions taken by India at the origin of the rivers.

The problem has become acute with the floodplains more heavily populated and their economic assets ever increasing. Consequently, the extent of flood damage is increasing. In 2007 the population of Bangladesh was estimated at more than 146 million. Urban population growth rate was extremely high in the 1980s and 1990s, at over 7 percent annually (figure 12.1). It has fallen since then but still remains at over 4 percent. The level of urbanization in 2005 (25 percent) in Bangladesh remained low compared to an average low-income country (30 percent) and to middle-income (54 percent) and high-income economies (78 percent) (World Bank 2008). The urban population in 2007 was more than 36 million and is expected to reach 74 million by 2035 (K. M. Islam 2006). More than half of the population will then live in urban areas.

Against this brief background, the major objective of this chapter is to reveal, conceptualize, and categorize various urban and nonagricultural impacts of flooding in Bangladesh, and thereby acquire a sound knowledge of the magnitude of major nonagricultural impacts so that consistent well-informed decision making is possible in

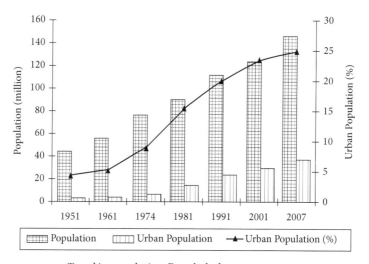

FIGURE 12.1 Trend in population, Bangladesh

Source: Based on data from K. M. Nabiul Islam (2006). *Impacts of Flood in Urban Bangladesh: Micro and Macro Level Analysis*. Dhaka, Bangladesh: A H Development Publishing House and Community Development Library.

relation to flood action. The chapter focuses on flood-loss potential in three of the major sectors of the urban economy: the residential, business, and industry sectors, based on investigations of flood-affected households and entrepreneurs in three urban areas using three reference floods: a major river flood, a flash flood, and a tidal flood. The author collected the primary data at different times during his Ph.D. research (1997), with updates in 2005 and 2006.

The current rate of population growth in Bangladesh is in the range of 1.4 percent per annum, which means that urbanization is increasing at nearly three times the rate of population growth. With already huge populations, most cities have alarmingly expanded into the low-lying areas on their peripheries. The rapid population growth compounded by perpetual changes in the "human-use system" has contributed to hazard effects by exposing more people and properties to risk, giving rise to ever more serious consequences.

The contribution of the urban sector to national GDP grew to nearly 42 percent in 1998/99 from only 26 percent in 1972/73. This share is probably close to 50 percent at present (Islam 2006).

Comparative statistics for selected countries show that with a population of 146 million (2007), Bangladesh has one of the highest population densities (1,042 people per km^2) in the world, in marked contrast, for example, to Australia, Brazil, the United Kingdom, or India (table 12.1). The most striking feature is that even with one of the lowest per capita incomes, Bangladesh has an enormous GNP/km^2 ($465,000)—much higher than that of low-income ($47,000) and middle-income countries ($116,000), and even that of an average world economy ($337,000).[2] This statistic for Bangladesh far surpasses even those of many advanced countries, Australia ($87,000), for example. This implies a very high intensity of land development and

TABLE 12.1 } Comparative Statistics on Population and GNP for Selected Countries

Countries	Population per km²	GNP per km² (000 US$)
Australia	3	87
UK	246	9,316
USA	31	1,341
Canada	3	105
Brazil	22	78
India	333	244
Bangladesh	1,042	465
Low-income	83	47
Mid-income	45	116
High-income	31	1,034
World	50	337

Source: World Bank, World Development Indicators.

TABLE 12.2 } Major Effects Caused by Selected Floods in Bangladesh

Damage item	Flood years					
	1974	1987	1988	1998	2004	2007
Percentage of country affected	37	40	62	68	38	42
Population affected (mil)	30	30	47	31	33	16
Loss to human lives (no.)	Several lacs[a]	1,657	2,379	918	285	1,071
Crop (mil ha)[b]	n.a.	2.1	7.5	1.37	1.1	1.1
Cattle heads (000)	n.a.	64	172	27	15	41
Houses (000)[b]	n.a.	2,467	4,358	2,647	4,284	1,100
Metalled roads (km)	n.a.	1,523	13,000	12,666	26,941	10,311
Educational institutions (no.)	n.a.	n.a.	8,481	22,600	25,571	8,753

Sources: BBS (various yearly issues); K. M. Islam 2005, 2006.

[a] Lac = 100,000.

[b] Fully and partially.

area-wise concentration of crops, assets, and properties in Bangladesh. In other words, it suggests immense competitive advantages from living in flood plains, perhaps partly justifying the high population density. This demonstrates that flood-loss potential in Bangladesh is enormous.

An account of "official" and "reported" damages from a few selected floods suggests that even "official" damages to crops, properties, and infrastructure are colossal, although the full account of losses is not available (table 12.2). More than 30 million people were directly affected averaged across the six selected flood events. In 1974, several hundred thousand people died in the famine, which was largely, though indirectly, due to flooding (table 12.3).[3] The full scale of damages caused by flooding, though unknown, was certainly large. For tidal flooding, the magnitude of the destruction is largely unknown. The death toll of more than half a million in 1970 and more than 150,000 in 1991, for example, suggests the scale of property losses even in this poor country (not shown in table 12.2) (K. M. Islam 2006).

The contribution of agriculture to GDP has declined, while the contribution from the service sector has markedly increased. The industrial sector has great unfulfilled development potential. Additionally, because the amount of land that can be irrigated is finite, GDP growth in the long run depends particularly on the growth of industries, which is expected to increase in urban areas as a result of improved infrastructure.[4] Such developments will greatly increase the rate and level of urbanization in the near future.

Thus, the urban and nonagricultural sectors of the Bangladesh economy are highly vulnerable to floods. Inordinate pressure on agricultural land resulting in widespread out-migration is another reason for such increased vulnerability.

Flood research in developing countries, let alone in Bangladesh, is rare and, where it exists, it is mainly limited to appraisal or evaluation studies that tend to focus on agricultural losses. There is no systematic flood-loss data collection, especially for nonagricultural sectors. As a result of this lack of damage data and methodology in Bangladesh, the loss assessments carried out by various agencies and the government appear to have been based on arbitrary methods.[5]

Against this background, this chapter attempts to answer the following important questions:

1. Can the flood loss assessment methods developed in advanced societies be applied in a developing country such as Bangladesh?
2. Compared to other economic sectors, are nonagricultural impacts more important in Bangladesh, even though it is currently an agricultural country?
3. If so, what effects does flooding have on nonagricultural sectors and on what scale? Which economic sectors are more vulnerable, and is there any relationship between poverty and natural hazards such as floods?

Bangladesh is selected as a case study as a predominantly agricultural country with high levels of poverty[6] and increasing urbanization, which is extremely susceptible to natural hazards, particularly floods. An account of historical damages to the economy caused by floods shows a marked rising trend of economic losses (see also Guha-Sapir, Hargitt, and Hoyois 2004). It is encouraging, however, to note that the reported number of people killed in river floods in Bangladesh is decreasing, thanks to better flood forecasting and warning systems (figure 12.2).[7]

Flood Impact Assessments in Bangladesh

FLOODS IN BANGLADESH

Before getting into issues relating to flood impacts and impacts assessment, this section seeks to conceptualize (or reconceptualize) flood impacts from the perspective

(a)
Economic losses in Bangladesh (US $ million: current values)

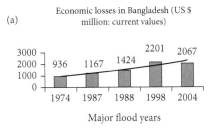

Major flood years

(b)
Reported human casualties in Bangladesh

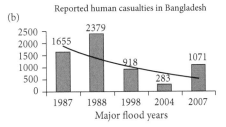

Major flood years

FIGURE 12.2 Economic losses during 30 years of river floods, Bangladesh

Note: Major floods occurred in the years 1974, 1987, 1988, 1998, 2004, and 2007, inundating 37, 40, 62, 68, 38, and 42 percent of the country's area, respectively.

Source: K. M. Nabiul Islam (2005). *Flood Loss Potentials in Non-agricultural Sectors, Assessment Methods and Standard Loss—Database for Bangladesh*. Dhaka, Bangladesh: Palok Publishers; K. M. Nabiul Islam (2006). *Impacts of Flood in Urban Bangladesh: Micro and Macro Level Analysis*. Dhaka, Bangladesh: A H Development Publishing House and Community Development Library; and CPD (2005). *Options for Self-Reliant Resurgence: Rapid Assessment of Flood 2004*. Dhaka, Bangladesh: UPL.

of a developing country such as Bangladesh. This conceptualization is important in order to increase the understanding of the short and long run, intangible, and "unconventional" nonagricultural effects of floods, which are not easily discernible in the society, and thereby contribute to policy making, especially in respect to efficient disaster response.

Four types of floods (usually not mutually exclusive) are commonly encountered in Bangladesh. These are seasonal floods, major river floods, flash floods, and storm-induced tidal surges. Floods caused by high-intensity rainfalls in the monsoon season generate "normal" seasonal floods. People can often adjust to these typical floods (e.g., through changes in cropping patterns), which are seldom harmful to agriculture or other sectors of the economy.

Major river floods, caused by spilling of water over the banks of major rivers due to heavy rains and other externalities in the upstream areas, are often catastrophic especially when the three major rivers rise simultaneously. Despite their short duration, flash floods, characterized by high discharge velocities with quick rises and recessions, can be very destructive at local levels in hilly regions. The fourth type of flood is the cyclone-induced, dangerous tidal surge that occurs in coastal areas.[8] As well as these four flood types, another type, which may be called urban floods, has recently emerged. Urban flooding is created by water-logging through a drastic reduction of low-lying areas and the consequent destruction of the natural drainage system resulting from usually unplanned rapid urbanization and infrastructure development. This type of flood is a threat to health and the environment in the major metropolis of the country.[9]

There has been a shift in the conceptualization of floods in Bangladesh. Until recently, floods were largely considered to be random geographical events, with the main focus on temporary relief and rehabilitation measures during and after the disaster. Floods have now started to be conceptualized, however, by the government and donors, as part of the development continuum, with consequent attention to mitigation, preparedness, vulnerability, marginality, and community participation.

In Bangladesh, floods may have multidimensional and multisectoral effects. There are enormous losses of loved ones, properties, livelihoods, community relationships, and heritage, which cause feelings of fear, helplessness, dependency, and mental stress. Unfortunately, such aspects as post-traumatic stress and psychological disorder due to flood hazard have not received adequate attention in Bangladesh. In severe floods, for example, males—particularly from the poorest social groups— often desert their wives.[10] Destitute women without any employment are sometimes compelled to migrate elsewhere and face acute conditions of physical and social insecurity. Often, an entire household is uprooted by floods and forced to migrate to urban areas. Many of the younger women refugees remain unmarried because of an inability to provide the kind of dowry customarily needed for their marriages. Often, some of them are even lured away by miscreants with promises of jobs elsewhere. One study indicates that about 9 percent of pavement dwellers and 18 percent of slum dwellers were uprooted from rural areas, and had migrated to Dhaka's urban centers because of floods (Begum 1999).

Deterioration of law and order, increased incidence of theft and robbery, price hikes of essential commodities, and an increased incidence of waterborne diseases are part of the normal scenario during and after floods, the impacts of which are enormously accentuated by lack of access to safe water and sanitation. The few and inadequate flood or cyclone shelters are very often monopolized by influential people. More often than not, even the location choice of flood shelters, either in urban or rural areas is dictated by powerful elites during their construction (Islam et al. 2006). The most vulnerable groups are the elderly, the disabled, children, and women. Women, for example, face severe difficulties in fulfilling their daily chores, such as cooking, collection of firewood, drinking water, and sanitation.

The physical and direct damage to roads has been an important nonagricultural flood impact, which has not been well researched, even in advanced countries.[11] In Bangladesh, road networks can be substantially damaged, depending on factors such as construction quality and the flood duration and depth (Islam and Mechler 2007; Siddiqui and Hossain 2006). Floods also cause indirect impacts such as traffic and communication disruptions. These include additional (marginal) transport costs incurred in the undertaking of an alternative route or journey, and the opportunity cost caused by deferment or delay of a journey.

In the case of Bangladesh, however, the negative indirect effects due to floods, created in the form of disruptions in travels, are likely to be largely offset by "natural redundancies" (automatic opportunities) created by widespread waterways through a large number of water transports on numerous river networks. Hence, indirect impacts on roads may not be considerable while direct damage to roads and infrastructure can be huge in Bangladesh.

INTERFACE BETWEEN ECONOMIC LINKAGES AND FLOOD IMPACTS IN BANGLADESH

While the direct impacts of flooding are those caused by direct contact with water, indirect impacts of flooding arise from the interruption and interaction between various social and economic activities that exist in an economy. In an economy such as that of Bangladesh, particularly with an open market structure, there can be innumerable directions and dimensions to these interactions among various sectors, in the form of "flows" and "stock" (figure 12.3). These intersectoral

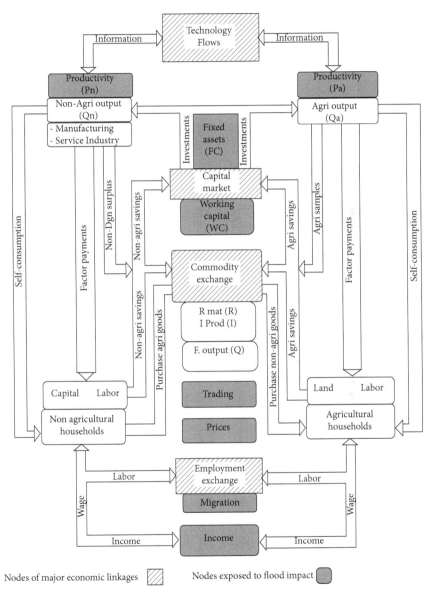

Nodes of major economic linkages ▨   Nodes exposed to flood impact ⬤

FIGURE 12.3 Link between intersectoral economic linkages and flood impacts for Bangladesh

Source: Adopted from K. M. Nabiul Islam (2000). "Micro and Macro Level Impacts of Urban Floods in Bangladesh." In *Floods*, Vol. 1, edited by D. J. Parker. UN-International Decade for Natural Disasters Reduction (UN-IDNDR). London: Routledge; and K. M. Nabiul Islam (1997a). "The Impacts of Flooding and Methods of Assessment in Urban Areas of Bangladesh." Ph.D. diss., Flood Hazard Research Centre, University of Middlesex, London.

relationships, or linkages as they are usually called, play a crucially important role in the growth of an economy, as well as in the creation of flood-loss potentials. The salient intersectoral economic linkages are merged into four broad types: technological flows, capital market, commodity exchange, and employment flows (Ranis et al. 1990). As depicted in the figure, the major economic interactions are between the two primary supply premises (agricultural and nonagricultural output sectors), on one hand, and the two major demand premises (agricultural and nonagricultural households), on the other.

Within the linkages, the major "nodes" that are likely to be exposed to flooding in Bangladesh are displayed in figure 12.3. Out of the four major nodes, commodity and capital nodes are relatively more exposed to flooding. Flooding is postulated to point to two major economic effects, one from the supply side (productivity) and the other from the demand side (income). Having considered the two broad sectors, flooding in the agriculture sector first (usually) means a fall in output and land productivity, leading, in turn, to a fall in agricultural surplus. This results in adverse effects on savings and hence investment, which, in turn, contributes to adverse indirect impacts on the wage and income of households in the nonagricultural sector, and the agriculture sector itself. As a result of flooding in agriculture, the nonagricultural sector is likely to suffer from a shortage of inputs and intermediate products.

From the demand side, the effects move in the other direction: a fall in income in agricultural households, less demand for nonagricultural goods (usually) and a consequent fall in output and productivity in nonagricultural sectors. This leads to unemployment and a fall in wages with subsequent adverse effects on income and savings. On the other hand, with the fall in employment, both wages and incomes in agricultural households are also likely to fall. Flooding in the nonagricultural sector affects the agriculture sector in a similar direction.

The decline in income may eventually contribute to malnutrition, and shortage of production inevitably results in a price increase in food and other commodities, especially those with inelastic demand. Thus, the adverse flood impacts—owing to interdependencies between the two sectors—progress in a vicious and never-ending circle. These interactions are explored in more detail below.

In Bangladesh, demographic and social characteristics such as community cohesion, friendliness and kinship also form a kind of linkage, a "social" linkage, which is likely to have a bearing on flood losses. Such linkages, however, are likely to act contrary to economic linkages. Considering only economic linkages, the more dependence and ties that exist across sectors in the system, the larger are the likely indirect impacts of a flood. From the point of view of social linkages, however, the more the community is socially linked, the stronger will be the extent of "transferability" (ability to respond) of burdens in the society, reducing the seriousness of the final impacts. An analysis of the 1998 flood in Bangladesh, for example, shows that family kinship along with community cohesion, as a whole (especially, the richer section, political activists and local community-based organizations) played a significant role in positive response to flood hazards (K. M. Islam 2006). Unfortunately, however, noncooperation from political leaders (due to military-backed interim government) led the local community to play a passive role during the 2007 flood, resulting in untold sufferings of the flood victims. Thus, community cohesion can serve as an informal insurance mechanism to help cope with shocks, as suggested by Santos (see chapter 10), who found that "inter-household transfers (e.g. informal loans) served as insurance against exogenous shocks such as Hurricane Mitch in Nicaragua" (see chapter 10).

NONAGRICULTURAL FLOOD IMPACTS EVALUATION: DEVELOPED COUNTRY PERSPECTIVE

This chapter deals with tangible and monetary impacts. However, flooding also leads to welfare loss to households through impacts on public nonmarket goods among others. The available nonmarket valuation methods, with a special focus on how they can be applied in developing countries, are discussed in chapter 3 of this book (e.g., Navrud and Magnussen 2008).[12] The following section briefly discusses nonagricultural flood impact evaluation from the perspective of developed countries.

Residential Sector

Research on flood impacts in developed countries is divided into three broad groups:

(1) impacts assessment methods;
(2) depth-damage functions and data sets construction; and
(3) project appraisal methods.

Flood damage assessments in the residential sector involve two principal techniques: stage-damage curves based on surveys of actual floods, and synthetic techniques. While the first approach involves damage assessments during or after the actual events, the second approach involves methods synthesizing damage information from multiple sources through constructing susceptibility matrices for different damage components.

Flood hazard research is relatively recent and oriented mainly toward advanced countries such as the United States, the United Kingdom, and Australia. The methods of modeling damages to residential buildings used in the 1960s in these countries were rudimentary. The actual damages assessed were used mainly for appraisals of flood control projects at regional levels, having few applications at the national level.

The approach of extrapolating future damages from actual floods was subsequently modified, and the "synthetic approach" of flood damage assessment started to be adopted in the United States.[13] In the United Kingdom (and perhaps the United States), the construction of consistent potential flood damages based on actual events was found to be impracticable for various reasons.

The only comprehensive study of flood loss potential in the residential sector in the United Kingdom is the one by Penning-Rowsell and Chatterton (1977), popularly known as "Blue Manual," which adopted a synthetic approach to residential flood-loss assessments.

Commercial Sectors (Business and Industries)

Research on flood losses in commercial sectors is centered on indirect losses, as assessment methods for direct losses are relatively straightforward. Until recently, industrial flood loss potentials for future floods in the United Kingdom or United States were predicted on the basis of actual events. This approach used to suffer from many estimation biases, such as those arising out of the tendency to record replacement cost rather than depreciated costs. Projections of indirect losses in future floods used to be made through obtaining crude ratios between direct losses and production disruptions.

Pioneering research on loss assessment in commercial sectors was conducted by Parker, Green, and Thompson (1987), popularly known as "Red Manual." The research overcame some of the problems associated with the approaches used in the past, such as distinguishing national economic losses from the financial losses of firms, through incorporating production transfers within the economy. It also addressed the problem of overestimation of direct loss potential through incorporating "average remaining values." The production loss in industries was the loss to value added, and the turnover loss in business amounts to the loss to gross margin.

As regards the multiplier effects of flooding, research has been far more limited. It is often argued, however, that multiplier effects are likely to be counterbalancing in many economies;[14] further research is needed on this.

EVALUATION OF FLOOD IMPACTS IN URBAN BANGLADESH: CAN WE APPLY DEVELOPED COUNTRIES' METHODS?

Residential Sector

PROBLEMS OF ASSESSMENTS

The major challenge in flood hazard appraisals relates to the generation of appropriate loss data sets to serve as an input to flood defense appraisals and the modeling of expected annual damage in an urban area. Damage data collection based on actual events through interviewing is dependent upon occurrence of flood events. The generation of data sets at disaggregated levels of depth and duration is often not feasible mainly because of the lack of adequate variations of depth and duration in a specific flood in a given area. Stable depth-damage curves are difficult to establish in these circumstances. Moreover, the properties vary greatly in type and quality so that damages are also subject to large variations. The relationship between damage and flood characteristics (e.g., depth and duration) is often further complicated by the presence of factors such as perception, warning, and emergency actions.

One of the problems of flood damage assessments in Bangladesh involves quantification of damage values. Flood damages are the cost of returning the relevant property to pre-flood conditions, through (a) repair works already undertaken (b) replacement works already undertaken, and (c) the remaining damages, if any, that are to be carried out in the future.

The replacement values are usually likely to be arbitrary and exaggerated. On the other hand, resale values are also subject to arbitrary considerations. In spite of this, the "resale value" approach may be adopted for Bangladesh, having the advantage that such values at existing conditions can capture the "average remaining values" of the properties, which is a major issue in flood damage research.[15]

Commercial Sectors

PROBLEMS OF ASSESSMENTS

In the commercial sectors, the major problem of using actual damage to construct standard damage data sets relates to the wide variations of these sectors in terms of type, stock, capital, output, and technology. This is true both for developing and developed countries. Another practical problem associated with the assessment of flood loss potentials involves converting actual to potential losses through adjustments with damage-saving activities. Obviously, sample size is a crucial determining factor in constructing a representative damage data set. On the other hand, the construction of average data in the commercial sector based on the synthetic approach is almost impossible not only in Bangladesh but also in developed countries. The major reason is the lack of appropriate secondary information required to construct susceptibility matrices for different damage items.

As is also true for residential damage assessments, the damage data "arithmetically" averaged from the actual flood survey can hardly lead to consistent stage/damage functions. This implies that an extremely large sample size is required to ensure that the data are consistent. This dictates the need for an approach that involves predicting damages through establishing functional relationships with flood variables, which can only lead to fairly consistent damage data sets. The approach may be termed the "regression approach." Besides "averaging" the results through a regression, which is more appropriate, such an approach is capable of working out estimates at any conceivable depth or duration based on some assumptions.

Thus the impact assessment methods used in developed countries, with some modifications, can largely be applied in a developing country such as Bangladesh. However, few alternatives to the synthetic approach are available in assessing residential damages in the United Kingdom or perhaps elsewhere in advanced countries. In Bangladesh, on the other hand, it appears that there is no alternative to survey techniques because of a lack of informed secondary sources for adopting the synthetic techniques.

FLOOD LOSS MODELS

The basic structure of modeling flood impacts is to employ a combination of the "unit-loss" method (Parker, Green, and Thompson 1987), multiple regression, the Cobb-Douglas model, and the input-output model (figures 12.4 to 12.6).[16] It consists of three major components for evaluating

(1) direct loss,
(2) primary indirect loss, and
(3) multiplier effects.

The direct loss component of the model is applicable to both residential and commercial sectors, while the indirect loss component comprising primary indirect and multipliers is applicable to commercial sectors.

Direct Loss Model

Physical direct losses are determined mainly by indices of flood intensity, depth, and duration. Nevertheless, even with the same flood intensity, damages are expected to significantly vary following variations in (1) the prevailing stock, type, and quality of assets, and (2) area of premises. Thus, stock of assets and area of space may also be considered two other explanatory variables in the model.

The direct loss model uses multiple regression analysis to estimate the potential damage to various damage components (e.g., structure, machinery/equipment, and stock (input and output)) at disaggregated levels of depth and duration. The model can use either absolute or proportional damages to regress on explanatory variables (box 12.1). Unlike in the residential sector, not surprisingly, the proportional approach

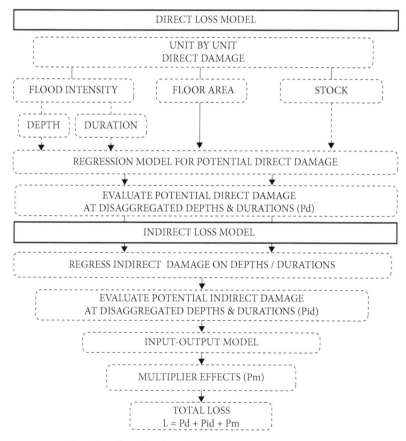

FIGURE 12.4 Flood loss (total loss) model 1

Source: Author.

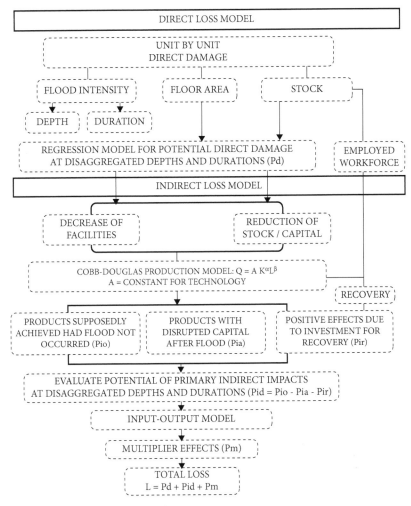

FIGURE 12.5 Flood loss (total loss) model 2

Source: Author.

has not proved feasible in the case of commercial sectors, both for industry and business. Instead, the flood-loss models using absolute damages generally fit well.

In both industries and business, the double logarithmic form of models shows higher correlation coefficients, implying more explanatory power of the models. For structural damages, it is assumed that no measures are undertaken to reduce such damages so that actual and potential damages are equal. For the assessment of potential damages to components, such as stock or machinery, damage-reducing activities are taken into account.

Indirect Loss Model

The indirect loss model, applied to industries and commercial sectors, has two components: the model for evaluating (primary) indirect impacts (either through

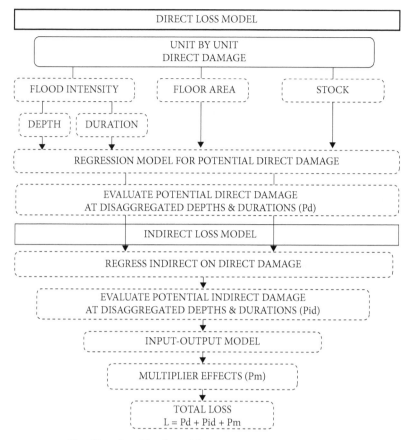

FIGURE 12.6 Flood loss (total loss) model 3

Source: Author.

regressing on independent variables, e.g., depth and duration, or through the Cobb-Douglas production model), and that for assessing multiplier effects (through Input-output Table). The primary indirect impacts, which are actually the indirect impacts of the first order, can directly be assessed like the direct ones.

The Cobb-Douglas model is based on the Cobb-Douglas production function, which is of the form:

$Q_t = A_t K_t^\alpha L_t^\beta$, where Q_t = output, A = constant for technology, K = capital stock, L = input for labor, and t = time. α is the partial elasticity (responsiveness) of output with respect to capital (holding labor constant), and β is the partial elasticity of output with respect to labor (holding capital constant).[17]

Following that output, capital, and labor input are known at time t (before flood) from enterprise level data, the parameters A, α and β are estimated empirically. Once the function is estimated for a before-flood situation, primary losses to output caused due to flood can be estimated through imputing disrupted (reduced) capital and labor into the function. The output loss in an industry or turnover loss in a business is termed as "indirect loss," as is commonly used in flood-loss literature (since

BOX 12.1 } Single Equation Models Used to Generate Potential Damage Data Set for Industries and Business Units

Direct Loss Models

(applicable to residential houses/industries/business units)

1 $D_m = A + B\,(DEPTH) + C\,(AREA) + H\,(D_1) + U_i$

2 $D_m = A\,(DEPTH)^c\,(AREA)^g\,e^{[h(D1)+k(Ii)]}\,U_i$

Or, $Log(D_m) = Log(A) + c\,Log(DEPTH) + g\,Log(AREA) + h\,(D_1) + k\,(I_i) + U_i$

where,

D_m = Direct damage
Depth = Depth of flooding above floor; Area = Area of relevant premises
A, B, C etc = Parameters to be estimated; e = Natural logarithm,
D_1 = A dummy variable for Duration, so that
D_1= 1 when duration more than 7 days; D_1 = 0 for duration for up to 7 days.

Likewise, I_i are dummy variables for residential house/commercial groups so that
I_i = 1, for houses/industries/business group I; I_i = 0, for otherwise, and U_i = Disturbance factor

Indirect Loss Models

(Applicable for industries/business units)

1 $V_a = A + B\,(DEPTH) + D\,(DURATION) + I_i + U_i$

2 $V_a = A\,(DEPTH)^c\,(AREA)^g\,e^{[h(D1)+k(Ii)]}\,U_i$

Or, $Log(V_a) = Log(A) + c\,Log(DEPTH) + g\,Log(AREA) + h\,(D_1) + k\,(I_i) + U_i$

3 $V_a = A\,(D_m)^c\,e^{Ii}\,U_i$

Or, $Log\,(V_a) = Log\,A + c\,Log\,(D_m) + I_i + U_i$

where,

V_a = Value added loss, D_m = Direct damage, and other variables as defined earlier.
4 Cobb-Douglas Production model

$Q = A\,K^\alpha\,L^\beta\,U_i$

Or, $LOG\,(Q) = LOG(A) + \alpha\,LOG\,(K) + \beta\,LOG\,(L) + U_i$

where,

Q = Production, K = Capital and L = Labor input used in the production process.
$\alpha + \beta, (\alpha, \beta > 0)$, the economies of scale.
I_i are Industries group, i = 1 to i.

The same set of models are applied to business units, replacing Production with Turnover, Value Added with Gross Margin, and replacing Industries groups, (I_i) with Business groups, B_i. For other assumptions, see Islam (1997a).

BOX 12.2 } Formulae for Evaluation of Primary Indirect Losses in Commercial Sectors

1. Production loss during complete closure (TK):

PDCCLOSE = (CCLOSE * OUT/30).

2. Production during partial closure (TK):

PDPCLOSE = (PCLOSE * OUT/30) * AVPROD/100.

3. Production loss during partial closure (TK):

PDPCLOS = (PCLOSE * OUT/30) * (1 – AVPROD/100).

4. Total production loss during complete and partial closure (TK):

TOPDLOS = (PDCCLOSE + PDPCLOS).

5. Production loss made up (TK):

PDMAKUP = (TOPDLOS * MADEUP/100).

6. Total net production loss (TK):

NTPDLOS = TOPDLOS – (PDMAKUP – ADCOST).

where,

CCLOSE = completely closed due to flood (days)
OUT = monthly output (TK)
PCLOSE = partially closed due to flood (days)
AVPROD = average production during partial closure (percent)
MADEUP = percent of lost production recovered
ADCOST = additional cost incurred for recovery (TK).

this is caused not due to direct contact with water). The indirect loss for industry is the loss to value added on production. Similarly, turnover loss in a business is the loss to gross margin.

Recovery of production, if any, is incorporated; additional costs of recovery or working less efficiently are added to calculate a firm's total indirect flood losses. The following formulae (box 12. 2) are used to estimate net losses in output, but the ultimate indirect loss to a firm is the loss to the value added/gross margin.

Indirect loss is generally found to be a function of depth, duration, and floor space, with only a few exceptions. The Cobb-Douglas production function, using empirical data on capital and labor inputs, is generally found to fit extremely well, indicated by values of R squared.

Indirect loss is related to direct damage in almost all the models.[18] The explanatory powers of these models (indicated by higher R squared values) are relatively higher than those of the models regressed on depths, durations and floor space. Because the indirect impacts are logically functions of direct losses, the modeling of indirect losses through regressing on direct losses is considered more suitable (thus illustrating higher explanatory powers).

TABLE 12.3 } Estimated Linkage Effects for Groups of Industries under Investigation

Industries groups	Output multipliers (MLT)	Recovery factor (RF)	Overall demand (decline) factor (DF)	TYPE 1 multiplier effects (Effect 1)	TYPE 2 multiplier effects (Effect 2)	TYPE 1 linkage effects (% of indirect loss)	TYPE 2 linkage effects (% of indirect loss)
Food and agro-based	2.6472	.55	.30	1.1912	1.9854	74.1	123.5
Cotton and textiles	3.1729	.34	.31	2.0941	3.0777	143.4	210.8
Timber and furniture	3.0151	.51	.22	1.4774	2.1407	98.7	143.1
Engineering	2.8487	.46	.41	1.5383	2.7063	99.8	175.6
Misc. and service	2.4890	.40	.36	1.4934	2.3894	89.3	142.9
ALL INDUSTRIES	2.8346	.48	.34	1.4740	2.4378	95.4	157.8

Note: Overall Demand (decline) Factor (DF) is estimated after adjusting for rise in demand, if any.

Modeling Multipliers and Linkage Effects of Flood Losses

The Input-Output (I-O) Table for the Bangladesh economy, as available for 1993/94 (BIDS 1999), partitioned the national economy into 79 production sectors.[19] These sectors are rearranged and consolidated by incorporating the sample industrial units (in five broad activity groups) under investigation.[20]

Output multipliers (Multipliers—MLT, as shown in table 12.3) for various economic sectors, as estimated from the national I-O Table with fixed coefficients, lead to what theoretically might be the linkage effects of flooding at the national level due to production loss at firm level. Such an approach is potentially inappropriate as a result of demand-side factors and recovery/restoration factors, the former leading to higher values and the latter leading to lower values of linkage effects. Field investigation (Islam 1997a) shows that a regional economy (town economy in this case) is significantly resilient and thus an approach of assessing linkage effects is required to capture this resiliency. Additionally, some of the industrial units experience a fall in demand while some experience increases in demand for their products in the aftermath of floods, presumably due to the loss of income and the act of diverting money to meet other consumption (in the case of falls in demand) or due to increased rebuilding activities (increases in demand).

Since this chapter is aimed at national economic efficiency analysis, the two factors—Demand Factor (DF) and the Recovery Factor (RF)—need to be incorporated into the assessment of linkage effects. The recoveries include the incorporation of factors such as "deferment," "transferability," and utilization of idle capacity, especially by nonflooded firms.[21] Hence, linkage effects, which are actually the spillover effects of various trade adjustments, should be seen from a national perspective. Thus:

(1) Type 1 multiplier effects (Effect 1) = MLT * (1–RF); and
(2) Type 2 multiplier effects (Effect 2) = MLT * [(1–RF) + DF].

Two types of linkage effects are estimated:

(1) by incorporating RF and
(2) by incorporating RF and DF.

Thus, linkage effects are defined as:

(1) Type 1 Linkage effects = [MLT–1] [(1–RF)] * 100 = [Effect 1–(Effect 1/ MLT)] * 100
(2) Type 2 Linkage effects = [MLT–1] [(1–RF) + DF] * 100 = [Effect 2–(Effect 2/MLT)] * 100.

It is more appropriate to contemplate the Type 2 linkage effects while construct-ing potential damage data sets. The estimates of multipliers and linkage effects are shown in table 12.3. The table shows that if the primary output loss in the industrial sector overall is 100, for example, the linkage effects of flooding would be 158. This means that linkage effects of flooding would be nearly 1.6 times that of the primary output loss.

Vulnerability of Economic Sectors to Floods in Bangladesh

AGRICULTURAL SECTOR

Semi-logarithmic trends for major rice crops, both in terms of acreage and output, for the period 1972 to 2003 are estimated. The analysis of damage to the wet season's rice crops shows that Bangladesh is prone to damage equivalent to 3.7 percent of production annually (averaged over 37 years). Of this, *aus* is subject to annual dam-age equivalent to 4.4 percent and *aman* to 3.4 percent (Islam 2005).[22]

As also argued in various contemporary studies (e.g., K. M. Islam 2006; Haruhisa, Matsumoto, and Rahma 2005; Hossain 1990), some floods can be absorbed by agriculture (e.g., through changes in cropping patterns) and are seldom harmful. Flooding often increases the productivity of agricultural land through increases in soil fertility.

In order to examine the link between flooding and damage to agricultural pro-duction, the first hypothesis is formulated as follows: the larger the areas affected by floods, the greater the negative deviations expected below the estimated (nor-mal) trend. In that case, the second hypothesis is as follows: a negative correlation is expected of the deviations with flood-affected areas.

The estimated semi-logarithmic trend lines (1981–2004) are considered as base figures for this analysis. The deviations of the actual production from the trend lines shows that in the disastrous flood of 1998, for example, *aman* production fell short by nearly 21 percent below the normal trend production (table 12.4). The shortfall in wet-season rice crops together (*aus* + *aman*) was 20 percent below the trend pro-duction. By contrast, the production of the dry-season rice crop (*boro*) was 10 per-cent above the normal trend in the same year. The findings are similar for the flood of 2004 when the shortfall in wet-season rice crops together (*aus* + *aman*) was 6 percent below the trend production. The production of the dry-season rice crop

TABLE 12.4 } Fluctuation in Trend of Rice Production from 1981 to 2004

	Fluctuation from estimated trend (%)			
	Wet-season rice crops			Dry-season rice crop
Flood years	*Aus*	*Aman*	*Aus + Aman*	*Boro*
1986	14.9	2.4	5.0	−9.1
1987	**13.6**	**−6.3**	**−2.1**	**0.5**
1988	**11.9**	**−17.7**	**−11.5**	**16.1**
1989	0.7	8.7	5.9	15.1
1997	−1.5	−7.9	−7.3	−9.5
1998	**−12.2**	**−20.8**	**−19.6**	**10.0**
1999	−2.7	3.9	2.9	7.7
2003	17.1	9.0	11.5	−3.2
2004	**−0.9**	**−8.6**	**−6.1**	**2.2**

Source: BBS (Agricultural Statistics), various issues.
Note: Trends for the years of flood are **in bold.** N = 24 (1981–2004).

(*boro*), however, was 2 percent above the normal trend. Similarly, in all the years of flood and years in the aftermath, the *boro* productions were above the normal trend (table 12.4). Thus, the agricultural shortfalls in the years/seasons of floods are to some extent compensated by above-normal production in the following years.[23]

Evidently, for *aman* individually and wet-season (*aus* + *aman*) rice crops together, the correlations are found to be negative (−0.38 and −0.63, respectively), as expected, and are also statistically significant. For the dry-season crop (i.e., *boro*) the correlation, as expected, is found to be positive (+0.45) and highly significant.

This suggests that farmers put additional effort into the production of the dry-season crop (*boro*) to make up for losses of wet-season crops. Replanting after flood damage is also frequently helpful in compensating for seasonal losses. The recovery process is also often facilitated by increased provision of irrigation and modern inputs and other extension services. In other words, the crop sector has demonstrated substantial resilience against floods, as compared to flood losses experienced by nonagricultural sectors or the urban economy in Bangladesh, which are analyzed in the following section.

NONAGRICULTURAL SECTORS

The flood loss caused to nonagricultural sectors appears to be enormous. An account of the flood losses to the whole economy caused by the 1998 flood, for example, shows that the nonagricultural sectors together (e.g., infrastructure and commercial sectors), including the noncrop sector, suffered enormous losses, amounting to 51 percent of the total loss, with the agricultural sector (crop plus noncrop) suffering 49 percent of the total loss. The 2004 flood scenario is yet more significant: the nonagricultural sectors suffered losses accounting for as much as 74 percent of the total loss, with the remaining 26 percent accounted for by the agricultural (crop

TABLE 12.5 } Flood Damage to Selected Sectors in Two Selected Floods (1998 and 2004)

Sector	1998 Flood		2004 Flood	
	% of total damage	% of GDP	% of total damage	% of GDP
Infrastructure	**38.6**	1.8	**69.7**	**2.36**
Roads, railways, institutions, etc.	18.2	0.85	37.2	1.26
Residential Sector	20.4	0.95	32,6	1.10
Industrial Sector	**12.0**	**0.56**	**4.7**	**0.16**
Agricultural Sector	**49.4**	**2.31**	**25.6**	**0.87**
Crop Sector	42.8	2.0	22.2	0.75
Noncrop Sector	6.6	0.31	3.4	0.12
Total	**100.0**	**4.7**	**100.0**	**3.4**

Sources: Islam, Chowdhury, and Bhattacharya 1999 (for 1998 flood); CPD 2005 (for 2004 flood).

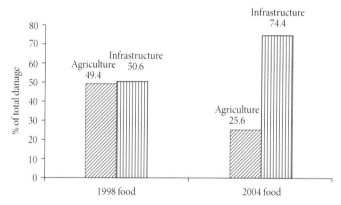

FIGURE 12.7. Percentage of total damage in two selected floods, 1998 and 2004

Source: Author.

plus noncrop) sector (table 12.5, figure 12.7).[24] The effects of the two floods were equivalent to 4.7 and 3.4 percent of Bangladesh's GDP, respectively.

The damage from the 1998 flood was similar to that caused by the super cyclone Sidr that struck the coastal districts. The total damage caused by the cyclone was estimated at Taka 113 billion (US$1.6 billion), which is equivalent to 2.8 percent of Bangladesh's GDP (GoB-WB 2008). Damage to nonagricultural sectors was enormous, amounting to 71.5 percent of the total damage, with the agricultural sector bearing the remaining 28.5 percent of the total damage.

FLOODING AND INDUSTRIAL PRODUCTION: A MULTIVARIATE ANALYSIS

An analysis of major sectors of the economy demonstrates that the deviations (from trend on value added) in small, large, and all industrial (combined) sectors are strongly related to deviations in value added in the agricultural sector. Despite these strong linkages in the economy, the deviations from the trend for agriculture, industry, and national GDP are found to be least related to flood-affected areas (Islam 2000; K. M. Islam 2006).

What follows from this analysis is that there are reasons to believe that the fluctuations in industrial production are due to factors other than flooding. In order to pursue this, a multivariate analysis is carried out incorporating other possible variables that are likely to influence the dependent variable—industrial production (box 12.3).[25]

Most industries show high coefficients of determination (detailed results not shown here). Out of 16 large industries, 15 have significant coefficients at more than a 5 percent level, with only one (cigarettes) being not significant at any level.

It appears that flood-affected areas have hardly any significant influence on the production of selected large industries, although for some of the industries the signs of the flood variable coefficient are negative, as expected. Except for the sugar industry, none of these are statistically significant at an acceptable level. Despite the fact that the two sectors, agriculture and industry, are strongly interrelated (K. M. Islam 2006), in terms of value added, surprisingly, the variable Agricultural Fluctuation does not show any significant and positive relationship for any of the industries under investigation.

As expected, urbanization has a positive and significant influence on production for many of the industries under investigation (paper, matches, newsprint, and iron/steel). The Income variable (per capita income) has a positive coefficient for only one industry (yarn). As expected, Political Instability (measured in terms of work-strike) has a negative influence for a considerable number of industries, but significant influence is found for only two industries: matches and agricultural

---

BOX 12.3 } The Multivariate Model Postulated

Q = f (FLOOD, AGFL, URBINDX, INCOME, PRINDX, POLINS, NPS)

where,

Q = Production (quantity in individual units) of selected large industries
FLOOD = Flood Affected Areas (in the country)
AGFL = Agricultural Production Fluctuations
URBINDX =Urbanization Index (share of urban to total population)
INCOME = Per Capita Net National Product (NNP)
PRINDX = Price index (for industrial products)
POLINS = Political Instability (work strike in hours)
NPS = Net Power Supply in the system (measured in MWH).

The reference period is 1973/74 to 2002/03.

Source: BBS, *Statistical Year Book* (various issues); BBS, *Report on Bangladesh Census of Manufacturing Industries* (CMI) (various issues); *The Year Book of Agricultural Statistics of Bangladesh* (various issues).

machinery. Despite the considerable variation in Power Supply (net of system loss) over the years, its coefficient is positive and statistically significant for only one of the industries (food). It may, however, be mentioned that large industries in general have their own power plants to avoid power disruption, which is a common phenomenon in Bangladesh. As expected, Price Index (for industries) has an apparent positive influence on production for many of the industries under investigation, but a significant and positive influence can be found only for three industries: fertilizers, urea, and readymade garments (export-oriented). A negative but significant coefficient is found for two industries, cloth (domestic) and iron/steel.

Thus, Bangladeshi industries appear to be resilient against exogenous factors. Although the industry and infrastructure sectors suffer enormous damage from flooding, their adjustment and recovery mechanisms appear strong. It can also be argued that the undercapacity of the industrial sector might have subsequently helped to overcome the losses occurred by any of the disturbances discussed above.

Concluding Remarks

Bangladesh seriously lacks flood damage data and assessment methodologies. In order to deal with a natural hazard such as flood, it is important to build knowledge and data networks that can be employed to enhance economic resilience. Experience shows that while the agricultural sector can often absorb the impacts of some floods, the size of urban and nonagricultural flood losses is greatly increasing.[26] Given the strong relationship between economic development and urbanization, potential urban flood losses will continue to sharply increase in Bangladesh in the years to come. Hence, adequate attention needs to be given to urban flood hazards, especially in the context of potential "disaster vulnerabilities" due to the rapid urbanization process, flawed development activities, and climate change.

On average, the poorest households suffer (in terms of losses proportional to values) nearly 4, 5, and 3 times as much, compared to the losses suffered by the richest households, in river, flash, and tidal floods, respectively. Hence, in Bangladesh, and perhaps in most other developing countries, natural hazards such as floods not only exacerbate poverty but they may help widen the income gap between the rich and the poor.[27] In respect of its national poverty reduction strategy and objective of attaining the Millennium Development Goals, Bangladesh can hardly afford to ignore the adverse impact of floods on the process of poverty reduction and growth. The primary and long-run indirect effects of floods on the poor need to be taken into careful consideration when formulating mitigation plans.

Historically, water and flood management policies have been dominated by structural measures. Following the failure of structural measures to provide full security, increased flood losses due to a "false sense of security," inadequate maintenance, and associated environmental issues,[28] nonstructural measures have to be given proper emphasis because such measures have enormous damage-reducing effects (K. M. Islam 1997b, 2000, 2006). The 2007 flood and Sidr serve as further reminders to Bangladesh of their importance.

In the context of disaster response, particularly to tidal surges, the potential for future sea-level rise is of great concern to Bangladesh, a country with vast low-lying, densely populated areas, especially in coastal regions.[29] Climate change may lead to a further increase in already rapid rates of urbanization through rural migrations and the coastal areas will come increasingly under threat, especially from tidal floods, which can be very destructive.[30]

The management of transboundary river flows is crucially important for Bangladesh. The importance of regional cooperation in ensuring effective early warning systems can hardly be overemphasized.[31] Bangladesh needs to exchange updated scientific data and information (e.g., on rainfall patterns) among its riparian neighbors.

Bangladesh, perhaps, has little option but to live with floods. Hence, it is important that they are managed and adjusted to successfully. The country has a long experience of flood disaster management. It is important to update lessons learned from disasters. Ironically, there has been a persistent disregard for emergency preparedness, which has not yet adequately been reflected in annual or long-term development plans. It is important for Bangladesh to concentrate on emergency preparedness and rehabilitation works in a planned, institutional, and coordinated way in order to avoid wasting resources in the aftermath of every occurrence.

Notes

1. Major floods in Bangladesh are defined as those which inundate more than 20 percent of the country's area. Major tidal surges, induced by storms in coastal areas, are those having more than 2 meter surge height.

2. These comparative statistics refer to 2005 (World Bank 2008).

3. Sen (1981) found that, even with no significant fall in food availability per head, "lack of entitlement to food" with sudden price hikes associated with a major fall in employment opportunities was the main reason for the starvation, which occurred immediately in the aftermath of 1974 flood.

4. Urbanization is viewed "as an inevitable concomitant of industrialization" (Ranis, Stewart, and Angeles-Reyes 1990).

5. National loss estimates for the 2004 flood, for example, carried out by various agencies based on arbitrary methods ranged from 10,000 crore to 42,000 crore Taka (K. M. Islam 2006); US$ = Taka 68 (2008).

6. The percentage of the population living under the poverty line in 2007 (Direct Calorie Intake [DCI] method) in rural and urban Bangladesh was 39.5 and 43.2, respectively (BBS 2007).

7. The trend, however, does not include human casualties caused in 2007 by Sidr (November 15) in coastal Bangladesh, which claimed around 4,400 human lives.

8. In terms of proportional damage, the most devastating flood is the tidal type—it destroys about 34 percent of the total assets in houses—followed by a flash flood, which accounts for 11 percent compared to 10 percent in the case of a major river flood (K. M. Islam 2006).

9. Following the 2007 flood, for example, the incidence of diarrheal diseases (recorded in International Centre for Diarrhoeal Disease Research, Bangladesh) increased threefold, compared to the yearly average incidence.

10. A participatory study (under NWMP 2000) conducted by the author demonstrates that the post-monsoon flood in 2000 across the southwest region caused huge damage to vegetables cultivated by women, subsequently causing a drastic fall in income and nutrition levels among women in the Satkhira district, which was reported to have resulted in higher divorce rates at that time.

11. One of the other major economic sectors is roads, which has not been covered in this chapter (see Islam 1997, 2005).

12. The methods include, among others, Stated Preference, Contingent Valuations, Hedonic Price Analysis, and Benefit Transfer methods (Navrud and Magnussen, 2008; see also Tunstall, Green, and Lord 1988; Green et al. 1988).

13. The synthetic approach in the United Kingdom used a combination of data sources, including loss adjusters who were engaged in calculation of insurance payments for flood damages.

14. In the United Kingdom, intuitively (perhaps because of more "transferability" or "redundancy") (Parker, Green, and Thompson 1987), multiplier effects of flooding are insignificant.

15. For a discussion on the replacement/restoration cost method in relation to loss of ecosystem functions, see chapter 3 by Navrud and Magnussen.

16. The unit-loss method is concerned with unit-by-unit loss estimates at an individual household or firm level.

17. The sum of the partial coefficients gives the scale of returns. $\alpha + \beta = 1$ represents constant returns, $\alpha + \beta > 1$ represents increasing returns and $\alpha + \beta < 1$ represents decreasing returns.

18. The variables, Depth and Duration, are not included in this model mainly because of the potential presence of multicolinearity with variable Direct Damage.

19. This includes 20 in agriculture, 39 in manufacturing, 6 in construction, 3 in energy, and 11 in service sectors.

20. It is obvious that the sample size (58 in five groups) is too meager to be represented in the national economy, so the estimated multipliers are to be used with some caution.

21. "Transferability" refers to the ability of an activity/farm to respond to a disruptive threat by overcoming dependence either by deferring or using substitutes or relocating.

22. *Aus* and *aman* are two wet-season rice crops while *boro* is a dry-season rice crop. Usually, flood causes huge loss to the *aman* crop (Islam 1999b).

23. Similar findings were reached by Haruhisa, Matsumoto, and Rahman (2005); Hossain (1990).

24. The UNDP-sponsored appraisal gives a similar picture demonstrating that in the capital city the loss caused to properties in two sectors (industry and trade) alone was estimated in the range of six billion Taka; US$ = Taka 68 (2008) (Islam 1999a).

25. The analysis is carried out on 16 selected large industries, the dependent variable being quantity of output, measured in individual units.

26. This does not in any way underestimate agricultural losses, which even though relatively smaller in size, have a large impact on relatively disadvantaged rural communities in terms of income and living conditions.

27. Another analysis (Islam 2005) shows that land-poor people (also lower income categories) suffer higher inundation levels and are more exposed to flood risks. From an analysis on WFP-Bangladesh data (2006) one can find a close positive relationship between the percentage of flooded areas and the percentage of most severely affected poor ($r = 0.33$, $p < 0.001$) (K. M. Islam 2006).

28. The duration of the 2000 flood over southwest Bangladesh was as long as four months, largely due to unplanned roads, polders, and shrimp *ghers* (earthen enclosures) in the region.

29. See, e.g., chapters 4 and 12 in this book.

30. More than 53 percent of total world deaths due to tidal floods occurred in Bangladesh (Hassan and Conway 2007).

31. See Islam (2000, 1997b) for damage-reducing effects of warning.

References

Asian Development Bank (ADB) (2006). *Urbanization and Sustainability in Asia; Good Practice Approaches in Urban Region Development.* Cities Alliance (Cities without slums). Dhaka, Bangladesh.

Bangladesh Bureau of Statistics (BBS). (2007). *Report of the Household Income and Expenditure Survey 2005.* Dhaka, Bangladesh: Ministry of Planning, Government of Bangladesh, BBS.

———. Various Yearly Issues. *Statistical Year Book of Bangladesh.* Dhaka, Bangladesh: BBS.

———. Various Yearly Issues. *Report on Bangladesh Census of Manufacturing Industries (CMI).* Dhaka, Bangladesh, BBS

———. Various Yearly Issues. *The Year Book of Agricultural Statistics of Bangladesh.* Dhaka, Bangladesh: BBS.

Begum, A. (1999). *Destination Dhaka, Urban Migration: Expectation and Reality.* Dhaka, Bangladesh: University Press Limited.

Benson, C., and Clay, E. (2004). *Understanding the Economic and Financial Impacts of Natural Disasters.* Washington, D.C.: World Bank.

BIDS (1999). *An Input-Output Table for Bangladesh Economy, 1993–94.* Dhaka, Bangladesh: General Economics Division, Planning Commission, Government of Bangladesh.

Centre for Policy Dialogue (CPD). (2005). *Options for Self-Reliant Resurgence: Rapid Assessment of Flood 2004.* January. Dhaka, Bangladesh: University Press Limited.

Dorosh, P., Shahabuddin, Q., and Farid, N. (2004). "Price Stabilization and Food Stock Policy." In *The 1998 Floods and Beyond: Towards Comprehensive Food Security in Bangladesh*, edited by P. Dorosh, C. del Ninno and Q. Shahabuddin. Dhaka, Bangladesh: UPL-IFPRI.

Government of Bangladesh—World Bank (2008). *Cyclone Sidr in Bangladesh: Damage, Loss and Needs Assessment for Disaster Recovery and Reconstruction.* Dhaka: Government of Bangladesh.

Green, C. H. (2003). *The Handbook of Water Economics, Principles and Practice.* London: University of Middlesex, Wiley Publication.

Green, C. H., Tunstall, S., Emery, J. P., and Bossman-Aggrey, P. (1988). "Evaluating the Non-monetary Impacts of Flooding." Annual Meeting of the Society for Risk Analysis, UK.

Guha-Sapir, D., Hargitt, D., and Hoyois, P. (2004). *Thirty Years of Natural Disasters 1974–2003: The Numbers.* Brussels: UCL Presses Universitaires de Louvain.

Haruhisa, A., Matsumoto, J., and Rahman, R. (2005). "Impact of Recent Severe Floods on Rice Production in Bangladesh." *Geographical Review of Japan* 78(12): 783–793.

Hassan, A., and Conway, D. (2007). "Secondary Impacts of Climate Change in Bangladesh." ORCHID: Piloting Climate Risk Screening in DFID, Dhaka, Bangladesh.

Hossain, M. (1990). "Natural Calamities, Instability in Production and Food Policy in Bangladesh." *Bangladesh Development Studies* 18(4) (December): 33–54.

Islam, K. M. Nabiul (1997a). "The Impacts of Flooding and Methods of Assessment in Urban Areas of Bangladesh." Ph.D. diss., Flood Hazard Research Centre, University of Middlesex, London.

———. (1997b). *The Role of Perception, Warning and Human Factors in Flood Losses*. Research Report 152. Dhaka, Bangladesh: BIDS.

———. (1999a). *The Assessment of Environmental Impacts of Flood 1998 on Dhaka City*. Dhaka, Bangladesh: Economic Impact Study, Industry, Trade, Commerce and Crops, Ministry of Environment, Government of Bangladesh.

———. (1999b). *Rapid Appraisal on Aman Crop Damage and Prospect of Aman due to 1998 Flood*. Dhaka, Bangladesh: FMRSP, BIDS-IFPRI.

———. (2000). "Micro and Macro Level Impacts of Urban Floods in Bangladesh." In *Floods*, Vol. 1, edited by D. J. Parker. UN-International Decade for Natural Disasters Reduction (UN-IDNDR). London: Routledge.

———. (2005). *Flood Loss Potentials in Non-agricultural Sectors, Assessment Methods and Standard Loss—Database for Bangladesh*. Dhaka, Bangladesh: Palok Publishers.

———. (2006). *Impacts of Flood in Urban Bangladesh: Micro and Macro Level Analysis*. Dhaka, Bangladesh: A H Development Publishing House and Community Development Library.

Islam, K. M. Nabiul, Chowdhury, O. H., and Bhattacharya, D. (1999). "The Assessment of Impacts of Flood 1998." Dhaka, Bangladesh: Asian Development Bank.

Islam, K. M. Nabiul, et al. (2006). *Stakeholder Consultation on Institutional and Partnership Issues in Coastal Districts*. Integrated Coastal Zone Management Plan Project (ICZMPP), WARPO, Ministry of Water Resources, Government of Bangladesh, Dhaka.

Islam, Nazrul (2006). "Bangladesh." In *Urbanization and Sustainability in Asia: Good Practice Approaches in Urban Region Development*, Cities Alliance (Cities without slums), Dhaka, Bangladesh.

Islam, N., and Mechler, R. (2007). "ORCHID: Piloting Climate Risk Screening in DFID Bangladesh: An Economic and Cost Benefit Analysis of Adaptation Options." Institute of Development Studies, University of Sussex, UK.

Mechler, R. (2005). "Cost-Benefit Analysis of Natural Disaster Risk Management on Developing Countries." Disaster Risk Management in Development Cooperation, Working Paper, August, Eschborn, Germany: GTZ.

Navrud, S., and Magnussen, K. (2008). "Damage Costs of Natural Disasters and the Benefits of Preventing Them: A Review of Valuation Methods." Working paper.

NWMP (2000). *National Water Management Plan*. Dhaka, Bangladesh: Ministry of Water Resources, Government of Bangladesh.

Parker, D. J. (ed.) (2000). *Floods*, Vol. 1. London and New York: Routledge.

Parker, D. J., Green, C., and Thompson, P. (1987). *Urban Flood Protection Benefits: A Project Appraisal Guide*. Aldershot, UK: Gower Technical Press.

Penning-Rowsell, E. C. (1997). "Testing the Contextual Models of Hazard-Response." *Geographical Review*, UK.

Penning-Rowsell, E. C., and Chatterton, J. B. (1977). *The Benefits of Flood Alleviation: A Manual of Assessment Techniques*. Aldershot, UK: Gower Technical Press.

Penning-Rowsell, E. C., and Green, C. (1990). *Benefit-Cost Analysis of Flood Alleviation: A Changing Art*. London: Flood Hazard Research Centre.

Ranis, G., Stewart, F., and Angeles-Reyes, E. (1990). *Linkages in Developing Economies: A Philippine Study*. San Francisco, Calif.: International Center for Economic Growth, ICS Press Publication.

Santos, I. (2008). "How Do Households Manage the Effects of Natural Disasters? The Role of Inter-Household Transfers in Nicaragua." Working paper.

Sen, A. (1981). *Poverty and Famine: An Essay on Entitlements and Deprivation*. Oxford: Oxford University Press.

Siddiqui, K. U., and Hossain, A. N. H. A. (eds.) (2006). *Options for Flood Risk and Damage Reduction in Bangladesh*. Dhaka, Bangladesh: University Press Limited.

Tunstall, S., Green, C. H., and Lord, J. (1988). *The Evaluation of Environmental Goods by the Contingent Valuation Method*. London: Flood Hazard Research Centre, University of Middlesex.

World Bank. (2008). *World Development Indicators*. Washington, D.C.: World Bank.

13 }

The Economics of Flood Disaster Management in the Netherlands
Roy Brouwer and Marije Schaafsma

Introduction

Climate change poses new challenges in terms of flood risk mitigation and disaster management in countries situated below sea level such as the Netherlands. Among the most important consequences of climate change are rising sea levels—expected to be in the range of 15 to 35 cm in the next 50 years—and an increase in extreme river discharge levels. For the Rhine, the largest river flowing through the Netherlands, this increase is expected to be between 20 and 115 cm (Middelkoop et al. 2001). Three quarters of the Netherlands is protected by dykes and embankments. Over the centuries, 53 such protected areas have been constructed. Safety standards for these areas are set out in the 1996 Water Act. Safety levels are highest in the western part of the country, where the flood return period is officially once every 10,000 years. But this reduces when moving eastwards. Near the border with Germany, the flood return period is once every 1,250 years. The western part of the country is the most densely populated and includes large cities like Rotterdam, The Hague, and Amsterdam, where Dutch economic activity is concentrated (Brouwer and Kind 2005). Hence, the safety levels are relatively higher in this part of the country. Safety levels are also higher along the coast because of the shorter warning period for sea-flood disasters (hours), compared to river-flood disasters (days).

The Netherlands has a long history of flood disasters. In 1953, a North Sea storm surge caused widespread flooding, resulting in the deaths of more than 1,800 people in the southwestern part of the country. More recently, in 1993 and 1995, large-scale evacuations of 200,000 people along the rivers Rhine and Meuse prevented flood disasters resulting from extremely high river discharge levels.

As a result of the 1953 disaster, the so-called Delta Plan was implemented. One of the most expensive public infrastructure investments ever made in the Netherlands, the plan closed off the gateways to the southwestern estuaries. After the events in 1993 and 1995, dykes were raised higher and made stronger. The government—traditionally

Part of this chapter was previously published in R. Brouwer and D. W. Pearce, *Cost-Benefit Analysis and Water Resources Management* (Cheltenham, UK: Edward Elgar Publishing, 2005).

responsible for flood control and flood disaster management in the Netherlands—provided compensation for most of the damage in 1993 and 1995. The cost of flood damage in these years was €115 million and €64 million, respectively (Kok and Barendregt 2004). The current Calamities and Compensation Act, adopted in 1998, details the circumstances under which the Dutch government will cover future flood damage.

In order to anticipate increased flood risks due to climate change, a new flood control policy was put in place in 1998. This is based on the principle of managed realignment and restoring river system dynamics (Brouwer and van Ek 2004). Moreover, flood disaster zones, which can be used in emergencies, were identified in the eastern part of the country (Commissie Noodoverloopgebieden 2002). The government is examining both adaptation and mitigation through "hard" physical infrastructure and "soft" adaptation, and mitigation mechanisms such as private insurance. Flood risk insurance is expected to be an efficient means of sharing between private and public institutions the financial burden of flood risks (Pearce and Smale 2005). Currently, no private flood risk insurance exists in the Netherlands (Botzen and Van den Bergh 2008).

In view of the spatial differentiation of flood calamity risks and the protected economic interests, flood disaster policy is increasingly subject to economic review and evaluation, such as cost-benefit analysis (CBA). Generally, the benefit to cost ratio of disaster risk reduction ranges from two to four (Mechler 2005), but the valuation of the costs and benefits involved is fraught with difficulties (Bouwer et al. 2007). Moreover, benefit to cost ratios based only on avoided property damage costs may substantially underestimate the total benefits, since they do not account for public risk aversion. These latter well-being effects, measured in economics through the concept of a society's willingness to pay (WTP) to avoid a specific risk when people are not entitled to risk protection, or society's willingness to accept compensation (WTAC) if they are, or believe they are, entitled to compensation, should be added to the expected damage costs (e.g., Jones-Lee 1989). Tol (1999) presents estimates of marginal damage costs that are adjusted to reflect risk aversion; these are around three times higher than the unadjusted costs.

The main objective of this chapter is to present an example of the Dutch experience of managing disasters related to climate change, and the use of CBA in this specific domain. Special attention will be paid to the residual risks of flooding over and above existing safety levels in the Netherlands, and the costs and benefits of potential emergency measures based on so-called designated flood disaster zones. In addition, the results of a public survey are presented, assessing public perceptions, support, and WTAC for controlled flooding, should emergency areas actually be employed in situations of disaster flooding.

The Use of Cost-Benefit Analysis in Flood Disaster Management

One of the first CBAs carried out in the Netherlands for a large-scale water management project was in the 1960s, for the so-called Delta Commission (Tinbergen

1960), which was established after the 1953 flood disaster. The Delta Plan involved the closing off of the gateways to the southwestern estuaries in the southwest of the Netherlands, except for the Rotterdam Waterway and the Western Scheldt. The net costs of the implementation of this plan were estimated at about 1.1 billion Dutch guilders (price level 1955), which was around 4 percent of net national income (NNI) at that time. The total direct costs were 1.8 billion guilders. Although these direct costs were only 200 million guilders higher than the cost of the improvement of the area's existing dyke system, the Delta Plan was expected to result in considerably more indirect gains, including nonpriced benefits such as public safety, drought damage reduction, and recreation. The study concluded that the incremental costs of 1.1 billion guilders were lower than the material damage of the 1953 floods, and the Delta Plan could therefore be justified. As a result of insufficient knowledge at that time, the study did not include a probabilistic analysis of future flooding events and their impact in terms of future economic damage avoided. It acknowledged the importance of such an analysis for the outcome of the CBA, as well as the fact that the economic value of the probability of future damage avoided, diminishes at positive discount rates.

Although knowledge and information about flood risks were limited in the 1950s and 1960s, and the study by Tinbergen was unable to quantify these risks, the study was amazingly comprehensive in its coverage of the relevant issues, when carrying out a CBA in the context of flood control. The concept of risk is central to a CBA that looks at alternative flood control options and scenarios. Risk can be defined as the product of the probability of flooding, which is a function of a variety of factors, including water levels, wind, geomorphology, strength of dykes and other water-retaining structures, and the financial and economic consequences of flooding, which are a function of the economic value of buildings and activities in flood-prone areas. A reduction in flood risks is therefore the main economic benefit in a CBA conducted in the context of flood control. However, it was not until the end of the 1990s that these benefits could actually be quantified in a CBA of large-scale flood control projects. This is done now with the assistance of advanced hydraulic and flood probability models, and a national information system that enables assessment of the damage costs of flooding with the help of damage functions (e.g., Jonkman et al. 2008).

Another area that has received heightened attention is the estimation of other socioeconomic benefits of nontraditional flood control alternatives, such as managed realignment. This has especially been the case since the publication of the Fourth National Water Policy Document (V&W 1998). In this policy document, the government for the first time addressed not only the issue of the costs of water management measures but also their financial and economic consequences for society as a whole. The benefits of a water management policy were set out even more explicitly by the Advisory Committee on Water Management Policy in the Twenty-First Century in their report, published in 2000. The committee concluded that awareness of the benefits of water management measures among both policy makers and the general public was low, and benefits should be addressed more explicitly in the future.

In CBA of flood control projects, the inclusion of the economic value of benefits other than material damage avoided is expected to play an important role, as this economic value can be decisively in favor of managed realignment, compared to traditional "hold the line" solutions. However, their estimation and valuation is not without problems. The hydrological and ecological functions of floodplains and fluvial wetlands, such as flood water retention, the provision of wildlife habitat and nutrient assimilation—nonpriced public goods—are difficult to translate into economic terms. Although various economic methods and techniques have been developed over the past decades to value nonpriced public goods in monetary terms, for instance, the restoration of wetlands and floodplains (e.g., Brander, Florax, and Vermaat 2006), there are few studies that estimate the nonpriced public benefits of risk reductions due to managed realignment, compared to traditional dyke strengthening. Economic valuation of these benefits can furthermore be a costly and time-consuming undertaking. In practice, benefits transfer is often used as a cost-effective alternative for the valuation of these benefits. Benefits transfer implies that previous valuation results, usually found under different geographical, socioeconomic, institutional, and political circumstances, are used to estimate the benefits of environmental changes in a new context (Brouwer 2000).

Nonpriced benefits such as ecological quality and the public perception and valuation of life-threatening risks were considered in a prefeasibility study of six different coastal and fluvial managed realignment projects, which was carried out by the Central Planning Agency (Centraal Planbureau—CPB) on behalf of the Ministry in 2000. The benefits could not be monetized (CPB 2000), but nevertheless, the prefeasibility study paved the way for a new policy based on other techniques (managed realignment), rather than conventional flood control measures (dyke strengthening). The CPB concluded for most of these projects that the socioeconomic benefits of managed realignment exceeded their costs and are thus likely to be beneficial to society as a whole. The study was quoted by the government in their official policy document "A Different Approach to Water," which was published one month later. The study was considered to provide sufficient evidence to justify continuation of the new flood control policy. The use of CBA in water management policy was given a major impetus in this policy document, with the government stating that "concrete (managed realignment) measures will have to be tested based on their costs and benefits. In this test also nonpriced costs and benefits will be taken into account, such as costs and benefits related to nature and spatial quality."

At the same time, the Ministry of Transport, Public Works and Water Management together with the Ministry for Spatial Planning also issued a new policy "Space for Water," which outlined the next steps from policy formulation to policy implementation and project planning (V&W 2000). Again the government referred explicitly to the study carried out by the CPB, which showed that alternative, nontraditional flood control measures are likely to be beneficial to society as a whole. It was furthermore emphasized that in the policy implementation and project planning phases, flood control alternatives should be evaluated and compared on the basis of their costs and benefits.

A Cost-Benefit Analysis of Designated Flood Disaster Areas

In May 2002, the Luteijn Commission presented its report "Controlled Flooding" to the Dutch government (Commissie Noodoverloopgebieden 2002). The Commission was established after the 1995 evacuations of flood-prone areas along the Rhine and Meuse. The Commission's aim was to advise on "controlled flooding" as a means of limiting the consequences of disastrous flooding in extreme hydraulic situations along the rivers Rhine and Meuse.

The Commission recommended the designation of three flood disaster zones— Rijnstrangen and Ooijpolder for the Rhine basin and Beersche Overlaat for the Meuse basin. These areas, measuring some 6,000 ha along the Rhine and 7,000 ha along the Meuse, are relatively sparsely populated with mainly extensive agricultural activities. Rijnstrangen has approximately 500 inhabitants, Ooijpolder 13,000, and Beersche Overlaat about 26,000. The flood disaster zones are to be used under extreme weather and hydraulic conditions, that is, when river discharges exceed the maximum levels that are used in the design of dyke infrastructure. Such extreme discharges present acute dangers of flooding due to dyke breaches, the locations of which are usually unknown in advance. Through the principle of controlled flooding in designated flood disaster areas, the risk of uncontrolled downstream flooding of densely populated, economically important areas is reduced. For example, if the upstream dyke enclosure along the river Rhine on the border with Germany (Ooij and Millingen) is flooded, the estimated damage costs are a factor of 60 lower than if the directly affected downstream dyke enclosure (Kromme Rijn) is flooded (CPB 2000). The frequency of using one of the flood disaster areas is estimated by the Commission at once every 1,250 years.

The costs of establishing flood disaster zones are mainly incurred for constructing new dykes, heightening existing dykes around the flood disaster areas, and building inlet and outlet structures and dykes in the areas to prevent villages located in these areas from flooding when the flood disaster areas are actually used. The total cost of constructing the three flood disaster zones was estimated at €1.25 billion. These costs were expected to be justified by the economic damage avoided downstream.

The Commission's report provoked much criticism, however, mainly questioning the effectiveness and efficiency of the proposed areas, the estimated costs and benefits, and the fact that alternatives to the flood disaster areas had not been sufficiently studied. Following the Commission's report, the Dutch government commissioned further prefeasibility studies of the costs and benefits of strategies dealing with residual risks in the Rhine and Meuse river basins. Hereafter we will discuss some of the results of the study carried out for the Rhine basin, based on Kind (2005).

In the follow-up prefeasibility study, a distinction was made between different flood disaster strategies: traditional dyke strengthening and overflow resistant dykes (the original flood disaster strategy advocated by the Luteijn Commission), and two variants of the latter, namely designated flood disaster zones in the upper part of the river basin without the construction of additional dykes or other protective structures, and designated flood disaster zones in the upper part of the river basin with only an inlet structure.

The costs of the different strategies vary considerably, as illustrated in table 13.1. Benefits were calculated in terms of a decrease in risk, that is, avoided material damage, as well as avoided damage resulting from the temporary disruption of business, due to flooding with and without the strategies. Without the strategies, the present value of the residual risk, calculated over an infinite period of time at the government-prescribed 4 percent discount rate for these types of investment decisions and an annual real GDP growth rate of 2 percent, is estimated at approximately €1.1 billion.

Traditional dyke strengthening has a major impact on the probability of flooding, reducing the disaster flood return period from 1 in 1,250 years to 1 in 6,250. However, the impact of flood disaster zones with no further protective structures is dramatic, as the residual risk of flooding actually increases by 10 percent. According to the hydraulic analyses that were carried out, several dyke enclosures along the river are expected to breach one after another, due to their limited storage capacities. Overflow-resistant dykes, the flood disaster zones originally proposed by the Commission, and those with only an inlet, limit the damage in the area where the emergency strategy is put in place, and reduce the local probability of flooding, but not the consequences outside those areas. In table 13.1, the increase in risk due to flooding in dyke enclosures or flood disaster zones is included as a "cost," whereas the decrease in risk in another area is included as a "benefit."

Table 13.1 shows that most risk reduction over and above the present legal safety levels results from traditional dyke strengthening. Based on this strategy, the residual

TABLE 13.1 } Costs and Benefits of Different Flood Disaster Mitigation Strategies in € Millions (Price Level 2000)

	Additional dyke strengthening	Overflow resistant dykes	Original FDZ	FDZ without further protection	FDZ with inlet only
Total costs	600	100	445	620	40
Investment, operation, and maintenance	600	90	440	–	5
Increased risk	–	10	5	620	35
Total benefits (decreased risk)	750	360	170	535	165
Net benefits	150	260	–275	–85	125
B/C ratio	1.3	2.6	0.4	0.9	4.1
Residual risk without strategy	1,100	1,100	1,100	1,100	1,100
Net reduction in residual risk	750	350	165	–85	130
Residual risk	350	750	935	1,185	970
Percentage residual risk reduction	–70%	–30%	–15%	+10%	–10%

Source: Adapted from Brouwer and Kind 2005.

Note: FDZ = flood disaster zone.

risk of €1.1 billion can be reduced by 70 percent. The strategies of overflow-resistant dykes and flood disaster areas with only an inlet deserve further attention in view of their high benefit-cost ratios, even though the first hydraulic assessments showed that they reduce the residual risk by less than traditional dyke strengthening (10–30 percent).

The results of this pre-feasibility study support the general conclusion of the Luteijn Commission that controlled flooding is preferable to uncontrolled flooding. After careful reconsideration, however, the investments originally proposed by the Commission to establish flood disaster zones along the river Rhine cannot be justified based on the estimated benefits of the associated risk reduction. However, an important question remains. To what extent does this outcome change when the immaterial damage costs are also taken into account? It has been argued that these are strongly and positively correlated with the size of the material damage costs (Baan 2004).

Economic Valuation of Immaterial Damage Costs

In a survey carried out in June 2006 in two different potential flood disaster zones along the rivers Meuse (Beersche Overlaat) and Rhine (Ooijpolder), 200 households were interviewed about their opinion and perception of living in a designated flood disaster zone. Face-to-face interviews were carried out door-to-door in seven villages, three along the river Meuse and four along the river Rhine. The study's main objective was to measure the perceived risks of climate change and public WTAC for an increase in disaster flood risk and associated welfare loss. The *a priori* expectation was that public WTAC would be positive and substantial, providing important additional information for CBA of climate change adaptation and mitigation. Special attention was paid to the estimation of the economic value of intangible welfare effects, such as feelings of discomfort, fear, and social disruption.

The questionnaire had three main parts. The first focused on flood risk perception, in absolute and relative terms, that is, compared to other risky events and activities, and experiences of flood events, including evacuations. The second part introduced a choice experiment, in which households at risk of flooding were asked to choose between controlled and uncontrolled flooding alternatives in the area where they live, under different possible climate change conditions. The third and final part contained questions about respondent demographic and socioeconomic characteristics, along with a number of debriefing questions, to assess the understanding of respondents of the choice experiment. The results on public perception and experiences will be presented first, followed by the results from the choice experiment.

The demographic and socioeconomic characteristics of the sample are presented in table 13.2. Fifty-five percent of the respondents were women, and the respondents' average age was 50. Most respondents (45 percent) fall in the 40–60 age group. Thirty percent of the sample was younger than 40, and 25 percent older than 60. About 45 percent of the respondents had children. The average household size was 2.8, which is slightly higher than the national average of 2.3 (Statistics Netherlands 2007).

TABLE 13.2 } Sample Demographic and Socioeconomic
Characteristics

Sample characteristic	
Share male respondents (%)	44.6
Average respondent age (years)	49.7
Average household size	2.8
Percentage households with children	41.5
Percentage higher educated	36.9
Average net monthly household income (€)	2,225
Percentage house owner	64.0

Source: Authors' own work.

Average household income was €2,225 per month, which is more or less the same as the national average disposable income of €2,335 (Statistics Netherlands 2007). Forty percent were highly educated, meaning that they had a college, university, or higher professional degree. Almost two thirds owned the houses in which they lived, with one third renting. As expected, household income and home ownership were significantly correlated (Pearson r = 0.465; $p < 0.001$).

Household perception of climate-change-induced flood risks is of particular interest here. A number of indicators and measurement scales were used in the survey. About one in every five respondents in the sample had experienced one or more flood disasters, while 46 percent had been evacuated due to flooding or the risk of flooding. Flood risk perceptions were drawn out compared to other risky events and activities, including smoking, driving a car, flying, sunbathing, and a terrorist attack. Forty-five percent of the respondents living in the potential designated flood disaster zones perceived climate-change-induced flood risks as riskier than or an equal risk to these other risks that people face in their daily lives. Seventy percent of the sample believed it to be unlikely that they will face a dyke breach in the next 10 years in the designated flood disaster zone. Ten percent of the sample felt unsafe where they live, while half of the sample felt very safe and one third somewhat safe. A remarkable finding was that almost 30 percent did not know whether a flood disaster emergency plan existed for the area in which they lived. Fifteen percent of the sample had no trust whatsoever in existing flood emergency plans. Almost 90 percent had heard of the principle of controlled flooding in designated flood disaster zones, mainly through the media (63 percent). Sixty percent thought controlled flooding was a good idea, 30 percent did not, and 9 percent did not know what to think of this or had no opinion.

Another interesting finding was that there were significant flood risk perception differences between men and women, and between higher and lower education and income groups. Women rated the risk of flooding significantly higher than men. Lower educated and lower income groups also perceived flood risks to be significantly higher. By the same token, lower educated and lower income groups felt less protected from flooding than higher educated and higher income groups.

Turning to the choice experiment, households at risk of flooding were asked whether they would be willing to accept compensation for the immaterial damage caused by the increased risk of controlled flooding under different possible climate change conditions. The climate change scenarios were represented by the following three attributes:

(1) "flood return period" measured in years (flood probabilities),
(2) "inundation level" measured in centimeters, and
(3) "evacuation period" measured in weeks.

Inundation and evacuation were used as indicators of discomfort, stress, and fear. Together they represented the immaterial damage cost due to flooding. Life-threatening risks were ruled out explicitly, and it was emphasized that the financial compensation would be for the experienced discomfort, stress, and fear only, over and above the fully-compensated material damage to houses and other assets. These possible future situations were combined with different compensation payments. Financial compensation was offered in the case of controlled flooding in the area where respondents lived. Households rejecting the idea of controlled flooding in designated flood disaster zones accepted the financial risk of uncontrolled flooding under different climate change conditions.

The economic value of a risk increase due to climate change was derived by examining individual WTAC for controlled flooding. In expected utility theory, which underpinned the study, the basic assumption underlying individual choice behavior facing uncertainty is that people are risk-averse when their decision involves potential losses under low probability, high impact conditions. The WTAC welfare measure is not universally transferable. As well as uncertainty, subjective emotional aspects play an important role, as does the extent to which the risk is regarded as voluntary, under one's own control and responsibility, familiar and well-understood (Beattie et al. 1998). Furthermore, risk perception and perspectives differ among individuals in the same situation and are relative and dependent on personal experience, consequently leading to different decisions (Wilson 1991). These factors were controlled for as much as possible in the choice model estimation procedure.

A card displaying the attributes and attribute levels was used to help respondents understand the idea and objective of the choice task, and to demonstrate the possible variations in the scenarios. The design of the experiment is presented in table 13.3. A main-effects fractional factorial design was generated, consisting of 28 choice sets, which were blocked into seven versions of four choice sets each. Each respondent was randomly shown one of these seven versions and hence answered four choice cards.

Each choice card showed two alternatives describing the climate change scenarios and the associated flood risks and risk mitigation possibility, along with the option to choose none of the two. This latter "opt-out" option, as it was explained to respondents, implied facing the increasing climate-change-induced flood risks in the future and choosing not to mitigate them through compensated controlled flooding. The card showed that the cost of the opt-out alternative is zero. In order to make sure respondents had a clear understanding of the choice task, they were first asked

TABLE 13.3 } Overview of Choice Experiment Attributes and Levels

Attribute	Levels			
Flood probability	Once in your life	Once every 25 years	Once every 10 years	Once every 5 years
Inundation depth	10 cm	100 cm	150 cm	200 cm
Evacuation period	1 week	2 weeks	4 weeks	8 weeks
Compensation for controlled flooding	€10,000/flood event	€50,000/flood event	€100,000/flood event	€150,000/flood event

Source: Authors' own work.

to make their choice using an example card, allowing them to ask questions about the task before the experiment started. Figure 13.1 shows an example of a choice card.

A large majority of the respondents living in potential flood disaster zones preferred controlled flooding and compensation compared to uncontrolled flooding and no compensation in the face of climate change and an increasing risk of catastrophic flooding. In 96 percent of the 676 choice occasions, one of the two alternatives with controlled flooding and compensation was preferred over the opt-out alternative.

Table 13.4 summarizes the results. As expected, flood probability and inundation level influence choices in a negative way. The higher the probability of flooding or the greater the inundation level, the lower the likelihood of a respondent choosing the option of controlled flooding and compensation. The compensation amount has a significant positive effect on choice behavior. The higher the offered compensation for the experienced discomfort and stress, the higher the probability of a respondent preferring controlled flooding.

A significant linear and quadratic effect was found for flood probability. Figure 13.2 shows the compensation demanded at different (controlled) flood probability levels, based on the estimated choice model. The graph clearly reflects nonlinearity in the compensation needed to offset the immaterial welfare loss (discomfort, distress, and fear) associated with controlled flooding.

The differences between the inundation levels are not statistically significant, except for the parameter estimates for one and two meters. This suggests that this jump in inundation level evokes additional stress and fear, even though it was emphasized that controlled flooding poses no threat to human life or livestock in these predominantly agricultural areas.

Contrary to expectations, evacuation period did not exercise a detectable significant influence on choice behavior. None of the evacuation periods were statistically significant at the 10 percent level, irrespective of how they were included in the estimated choice model, that is, as a continuous or a dummy variable.

Hence, the findings show that WTAC is substantial, varying roughly between €185,000 and €370,000 per household per flood event, depending on flood probability and inundation depth, but also on respondent characteristics (house ownership, evacuation history, trust in existing flood emergency plans, and fear of flooding)

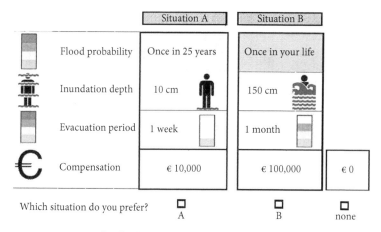

FIGURE 13.1 Example of a choice card
Source: Authors' own work.

TABLE 13.4 } Estimated Discrete Choice Model for Controlled Flooding and Compensation

Attribute		$\hat{\beta}$	*s.e.*	*p* <
Constant	Constant	3.708	0.275	0.001
Compensation	Linear	0.006	0.002	0.001
Flood probability	Linear	−23.372	5.590	0.001
Flood probability	Quadratic	68.169	23.330	0.003
Inundation depth 100 cm	Dummy	−.617	0.176	0.001
Inundation depth 150 cm	Dummy	−0.796	0.202	0.001
Inundation depth 200 cm	Dummy	−0.943	0.216	0.001
Evacuation 2 weeks	Dummy	0.169	0.165	0.306
Evacuation 4 weeks	Dummy	−0.144	0.207	0.488
Evacuation 8 weeks	Dummy	−0.069	0.184	0.707
Model summary				
Log likelihood function		−503.025		
Adjusted R^2		0.318		
N		676		

Source: Authors' own work.

and their subjective risk perception (not presented in table 13.4, but results available from the authors). *Ceteris paribus*, homeowners are less likely to choose one of the alternatives with controlled flooding and compensation compared to the current situation of uncontrolled flooding. The same negative relationship is found for respondents who experienced an evacuation before, suggesting negative experiences with evacuations in the past. Respondents who had been through an evacuation were less likely to be in favor of controlled flooding with compensation than respondents who had never experienced an evacuation. Respondents who feared flooding, even under controlled circumstances, demanded significantly higher compensation to offset the negative impact of flooding on their well-being, such as fear and distress. On the

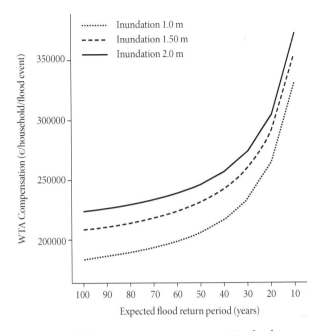

FIGURE 13.2 Willingness to accept compensation for the discomfort, fear, and stress experienced during controlled flooding at different flood probability and inundation levels
Source: Authors' own work.

other hand, respondents who trusted existing disaster plans for the area in which they lived were less likely to be influenced by the amount of compensation offered, compared to respondents who did not trust existing disaster plans.

The Economics of Disaster Management: Conclusions and Caveats

People living in potential flood disaster zones and at risk of catastrophic flooding are willing to accept compensation for immaterial damage due to the increased risk of controlled flooding. However, the required compensation to offset the immaterial welfare losses associated with controlled flooding increases exponentially as the probability of flooding increases. Subjective risk perception also affects choice behavior. Fear of flooding leads, as expected, to an increase in the amount of compensation demanded for the welfare loss involved. The study shows that WTAC for controlled flooding does not depend on the evacuation period once inundation levels are accounted for. Although evacuation period is not a significant influential factor in this study, it would be premature to conclude that welfare losses due to evacuation discomfort and distress do not exist. A possible explanation might be that evacuation is considered a flood risk reduction strategy rather than an event causing discomfort. More research in this area is needed in order to better capture these specific evacuation-induced well-being effects.

The results of the study presented here imply that external social damage costs should play a more prominent role in CBA of climate change and flood mitigation policies. In theory, the estimated WTAC should be considered an indicator of the expected welfare loss due to fear, stress, and social disruption, and should be added to the material damage costs of controlled flooding, and compared with public WTP to avoid the material and immaterial damage costs due to uncontrolled flooding downstream. The skewed distribution of the welfare losses and disruption costs upstream in case of controlled flooding, and the corresponding economic benefits downstream pose a number of interesting challenges to policy and decision makers who are attempting to manage the relevant spatial equity issues across the public and private parties involved.

We conclude with some final remarks regarding current caveats in the economics of disaster management. Central to the economics of natural hazard and disaster management, including catastrophic flooding and climate change, is the concept of risk and uncertainty. Risk means that a certain event can be predicted with a certain probability. Uncertainty can be fundamental in that there is little or no prior knowledge and information about the exact nature or consequences of the event, and the probability that it will actually take place. The well-known economist Keynes phrased the distinction as follows (Keynes 1937, 148):

> By "uncertain" knowledge, I do not mean merely to distinguish what is known for certain from what is only probable. The game of roulette is not subject, in this sense, to uncertainty. The sense in which I am using the term is that in which the prospect of a European war is uncertain, or the price of copper and the rate of interest twenty years hence. About these matters there is no scientific basis on which to form any calculable probability whatever. We simply do not know.

Most decision theories and economic policy assessments treat uncertainty as a state that can in principle be known through objective or subjective probability distributions and preferences for specific probability distributions (e.g., risk-averse or risk-neutral attitudes and behavior). In assuming that all uncertainty can be quantified by given probabilities, most approaches treat the problem as an analysis of risk rather than true uncertainty (Brouwer and Deblois 2008). Although this is a powerful approach, it may be inadequate when dealing with stochastic events like catastrophic flooding, which are hard to predict, both in terms of probability and socioeconomic consequences.

Although flood damage cost modeling was not addressed explicitly in this chapter, most damage cost models only assess the direct costs of flooding. This is also the case for the damage costs presented in this chapter. Part of the indirect costs associated with temporary business disruption were accounted for in the CBA of alternative flood disaster zones, but not the possible change in economic behavior as a result of a stochastic shock to the economic system, such as a catastrophic flood event. Constant economic growth rates are usually used to estimate future (avoided) damage costs. Adaptation to, and resilience in the face of, new circumstances based on socioeconomic learning processes are expected to play an important role, and may significantly moderate and mitigate the longer term economic effects of environmental change. These learning experiences are currently inadequately captured in existing damage cost models, and merit more attention in future research.

References

Baan, P. J. A. (2004). "Flood Risks along Rivers More Than Probability Times Effect: Perception and Implications for a Safety Strategy" (in Dutch). Research report Q3673.20, Delft Hydraulics.

Beattie, J., Covey, J., Dolan, P., Hopkins, L., Jones-Lee, M., Loomes, G., Pidgeon, N., Robinson, A., and Spencer, A. (1998). "On the Contingent Valuation of Safety and the Safety of Contingent Valuation: Part 1—Caveat Investigator." *Journal of Risk and Uncertainty* 17: 5–25.

Botzen, W. J. W., and van den Bergh, J. C. J. M. (2008). "Insurance against Climate Change and Flooding in the Netherlands: Present, Future and Comparison with Other Countries." *Risk Analysis* 28(2): 413–426.

Bouwer, L. M., Crompton, R. P., Faust, E., Höppe, P., and Pielke, Jr., R. A. (2007). "Confronting Disaster Losses." *Science* 318: 753.

Brander, L. M., Florax, R. J. G. M., and Vermaat, J. E. (2006). "The Empirics of Wetlands Valuation: A Comprehensive Summary and a Meta-analysis of the Literature." *Environmental and Resource Economics* 33: 223–250.

Brouwer, R. (2000). "Environmental Value Transfer: State of the Art and Future Prospects." *Ecological Economics* 32: 137–152.

Brouwer, R., and De Blois, C. (2008). "Integrated Modelling of Risk and Uncertainty Underlying the Selection of Cost-Effective Water Quality Measures." *Environmental Modelling & Software* 23: 922–937.

Brouwer, R., and Kind, J. (2005). "The Costs and Benefits of Flood Control Policy in the Netherlands." In *Cost-Benefit Analysis and Water Resources Management*, edited by R. Brouwer and D. W. Pearce. Cheltenham, UK: Edward Elgar Publishing.

Brouwer, R., and van Ek, R. (2004). "Integrated Ecological, Economic and Social Impact Assessment of Alternative Flood Protection Measures in the Netherlands." *Ecological Economics* 50(1–2): 1–21.

Commissie Noodoverloopgebieden. (2002). "Controlled Flooding. Advise from the Commission Flood Disaster Zones" (in Dutch). *The Hague*, May 29, 2002.

CPB (2000). "Space for Water: Costs and Benefits of Six Projects and Some Alternatives" (in Dutch). The Hague, The Netherlands: CPB.

Jones-Lee, M. W. (1989). *The Economics of Safety and Physical Risk*. Oxford: Blackwell.

Jonkman, S. N., Bockarjova, M., Kok, M., and Bernardini, P. (2008). "Integrated Hydrodynamic and Economic Modelling of Flood Damage in the Netherlands. Special Issue Ecological Economics Integrated Hydro-Economic Modelling for Effective and Sustainable Water Management." *Ecological Economics* 66(1): 77–90.

Keynes, J. M. (1937). *The General Theory of Employment, Quarterly Journal of Economics, February 1937*, reprinted in *The Collected Writings*, Vol. 14. Cambridge: Macmillan & Cambridge University Press.

Kind, J. M. (2005). "Disaster Management Strategy: Flooding Rhine and Meuse. RIZA report 2005.025" (in Dutch). Lelystad, The Netherlands.

Kok, M., and Barendregt, A. (2004). "Responsibility and Liability in the Case of Water Damage" (in Dutch). Report for the Directorate-General Water, Ministry of Infrastructure, Public Works and Water Management. HKV Lijn in Water, Lelystad, The Netherlands.

Mechler, R. (2005). "Cost-Benefit Analysis of Natural Disaster Risk Management in Developing and Emerging Countries." German Society for Technical Cooperation (GTZ), Eschborn.

Middelkoop, H., Daamen, K., Gellens, D., Grabs, W., Kwadijk, J. C. J., Lang, H., Parmet, B. W. A., Schädler, B., Schulla, J., and Wilke, K. (2001). "Impact of Climate Change on Hydrological Regimes and Water Resources Management in the Rhine Basin." *Climatic Change* 49(2–3): 105–128.

Pearce, D. W., and Smale, R. (2005). "Appraising Flood Control Investments in the UK." In *Cost-Benefit Analysis and Water Resources Management*, edited by R. Brouwer and D. W. Pearce. Cheltenham, UK: Edward Elgar.

Statistics Netherlands. (2007). http://www.cbs.nl.

Tinbergen, J. (1960). *The Economic Balance of the Delta Plan* (in Dutch). Bijdrage VI, Deltacommissie, The Netherlands.

Tol, R. (1999). "The Marginal Costs of Greenhouse Gas Emissions." *Energy Journal* 20(1): 61–81.

V&W (1998). "Fourth National Water Policy Document" (in Dutch). Ministry of Transport, Public Works and Water Management, December 1998, The Hague, The Netherlands.

———. (2000). "Space for Water: View Point to the Chair of Parliament" (in Dutch). Ministry of Transport, Public Works and Water Management, December 2000, The Hague, The Netherlands.

Wilson, A. R. (1991). *Environmental Risk: Identification and Management*. Chelsea, Mich.: Lewis Publishers.

CONCLUSION

The economic impact of natural disasters has been increasing in the last decade. Lives are lost and people are disabled, sometimes for life. Even if lives are spared, harvests and livelihoods are lost, marginalizing large sections of the already poor in many countries.

This book has been a step toward bringing together varied expertise in the field of the economics of natural disasters from north and south, and to look at what future research is needed in order to improve our management of disaster risks.

We conclude here with five pointers for research that could contribute most to reducing these risks and providing a clearer picture of the real costs of disasters.

1. Being poor makes one substantially more vulnerable to natural disasters—probably more significantly than physical factors, such as distance to an earthquake's epicenter or to a flooded river. Although systematic studies are rare in bringing clear evidence on the relative importance of different factors determining impact, vulnerability of the poor to disasters has been emphasized widely without many attempts at understanding the pathways and mechanisms that define these associations or the mitigating factors that protect the poor against shocks.

   Epidemiologists have started undertaking studies to determine risk factors for death, injuries, and disease, but this agenda is still relatively nascent. Much work needs to be done to develop practical economic methods that estimate value of assets in poor communities after a disaster. In postdisaster situations, the economic assessment typically has to be done in a hurry and without easy access to standard data sources. Frequently, the little that is done comes from results of population-based surveys, which have major limitations in the field in such circumstances. Other assessments take a very long time and require significant investment of highly skilled staff on the ground for weeks.

   The affected regions are increasingly in poor and often in remote areas of developing countries and in the absence of proper economic impact tools, these disasters are vastly underestimated. More research to develop and field test effective operational tools that could rapidly establish broad economic losses, is a priority issue in this agenda.

2. Natural disasters can also have an impact on poverty by increasing the proportion of the poor in a low-income region. Most people living in disaster-prone areas, such as flood banks in Cambodia or Haiti lack appropriate insurance and credit mechanisms and have even less reserves to absorb shocks to their family income. Natural disasters

can take away their few assets, affect their health status, remove a key member of the family, and reduce their accumulation of human capital. Every successive disaster (frequently in the case of floods) has a pernicious effect of marginalizing already marginalized communities, finally pushing them into ultra poor groups or inciting rural to urban migration in search of survival. A better understanding of the relationship between marginalization and natural disasters is required, as well as a more thorough discussion of the possible policy measures necessary to break the vicious circle between poverty and vulnerability.

3. Given that the size of disaster-affected populations is increasing—especially in poor countries, the reality is that not much increase in resources can be expected for disaster mitigation or prevention measures. This is even truer now when the economic and financial crises effects are likely to be felt for some time. In these circumstances, better research on creative forms of social insurance and microinsurance need to be developed to take into account the existing resource constraints. Mechanisms that are community based and small scale are likely to work better than nationwide models in locations where formal insurance and credit markets do not exist or do not work well. This is evidenced by ongoing projects such as the Microinsurance Agency and the Microinsurance Innovation Facility discussed in this volume.

4. Fourth, better indicators of coping capacity at the micro level are urgently required. Given equal exposure to a disaster in a village, for example, some households suffer less than others due to their coping instruments. These successful, locally appropriate, and frequently time-tested interventions should be systematically studied and brought out for others to learn and use. Policy options should also be developed based on this understanding of coping mechanisms in communities that reinforce these home-grown measures and progressively reduce dependence on and expectations of aid.

5. Finally, there is an urgent need for better assessing the short- and the long-term impacts of natural disasters on communities. Better instruments to measure the effects on nonmarketed goods, for example, will allow for an improved understanding of the true costs of natural disasters.

The phenomenon of natural disasters has high moral imperatives linked to the tragedies of households and families. But it also has an important economic development imperative. We would like this book to encourage young economists in the future to look into this field and work on reducing the effects of natural disasters on the poor of the world.

INDEX

About-Ali, H., 68
Abramovitz, J., 42
AC method. *See* averting cost method
adaptation, 52, 112–117, 155*f*
adaptive capacity, 39
Adger, W.N., 184, 188
Africa
    disaster losses in 2007, 166*t*
    disaster occurrence in, 9, 10, 10*f*, 11*f*, 50, 51*f*
    disaster preparedness in, 50, 51*t*
    economic damage data from natural disasters, 14, 21*f*, 22, 23*f*, 25*f*
    EM-DAT classification, 15*t*-16*t*
    insurance in, 165*t*
    mortality from natural disasters, 13
    natural hazard risk levels by country, 50, 51*f*
    property insurance in, 134
    Sahel drought (1972–73), 38–39
Aghion, P., 30
agriculture
    Bangladesh flooding and, 286–287, 287*t*, 288*f*, 288*t*, 292*n*22
    estimating crop damage's, 59–60
    Vietnam natural disasters and, 184–186, 194
    weather index-based insurance for Indian farmers, 47
    Windward Islands Crop Insurance (WINCROP), 45–46
Albala-Bertrand, J.M., 30, 32, 33
Albarran, P., 245
Alberini, A., 68, 71
Alderman, H., 34
Allen, K., 41
Allen, M.R., 111
alternative methods of risk transfer (ART), 148–150
Altonji, J., 254
altruistic model, interhousehold transfers, 243–244, 245
Americas
    disaster occurrence in, 9, 10, 10*f*, 11*f*
    economic damage data from natural disasters, 14, 21*f*, 22, 23*f*, 25*f*
    EM-DAT classification, 16*t*-17*t*
    mortality from natural disasters, 13
Angola, natural hazard risk levels, 51*f*

animal husbandry, Vietnam natural disasters and, 185
aquaculture, Vietnam natural disasters and, 185
Arrow, K., 64, 103*n*4
ART. *See* alternative methods of risk transfer
ASEAN countries, insurance in, 165*t*
Asia
    disaster losses in 2007, 166*t*
    disaster occurrence in, 9, 10, 10*f*, 11*f*
    earthquakes in, 9
    economic damage data from natural disasters, 14, 21*f*, 22, 23*f*, 25*f*
    EM-DAT classification, 17*t*-18*t*
    floods in, 9
    human impact of natural disasters, 13
    insurance in, 165*t*
    mortality from national disasters, 12, 13
    storms in, 9
Attanasio, O., 245
Australia, disaster losses in 2007, 166*t*
Australia and New Zealand
    economic damage data from natural disasters, 14, 21*f*, 22, 25*f*
    EM-DAT classification, 20*t*
    property insurance in, 135
aversion to inequality, 122
averting cost method (AC method), 61

"backward class", 223*n*12
backward-looking framework, 89*t*, 90–91, 92
Badola, R., 72
Balhaj, M., 68
Bandyopadhyay, S., 3, 199
Bangladesh
    agriculture, 286–287, 287*t*, 288*f*, 288*t*
    economic impacts of disasters, 35, 252*t*, 269–291, 272, 273*f*, 274–277, 275*f*
    economy, 272, 285
    flood loss models, 279–286, 280*f*-282*f*, 285*t*
    flood risk reduction in, 71–72
    geography, 269
    gross national product (GNP), 270, 271*t*
    micro-credit, 48
    mortality from national disasters, 12, 13
    nonagricultural flood impact, 277–279, 287–288, 288*f*, 288*t*

313